Windows NT® DNS

New Riders

New Riders Professional Library

New Riders Professional Library

Windows NT Registry
Sandra Osborne,
ISBN: 1-56205-941-6

Windows NT DNS
Michael Masterson & Herman L. Knief,
ISBN: 1-56205-943-2

Windows NT Performance Monitoring
Mark Edmead,
ISBN: 1-56205-942-4

Exchange System Implementation and Administration
Excell Data Corporation,
ISBN: 1-56205-931-9

SQL Server System Administration
Sean Baird, Chris Miller, et al.,
ISBN: 1-56205-955-6

Windows NT Thin Clients
Ted Harwood,
ISBN: 1-56205-944-0

Windows NT Technical Support
Brendan McTague & George Neal,
ISBN: 1-56205-927-0

Windows NT Security
Richard Puckett,
ISBN: 1-56205-945-9

Windows NT Administration Handbook
Eric Svetcov,
ISBN: 1-56205-946-7

Linux System Administration
James T. Dennis,
ISBN: 1-56205-934-3

Domino System Administration
Rob Kirkland,
ISBN: 1-56205-948-3

Windows NT® DNS

Michael Masterson
Herman Knief
Eric Roul and
Scott Vinick

New Riders
201 West 103rd Street,
Indianapolis, Indiana 46290

TAOS MOUNTAIN
www.taos.com

Windows NT® DNS

Michael Masterson

Copyright © 1998 by New Riders Publishing

All rights reserved. No part of this book may be reproduced or transmitted in any form or by any means, electronic or mechanical, including photocopying, recording, or by any information storage and retrieval system, without written permission from the publisher, except for the inclusion of brief quotations in a review.

International Standard Book Number: 1-56205-943-2

Library of Congress Catalog Card Number: 98-86490

Printed in the United States of America

2001   00   4   3

Interpretation of the printing code: The rightmost double-digit number is the year of the book's printing; the rightmost single-digit, the number of the book's printing. For example, the printing code 98-1 shows that the first printing of the book occurred in 1998.

Composed in Bembo and Rotis Sans Serif by Macmillan Computer Publishing

Trademark Acknowledgments

All terms mentioned in this book that are known to be trademarks or service marks have been appropriately capitalized. New Riders Publishing cannot attest to the accuracy of this information. Use of a term in this book should not be regarded as affecting the validity of any trademark or service mark.

Warning and Disclaimer

This book is designed to provide information about Windows NT DNS. Every effort has been made to make this book as complete and as accurate as possible, but no warranty or fitness is implied.

The information is provided on an as-is basis. The authors and New Riders Publishing shall have neither liability nor responsibility to any person or entity with respect to any loss or damages arising from the information contained in this book or from the use of the discs or programs that may accompany it.

Executive Editor
Linda Ratts Engelman

Acquisitions Editor
Karen Wachs

Development Editor
Christopher Cleveland

Managing Editor
Caroline Roop

Project Editor
Brad Herriman

Copy Editor
Krista Hansing

Indexer
Joy Dean Lee
Cheryl Jackson

Technical Reviewers
John Engelhart
Sanjiv Raja
Scott Vinick

Production
Terri Edwards
Brad Lenser
Donna Martin

About the Authors

Mike Masterson is currently the Director of Technical Services at Taos Mountain, Silicon Valley's largest provider of system administration services. A Microsoft Certified Professional, he is also the founder and president of the Silicon Valley NT Engineering Association. Michael is a member of the Editorial Board of NT Systems Magazine, and has spoken at several conferences, including the SAGE/USENIX Large Scale NT Systems Administration Symposium.

Herman Knief is a Senior Technical Advisor at Taos Mountain. He's provided system and network administration services for various clients, including Netcom and Bay Networks. Herman's broad system architecture and administration background includes work at GTE Government Systems Corp., the USC/ISI office at the Defense Advanced Research Projects Agency (DARPA), and the Corporation for National Research Initiatives (CNRI).

Eric Roul is a Taos Mountain Information Technology Consultant with several certifications: Microsoft Certified Systems Engineer, Citrix Certified Professional, Compaq and HP Certified Professional. An accomplished systems and network administrator, he has been teaching system administration and managing diverse systems and networks for over 13 years. He has a master's degree in Civil Engineering and a master's degree in computer science from the Conservatoire National des Arts et Metiers in France.

Scott Vinick is a Systems and Network Administrator with Taos Mountain, Inc. in the San Francisco Bay area. Scott has worked on Windows NT cross-platform projects for a number of companies, helping them migrate from or integrate with UNIX, Macintosh, and Novell-based networks. He also owns and operates an Internet Service Provider, SCV Consulting, providing DNS, email, and Web Services for a number of organizations. Scott has been working with Windows NT since its release and is a Microsoft Certified Engineer (MCSE). He is also involved with several NT user groups. Scott studied Mechanical Engineering at Cleveland State University.

About the Technical Reviewers

These reviewers contributed their considerable practical, hands-on expertise to the entire development process for *Windows NT DNS*. As the book was being written, these folks reviewed all the material for technical content, organization, and flow. Their feedback was critical to ensuring that *Windows NT DNS* fits our reader's need for the highest quality technical information.

Sanjiv Raja has been heavily involved in the networking industry working with blue-chip companies in England and Europe. Sanjiv began his work in the networking field by designing Novell Netware systems. He is currently certified to CNE 4.x and a Master CNE (MCNE). Recently, Sanjiv has been concentrating on Microsoft and BackOffice products where he holds an MCSE. Sanjiv is currently the lead architect at a specialist bank designing BackOffice solutions including MS Exchange, MS SMS, and Windows Terminal Server. In his spare time, Sanjiv enjoys skiing, golf, and good theatre.

Joe Dial is a Computer Scientist currently involved in the creation of a complete network infrastructure including DNS, DHCP, WINS, and all of the TCP/IP protocols to integrate his company's Gloabl WAN with Windows NT, 95, and UNIX hosts. Someday, he hopes to have time to remember what it is that he does when not working.

Larry Gandy's background includes 7 years experience as a technical trainer. Presently a Microsoft Certfied Technical Trainer for the Microsoft Enterprise and Support Training organization specializing in Windows operating systems and Internet/Web Development Technologies. Also a Microsoft Certified System Engineer.

Dedications

This is for my lovely wife, Julie, who still gives me lots of love and too few complaints after 20 years of marriage; for Janelle, who's given us both the incomparable privilege of watching her grow from nothing into a beautiful and responsible college-age adult; and for Ryan, who's old enough to be a friend but still young enough to do kid stuff with his dad.
Mike Masterson

To my wife and son, who gave me the time and quiet I needed to work and do research for this book.
Herman Knief

For my wife Betty, for my brother Robert and for Jo-Anne and Terri, with love.
Eric Roul

To Sarah :-)
Scott Vinick

Contents

Introduction xv

I Understanding Windows Name Services

1 Introducing the Domain Name System 3
Name Registration, Resolution, and Distribution 4
Host Name Characteristics 13
Fully Qualified Domain Names 16
Summary 17

2 Introducing NetBIOS 19
NetBIOS 20
Resolving NetBIOS Names 24
A Flat Namespace 29
NetBIOS Name Characteristics 30
NetBIOS Names and Resource Codes 31
Summary 32

3 How Windows Clients Use DNS and WINS 33
Introducing the Windows Resolver 34
How WINS Serves the Windows Name Resolver 35
How DNS Serves the Windows Name Resolver 35
How the Resolver Works 40
Summary 51

4 WINS and DNS: Making the Most of Both Services 53
What the Future Holds for NetBIOS 54
WINS Purpose and Limitations 55
The Benefits of Combining WINS and DNS 56
Multihoming PDCs, WINS, File, and Print Servers 57
Browsing: The NetBIOS Discovery Service 58
Summary 60

Contents

II Introducing Windows NT DNS

5 How DNS Works 63
A Hierarchy of Hosts and Domains 64
Domains and Zones 68
Resolving Client Requests 71
Summary 79

6 Name Server Types 81
Primary Domain Servers 82
Secondary Name Servers 85
Caching Name Servers 86
Passing Queries: Forwarders and Slaves 87
Determining DNS Type 90
Summary 92

7 What DNS Knows 93
Database Resource Records 94
The Cache File 108
Delegation 110
Distributing Names 110
Summary 111

8 Dissecting Name Queries 113
Iterative and Recursive Queries 113
Sending the DNS Query 114
Time-to-Live 120
Summary 120

9 How MS DNS Works with Other Servers 121
Communication Between MS DNS and Other Name Servers 121
Migrating from BIND to MS DNS 122
Boot Files and Other Differences 123

III Using Windows NT DNS

10 Designing Your DNS Service(s) 127
DNS Server Capacities 128
Deciding How Many Domains to Have 129
Deciding How Many DNS Servers to Have 130
Practical Design Examples 131
Summary 136

11 Installing and Setting Up DNS 137
Installing the DNS Service 138
Configuring the DNS Server 139
Creating Virtual Servers 150
Summary 151

12 Integrating DNS with WINS 153
How Integration Works 154
Enabling WINS Lookups 158
Testing WINS Lookups 161
Reverse Lookups with WINS 162
Multihomed Servers 165
Summary 169

13 Configuring Clients 171
Configuring the Client to Use WINS 171
Configuring the Client to Use DNS 185
Summary 193

14 Working with Service Providers 195
Domain Name Registrations 196
Internal and External Servers: Primary, Secondary, and Caching 198
Zone Transfers: Which Way, and Why? 200
Interpreting the Event Log 200
What to Expect in the DNS Database 202
Summary 204

Contents

15 Maintenance Tasks 205
Moving Zone Files Between Servers 205
Managing Multiple Zones 212
Changing a DNS Server's IP Address 219

16 Security Issues 223
Spoofing Name Queries 224
Firewalls 225
WWW Security 227
FTP Security 228
Mail Security: SMTP, POP, and IMAP 229
Summary 229

17 Troubleshooting Tools and Utilities 231
nslookup 232
dig 240
ping 242
traceroute (tracert) 243
Netlab 243
ipconfig 244
winipcfg 245
netstat 246
nbtstat 247

18 Dynamic Host Configuration Protocol (DHCP) 249
It's Not Dynamic DNS 250
What is DHCP? 250
How DHCP Configures a Client 253
Installing a DHCP Server 254
Configuring a DHCP Server 257
Configuring Clients to Use DHCP 261
Checking the Registration in WINS and DNS 261
Summary 262

IV Appendices

A Third Party Utilities and DNS Servers 265
Utilities 265
DNS Server Software 266
DNS and IP Version 6 (IPv6) 269

B RFCs on DNS, BIND, and NetBIOS 271

C Top-Level Internet Domains 275

D Registering Addresses on the Internet 281

E Sample Network Traces for DNS Resolutions 301
DNS Query Trace: The Question 301
DNS Query Trace: The Answer 302
DNS Query Trace: DNS Questions WINS 302
DNS Query Trace: WINS Answers DNS 304

F Resource Records and the InterNIC Cache File 307
Resource Records 307
The InterNIC Cache File 311

Index 313

Acknowledgments

Mike Masterson: I'm grateful to my boss, Cindy Lee Smith, for understanding that writing occasionally conflicts with work's routine. Cindy believes in people and their talent. With her awesome team of recruiters, she's launched more technical careers in Silicon Valley than anyone I know.

Thanks to Herman Knief, my co-author and co-worker. If all system and network administrators were like him, people would never know how problematic computers and networks can be. He does great work, sometimes under stress, then shrugs out a smile and says, "no big deal."

Thanks to Eric Roul and Scott Vinick whose help in the later stages of this project got it over the finish line. Sanjiv Raja and Scott Vinick did great review work. Readers will have them to thank for fewer errors and for clarity in many once-hazy phrases.

I also appreciate the assistance of Guy Tal, an awesomely talented co-worker who typifies quiet productivity. He writes some of the best Java code around, always producing ten times more work than words. I'm privileged to benefit from his time and efforts.

Linda Engelman, Karen Wachs, and Chris Cleveland at Macmillan make a great team whose combined skills include visioneering, cheerleading, psychology, coaching and motivation, lawyering, wordsmithing, and maybe even animal training for stubborn beasts like me. Together, they produce some of the greatest publications on earth.

Thanks to the hundreds of talented techncial staff members who make Taos Mountain the greatest place on earth to work. I don't take lightly the privilege of working with the brightest and the best. My motivation to write this book comes mostly from them. And to the directors, volunteers, and members of the NT Engineering Association I owe the abiding satisfaction of friendship, collaboration, and the enjoyment of much good, hard work done well to benefit a great group of people. Finally, I owe the greatest debt to any reader who looks past this book's imperfections to learn something new. They prove that learning still happens. And at my age, that's a comforting thought.

Herman Knief: Writing this book has been one of the most difficult experiences of my life, and if Michael had not been so persistent, I probably wouldn't have completed my portion of this work. I would like to thank my co-authors for enduring the same hardships and making this possible. Of course, without the wonderful people at Macmillan none of this would have been possible. Much thanks to the technical reviewers for helping to make this a better book.

Eric Roul: First, I would like to thank the entire team at Macmillan for their assistance, guidance, and patience in this new project for me. I would also like specially to thank Michael Masterson at Taos Mountain who got me started in this project in the first place. He put me in a very challenging position that finally give me a very precious opportunity to contribute to the high-tech community. I am very proud to be part of this.

And finally thanks to my Mom and Dad, with love and respect.

Scott Vinick: Thank you to Mike Masterson, and everyone at Macmillan, for helping me make it through my first authoring experience.

Introduction

The domain name system is a global registry of computer names and addresses, and it is as necessary for the Internet as telephone directories are for the phone system. DNS is how computers find each other in the vastness of cyberspace where everything's really numbers. If DNS name servers weren't always busy in the background finding numeric addresses when our computers needed them, web browsing and email wouldn't work.

DNS relies on many administrators who know what they're doing, both individually and together. By learning about the DNS namespace and how name servers are supposed to interact, an administrator can not only keep his own services running, he also can avoid causing problems for other's DNS servers.

Just as truck drivers need to know the rules of the road before going on the highway, system administrators need to know how the Domain Name System works before they operate a server on the public network.

Through this book, Windows NT administrators can learn to design and run reliable DNS services using Microsoft's DNS Server for Windows NT. This book has the kind of information you can use to make good DNS design decisions. It covers DNS thoroughly, and it says enough about WINS to help administrators integrate the two name services.

UNIX administrators can read this book to add Microsoft's DNS to their name server repertoire, and its coverage of NetBIOS, WINS, and the Windows name resolver may be particularly enlightening because the Windows resolver is complex compared with straight DNS resolvers.

DNS isn't the only naming scheme around. Windows computers are complex and capable of using other methods as well, such as WINS, the Windows Internet Name Service. WINS has advantages for users in local and wide area networks because it supports NetBIOS, the layer of network services that make it so easy for Windows computers to share resources in small networks. The Network Neighborhood's computer browsing list, for example, is made possible through NetBIOS. But WINS isn't capable of handling all the Internet's names. To be fair, it wasn't designed to.

Harmonizing WINS and DNS gives Windows users the benefits of both worlds by allowing them to get on the Internet, and it lets UNIX hosts resolve Windows computer names easily, which is no small accomplishment. Abandoning either name service isn't sensible as long as they're both providing something our users value or need.

The first section of this book, "Understanding the Windows Name Services," covers the DNS system in a nutshell and explains NetBIOS and the NetBIOS name server, WINS.

The second section, "Introducing Windows NT DNS," describes in more detail how DNS works, explains the different server types and how they work together. All of this provides background for your own designs.

The third section, "Using Windows NT DNS," shows you how to design and implement a system of your own. It covers practical techniques for installing, configuring and managing Microsoft's DNS Server, including how to cooperate with other DNS administrators and Internet service providers. Finally, this section explains techniques and tools for troubleshooting DNS.

I

Understanding Windows Name Services

1 Introducing the Domain Name System
2 Introducing NetBIOS
3 How Windows Clients Use DNS and WINS
4 WINS and DNS: Making the Most of Both Services

Introducing the Domain Name System

This chapter will review:

- **Name Registration, Resolution, and Distribution.** The Domain Name System (DNS), above all, is a directory of registered computer names and IP addresses that can be instantly located. This section provides an overview of how the name service that's a critical part of the DNS registers, resolves, and distributes computer names.
- **Host Name Characteristics.** The rules for DNS host naming are important to consider when you choose just one name or you're planning to name thousands of computers. Windows computers have special requirements. This section describes the rules you need to know and has suggestions for making good name choices.
- **Fully Qualified Domain Names.** Computers on the Internet are all members of a domain. This section describes domain names and fully qualified domain (host) names and how they're formed.

TCP/IP (TRANSMISSION CONTROL PROTOCOL/INTERNET PROTOCOL) communication happens between computers using their Internet Protocol (IP) addresses. For this reason, an IP address is required for every computer on the Internet to give it a unique identity. The *Domain Name System* (DNS) is the de facto method for registering computer names and IP addresses. The DNS was developed by the Internet community to enable computer hosts anywhere to locate others by friendly names instead of their more cryptic IP addresses.

Note
Every computer on the Internet has an IP address. An IP address is four numbers in a row, each ranging from 0-255 and separated by dots, such as 123.21.99.1, or 10.1.1.3. Individual IP addresses can be assigned automatically or manually. For most purposes, DNS doesn't care about the way they're assigned.

Note
A DNS *domain* is not related to a Microsoft Windows NT domain. Primary Domain Controllers (PDCs) and Backup Domain Controllers (BDCs) authenticate users. They don't provide name service like a DNS server.

Don't confuse a Domain Name System (DNS) server with DNS itself. DNS servers are merely tools of the Domain Name System, or its robots, so to speak, doing the routine work needed to make the Domain Name System function. This chapter covers the Domain Name System and DNS servers. It's important to keep the difference in mind.

This chapter introduces the Domain Name System without making any assumptions about your prior knowledge except that you know a bit about how computers work and how they interact with the Internet. Those who need an introduction or refresher on DNS and DNS servers can benefit from reading it. Here you can learn conceptually, and in some small degree of detail, what the Domain Name System is and how DNS servers make it work for millions of computer users in homes and businesses around the world.

Name Registration, Resolution, and Distribution

DNS servers give clients—individual users, application servers, and even other DNS servers—a way to store and retrieve the host names and IP addresses of other hosts. *Host* is another name for a computer, and a *host name* is the name a computer goes by in the Domain Name System.

Every host name and its Internet Protocol (IP) address are stored in one or more DNS servers, enabling everyone in the world with Internet access to retrieve a host's IP address simply by name. For this to work, DNS servers must communicate reliably with each other to bind every branch of the Internet domain name tree together into one comprehensive system.

Perhaps the two most fundamental name service concepts you can learn are *registration* and *resolution*. They are important requirements for understanding DNS names and DNS servers. But first, let's take a quick look at what we register and resolve: host names and IP addresses.

Host Names and IP Addresses

DNS data files match names with numbers. Telephone directory services resemble the Domain Name System in the sense that they, too, are systems in which names are stored and matched with numbers to identify destinations.

Even though there are other parts to DNS records and some complicated aspects to the DNS system itself, the most fundamental use of DNS, and its highest value to most users, is its capability to match host names with the numeric IP addresses to which they belong, and to give out that information on demand.

Host Name Registration

Host's names and IP addresses have to be registered. *Registration* involves simply recording a name and IP address in a directory or listing. Registration methods can be manual or automatic, static or dynamic. DNS servers, with rare exceptions, get original host registrations manually, which means that hosts in a DNS server's list must be put there, or *registered*, by someone entering them at a keyboard.

Typical DNS registrations are not only manual, they're static. Someone must manually update a host's record when any of its information changes. Figure 1.1 depicts individual hosts that have been registered with a DNS server. Fortunately, the most critical information in a DNS server is just a name and an IP address. (Some important exceptions are introduced in Chapter 7, "What DNS Knows.")

Figure 1.1 doesn't show how host names are registered because there isn't just one way. Manual registrations are most common, and there are a few ways to register names automatically. One way to register automatically is for a DNS server to refer to a WINS server. The WINS registration method is described in Chapter 12, "Integrating DNS with WINS."

Another method of registering automatically occurs when a DHCP server registers names with DNS servers that are capable of handling Dynamic DNS. DHCP (Dynamic Host Configuration Protocol) servers automatically issue IP name and address information to clients when they start up. MS DNS does not support this method.

Host Address Resource Records

The main purpose of name registrations, regardless of how they're performed, is to record the name of a host and its IP address in a place that's accessible to other machines that need the information. An entry is called a *Resource Record* (RR). RRs come in many varieties, which Chapter 7 describes in more detail.

Figure 1.2 shows the host records of several machines as they appear in DNS Manager.

6 Chapter 1 Introducing the Domain Name System

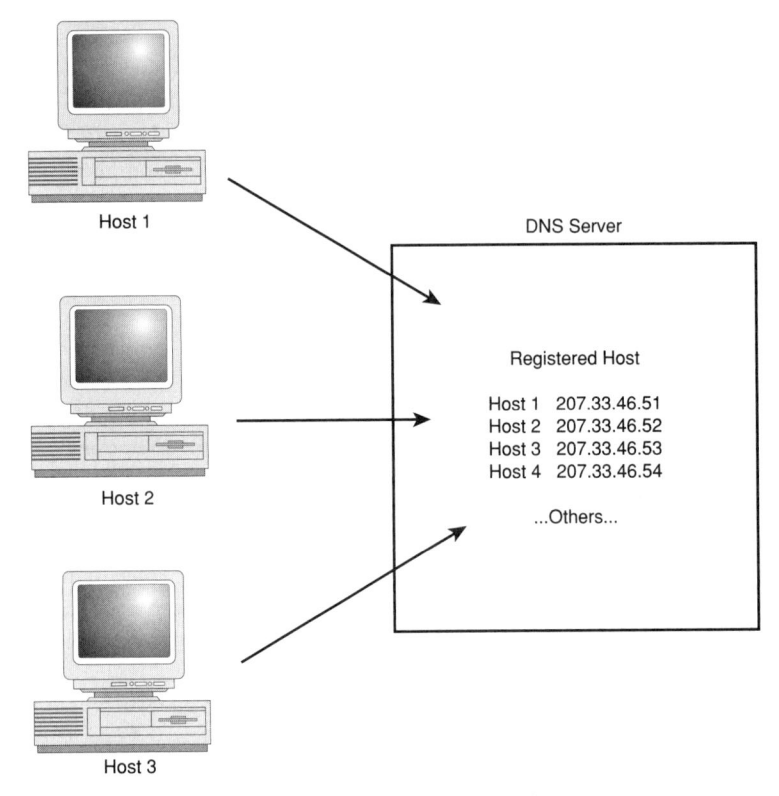

Figure 1.1 Individual hosts are registered with a DNS server.

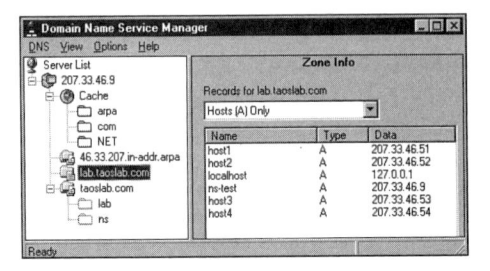

Figure 1.2 Viewing host address (A) Resource Records (RRs).

If you used a UNIX DNS server with text-based configuration files, the entries would look something like the hosts recorded in these records (*IN* means *Internet* and *A* means *Address*):

```
host1    IN    A    207.33.46.51
host2    IN    A    207.33.46.52
host3    IN    A    207.33.46.53
```

Most computers are manually registered with one DNS server, which is usually in the same building, campus, or at least in the same organization. Mid- and large-size organizations almost always have their own DNS servers because it's often faster and easier to edit your own host list than it is to call someone else, such as an Internet service provider (ISP), to record every change for you.

Hosts must be registered in one DNS server: the *primary*. *Secondary* servers automatically get all their data from a primary DNS server. Administrators like the backup this gives them, and it lets them place servers with identical databases in several locations. A headquarters office, for example, might have a primary DNS server, while remote locations could each have a local secondary server for speedy lookups and to protect against network failures that would make the primary server unavailable.

Host Name Resolution

Once registered, a host's name can be resolved. *Resolution* is the client's process for looking up the registered name or service in order to learn its IP address. After the client gets a target host's IP number, it can communicate with it directly on a local network or subnetwork, or it can reach out through one or more routers to a remote network or subnetwork.

It may seem obvious that there's usually a single DNS server for many registered hosts. It's worth noting, though, how this fact makes it a quick matter to resolve the names of other hosts also registered in the same server. Organizations with thousands of hosts need only a few DNS servers. Sparseness of servers also keeps local resolution traffic off the Internet.

Figure 1.3 illustrates how a DNS client resolves the names of other hosts listed in the DNS server where it, too, is registered.

Resolvers

The explanations of name queries in this chapter may seem to imply that DNS servers do all of the name-resolving work. Let's clarify this. The main actor is actually an invisible *resolver* program that runs on all DNS-enabled computers that use TCP/IP. Resolvers convert compatible path statements involving networked host domain names into queries. Resolvers can even cache previously located hosts, speeding up connection times.

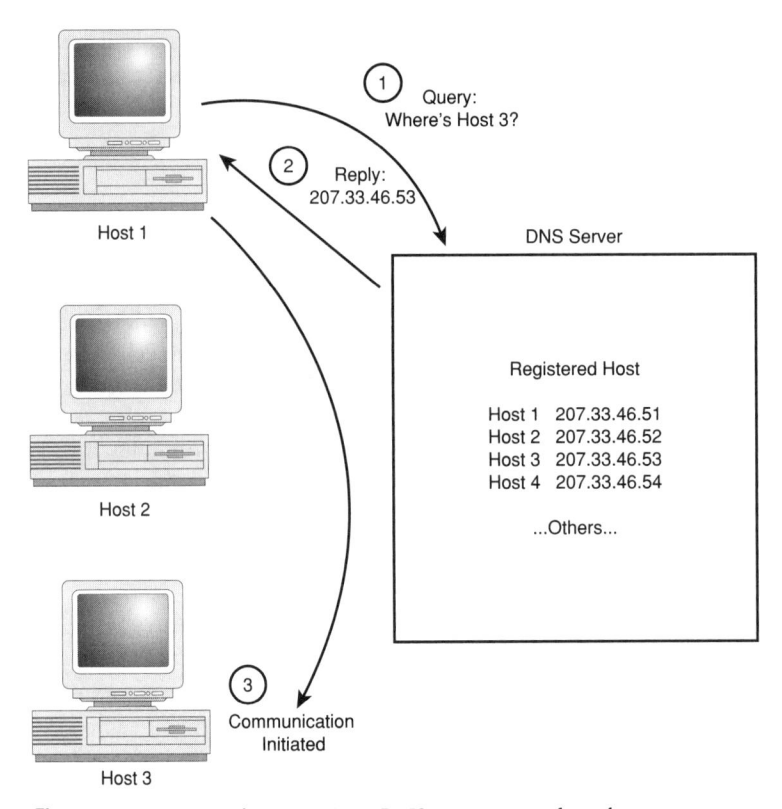

Figure 1.3 A DNS client queries a DNS server to resolve a host name.

Resolvers are everywhere, local and remote, on clients and DNS servers alike. DNS servers use a resolver to query other DNS servers when called upon to do so, which can be often. When a DNS client acts like a client, its resolver is busy. When a DNS server acts like a client, its resolver is busy. When a DNS server acts like a server, it's responding to a client's resolver, and the client may be another DNS server.

Requests for Comments (RFCs)

International standards-setting authorities and voluntary regulating bodies work together to preside over the Internet. These regulating bodies use *Requests For Comments* (RFCs) and working committees to openly evaluate new ideas for standards, receiving them from bright individuals and commercial interests. Some RFCs become standards. To view RFCs, visit the *Domain Name Services Resource Directory* at http://www.dns.net/dnsrd/.

Agencies with standard-setting influence over DNS, Internet protocols, and the Internet itself include the following organizations:

Name Registration, Resolution, and Distribution 9

- Internet Architecture Board (IAB)
- Internet Assigned Numbers Authority (IANA)
- Internet Engineering Steering Group (IESG)
- Internet Engineering Task Force (IETF)
- Internet Society (ISOC)
- InterNIC (Internet Network Information Center)

RFC 1034 indicates that resolvers require access to at least one name server for their information directly, or to pursue the query using referrals to other name servers. On pages 5 and 6, RFC 1034 says, "From the resolver's point of view, the domain system is composed of an unknown number of name servers. Each name server has one or more pieces of the whole domain tree's data...."

Resolvers usually have one of the following results to pass back after queries (from RFC 1034, page 29):

- *One or more RRs giving the requested data:* In this case the resolver returns the answer in the appropriate format.
- *A name error (NE):* This happens when the referenced name does not exist. For example, a user may have mistyped a host name.
- *A data not found error:* This happens when the referenced name exists, but data of the appropriate type does not.

Resolvers are located on the same machine as the program that requests the resolver's services, but it may need to consult name servers on other hosts. On page 28, RFC 1034 says, "Because a resolver may need to consult several name servers, or may have the requested information in a local cache, the amount of time that a resolver will take to complete can vary quite a bit, from milliseconds to several seconds."

Reverse Lookups

So far, all our discussion has illustrated is how DNS maps names to numbers. But it can also map numbers to names. Because the data files in DNS servers are automatically ordered or indexed to quickly find names, *reverse lookups* on numbers would require a special numbers-first database order as well. Reverse lookups are also sometimes called *inverse queries*.

The database DNS servers use to perform reverse lookups is called an in-addr.arpa zone, or *Internet address zone in the ARPA domain*. If you look at Figure 1.2 carefully, you'll see the 46.33.207.in-addr.arpa zone belonging to the 207.33.46.9 name server. This in-addr zone contains a database of numbers to names that the server can use if you need to look up a number instead of a name. MS DNS server can automatically create an in-addr.arpa zone for you for any domain where it's the primary DNS server.

Reverse lookups are not nearly as useful as forward lookups, but they do happen. Most reverse lookups are performed to find the name of a local host when the user, such as a system administrator, already knows its IP address. The practical use of reverse lookups is to discover the fully qualified domain name of a known host. File Transfer Protocol (FTP) servers sometimes use reverse lookups to verify that connecting hosts are actually who they say they are. Otherwise, such tools as nslookup are required to use the reverse lookup feature (see Chapter 17, "Troubleshooting Tools and Utilities").

DNS Server Search Order

You can configure where DNS clients seek to resolve names first, second, and so on. Figure 1.4 shows the search order used by a Windows 95 client. The first DNS server listed, `207.33.46.9`, is where the client itself is registered as a member of the `lab.taoslab.com` domain. If the client can't quickly resolve a host by querying the first server on the list, a second search will be initiated with the second server listed, `204.88.112.62`. After that, the third server will be searched, and so on.

The DNS server where your clients need to be registered is a primary server for their own domain, and most administrators set their clients' search server to the IP address of the same server. But there's no reason why the search servers must be the same.

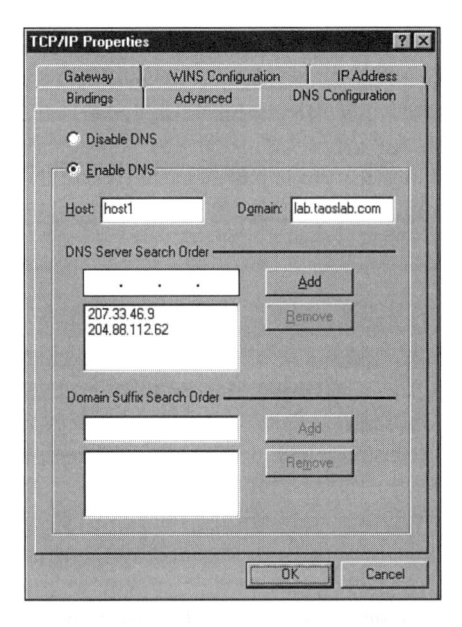

Figure 1.4 DNS Server search order is optional.

The search order is entirely up to you. The DNS servers that your machine queries for resolutions and the DNS servers where it's registered do not have to be the same. Second and third search servers can also be any you like, such as one in another domain, an ISP's name server, or any other that'll respond quickly to queries. Searching through the list will halt as soon as a server responds with an answer that satisfies the client.

Host Name Distribution

No single DNS server holds the names of all the world's hosts. That would be impossible. The distance it would create between you and such a master DNS server, if one existed, could be enormous. Imagine the computing power and bandwidth that it would take to make a single central DNS server work for the whole Internet. Instead, host names are distributed among many DNS servers.

Name distribution solves one problem, but it creates another problem for clients. How can a client know which DNS server to query? The Domain Name System solves this by using a top-down tree structure for host names, where each host is a leaf on some branch and each branch has a domain name. It's important to realize that every host you'll have is associated with a domain.

How many DNS servers are needed then? Although the real number is unknown and varies for practical reasons, the theoretical need is for one DNS server for each branch in the domain name tree.

When a client needs another host's IP address, it will usually query its own DNS server first, that is, if it's the first in search order. If that server doesn't have a record for the host being sought, as is often the case, the query gets referred—passed up the tree, so to speak—to a higher server. Eventually, one with the capability to answer the query is found. To fully understand this co-dependence of DNS domains and servers, it might help to imagine the domain name tree itself as a hierarchy of names, as Figure 1.5 illustrates.

> **Not Quite One DNS Server per Domain**
>
> Figure 1.5 illustrates how DNS servers are placed in the domain name tree. There must be at least one server to manage the records of every domain, and every domain represents a logical branch in the tree. Such is the logic. But actually, one DNS server can handle multiple domains or multiple parts of one or more domains, called subdomains. Don't be concerned about this distinction now. *Zones*, which are introduced in Chapter 5, "How DNS Works," will make it clear how to relate DNS servers with their domains in a variety of ways.

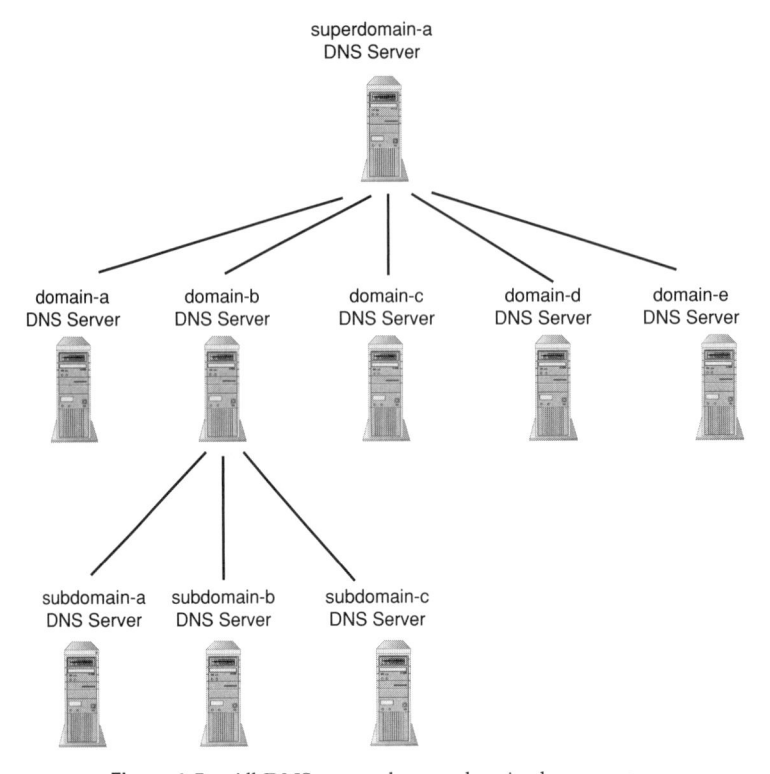

Figure 1.5 All DNS servers have a place in the name tree.

Every DNS server, unless it's isolated for a special reason, fits somewhere into the overall Internet domain hierarchy with other servers. No DNS server is an island unto itself. Each one assumes responsibility for domain name-service duties, even if only for the names that belong to a small organization or some part of a large one.

Private DNS Servers

It's possible to operate DNS servers in private networks unconnected to the Internet. You can even physically connect servers to the Internet, but not let them participate in the public namespace. Unless private servers are isolated, they can cause serious conflicts. IP numbers get allocated (see Chapter 14, "Working with Internet Service Providers"), and domain names must be registered (see Appendix D, "Registering Addresses on the Internet").

To establish a private network, you must isolate it from the public network and use IP numbers reserved for private use only. RFC 1597, "Address Allocation for Private Internets," examines these issues. Like the public network, private networks also need root name servers. Appendix B, "RFCs on DNS, BIND, and NetBIOS," explains RFCs and tells you how to get them. Public root servers are described in RFC 2010, "Operational Criteria for Root Name Servers," and root server design in RFC 1034, "Domain Names—Concepts and Facilities."

Host Name Characteristics

Following the most restrictive advice of Internet RFCs, domain host names (such as those given to UNIX computers) can be up to 24 characters long. Note that Windows computers can have two names! Figure 1.4 shows the Windows 95 Network Control Panel where you can enter host and domain names, but the Windows computer name doesn't go there. It goes in the Identity panel and can't be any longer than 15 characters. Windows computer names are short and simple, like the following:

`hostone`

`hosttwo`

`hostthree`

They could be long and complex, like the following, but then they'd be illegal in the Identity panel where the NetBIOS namespace surfaces:

`host1-o12s-3t4n5a6m7e8-1`

`host2-o23s-4t5n6a7m8e9-2`

`host6-o37s-8t9n0a1m2e3-3`

The wisest way to solve this dilemma is to choose a name that satisfies the criteria of both the domain namespace and the NetBIOS namespace. This means that names will have to be short—15 or fewer characters—and they'll have only characters legal in both spaces.

For servers and other frequently used hosts, you should choose names that people can remember. Simple, functional names are best. Before you implement DNS you can come up with an intuitive naming convention for user workstations, such as `tcarter-pc` for Trent Carter's PC, `hknief-ws` for Herman Knief's workstation, and so on. Servers should also follow a naming convention. You can first select a natural realm from which to select their names. This easily creates easy-to-remember associations between all like hosts, such as `titanic`, `enterprise`, and `mayflower` named after ships, and `paris`, `munich`, `seattle` named after cities. Users at a new site I, once set up, were delighted that I had named all their new printers after volcanoes.

Incidentally, InterNIC, or NIC as it's sometimes called, is the agency that manages domain name registrations. Chapter 14 explains how to register a new domain with NIC.

IP Host Names

The Internet community provides some rules for naming hosts. If you don't follow them carefully, you can create problems for users or applications that try to access your computers. RFC 952 is an authoritative standard defining valid host names, and it describes what makes names valid, or *legal*. RFC 1035 is also authoritative. The following are some practical naming guidelines excerpted from RFC 952:

- A *name* is a text string up to 24 characters drawn from the alphabet (A–Z), digits (0–9), minus sign (–), and period (.). Periods are allowed only when they serve to delimit components of *domain style names*.
- No blank or space characters are permitted as part of a name.
- No distinction is made between upper- and lower-case letters.
- The first character must be a letter of the alphabet.
- The last character must not be a minus sign or period.
- Single character names or nicknames are not allowed.

Some names don't follow the standard. Take `3com.com`, for example, which obviously violates the rule that the first character not be a digit. Although there are some contradictions between RFC documents and some practical relaxation of the standards, it's a good idea to follow them as closely as you can.

RFC 1035: Host Name Recommendations

RFC 1035, "Domain Implementation and Specification," provides a grammar for domain names that's especially helpful if you're familiar with formal computer language forms. Here's an excerpt from pages 6 and 7 of that document:

2.3. Conventions

The domain system has several conventions dealing with low-level, but fundamental, issues. While the implementor is free to violate these conventions within his own system, he must observe these conventions in all behavior observed from other hosts.

2.3.1. Preferred name syntax

The DNS specifications attempt to be as general as possible in the rules for constructing domain names. The idea is that the name of any existing object can be expressed as a domain name with minimal changes.

However, when assigning a domain name for an object, the prudent user will select a name which satisfies both the rules of the domain system and any existing rules for the object, whether these rules are published or implied by existing programs.

For example, when naming a mail domain, the user should satisfy both the rules of this memo and those in RFC-822. When creating a new host name, the old rules for **HOSTS.TXT** *should be followed. This avoids problems when old software is converted to use domain names.*

The following syntax will result in fewer problems with many applications that use domain names (such as mail, Telnet).

```
<domain> ::= <subdomain> | " "
<subdomain> ::= <label> | <subdomain> "." <label>
<label> ::= <letter> [ [ <ldh-str> ] <let-dig> ]
<ldh-str> ::= <let-dig-hyp> | <let-dig-hyp> <ldh-str>
<let-dig-hyp> ::= <let-dig> | "-"
<let-dig> ::= <letter> | <digit>
<letter> ::= any one of the 52 alphabetic characters A through Z in upper
 case and a through z in lower case
<digit> ::= any one of the ten digits 0 through 9
```

Note that while upper- and lowercase letters are allowed in domain names, no significance is attached to the case. That is, two names with the same spelling but different case, are to be treated as if identical.

You can find more information about the rules for creating valid host names in RFCs 1123 and 1912. Good sources for all Internet RFC documents are `http://www.isi.edu/rfc-editor/` and `http://www.merseyworld.com/techwatch/standards/`.

Windows (NetBIOS) Computer Names

Windows computer names must be 15 or fewer characters long to satisfy the NetBIOS length requirement. Don't depend on case to make names unique: `Host-One`, `HOST-ONE`, and `host-one` are equivalent on UNIX and Windows computers alike. Windows computer names can have characters that aren't allowed in DNS. Problems can arise if names with invalid characters are registered in DNS, either manually or through the automatic WINS feature, which is described in Chapter 12, "Integrating DNS with WINS." Windows computers should use valid DNS characters only so that problems can't arise. The following sample names are valid in WINS, but not in most DNS servers:

`1isAnumber` (begins with a digit)

`under_score` (underscore character not allowed)

`space ghost` (space character not allowed)

Although the MS DNS server accepts Windows host names with some invalid characters in order to support NetBIOS names via WINS, it is not a good idea to ignore DNS naming rules, even if for a seemingly good reason. Microsoft knowledge base article Q154554 explains it this way:

Windows NT 4.0 Domain Naming System (DNS) server does not enforce the name restrictions, and will do WINS lookup for host names containing invalid characters...

It continues, saying:

It is not recommended to use invalid host names.... Other DNS servers may have problems with names containing invalid characters.

This is good advice. Use only DNS-legal names for Windows computers.

Fully Qualified Domain Names

Host names aren't truly complete unless they include the domain the host belongs to. Of course, if you're using a computer in the same domain with the host you seek, your resolver will probably append the domain name for you after making the helpful assumption that you're in the same domain. But if the computer you seek is in another domain and DNS fails to find it, it may be that you're using an unqualified domain name—one that doesn't include domain membership information.

To locate a host totally outside your domain, you need to tell DNS the host's name and its domain. Calling for telephone directory assistance is no different: You have to know the country and city where a person lives if you want the operator to find the phone number. Ultimately, all host names are qualified by the membership in an organizational domain, a fact that adds length to their names:

```
host1.acmecompany          10.1.1.1
host2.acmecompany          10.1.1.2
host3.acmecompany          10.1.1.3
```

In the preceding example, `host1`, `host2`, and `host3` belong to the `acmecompany` organization, and hence, are members of its domain. As all hosts belong to some organization, all organizational domains belong to a top-level Internet domain, also called a *TLD*. The fully qualified host names for `acmecompany` hosts could look like the following:

```
host1.acmecompany.com      10.1.1.1
host2.acmecompany.com      10.1.1.2
host3.acmecompany.com      10.1.1.3
www.anysite.org            101.1.1.1
fileserver.anysite.net     110.1.1.10
```

A fully qualified domain name (FQDN) is the host name plus the full path, listing all domain memberships in a series. Domain names are joined together in series to indicate exactly where the host logically resides. Another way to put it is to say that FQDNs are fully expressed host names because they leave nothing unsaid. FQDNs contain directions leading to the very top of the domain tree where all domains and hosts are rooted. For example, the FQDN of a Web server at acmecompany might be www.acmecompany.com, or if the host www resides in the sales department's subdomain, its FQDN might instead be www.sales.acmecompany.com.

FQDNs are practical. Electronic mail, for example, uses fully qualified domain names in the recipient's email address. Take janicejones@acmecompany.com, for instance, in which the recipient's name, janicejones, is followed by the @ symbol. Following @ is the mail server's FQDN or alias, which in this case is the name of an organizational domain where the mail server resides, followed by its top-level domain: .com. The .com domain means that acmecompany is a commercial organization.

Summary

This chapter introduced fundamental DNS concepts and some rules for naming. The next few chapters will cover WINS, the Windows Internet Name Service, in some depth to help you understand how Windows computers natively handle name resolution without DNS, and to help you later integrate WINS with DNS, which is the subject of Chapter 12.

Introducing NetBIOS

This chapter will review:

- **NetBIOS.** NetBIOS is a legacy application interface with services designed to make peer-to-peer networking easy. NetBIOS works on more than one transport protocol. This section gives you an overview of NetBIOS so you can understand precisely what it is and how, for example, it's different from NetBEUI.

- **Resolving NetBIOS Names.** NetBIOS has many name-related services and six ways to resolve names. This section describes NetBIOS names and explains all the ways clients can resolve them, including WINS, the Windows Internet Name Service.

- **A Flat Name Space.** Unlike DNS, the NetBIOS namespace is flat. This section describes the namespace and explains its implications for name service administration and scalability.

- **NetBIOS Name Characteristics.** Some NetBIOS names have to be unique. This section describes NetBIOS names and explains the rules for naming users, computers, and groups.

- **NetBIOS Names and Resource Codes.** NetBIOS names contain hidden characters NetBIOS uses to identify special resources, such as message services and domain controllers. This section reveals those codes and explains how they're stored in WINS.

THERE'S NOTHING QUITE LIKE NETBIOS in the UNIX world, which is probably why it presents an awkward challenge to experienced UNIX DNS administrators who are learning to support Windows machines. Windows administrators can also struggle with NetBIOS in heterogeneous environments if its architectural limitations haven't been adequately accounted for by good service designs—which is too often the case.

At least two things make learning NetBIOS essential for system administrators: NetBIOS isn't going away soon and NetBIOS needs a non-DNS name server (WINS, the Windows Internet Name Service) to make all of its other services run properly in TCP/IP environments.

This chapter introduces NetBIOS services and its namespace to help experienced DNS administrators understand Windows, and it gives all readers a short and to-the-point overview. Chapter 3, "How Windows Clients Use DNS and WINS," builds on this chapter to round out our introduction of Windows name resolution methods, and Chapter 4, "WINS and DNS: Making the Most of Both Services," shows you how to use the two services concurrently to get the best out of both.

NetBIOS

The *Network Basic Input/Output System* is documented in RFCs 1001 and 1002.

NetBIOS isn't a name service, although it does have some related capabilities as well as a formalized facility called the *Windows Internet Name Service* (WINS) covered in Chapter 3. NetBIOS started out as an application programming interface (API) for MS-DOS computers in small single-segment networks, but it has become widely popular in recent years due to Microsoft's awesome success with Windows for Workgroups, Windows 95, and Windows NT.

NetBIOS Services

Some widely used and very convenient services depend on NetBIOS, such as *browsing* (which provides a list of computers in the Network Neighborhood window) and the capability to send *messages* to users with only their login name for reference (a vital administrative tool). There are services that depend on NetBIOS, but let's leave the particulars for a moment to describe NetBIOS more generally. NetBIOS is best described as a suite of *interprocess communication* (IPC) services falling into three categories:

- *Name services* get and release resource names. NetBIOS has unique (individual computer and user) names, and group (workgroup/domain) names. Names in its flat namespace commute through broadcasts, or in the case of WINS, through point-to-point communications with a persistent naming authority capable of addressing computers on any reachable IP network.

- *Session services* include messaging commands that give a pair of NetBIOS applications full-duplex, sequenced, and reliable connections. Multiple connections are supported, and names identify both participants.

- *Datagram services* transmit and receive messages between participants by broadcasting to group names or unicasting to unique, individual names. Unlike session services, datagram services are non-sequenced, unreliable, and connectionless.

NetBIOS supports broadcast name resolutions, a service that has a close relationship with DNS, the core subject of this book. NetBIOS broadcasts frequently, even on TCP/IP, but the broadcasts aren't always appreciated. Name service broadcasts have an architecturally imposed scope, limiting them to single network segments.

Users and administrators alike get frustrated. It's no surprise that name services, namely browsing and name resolutions, cause most of the problems people have with NetBIOS in routed networks and environments where port or packet filtering is aggressively applied. By default, all NetBIOS name services depend on broadcasts. Fortunately, NetBIOS session services usually work fine if name service issues are resolved.

A Nutshell History of NetBIOS

NetBIOS was developed in the personal computer environment to let programmers develop client/server programs and was implemented on the *NetBIOS Extended User Interface* (NetBEUI) by IBM in 1985. IBM packaged NetBIOS support with NetBEUI to give MS-DOS PC applications easy-to-use network services in local area networks (LANs).

NetBEUI uses a Token Ring type of source routing. NetBEUI is only practical for a few hundred computers, and doesn't scale to wide area networks (WANs) because it can't be routed. A frustrating example of this legacy is evident, even in new implementations of NetBIOS, when the list of computer names showing up in one Network Neighborhood window differs from another because the users are on opposite sides of a router.

3Com and Microsoft jointly developed LAN Manager to run as a process on OS/2. IBM's version, LAN Server, was slightly different, but they both used NetBEUI. In 1993, Microsoft abstracted NetBIOS from NetBEUI for binding to TCP/IP, and in 1995 for binding to Novell's IPX/SPX. This made NetBIOS services more useful in WANs, but it didn't remedy its architectural limitations. NetBIOS still uses more broadcasts than other TCP/IP service protocols, and uses an altogether different convention to name computers and services that we'll discuss in depth later in this chapter in the section "NetBIOS Names and Resource Codes."

Server Message Blocks and the Common Internet File System

In a historical overview of NetBIOS, we can't overlook the networking functions of *Server Message Blocks* (SMBs), which give Windows computers a native file redirection facility for accessing remote file systems. Some developers refer to SMB as the *Lanman* protocol because it was first popularized by 3Com's now defunct LAN Manager products.

Although SMB and NetBIOS have a closely related history, SMB is more enduring. It's now subsumed in the open *Common Internet File System* (CIFS) standard proposed by Microsoft, Network Appliance, and others. CIFS is much like the *Network File System* (NFS) common on UNIX computers, but with some significant feature differences. At the time of writing this book, CIFS is in the hands of an Internet Engineering Task Force (IETF) workgroup for discussion and endorsement.

CIFS is alive and well, and its popularity is still growing. A popular open-licensed application for UNIX named SAMBA implements CIFS, enabling UNIX hosts to share files and printers with Windows computers. SAMBA also makes UNIX hosts into clients using Windows shares.

Another use of CIFS best exemplified by Network Appliance, a company that ships one of the world's fastest fileservers for UNIX and Windows users alike, is network-attached storage. NetApp filers, as they're called, simultaneously and natively support the CIFS and NFS file protocols to share (export) a RAID subsystem without a general-purpose operating system like Windows NT or UNIX. A high-performance micro-kernel operating system does nothing but disk and network I/O.

NetBIOS and SMB/CIFS make it possible for SAMBA, NetApp filers, and other products like them, to join with Windows computers on the network.

NetBIOS on TCP/IP and Other Transport Protocols

NetBIOS over TCP/IP, documented in RFCs 1001 and 1002, is named NetBT, or NBT. NetBIOS provides the same suite of services on NetBEUI, IPX/SPX, or TCP/IP. It's important to note, though, that NetBIOS services operating on one transport protocol can't communicate with NetBIOS services operating on another transport protocol. You can use NetBEUI (which always includes NetBIOS) on one computer, for example, and NetBIOS over TCP/IP on another, but they won't communicate.

NetBIOS is segregated by transport because most of its features can only work on the first transport that binds to the network adapter; later NetBIOS bindings are ignored. If you require multiple protocols and expect NetBIOS to work properly, set all the computers needing NetBIOS to the same binding order and make the preferred NetBIOS transport protocol first in binding order. This requires a Registry edit on Windows 95 machines and an adjustment in the Network Control Panel on Windows NT.

A resulting limitation is that NetBIOS itself can't be multihomed reliability; that is, it cannot be functionally bound to multiple network adapters in one computer. Computers with NetBIOS can be multihomed, but it's recommended only for routers, and for file and print servers if clients already know the server's address or can resolve it. Such a server won't respond to broadcasts on every interface, but it will respond to a direct connection request on every interface.

Note

NetBIOS uses well-known ports:

- NetBT name services use UDP port 137.
- NetBT session services use TCP port 139.
- NetBT datagram services use UDP port 138.

Figure 2.1 compares OSI and TCP/IP network layers with common NetBIOS implementations, and it reveals how NetBIOS and NetBEUI differ. It's important to note that NetBIOS can operate on several transport protocols, including NetBEUI, TCP/IP, and Novell's IPX/SPX.

Because the subject at hand is name resolution, a question arises: How does a NetBIOS computer resolve the names it wants to connect with? The answer is that there are multiple methods. The next section, "Resolving NetBIOS Names," describes them all.

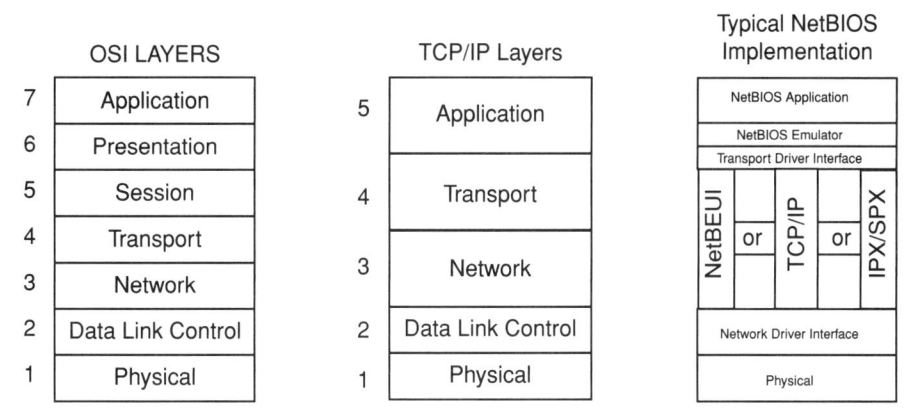

#	OSI LAYERS	#	TCP/IP Layers	Typical NetBIOS Implementation
7	Application	5	Application	NetBIOS Application
6	Presentation			NetBIOS Emulator
				Transport Driver Interface
5	Session	4	Transport	NetBEUI or TCP/IP or IPX/SPX
4	Transport			
3	Network	3	Network	
2	Data Link Control	2	Data Link Control	Network Driver Interface
1	Physical	1	Physical	Physical

Figure 2.1 Network layers and NetBIOS transport protocols.

Resolving NetBIOS Names

The browse service creates a list of NetBIOS computer names, sorted by a group name, that is viewable in the Network Neighborhood or with the NET VIEW command. The message service sends directed messages to NetBIOS unique (user or computer) names, or to whole groups using the NET SEND command.

The following are the kinds of names NetBIOS uses:

- *Unique NetBIOS names:* Identify individual computers or users.

- *Workgroup names:* NetBIOS *group* names that identify members of an ad hoc association. Unique names (users and computers) are workgroup members by default, or they may choose a group to belong to by its name.

- *Domain names:* Also NetBIOS *group* names, but they identify members with an authenticator, a Domain Controller, instead of an ad hoc workgroup. The distinction between workgroup and domain names means nothing to the name service: It treats them identically.

NetBIOS *name* services provide a way to register names via broadcast in small networks and via directed communications if they're available. It automatically registers names, queries names, responds to name queries, and releases registered names at shutdown. NetBIOS doesn't require a name server like DNS or WINS. Name servers are useful, and necessary under some circumstances, but they're only one of several name resolution mechanisms that NetBIOS is capable of using.

Six Name Resolution Methods

Windows computers can resolve names from six possible sources. Chapter 3, "How Windows Clients Use DNS and WINS," covers the sources in depth and describes the query order clients use depending on how they're configured and what methods they have at their disposal. Figure 2.2 shows what happens when three of the most popular methods are used. Notice that broadcast resolutions don't typically return the addresses of hosts outside the local network, a limitation that's best overcome by deploying a WINS server.

The rest of this chapter presumes that TCP/IP is the NetBIOS transport protocol being used. The following are some short descriptions of the six name resolution sources Windows computers employ:

- *NetBIOS name cache:* The locally stored cache of names gathered into each client's memory by preloading (see LMHOSTS in this list) or by successfully resolving an address. Subsequent queries from cache are quick, but cache life for an entry is only 10 minutes, after which it will have to be refreshed.

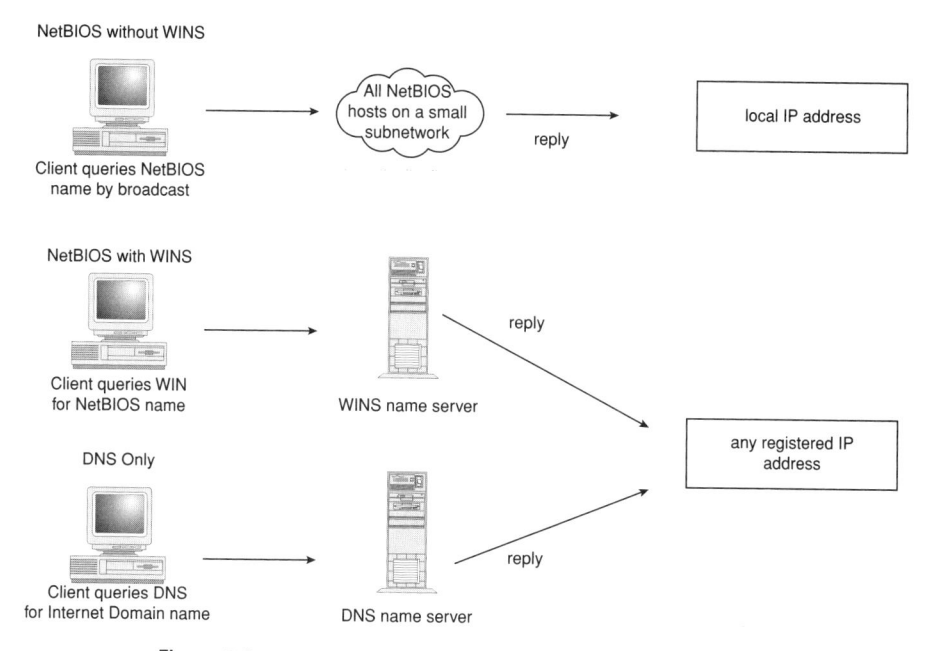

Figure 2.2 NetBIOS and DNS name query methods and results.

- *Broadcast queries:* Use the NetBIOS Datagram Distribution service (NDDS) on UDP ports 137 and 138 if names can't be found in cache and a WINS server (NBNS) is not configured. Broadcasts ask computers on the local network to search their name tables. The target host, if on the same network, will respond. Routers normally block NDDS broadcasts, limiting this method to single network segments.
- *WINS:* Microsoft's NetBIOS name server (NBNS). Clients will register and release their own names at the WINS server address they're configured to use. For resolutions, they query the same address. WINS/client communications are directed messages at UDP ports 137 and 138, enabling them to pass through routers. If WINS fails, clients can resort to broadcast queries.
- *LMHOSTS:* A locally stored LAN Manager-style hosts (text) file a client can query if broadcasts fail. LMHOST names can be preloaded into local NetBIOS name cache using the #PRE tag to prevent broadcasting for frequently queried hosts. #PRE is also useful for hosts outside the local network so that sure-to-fail broadcasts won't be attempted. Preloading a domain controller's address is required (using the #PRE and #DOM tags) if you're not using WINS, and the domain controller isn't on the client's immediate network.

- *HOSTS:* A locally stored UNIX-style hosts (text) file a client can also query if broadcasts fail. Clients use HOSTS as the last resort. Advantages of the HOSTS file is that it can store aliases and fully qualified domain names (FQDNs). A disadvantage is that it's used only if other query methods fail. Another disadvantage is that tags aren't supported.
- *DNS:* Clients will query a DNS server if the Enable DNS for Windows Name Resolution box is checked in the client's Network Control Panel. DNS servers are always queried last, even after a HOSTS file, which means that DNS is the least practical method for resolving NetBIOS names.

The NetBIOS query sources are local cache, broadcast, WINS, and LMHOSTS. Domain name query sources are DNS and HOSTS. If you use domain name resolution methods, DNS or HOSTS, IP host names *are* assumed to be NetBIOS names, meaning that the NetBIOS computer name and its IP host name must be identical.

Nothing prevents you from normalizing NetBIOS computer names with domain host names, but doing so is optional if you use name resolution methods selectively: NetBIOS name resolution methods for NetBIOS computer names and domain name resolution methods for IP host names. In any case, it's best to normalize names so that one method can resolve names in both spaces.

WINS

The Windows Internet Name Service (WINS) gives NetBIOS a real name server. Clients must be configured to use WINS. Figure 2.3 shows the Network Control Panel of a Windows 95 computer configured to use WINS. Windows NT configuration is similar.

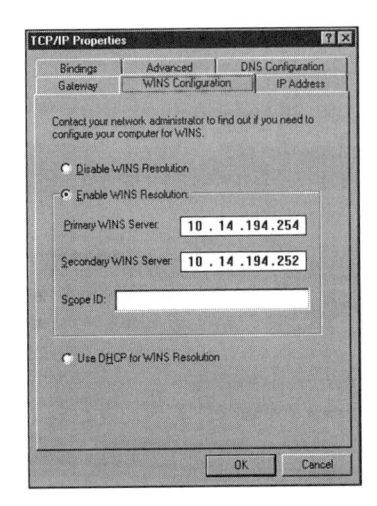

Figure 2.3 Client configuration for WINS.

Example 2.1 shows output from the `nbtstat -r` command on a Windows 95 computer. `nbtstat -r` reveals resolution statistics since boot up, illustrating in this case that a WINS server resolved all 18 of the name queries the client performed.

Example 2.1 **NBTSTAT -r Showing Name Resolution History**

```
C:\WINDOWS>nbtstat -r

NetBIOS Names Resolution and Registration Statistics
----------------------------------------------------
Resolved By Broadcast      = 0
Resolved By Name Server    = 18

Registered By Broadcast    = 0
Registered By Name Server  = 4
```

Example 2.2 shows output from the `nbtstat` command on the same Windows 95 computer, revealing what names it successfully registered on the name server:

Example 2.2 **NBTSTAT -n Showing Registered Names**

```
C:\WINDOWS>nbtstat -n

Node IpAddress: [10.14.194.8] Scope Id: []
          NetBIOS Local Name Table
     Name              Type         Status
    ---------------------------------------------
    WS-MASTERSON     <00>  UNIQUE    Registered
    TAOS             <00>  GROUP     Registered
    WS-MASTERSON     <03>  UNIQUE    Registered
    MMASTERSON       <03>  UNIQUE    Registered
```

Computer names are forced to be unique, but group names can be shared. Example 2.2 shows two instances of the *unique* WS-MASTERSON computer name, one instance of the *unique* MMASTERSON user name, and one instance of the TAOS *group* name. How can this be? The <00> (hostname) and <03> (messenger service) name suffixes are resource codes accounting for how two names appearing to be duplicates are actually unique. Resource code suffixes appended to NetBIOS names indicate what services are available at that name.

Figure 2.4 shows the contents of a WINS database listing more than computer names and IP numbers. At the end of each NetBIOS computer name you can see the resource codes between brackets [ ]. These resource codes will be described more fully a little later in this chapter, in the "NetBIOS Names and Resource Codes" section. For now, note that each code represents a resource or service that's running and available at that IP address.

Chapter 2 Introducing NetBIOS

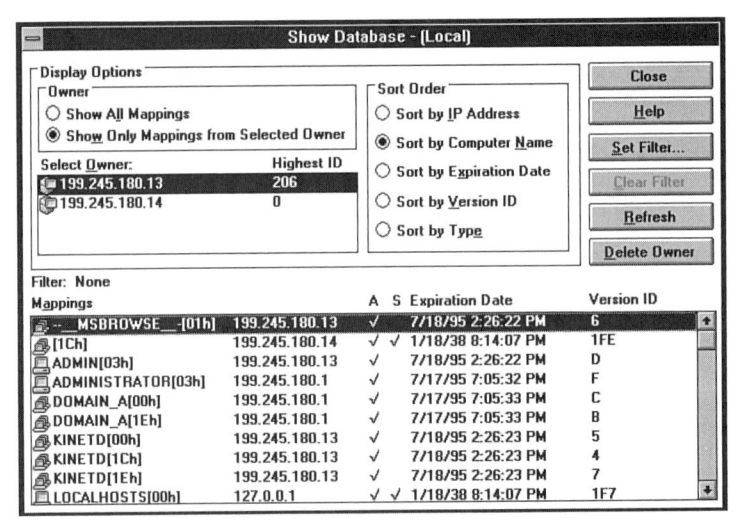

Figure 2.4 A WINS database contains more than computer names and IP numbers.

In the bottom half of the dialog box in Figure 2.4, the first column on the left is the NetBIOS computer's name, the name of a resource or a resource code. NetBIOS keeps a list of the services available at each computer name. The second column on each line is the Internet Protocol (IP) address.

The next columns (A and S) are checkmarks indicating how the record was registered. *A* indicates active (automatic, dynamic) registration, which happens at startup time as clients register their own IP addresses with the WINS server they're configured for. *S* indicates a static (manual) registration made by an administrator at the WINS console. Both types can be checked because a computer can be registered automatically and statically at the same time.

The fourth column in Figure 2.4 is a date indicating when the registration will expire. The client protocol automatically refreshes a registration before it expires if the client is still on the network. If not, it will refresh during the next startup.

The fifth and last column in Figure 2.4 provides a hexadecimal number representing the record's replication version. Created by the WINS server, this version ID helps the WINS replication protocol determine which records need to be updated on data-pulling partners and which ones don't because they're current.

Those who know a lot about database structures viewing WINS can quickly observe that the WINS database is not a *normalized* table of computer names and IP numbers. WINS isn't, perhaps, as well designed as it could be because of the non-IP NetBIOS legacy. Still, WINS does its job quite well in light of its unavoidable NetBIOS limitations.

Note

Windows NT 5 will be able to run without NetBIOS, but it will require that clients subscribe to MS Active Directory services. AD is Microsoft's server supporting the Lightweight Directory Access Protocol (LDAP). In practical terms, then, you can't plan to dump NetBIOS altogether until all clients are Windows NT 5.

There's no plan we know of to make AD client software available for legacy operating systems, such as Windows 95 and NT4. Until all clients can use Active Directory instead of the current built-in NetBIOS services, NetBIOS will need to exist in its present form and must be supported by current services.

A Flat Namespace

The NetBIOS namespace isn't hierarchical; it's flat, which creates some challenges for administrators. Limited capacity for names is one such challenge. Another challenge of a flat namespace is that no two computers can have the same name. Can you imagine what would happen if two companies couldn't name their Web servers www? There would be no www.taos.com, no www.cnet.com, and no www.yahoo.com.

DNS fortunately allows thousands of computers to be named www because each belongs to a different domain. The single, flat space of WINS doesn't have the same flexibility, and it increases the chance that duplicate names will occur because there are no qualifiers, such as DNS domains, to separate them. NetBIOS scopes are arbitrary numbers you can assign to computers in order to separate one set of NetBIOS names from another, effectively creating two or more entirely distinct namespaces. The problem with scopes is that, once separated, computers using different scopes don't communicate.

Figure 2.5 illustrates practical computer naming implications in a flat namespace.

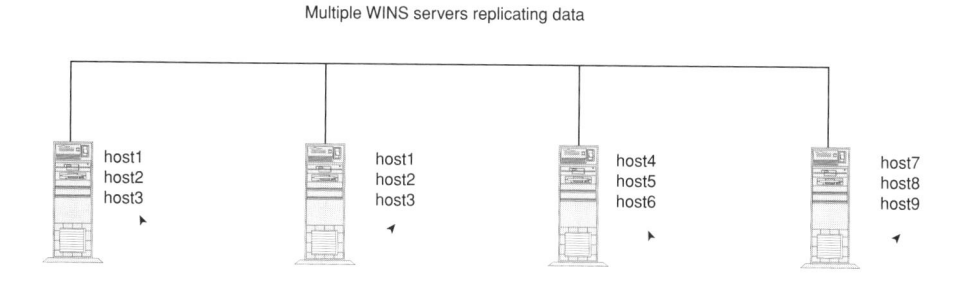

Figure 2.5 NetBIOS computers in a WINS system cannot have the same name.

To describe the flat namespace problem most accurately, no two computers with NetBIOS names sharing a single WINS server or a set of replication partners can have the same name. This is true even if the computers are in different DNS domains because the NetBIOS name service will issue error messages, and without hesitation, it will halt duplicate computer names from registering on the network, making it impossible for them to share resources or access services.

Figure 2.6 illustrates practical computer naming implications in a flat namespace. You can see in Figure 2.5 that NetBIOS names contend for recognition at only one level. Figure 2.6, by contrast, shows how the DNS namespace can support identical hostnames as long as they're not in the same subdomain because they're in different parts of the hierarchy.

NetBIOS Name Characteristics

NetBIOS computer and user names are always 16 byte strings. When a name is less than 15 characters, it's automatically padded out with space characters to 15 bytes in length, with one byte reserved for a suffix that's really a resource or service code. These are automatically appended after the 15th byte. The suffix is usually hidden unless you're looking at a WINS database or the output of a command like nbtstat.

Whenever you see a NetBIOS name shorter than 15 characters, such as in a WINS database, it has been truncated for display purposes by removing all white space after the last printable character.

NetBIOS names can be up to 15 printable characters long, consisting of alphanumeric characters only and the following special characters:

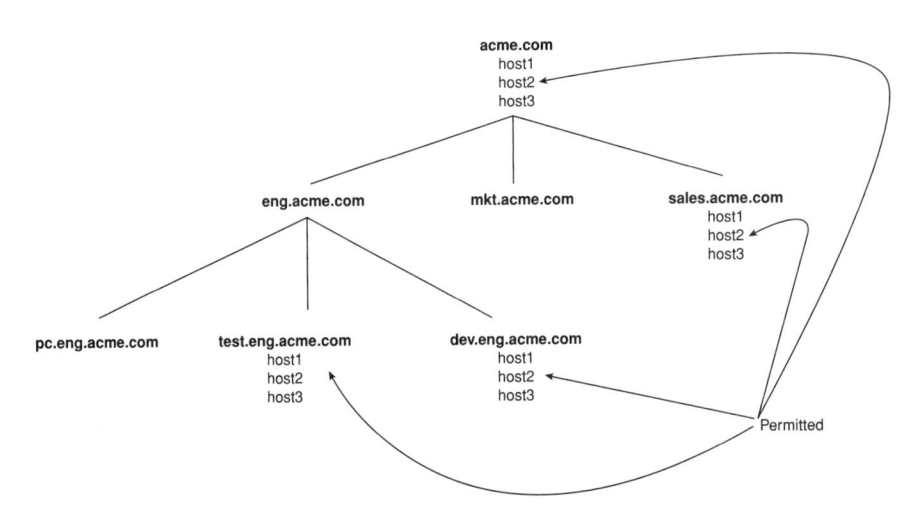

! @ # $ % ^ & ( ) - ' { } . ~

Figure 2.6 Host names in DNS can have the same name.

Some implementations of NetBIOS tolerate spaces in names (that is, embedded between two visible characters), but it's not advisable to use white space at all, especially if you want a computer's name to be valid in DNS too, where white space characters are invalid.

NetBIOS names can't start with an asterisk (*), which is reserved for broadcast addressing. Even though the period (.) is legal in NetBIOS, it's not valid for host names in the domain name space because it delimits portions of fully qualified domain names (FQDNs). Take a look at the "Host Name Characteristics" section of Chapter 1, "Introducing the Domain Name System," where there's more information about naming, particularly for compatibility with DNS.

NetBIOS Names and Resource Codes

Like DNS, WINS stores computer names—albeit NetBIOS computer names—and it maps them to IP address numbers. Also like DNS, WINS answers name resolution queries with an IP number so that the client can connect, even over routers.

Resource codes give NetBIOS the capability to register not only computers, but also standard services. Because NetBIOS already knows where services reside, that is, what IP number to use to reach them, clients can query WINS to reach those services by name without first having to know where they are.

Table 2.1 lists the NetBIOS service resource codes. Most of the codes are used only to identify computers and resources within one subnet—often by broadcast because NetBIOS was first designed to operate without routers on single, small networks. Some of the codes might never appear in a WINS database.

Table 2.1 **NetBIOS (16th Byte) Service Resource Codes**

Resource Code	Type of Entry	What's Registered; Service is Performing the Registration
<00>	A computer or domain name	NetBIOS computer name or domain of membership, by Workstation service
<01>	Literally: "_MSBROWSE_"	IP of local master browser for announcement to other browsers, by Browser service
<03>	A user or computer name	Message target: a NetBIOS username or NetBIOS computer name, by messenger service
<06>	A computer name	NetBIOS computer name running RAS, by RAS service

continues

Table 2.1 **Continued**

Resource Code	Type of Entry	What's Registered; Service Performing the Registration
<1B>	A domain name	Domain master browser, by the PDC's special domain master browser service
<1C>	A domain name	Domain group name, by PDC or BDC (up to 25 DCs can register per domain)
<1D>	A domain name	Local master browser publishing browse lists for retrieval by backup local browsers, by browser service
<1E>	A domain name	Normal group name targeted by broadcasts to elect local master browsers, by browser service
<1F>	A computer name	NetBIOS computer name capable of Network Dynamic Data Exchange, by NetDDE service
<20>	A computer or group name	NetBIOS computer name, or special administrative group name, by Server service
<21>	A computer name	NetBIOS computer name, by RAS client
<BE>	A computer name	NetBIOS computer name, by Network Monitor agent
<BF>	A computer name	NetBIOS computer name, by Network Monitor utility

Summary

This chapter introduced WINS and NetBIOS names, pointing out that NetBIOS uses a flat namespace. A flat namespace can be a severe impediment to administrators designing name services for organizations that are large or connected to the Internet. This doesn't, however, conclude our investigation of WINS. Arguing to abandon NetBIOS and WINS isn't wise at this time because they provide too many advantages in Windows networks. Chapter 3 identifies more WINS qualities while comparing its features to DNS.

How Windows Clients Use DNS and WINS

This chapter will review:

- **Introducing the Windows resolver.** This section introduces the Windows client resolver and also explains what a resolver is and how it differs from a name server.
- **How WINS serves the Windows name resolver.** WINS is the NetBIOS name server and, as such, provides an invaluable service to Windows clients by helping Windows computers find one another in a local area network and even over a WAN. This section explains the role WINS can play to help you resolve names.
- **How DNS serves the Windows name resolver.** DNS is the irreplaceable Domain Name Service that helps clients resolve Internet names. This section explains in some detail how this service works, including a description of iterative, recursive, and reverse queries.
- **How the resolver works.** The Windows client resolver is complex because it must deal with two different name types (DNS and NetBIOS) and can use up to six methods. This section explains how the resolver thinks—and how it actually works its way through three separate phases to resolve names depending on different configuration options at your disposal.

34 Chapter 3 How Windows Clients Use DNS and WINS

WINDOWS COMPUTERS HAVE SO MANY NAME-RESOLUTION OPTIONS to use that it's hard sometimes to predict just how they'll behave. The way in which the resolver is configured makes a huge difference. Sometimes a computer just can't find others on the network—even those listed in the Network Neighborhood. If you know how resolvers work, the mysteries behind a success or failure are easier to solve. Helping you understand the Windows resolver is the purpose of this chapter. For guidance on how to configure your computers to take advantage of all the resolver's options, take a look at Chapter 13, "Configuring Clients."

Introducing the Windows Resolver

A *resolver* is the collection of programs and processes a client computer uses to take advantage of available name services. A Windows resolver that asks a WINS or a DNS name server for an address stays engaged until an answer comes back, even if it means that other servers must also be queried or other methods invoked. Resolvers typically use all options at their disposal.

For the purposes of the discussion in this chapter, name-resolving is strictly a client function. This isn't to say that name servers don't help—they simply play a supporting role in the process. Clients resolve names.

UNIX resolvers deal almost exclusively with IP host names. By contrast, Windows resolvers must support two name types: NetBIOS computer names and IP host names. What's more, Windows resolvers must decide which of several possible options to use to resolve the names—and the resolvers also must know what to do if the first approach doesn't succeed, if the second doesn't succeed, and so on.

Note

Variations in resolver behavior among Windows 95, Windows 98, and Windows NT are not explored in detail here because the differences are too few.

Having said that, the main difference between Windows NT 4 and Windows 95 is that Windows NT queries DNS first if any periods (".") exist in the name, or if the name is more than 15 characters in length. Windows 98 acts more like Windows NT than Windows 95. By contrast, Windows 95 first attempts to use NetBIOS resolution methods, and only when these fail will it query the LMHOSTS and HOSTS files—and finally a DNS server lookup. The calling order and the method of deciding which are used or ignored are determined by configuration settings.

The general-purpose resolver facility inside a Windows operating system is available to any program that needs it—even those with no name-resolving capabilities. Most applications needing name service use the general purpose resolver by giving it computer names to resolve.

The Windows name resolver submits queries to name servers and handles the various possible responses they can return. When names are resolved, applications can usually proceed with their tasks. If, for any reason, the resolver does not succeed in locating a name, it sends an appropriate failure message to the local application that requested service. Most Windows applications are designed to handle these conditions gracefully; they'll warn the user about the failure instead of crashing.

Some applications have built-in resolver capabilities so that they don't even need the general-purpose resolver. Examples of this approach include ping and nslookup. The ping tool, which sends Internet Control Management Protocol (ICMP) echo requests to verify other computers on the network, parses names and numbers and can query a DNS server itself without calling its host's general-purpose resolver. The nslookup tool is a comprehensive, standalone DNS server diagnostic utility that also contains a resolver. Chapter 17, "Troubleshooting Tools and Utilities," can tell you more about ping and nslookup and explains how to use them.

A useful feature of Windows resolvers is that they automatically switch between various name services including WINS and DNS, saving users from having to decide. The following sections review what WINS and DNS servers can do for clients.

How WINS Serves the Windows Name Resolver

WINS servers have one simple query-handling behavior: They reply positively with the address and name sought, or they reply negatively with a `Requested Name Does Not Exist` message. WINS servers search through the names and addresses in their own database file of registered computers and any other databases they've received by replication from other WINS servers.

A Windows client sends up to three requests to a primary WINS server. The IP number (address) of WINS servers is set in the Network Control Panel under TCP/IP settings. If a secondary WINS server's address is included, the client then queries the secondary server at its address, sending up to three requests before giving up. If either server responds before all six queries are sent, the client will not query again. If all six queries fail, the client may or may not have alternatives, depending on its configuration. Using a DNS server is one possible option.

How DNS Serves the Windows Name Resolver

Windows computers can use DNS, too. You can even give a Windows client several DNS servers to choose from, specifying in the Network Control Panel which to use first, second, and so on. Figure 13.10 in Chapter 13 illustrates this.

If a Windows computer is configured to use DNS in the Network Control Panel (see Figure 3.1), it can request three types of queries:

- Recursive name queries
- Iterative name queries
- Reverse name queries

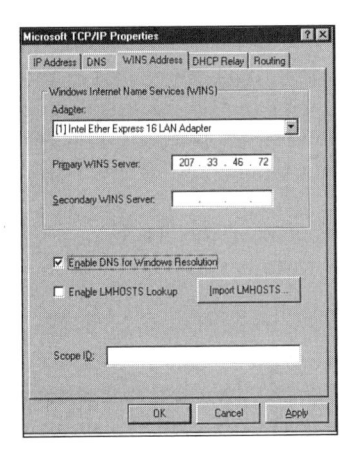

Figure 3.1 Windows NT 4.0 enabling DNS for Window resolution.

The Microsoft DNS server accepts all three kinds of queries, whether recursive, iterative, or reverse. DNS servers are configured by default to issue recursive queries to other DNS servers in the hope that they can off-load the burden to retrieve a final, authoritative answer. You can set a DNS server so that it won't attempt recursion by changing the `NoRecursion` Registry key from `0/False` to `1/True`, as in the following code:

```
HKEY_LOCAL_MACHINE\SYSTEM\CurrentControlSet\Services\DNS\Parameters\
NoRecursion
Value Type: REG_DWORD - Boolean
Default: 0 (Recursion Enabled)
Valid Range: 0,1 (False, True)
Description: Enables/disables if the DNS Server should
             do recursive lookups to other DNS Servers.
```

Other recursion options in the Registry are `RecursionRetry` (default=every 2 seconds) and `RecursionTimeout` (default=every 15 seconds).

Recursive DNS Queries

Recursive queries force the DNS server to take on the whole burden to retrieve an authoritative answer on behalf of the client. This is illustrated in Figure 3.2 where the client, `pc.acme.com`, issues a recursive query to the DNS server, `acme.com`.

In Figure 3.2, the DNS server `acme.com` itself becomes an iterative DNS client/resolver to four other DNS servers after it accepts a recursive query request from `pc.acme.com`.

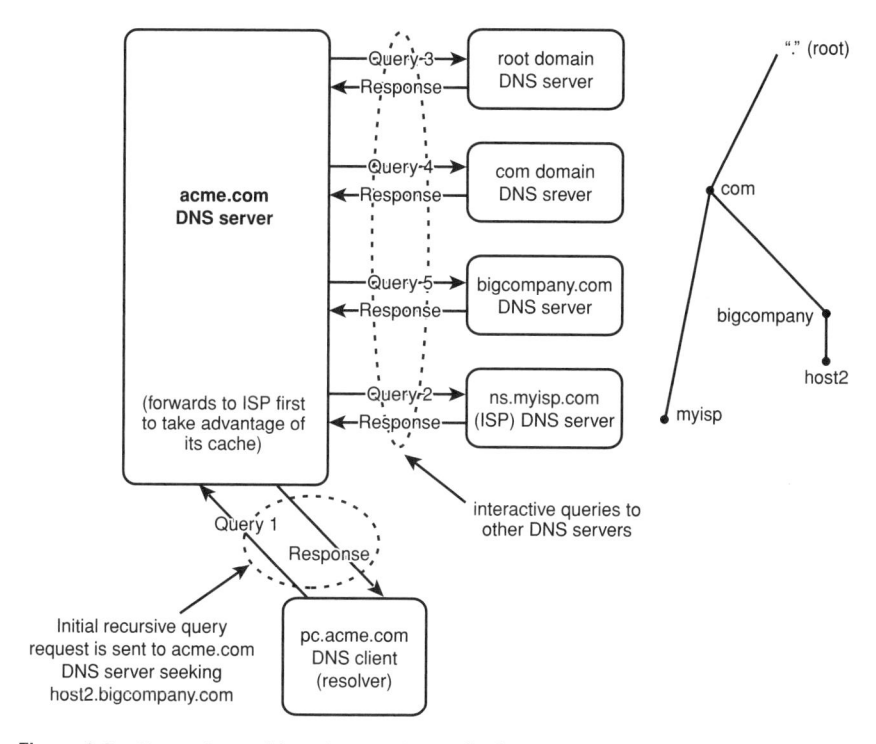

Figure 3.2 Recursive and iterative queries are both required to resolve some client requests.

When the `bigcompany.com` DNS server replies with an authoritative answer, `acme.com` passes it to `pc.acme.com`, which completely resolves the query. Resolution isn't final until the client is satisfied.

If `acme.com` had refused the recursive query request from `pc.acme.com`, `pc.acme.com` would have had to perform all the iterative queries for itself, going to each DNS server in turn, just as `acme.com` does in Figure 3.2. Client resolvers issue recursive requests almost exclusively, but they are sometimes refused.

The only reply a client will accept from a DNS server in response to a recursive query is success or failure. Until then, the client just waits. If the result isn't an authoritative IP address for the host sought but is instead a "hint" or referral to another DNS server, the client next queries the hint address looking for an authoritative reply.

Recursion means that a DNS server stays with the query on the client's behalf until it's resolved. The DNS server uses its own resolver, switching roles instantly from server to client and back again until it or another server can provide an authoritative reply. Ironically, the DNS server handling a recursive client query usually issues iterative queries to other DNS servers, following their pointers up and down the DNS name tree to reach a server with a match for the queried name, or until an end condition is met such as a timeout or error.

Recursion can happen only if the following conditions are met:

- The client requests recursion.
- The DNS server accepts recursive queries. (Most do, with the exception of root servers.)
- The client's DNS server can't answer out of its own cache or database.

If the client's DNS server could answer out of its own cache or database, it would reply immediately and authoritatively, eradicating the need to perform further queries.

Most resolvers attempt a recursive query first. If the server refuses recursive queries and can't return the address itself out of its own cache or data files, clients usually try again using an iterative query.

Iterative DNS Queries

Iterative queries enable the DNS server to pass back best-guess pointers, also called hints or referrals. An iterative query may not return a final result, but a recursive query does return a final result. An iterative query may return a partial result, or a suggestion about where to look next. The client (resolver) uses iterative queries to get closer to an answer, iteratively querying other DNS servers until a final answer (resolution), an error, or a timeout occurs. Iteration puts less work on DNS servers but requires more from clients.

Referring back to Figure 3.2, the second query to `ns.myisp.com` returns a hint referring `acme.com` to the root domain DNS server. This repeats until an authoritative answer is received from `bigcompany.com`'s DNS server in response to the fifth query.

If the first DNS server iteratively queried can't return an address, it tells the client which DNS server is the next best to query. The next best server is usually one somewhere up the name tree closer to the DNS root, or it may be a root server. After a root server is located, it usually takes very few queries to walk back down the name tree to an authoritative server for the domain sought, which returns the desired address or an error to conclude the original query.

> **DNS Servers can be DNS Clients**
>
> When talking about iterative and recursive queries, it's easy to get confused. The reason is simply that DNS servers also have a resolver, or client, and they instantly and frequently change roles from one client's server to another server's client. To satisfy one original client query, many queries can be performed by a series of DNS servers acting as servers and as clients to one another.
>
> If a DNS server sends a query, it acts as a client to another DNS server. It's helpful to view each query along the way individually, as a unique query with its own client and its own server.
>
> If you keep this in mind, it will help you remember who's the server and who's the client in any given query—and you're less likely to become confused by recursive and iterative queries.

Reverse DNS Queries

Reverse queries are another thing altogether. Recursive and iterative queries are both *forward* queries, which means that they take a domain name and return an IP number. A *reverse* query does the opposite—it takes an IP number from the client and returns a fully qualified domain name (FQDN). A special domain was created in the domain namespace for this purpose using reversed IP numbers instead of names. All registered IP numbers are joined to (made members of) the in-addr subdomain of the arpa domain.

Typically, host names can be duplicated because domain name qualifiers separate them sufficiently into domains and subdomains. Because no two hosts in the Internet can have the same registered IP address, they can all be members of one subdomain—but only by number. In this scheme, unique IP numbers replace host names in the domain name hierarchy. In the in-addr.arpa domain, host2.acmecompany.com would have a pointer (PTR) record appearing like the following:

```
2.1.1.10.in-addr.arpa     IN     PTR     host2.acmecompany.com
```

The matching address entry in the acmecompany.com subdomain for this PTR record would look like this:

```
host2.acmecompany.com     IN     A     10.1.1.2
```

In this example, the IP address for host2 is stored in the in-addr.arpa domain and is sorted along with all other registered Internet hosts. MS DNS creates a matching PTR record in the in-addr.arpa domain for every A record.

To reverse-query host2 (by IP number) requires only that a few numbers be reversed. The FQDN for host2 can then be returned simply by querying its reversed IP number in the in-addr.arpa subdomain, where all registered hosts are members known by IP address instead of their domain name.

When everything is working, the type of query a client or even a DNS server uses is more important to administrators than users. If you're having performance or resolution problems, you can try changing the default setting. Clients almost always attempt recursive queries—and the default for MS DNS is also to attempt recursive queries when going to other DNS servers—but recursive queries can be refused by other servers. If you want to change a server's default setting, refer to the discussion earlier in this chapter describing Registry keys.

> **Reverse Queries are IN. Inverse Queries are OUT.**
>
> Inverse queries are sometimes confused with reverse queries, but their method is radically different. Instead of scanning an index of names, inverse queries ask the DNS server to scan sequentially (no index) the IP addresses of A records to match a number the client provided. Inverse queries were supported in earlier versions of the popular BIND program (mostly a UNIX-based DNS server), but now inverse queries are rare. They're slow because A records aren't sorted by IP address like the PTR records in the in-addr.arpa domain designed for the purpose. What's more, inverse queries always fail if the IP number isn't stored directly on the queried DNS server because, unlike with other queries, the client cannot be referred to another server.

How the Resolver Works

DNS helps clients reach Internet hosts such as Web servers, and WINS servers help Windows clients reach local Windows computers. Querying name servers, however, is just one of several methods a Windows resolver can use.

Note
The resolver described in this chapter is the one in Windows NT 4.0. Prior versions of Windows NT and Windows 95 differ only slightly from Windows NT 4.0.

One difference is that the resolver in Windows NT 4.0 can handle an IP number or a domain-qualified host name in almost any place it takes a NetBIOS name.

Another difference is that the resolver in Windows NT 4.0 implements a new phase of resolution that other versions do not: Phase One, "Query DNS for obvious non-NetBIOS names," which is described in the text immediately following. Other Windows versions start at Phase Two, "Attempt NetBIOS methods." To understand these phases, read on.

Chapter 2, "Introducing NetBIOS," briefly described the six possible resolution methods:

- Name cache
- Broadcast
- WINS
- LMHOSTS
- HOSTS
- DNS

The remainder of this chapter describes each of these methods in more depth and explains how the resolver decides which to use.

The resolver works through three phases when trying to resolve a name, and it may use any or all of the six possible methods in the process. The three name-resolution phases are as follows:

1. Query DNS for obvious non-NetBIOS names.
2. Attempt NetBIOS methods.
3. Query local files LMHOSTS and HOSTS.

Phase One: Query DNS for Obvious Non-NetBIOS Names

If a name is greater than 15 characters in length or contains a "." it is not a NetBIOS computer name. This makes things simple; such a name must be resolved using one of the methods that works for domain host names.

DNS and the local mapping file, HOSTS, are the only options for resolving names such as the following:

- `webservertwentytwo.`   Consists of 18 characters.
- `webserver.isp.com.`   Is qualified by a domain name.
- `web.server.`   Contains the "." character.

If "Enable DNS for Windows Resolution" is not checked in the Network Control Panel (see Figure 3.1) resolution will quickly fail as Figure 3.3 illustrates.

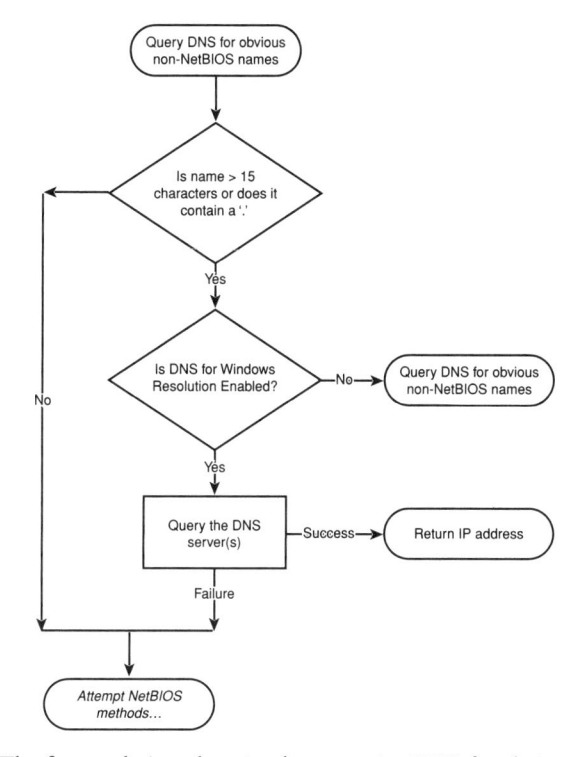

Figure 3.3 The first resolution phase involves querying DNS for obvious non-NetBIOS names.

To resolve these names, your client must be configured to "Enable DNS for Windows Resolution." The resolver then will query the DNS server(s) listed under the Control Panel's DNS tab.

Phase Two: Attempt NetBIOS methods

If the name could be either a NetBIOS name or a domain host name (containing 15 or fewer characters in length without any "." characters), its namespace can't be determined. In this case, the Windows client resolver provisionally assumes it is a NetBIOS name and begins to attempt to resolve the name using NetBIOS methods.

Because Windows doesn't know for sure what kind of service to use, it first checks the local NetBIOS name cache. If that doesn't work, Windows decides what to do next based on the client's node type. Let's briefly discuss the name cache and then cover node types in more detail.

The NetBIOS Name Cache

As mentioned previously, it doesn't matter what the node type is: The NetBIOS cache is checked first if the resolver thinks it might be a NetBIOS name. The address will be there if this is indeed a NetBIOS name that has been recently resolved.

There is no such thing as a remote NetBIOS name cache. A NetBIOS name cache is always local and belongs only to the machine it's on. Names and addresses previously resolved by that client remain in cache for 600 seconds (10 minutes).

TIP
You can preload addresses into cache to guarantee reliable and fast name resolution of any important computer. The technique requires that you use the #PRE directive in the LMHOSTS file. For an explanation of this technique, refer to the LMHOSTS section later in this chapter.

To check the name cache, use the `nbtstat -c` command, which is documented in Chapter 17.

The NetBIOS Node Types

The first thing to know about a Windows computer resolver is its node type.

Every NetBIOS computer has a node type. Node type has nothing to do with DNS domains and IP hosts name resolution; it is a configuration parameter for NetBIOS computers only.

Four possible node types exist, specifying which method is used to resolve NetBIOS computer names:

- **b-node.** Uses broadcasts only (also called *broadcast method*).
- **p-node.** Uses point-to-point with the name server only.

- **m-node.** Mixed; uses broadcasts first and then point-to-point.
- **h-node.** Hybrid; uses point-to-point first and then broadcasts.

Regardless of the node type, at this point in the process the resolver assumes that it's dealing with a NetBIOS computer name, even though it's not sure. That's why the resolver checks its own local NetBIOS name cache before taking any further steps to implement a specific node type behavior.

Configuring the Node Type

To configure a client to be an h-node, enter a WINS server address. To configure a client to be a b-node, leave the WINS address empty. It's that easy!

Windows NT node configuration is pretty reliable. Windows 95, though, has shown instability in that clients configured to use WINS (h-nodes) may fall back to b-node configuration. Although this problem is most likely to occur over dial-up networks, it has been observed even on computers with Ethernet connections.

To check your node type on a Windows 95 machine, just run `winipcfg.exe /all`, the configuration display utility, in the Start/Run... menu or in a MS-DOS prompt (command) window. Figure 3.4 shows the information you'll see. To check a Windows NT machine, run `ipconfig.exe /all` in a command window.

The node types you're most likely to encounter are b-nodes and h-nodes. The m-node and p-node types are rare and, in fact, don't even appear unless configured manually, as with a DHCP server (see Chapter 18, "Dynamic Host Configuration Protocol (DHCP)"). The following section briefly discusses p-nodes and m-nodes before moving on to a fuller explanation of the more common h- and b-node types.

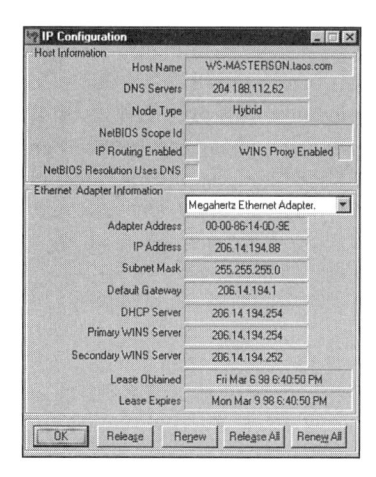

Figure 3.4   A Windows 95 client is configured to be an h-node.

The Rarest Node Types: p-node and m-node

The p-nodes don't ever broadcast to register themselves or find addresses. They only communicate point-to-point using directed User Datagram Protocol (UDP) datagrams and TCP sessions to register with a NetBIOS name server (WINS) and resolve names using the same server.

These p-nodes are a practical configuration to have for clients on the remote side of a WAN link from the main office, for example, where broadcasts would surely fail often because the computers being resolved live on the other side of a router. The downside of this node type is that all systems must know the IP address of the WINS server. Those that don't won't resolve. To configure a p-node, you use a DHCP server. Chapter 18 covers this in depth.

The m-nodes broadcast and then go directly to a WINS server if this fails. This is by far the least-used configuration because it's so impractical. The m-nodes might be useful in an instance in which a remote WAN site has no WINS server and the client mostly needs servers located in the same subnet. If a local broadcast name-resolution attempt fails, the client connects with a WINS server over the router, in the main office, to resolve a server there. The delays could be as long as several seconds, but if there's a slow WAN link anyway, the delay may not bother users.

As described in Chapter 18, DHCP covers node configuration in some detail. DHCP clients can be set to any node type: b, h, p, or m.

b-node Resolution

The b-nodes resolve names by broadcast only, which usually means that their effective scope is limited to the single subnetwork they're on. Because routers typically block broadcasts, they prevent b-nodes from resolving any computers on the other side. These b-nodes never use a name server, as Figure 3.5 illustrates.

A downside to b-nodes is that they put unnecessary traffic on the network that can be removed simply by employing a WINS server. If you don't want to use WINS and plan to rely mostly on broadcasts, you can still get the benefit of some direct addressing across routers by preloading addresses into the local NetBIOS name cache. To do this, just employ an LMHOST file and the `#PRE` directive. This technique also reduces broadcasts from b-nodes because every preloaded address that would otherwise require a broadcast will be first found in cache.

How the Resolver Works

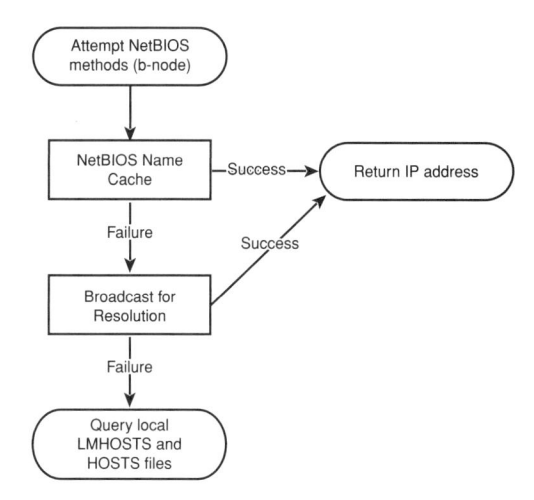

Figure 3.5 This second resolution phase involves attempting NetBIOS b-node method.

h-node resolution

The h-nodes, or hybrid nodes, resolve names by asking the WINS server. If that fails, they broadcast. The h-nodes overcome the limitations of b-node address resolution because the queries pass directly through routers to get to the name server. Because an h-node's resolver already knows the WINS server's address, it's easy to resolve a target computer's address. Then the client can pass through routers again to connect with the target computer. This is where h-nodes really shine. Figure 3.6 illustrates how h-nodes work. These nodes can locate any computer that's registered in their same WINS server, in contrast to b-nodes, which typically can't locate any addresses outside their own subnet.

There's little to dislike about hybrid nodes: Simply install a WINS server and use them! WINS is very easy to install and takes no configuration to get running. You can take some time to configure replication between the primary and secondary WINS server to provide a bit of redundancy, but that's all there is to it, and the benefits are many. The following sequence illustrates the operation of a typical h-node, from startup to shutdown.

1. **Registration.** At startup, the h-node *registers* its own name and address with the WINS server using point-to-point communications with the server via the address it already knows.
2. **Resolution.** Until shutdown, the h-node *resolves* names as often as necessary by asking the WINS server directly. The h-node uses addresses the WINS server sends back to directly contact other computers.
3. **Release.** At shutdown, the h-node *releases* its own registration from the WINS server to indicate that it is no longer available.

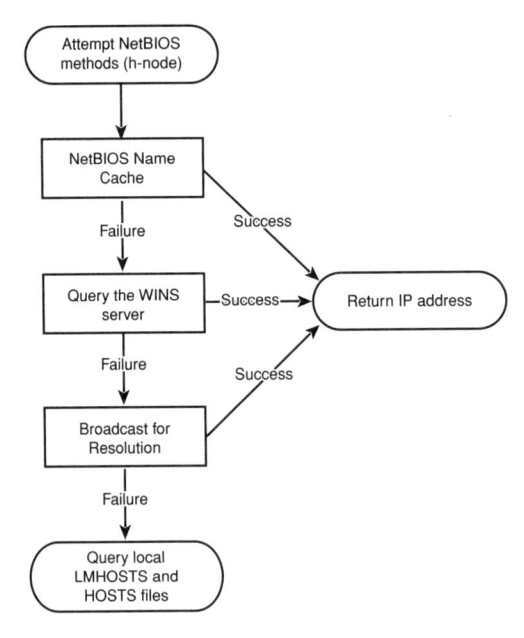

Figure 3.6 This second resolution phase attempts the NetBIOS h-node method.

The h-nodes always use the WINS server after checking the local NetBIOS name cache; they resort to b-node behavior only if that fails. The exception to this operation is if the WINS server doesn't respond or if, for some other reason, the client can't register itself upon startup. Even in one of these cases, or if the WINS server goes offline, the client continues to attempt to contact the WINS server to try to return to a direct addressing method.

Phase Three: Query Local Files LMHOSTS and HOSTS

Regardless of node type, the resolver has two last options if the NetBIOS methods fail: It can query one or two local files. The LMHOSTS file is usually checked first, before the HOSTS file. If the DNS server(s) is unable to locate a name and the NetBIOS methods fail, resolution fails unless the name exists in the LMHOSTS or HOSTS file. Figure 3.7 shows the decisions the resolver makes at this stage, assuming that NetBIOS methods have failed.

The difference between the LMHOSTS and HOSTS files is slight from a cosmetic perspective—they look almost identical. In fact, under certain circumstances, both files could actually be identical and function just fine. However, each file reflects a different namespace.

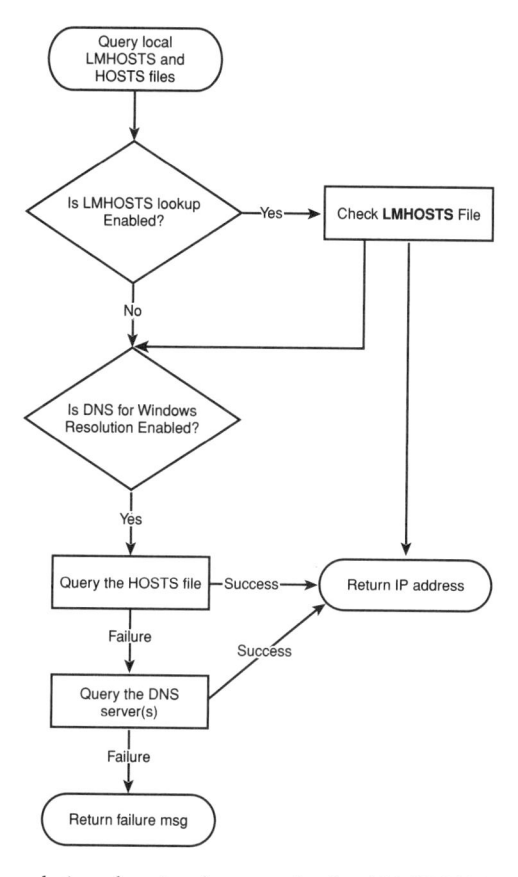

Figure 3.7 The third resolution phase involves querying local LMHOSTS and HOSTS files.

The LMHOSTS file is for NetBIOS names, and the HOSTS file is for domain host names. If you had only Windows computers, you wouldn't need a HOSTS file. If you had only one Windows computer and all the rest were UNIX hosts, you wouldn't need an LMHOSTS file because the UNIX hosts would be listed only in the HOSTS file.

LMHOSTS: A Local NetBIOS Name/Address Listing

The LMHOSTS file is always checked first if the Enable LMHOSTS Lookup checkbox is checked (refer back to Figure 3.1). If LMHOSTS is not enabled, it's not used at all.

LMHOSTS is kept in the \<systemroot>\system32\drivers\etc directory, where you'll find a sample named LMHOSTS.sam that Microsoft provides to get you started. If you decide to use the sample, remove the .sam extension.

LMHOSTS is much like a hosts file on UNIX, but, as mentioned earlier, it works with NetBIOS names and uses the same syntax as Microsoft LAN Manager 2.x. LMHOSTS is primarily a hosts file for simple name-to-address mappings, but it also supports directives that aren't allowed or aren't that meaningful in a HOSTS file.

The following is a sample of Microsoft's LMHOSTS file that's automatically installed on Windows NT computers:

```
# Copyright   1993-1995 Microsoft Corp.
#
# This is a sample LMHOSTS file used by the Microsoft TCP/IP for Windows
# NT.
#
# This file contains the mappings of IP addresses to NT computernames
# (NetBIOS) names.  Each entry should be kept on an individual line.
# The IP address should be placed in the first column followed by the
# corresponding computername. The address and the comptername
# should be separated by at least one space or tab. The "#" character
# is generally used to denote the start of a comment (see the exceptions
# below).
#
# This file is compatible with Microsoft LAN Manager 2.x TCP/IP lmhosts
# files and offers the following extensions:
#
#      #PRE
#      #DOM:<domain>
#      #INCLUDE <filename>
#      #BEGIN_ALTERNATE
#      #END_ALTERNATE
#      \0xnn (non-printing character support)
#
# Following any entry in the file with the characters "#PRE" will cause
# the entry to be preloaded into the name cache. By default, entries are
# not preloaded, but are parsed only after dynamic name resolution fails.
#
# Following an entry with the "#DOM:<domain>" tag will associate the
# entry with the domain specified by <domain>. This affects how the
# browser and logon services behave in TCP/IP environments. To preload
# the host name associated with #DOM entry, it is necessary to also add a
# #PRE to the line. The <domain> is always preloaded although it will not
# be shown when the name cache is viewed.
#
# Specifying "#INCLUDE <filename>" will force the RFC NetBIOS (NBT)
# software to seek the specified <filename> and parse it as if it were
# local. <filename> is generally a UNC-based name, allowing a
# centralized lmhosts file to be maintained on a server.
# It is ALWAYS necessary to provide a mapping for the IP address of the
# server prior to the #INCLUDE. This mapping must use the #PRE directive.
```

```
# In addition the share "public" in the example below must be in the
# LanManServer list of "NullSessionShares" in order for client machines to
# be able to read the lmhosts file successfully. This key is under
# \machine\system\currentcontrolset\services\lanmanserver\parameters\nullsessionshares
# in the registry. Simply add "public" to the list found there.
#
# The #BEGIN_ and #END_ALTERNATE keywords allow multiple #INCLUDE
# statements to be grouped together. Any single successful include
# will cause the group to succeed.
#
# Finally, non-printing characters can be embedded in mappings by
# first surrounding the NetBIOS name in quotations, then using the
# \0xnn notation to specify a hex value for a non-printing character.
#
# The following example illustrates all of these extensions:
#
# 102.54.94.97      rhino           #PRE #DOM:networking  #net group's DC
# 102.54.94.102     "appname   \0x14"                     #special app server
# 102.54.94.123     popular         #PRE                  #source server
# 102.54.94.117     localsrv        #PRE                  #needed for the include
#
# #BEGIN_ALTERNATE
# #INCLUDE \\localsrv\public\lmhosts
# #INCLUDE \\rhino\public\lmhosts
# #END_ALTERNATE
#
# In the above example, the "appname" server contains a special
# character in its name, the "popular" and "localsrv" server names are
# preloaded, and the "rhino" server name is specified so it can be used
# to later #INCLUDE a centrally maintained lmhosts file if the "localsrv"
# system is unavailable.
#
# Note that the whole file is parsed including comments on each lookup,
# so keeping the number of comments to a minimum will improve performance.
# Therefore it is not advisable to simply add lmhosts file entries onto the
# end of this file.
```

The # character appearing first on a line is the comment symbol, indicating that the line contains only comments for users to read. However, if the characters immediately following the # are reserved words, as shown in Table 3.1, they're directives, not comments.

Table 3.1 **Reserved words in the *LMHOSTS.sam* file**

Reserved word	Description
#BEGIN_ALTERNATE	Indicates the beginning of a section where #INCLUDE <filename> statements exist. The first <filename> successfully included (loaded) in any group during processing causes the others to be skipped.
#INCLUDE <filename>	Used to specify one or more LMHOST files on other computers to be read and included in the list of names and addresses. Uses UNC syntax.
#END_ALTERNATE	Indicates the end of a section where #INCLUDE statements exists, delimiting the group.
#PRE	Preloads an entry into the NetBIOS name cache, where it remains as long as the computer is running. It's required and must precede computer names that will be #INCLUDED. Up to 100 entries may be preloaded.
#DOM: <domain_name>	Identifies the name of a computer acting as a domain controller, either a PDC or a BDC. It's important, especially in the absence of WINS, that DCs be identified because of their name-integration role in browsing (as Domain Master Browser).
\0x*nn*	Specifies the hex value of a nonprinting character to be appended to the NetBIOS name at the 16th byte. This enables you to manually identify service codes with computers in a manner similar to the registrations in WINS. If you use this feature with a name less than 15 characters, enclose the name in quotes, pad it with spaces, and insert the \x*nn* within the quote marks beginning at the 16th character position. See Table 2.1 for the resource codes these represent. Other special application codes may also be used as documented in product literature. Note that this feature is not backward-compatible with LAN Manager.

The LMHOSTS file is really easier to use than it may appear from this description. Just remember to make sure the Enable LMHOSTS Lookup checkbox is checked, as indicated earlier in Figure 3.1.

HOSTS: A Local DNS Name/Address Listing

If the Enable LMHOSTS Lookup checkbox is not checked, or if the name isn't found there, the resolver can check the HOSTS file—but only if the Enable DNS for Windows Resolution checkbox is checked (refer back to Figure 3.1).

HOSTS is a reflection of the domain host namespace, not the NetBIOS namespace. The HOSTS file works exactly like a UNIX hosts file—and like LMHOSTS, this file is also stored in the \<systemroot>\system32\drivers\etc directory.

Here's the sample Microsoft HOSTS file that comes with Windows NT:

```
# Copyright   1993-1995 Microsoft Corp.
#
# This is a sample HOSTS file used by Microsoft TCP/IP for Windows NT.
#
# This file contains the mappings of IP addresses to host names. Each
# entry should be kept on an individual line. The IP address should
# be placed in the first column followed by the corresponding host name.
# The IP address and the host name should be separated by at least one
# space.
#
# Additionally, comments (such as these) may be inserted on individual
# lines or following the machine name denoted by a '#' symbol.
#
# For example:
#
#      102.54.94.97     rhino.acme.com          # source server
#       38.25.63.10     x.acme.com              # x client host
        127.0.0.1       localhost
```

Notice that the # symbols are only comment characters. Another difference from the LMHOSTS file is that the names can be fully qualified domain names (FQDNs).

Summary

This chapter presented an ambitious overview of the Windows NT name-resolution client and gives a thorough description of how it works, including what WINS and DNS do to help it get the job done. The next chapter, "WINS and DNS: Making the Most of Both Services," explains how WINS and DNS can be made to cooperate at the server level to functionally make the NetBIOS and domain namespaces appear as one.

WINS and DNS: Making the Most of Both Services

This chapter will review:

- **What the future holds for NetBIOS.** Windows NT 5 will, for the first time, provide another way to obtain the same kind of user-friendly services NetBIOS now provides. Eventually, the need for NetBIOS will disappear altogether. This section describes key NetBIOS services and how they'll be replaced.

- **WINS purpose and limitations.** WINS performs an invaluable service in helping clients resolve NetBIOS names in segmented networks, but its legacy and implementation impose some limitations. This section describes the most important WINS advantages and offers suggestions for dealing with its limitations.

- **The benefits of combining WINS and DNS.** DNS and WINS are similar in that they provide name resolution services, but they're very different in how they do it. Administrators have little choice but to support both services. Combining WINS and DNS takes a little work, but it's well worth it, as this section explains.

- **Multihoming PDCs, WINS, file, and print servers.** Not all services are created equal. Some work well multihomed, and others don't work well at all unless they're using only one network. This section offers some service architecture advice to help you design reliable services.

- **Browsing: The NetBIOS Discovery Service.** Browsing is the automatic service that collects names and presents them in the Network Neighborhood. The Computer Browser service is automatic but doesn't always work properly, such as when users see only partial lists of computers. In this case, browsing requires a knowledgeable troubleshooter. This section outlines some design rules for preventing browsing from breaking.

THIS CHAPTER COVERS A FEW THINGS every administrator should know—namely, WINS and browsing, what they do for you, and how to deal with them on a very practical design level.

WINS is included in this book about DNS simply because providing comprehensive name services for Windows computers requires familiarity with the *other* Windows name service, too. It's a mistake to view DNS and WINS as duplicates because they have different, although overlapping, capabilities. The benefits of adding WINS lookups to a DNS server are described later in the chapter.

What the Future Holds for NetBIOS

NetBIOS is built into all Windows operating systems and will be until NT 5.0, when the process of killing it off will begin in earnest. Microsoft has known for a long time that NetBIOS over TCP/IP is less than ideal and that it, in fact, creates problems because the program just wasn't designed for an expansive network such as the Internet: NetBIOS was designed for a small network and now operates on networks many thousands of times the size of those for which it was built.

Still, administrators should plan to support NetBIOS until all Windows 95, Windows NT 3.x, and Windows NT 4.0 computers are gone from their network. All these clients need NetBIOS, and they'll continue to need it. Only when NT 5.0 and its successors have completely replaced the earlier operating systems will we be free of NetBIOS. It's possible that Microsoft will build an add-in or alternative client for legacy clients, but this isn't yet known.

The name services, in particular, are crucial. For this reason, a later section in this chapter covers how to integrate WINS and DNS and outlines the benefits of doing so for your own network. If you don't need to integrate WINS and DNS, you may still benefit from knowing how it's done and why.

To orphan NetBIOS, Microsoft will move its discovery (browsing) service to Active Directory, which is the Windows implementation of the Lightweight Directory Access Protocol (LDAP) standard. Clients will register with the directory server and will be able to read computer listings through the new HTTP browser of the kind that's now in Internet Explorer 4.x.

Name services will also be based on Active Directory. Instead of registering with a WINS server, servers will register with an Active Directory, where all their important attributes and shares will be recorded alongside their name and address. It's also likely that Active Directory will be a repository for DNS server zone files. This probably won't change the DNS server functions much because DNS servers are designed to follow Internet standards, but it will change where and how DNS zone data is stored. The DNS server will optionally be able to store its data on an Active Directory server in addition to the local zone files and Registry options now available.

When Windows NT 5.0 ships, you'll have more options and more to learn.

WINS Purpose and Limitations

WINS is the NetBIOS name server, and DNS is the domain host name server. DNS and WINS differ greatly in several important respects, the most important being that DNS serves the domain namespace and WINS serves the NetBIOS namespace. The domain namespace is more extensible and better designed, but it isn't an adequate replacement for the other attractive NetBIOS services such as browsing (which enables you to see host lists by workgroup) or messaging (which enables you to send messages to users simply by addressing them by login name).

NetBIOS and WINS have serious limitations when compared with DNS, however. WINS can handle only as many host names as a single WINS server can support, even though several WINS servers can replicate data between themselves.

Microsoft recommends a good rule of thumb: If your network performs well and you have 10,000 or fewer computer names, a single primary WINS server and a single secondary WINS server for backup purposes are enough. The database size will be large, though—perhaps as big as 12MB.

Replicating the database from the primary WINS server to the secondary WINS server is crucial because it's the only good way to provide continuous service and protect all the registrations. If all WINS servers go down—which could easily happen if you don't have a secondary for backup purposes—you would go without service until a replacement comes online; even then all clients would have to re-register themselves with the replacement server. A secondary server that's receiving a copy of the primary's database by replication can prevent this problem from occurring.

TIP
WINS servers that have a large database and that also receive large replicated databases can experience data corruption. Because of this, large sites should use replication in only one direction: from primary to secondary.

On a positive note, WINS replication is pretty reliable for duplicating smaller databases, which helps distribute names in WANs with slow links.

Administrators can scavenge to clean up databases, and the Resource Kit contains a few utilities that can help you check and manage WINS data. Every administrator should have the latest Resource Kit for the version of Windows NT being run.

Even with its limitations, WINS has at least one tremendous merit: It makes NetBIOS computers accessible across IP routers, as Figure 4.1 shows. If broadcasts were the only means for resolving names, IP routers would prevent computers from reaching many others.

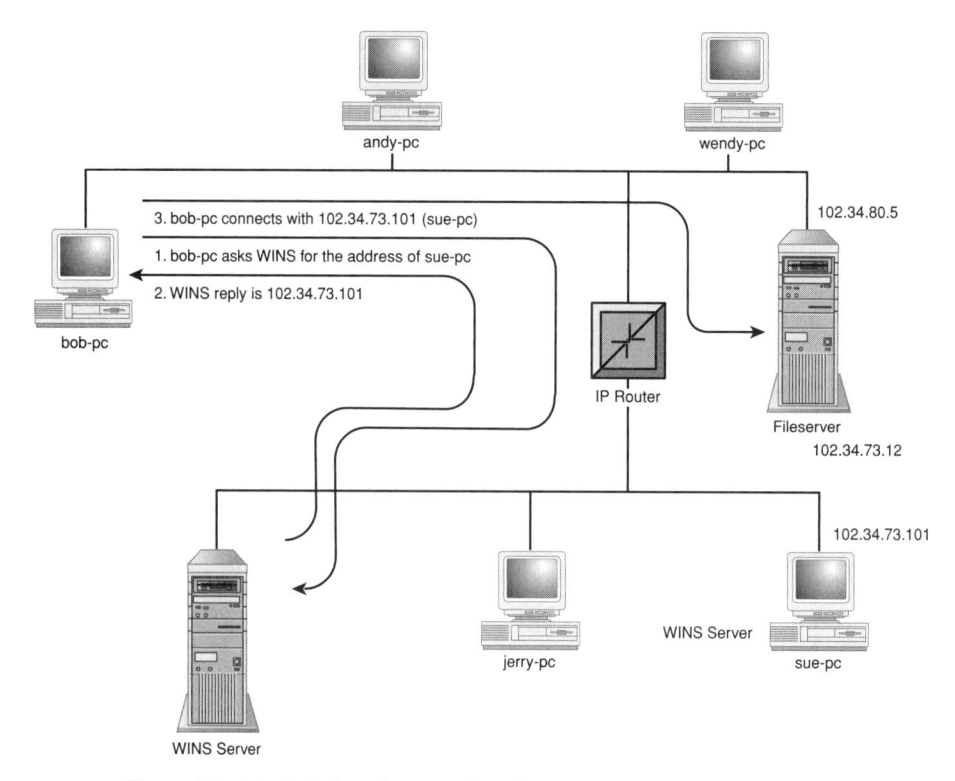

Figure 4.1 WINS helps clients resolve addresses even on remote networks.

The Benefits of Combining WINS and DNS

You can configure a Microsoft DNS server to use WINS for host name resolution because the host name part (leaf) of a fully qualified domain name is similar to a NetBIOS computer name. During the resolution process, the DNS client queries a Microsoft DNS server that refers the query to an associated WINS server.

Even though the name in WINS is a NetBIOS computer name, it is also the host name of the Windows computer in an IP domain name sense. This assumes, though, that the naming schemes are complementary—that you're using one name for both namespaces.

After the WINS server finds the correct host, it returns the address of that host to the DNS server, which then forwards an authoritative reply to its client. All the interactions between the WINS server and DNS server are transparent to clients. To the clients, the WINS/DNS transaction appears as though the DNS server handled the request by itself.

By using WINS and a Microsoft DNS server on an IP network, your clients can use NetBIOS or DNS names to locate and connect with other computers that have resources.

Integrating WINS and Microsoft DNS enables you to use the dynamic name services of WINS to reduce the number of static Resource Records (RRs) you would normally have to maintain in a DNS server's zone file. This is a particularly powerful option for Windows computers configured to use both DHCP and WINS because in such a case you don't even need to configure the Windows clients manually—the whole setup becomes dynamic.

You can run WINS and DNS Manager on the same computer or on different computers. The DNS Server service requires Windows NT Server 4.0.

Chapter 12, "Integrating DNS with WINS," includes more information about how to configure complementary name services.

Multihoming PDCs, WINS, File, and Print Servers

A multihomed computer consists of two or more network interface cards connected to two or more subnets. This type of computer is called "multihomed" because it has a "home" on more than one network. Figure 4.2 shows a file server with two network homes.

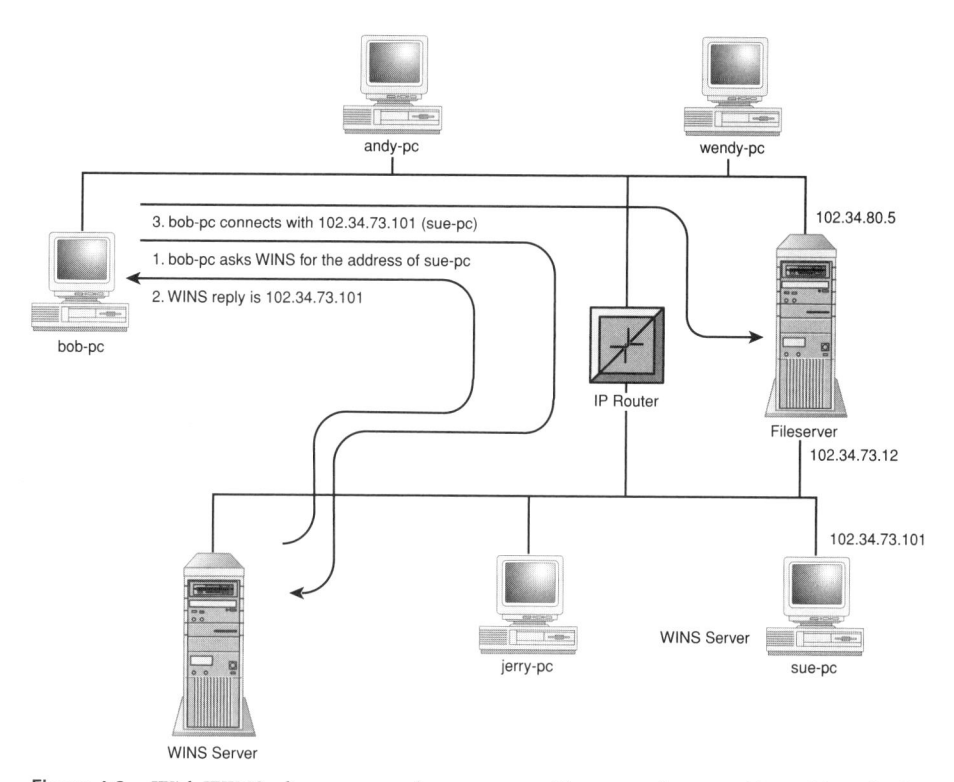

Figure 4.2 With WINS, clients can resolve a correct address even for a machine with multiple network homes.

WINS handles multihomed registrations well: A multihomed file server automatically registers all its interfaces with WINS. When a client then queries WINS for the file server's address, it obtains several addresses, as Figure 4.2 shows. This means that the client can resolve the file server's network interface address on the client's own subnet, if one exists. If not, the client resolves one on another subnet, so subsequent traffic between the two networks must cross a router.

Not all servers, however, should be multihomed. WINS servers, for example, should never be multihomed. WINS doesn't work reliably when multihomed, even though Microsoft has been working on this aspect, and even though the company claims the problem was fixed in a Windows NT 3.51 service pack and again in a Windows NT 4.0 service pack. Because all clients know how to find a WINS server by address, there's no compelling reason to multihome this type of server.

Domain controllers (DCs) also don't work well multihomed because they use NetBIOS broadcasts to participate in browsing. Primary Domain Controllers (PDCs) compete in the equivalent of computer elections—and they're supposed to win so that they become master browsers. However, NetBIOS over TCP/IP operates properly on only one interface—the one it binds to first. So, if a PDC isn't elected, it can't perform its duties as a Domain Master Browser (DMB), which include propagating browse lists across routers. If you multihome DCs, they confuse other browsers. NT-based routers, of course, are multihomed for obvious reasons.

File and print servers work great multihomed if you use WINS. What's more, multihoming a file server can improve overall network performance by reducing traffic in routers where bottlenecks can easily occur. If you now have a high-speed backbone where file servers reside and send all traffic through routers, consider instead putting one network card into a file server for each network where frequent users reside. The clients using WINS will resolve the file server's network interface on their own network, and none of the traffic will go through the routers.

Browsing: The NetBIOS Discovery Service

The Computer Browser service automatically discovers all the computers on the network and gathers them into lists organized by workgroup or domain name so that you can view them in the Network Neighborhood. This service has no address information, however. When you double-click on a name in the Network Neighborhood, for example, you call for name service to connect with the selected server directly and to ask it to enumerate all its shares for you. If this operation is successful, you'll quickly see what printers and files are available. If name service isn't successful, you'll get an error message saying the server can't be found.

Browsing works fine when there are no routers because it discovers computer names primarily using broadcasts. As soon as you introduce routers, browsing can become unreliable.

The way to establish reliable browsing is to first realize how it works, and second to design the support it needs to function properly.

At least one local master browser (LMB) exists for every subnet. There's also at least one LMB for every protocol (such as NetBEUI, TCP/IP, and IPX) if you have a computer using these protocols.

Note
Though this book uses the term "local master browser (LMB)," Microsoft's documents refer to the master browser—as distinct from the domain master browser (DMB)—in several ways, which leads to confusion. I prefer to call browsers either a local master browser or a domain master browser to emphasize the role they play. LMBs are responsible only for the names on one network segment, or subnet. DMBs function like LMBs, but they also merge and sort the names gathered by LMBs from the various network segments.

The LMB that NetBIOS binds to and uses for broadcast name service is the one bound first to the network adapter. It's a good idea to use only one protocol, or as few as are absolutely necessary. If you must have more than one, make sure that all the computers have the same binding order to ensure that NetBIOS name services will work. If you're using TCP/IP, you may also discover an LMB for each workgroup or domain name on the subnet. The rule of thumb here is to reduce the workgroup and domain names, if possible.

To make browsing reliable, you'll need at least one PDC with a domain member on each subnet where you want reliable browsing—a PDC is the only server that can act as a domain master browser (DMB). DMBs are critical because they merge the browse lists received from LMBs and then pass them back sorted (see Figure 4.3).

You'll also need a WINS server because the DMB and the LMBs on various subnets find one another through WINS. You can also use special entries in the LMHOSTS file. See Chapter 2, "Introducing NetBIOS," and Chapter 3, "How Windows Clients Use DNS and WINS," for more information about NetBIOS names and how the LMHOSTS file functions. On nomadic networks—such as those where users dial in but no permanent users exist—install a Windows NT server to act as the browser, and make all dial-in users' workgroup or domain names the same as that of the server.

Make sure that your DMB doesn't lose an election: Don't put a PDC on the same network on which a newer version of Windows NT Server is running because the newer Windows NT Server will win the election. This newer version will then become an LMB, thereby putting the DMB out of business. If you must put a Windows NT 4.0 server on a network with a Windows NT 3.51 PDC/DMB, for example, disable the Windows NT 4.0 server's Computer Browser service in the Network Control Panel.

To hide a Windows NT server from the browse list, change the following Registry key value from 0 to 1:

```
HKEY_LOCAL_MACHINE\System/CurrentControlSet\Services\LanManServer
\Paramters\Hidden
```

The server will still be active, and users will be able to connect, but the server won't appear in any browse lists or the Network Neighborhood.

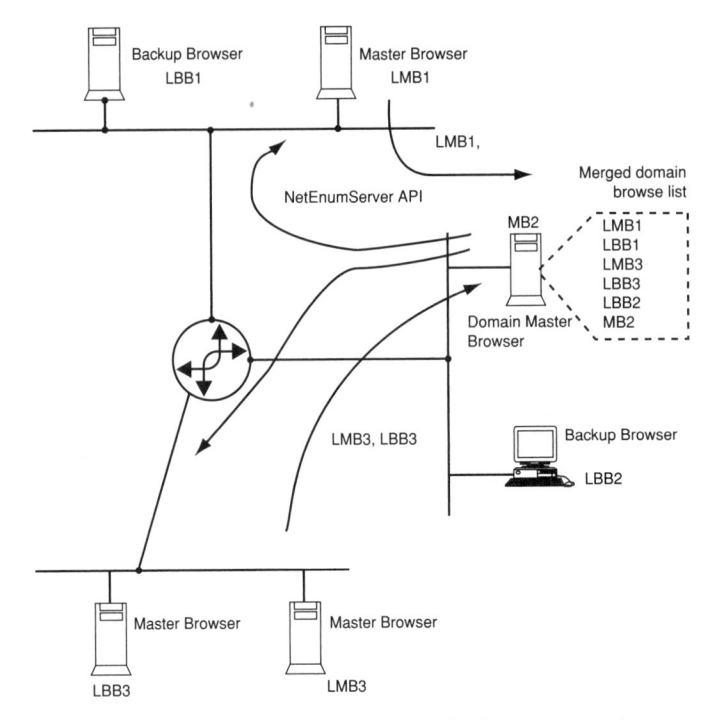

Figure 4.3 The local master browser's lists are sent to the domain master browser, which sends them back merged.

Summary

This chapter introduced some concepts to help administrators make design decisions affecting WINS, browsing, and other services, such as file and printer sharing. The next chapter, "How DNS Works," takes you into DNS itself to explain how it functions and to prepare you for other chapters that follow.

II

Introducing Windows NT DNS

5 How DNS Works

6 Name Server Types

7 What DNS Knows

8 Dissecting Name Queries

9 How MS DNS Works with Other Servers

5

How DNS Works

This chapter will review:

- **A Hierarchy of Hosts and Domains.** This section shows how the domain name space is like a tree, a hierarchy of computer names that are all related to organizations. It explains how subdomains divide the name space up into manageable units, and how delegations tell one DNS server how to query other servers when needed.

- **Domains and Zones.** The relationship between a domain and a DNS server can vary; it's not always one server per domain. DNS servers use zone files that determine precisely what domains and hosts they'll manage. Zones give DNS administrators enough flexibility to make one DNS server handle one or more domains, parts of one or more domains, or combinations. Zone files, which are at the heart of DNS administration, are introduced in this section.

- **Resolving Client Requests.** What happens when a client sends a name query? This section illustrates the client query resolution process in detail using an example query. It also explains the recursive and iterative query modes DNS servers can use. The example shows how a query can *walk up* the DNS name tree to the root server and back down another branch to satisfy a client's request.

D**NS IS A PRACTICAL REPOSITORY** and clearinghouse for network host and domain names, treating every host name as a symbolic address because names are convenient and easier to remember than numbers.

DNS client features are most apparent in the application networking layer where URL names, for example, open quickly in browsers to reveal Web pages from anywhere. The lower, transport layer communicates DNS information over the network. DNS clients and servers use the connectionless UDP protocol on port 53 for queries and responses, and the TCP protocol on port 53 for server-to-server connections.

This chapter describes how DNS servers work, how they work together, and how they respond to name queries.

A Hierarchy of Hosts and Domains

When the Internet (originally called the ARPAnet) was small, a single consolidated hosts.txt file was distributed around the network for the purpose of performing host lookups. As the Internet grew, the old model of host file distribution became inadequate. The DNS architecture was developed to replace the old file-based implementation of performing host lookups. DNS established a distributed data model that resembles a file system tree, as shown in Figure 5.1. Architecturally, the Domain Name System (DNS) is a distributed, hierarchical, client/server database management system.

The tree-like model is distributed because each registered domain provides its own database listings to contribute to the overall architecture, as shown in Figure 5.2.

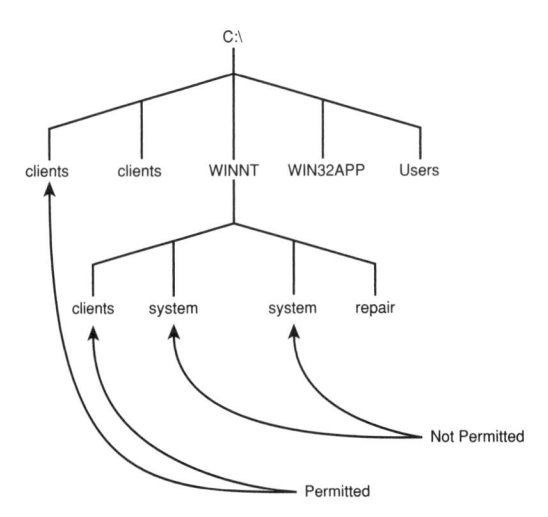

Figure 5.1 A DNS tree, like a file system tree, requires unique names at each level.

A Hierarchy of Hosts and Domains 65

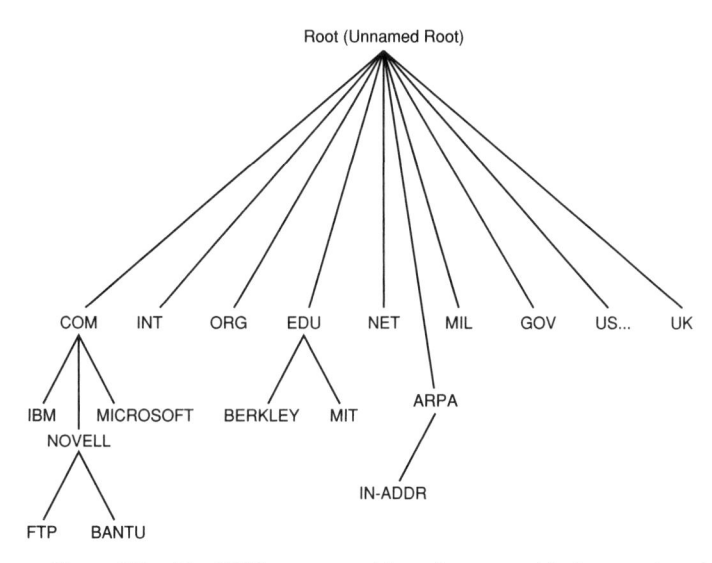

Figure 5.2 The DNS name tree hierarchy starts with the root domain.

At the very peak of the hierarchy is the root of the domain tree, consisting of root-level name servers. These root-level name servers have initial pointers heading down to the first-level, or top-level, domains, such as .com, .gov, .org, .net, .mil, .edu, and some having various other designations for geographic locations.

Note
First-level domains are actually at the second level when compared with the root, but they're called top-level domains, or TLDs. The root domain is not often thought of as a domain, even though it is one in every technical sense. The root domain's relatively few root-level members exist solely to support the name tree and its functions.

Hosts within the domain name hierarchy may exist at any level below the root. Because the name tree is a hierarchy and not flat, host names have to be unique only within each small branch of the domain. For example, www could be the host name of several Web servers within a single company as long as each machine resides in a separate branch of the domain hierarchy. For example, www.xyz.com, www.corp.xyz.com, and www.eng.xyz.com are all valid host names that will correctly resolve to unique hosts, even though each host has the same name. This basic principle also allows for uniformity in naming conventions for FTP sites, Web sites, name servers, and so on, across subdomains.

Root-level DNS servers are much like those used by corporations and educational institutions all around the world, but they reside at the most privileged place on the Internet—that is, above even the first level domains, such as .com and .org. Table 5.1 shows the all-important first levels in the domain name hierarchy.

Table 5.1 **Domain name hierarchy**

Domain Name	Position in Hierarchy
.	Root is the only domain with no name, represented by a terminating dot that's customarily implied
.com	A top-level or first-level domain name
isi.edu	A second-level domain name
East.isi.edu	A subdomain name, an organizational domain within another

An easy way to remember DNS levels is to recall that the root domain has only a dot (.). Top-level domains have one name, and second-level domains have two names.

A key difference between root-level name servers and an organization's name servers is that root servers contain pointers back down to all of the registered second-level domains, such as `taos.com` or `isi.edu`.

Second-level domains are organizational or geographic, categorized by the last part of the domain name, or *suffix*. For example, `taos.com` is owned by Taos Mountain, Inc., a commercial business based in the Silicon Valley. Most domain suffixes give a clue as to what kind of organization owns them.

An organization's type is not always that easy to determine, though, by looking at its suffix. Take the `.net` and `.org` domains, for example. These are not as clearly defined as the commercial `.com` domain. Although originally intended for ISPs and other networking organizations, the `.net` domain has been granted to a number of research projects, such as `handle.net` and `giga.net`.

The `.org` domain was intended for use by nonprofit and federally funded research organizations; however, it has also been used by such government organizations as the High Performance Computing Center (`hpc.org`) and the Integration Technology Office (`ito.org`).

> **Domains Versus Subdomains**
>
> A logical purist may call all domains underneath the root subdomains just because they're subordinate. But this usage of the term is too broad and doesn't adequately distinguish the upper levels. Commonly, administrators call any domain under the second level a subdomain—that is, those having three or more names separated by dots. This distinguishes the top-level domains, which are more permanent, from those at the third, fourth, and lower levels.
>
> In practical terms, *root-*, *top-*, and *second-level domains* refer to the firmly established domains high in the name tree, and *subdomain* refers to domains beneath the second level.

Subdomains

A domain underneath any other is a subdomain, so that even top-level domains are actually subdomains of the root. The variety of subdomains underneath second-level domains, however, is huge, and because this is where most subdomains reside, *subdomain* most often refers to one located anywhere beneath the second-level domain.

Organizations establish subdomains for their own internal reasons. East.isi.edu is a subdomain of isi.edu for use by the east coast division of ISI. Companies sometimes create subdomains to match the internal structure of their corporation. Figure 5.3, in the section "Domains and Zones," illustrates this by showing one subdomain each for Engineering, Marketing, Sales, and HR. Domain subdivisions like this may help improve the performance of mail servers, name servers, and other services, by distributing the workload over several machines in the company's internal network.

Delegation

This brings up the purpose of delegation—the formal method for distributing the workload among several servers within a domain, such as between the parent domain and its children, or subdomains. An authoritative server has an indisputable right to answer all queries for its domain, or to delegate some of that authority to other servers. Authoritative servers can contain all the data for their domains, or they can delegate part of that authority to other servers.

Every top-level domain is actually a small part of the root domain, and many top-level domains are divided even further. Delegation is the method root-level servers employ to share responsibility with all other name servers. The result is distributed authority for all the Internet's published host names.

If one DNS server can't answer a query, it can automatically point the client to another server that's been delegated to account for some of the domain's records, or a subdomain. Subdomains are often handled by delegated servers. Delegations determine what servers are called next, based on the name being queried, if the authoritative server doesn't have the data. Delegations advertise authoritative name servers for a domain, but, in reality, most queries need only be sent to one server. If a client (resolver) receives an answer back indicating that the host or domain does not exist, it immediately stops looking. The resolver does not follow any more delegations, and it doesn't matter how many name servers it may have formerly contacted.

Delegations tend to point downward from root-level servers, which are at the DNS pinnacle, to top-level DNS servers. Subdomain DNS servers are registered with parent domain servers through Name server (NS)records just as organizations register their second-level domains and DNS servers with InterNIC.

Delegations tend to point both laterally and downward. Lateral delegations identify other name servers at the same level, sharing authority for a single domain, and downward delegations identify subdomains (see Appendix C, "Top-Level Internet

Domains"). Any DNS server you have will presumably be delegated by a top-level DNS server as one of its many subdomains.

You delegate a name server by using the NS record (Chapter 7, "What DNS Knows," describes NS records and shows you how to use them). NS records can specify a list of authoritative servers for the domain. For example, to set up subdomains for an organization, you should make a delegation from the parent domain to the subdomains. If you don't, the subdomains will not be resolvable by any outside hosts.

From a DNS client computer's perspective, it's as though all registered host addresses are local to their own DNS server. But that's just the appearance. Delegation tells the local DNS server how to find hosts outside itself, which makes it possible for clients to resolve addresses outside their own domain.

Domains and Zones

Understanding the difference between zones and domains can take a bit of mental effort. The DNS domain name tree provides a branch for domain names and leaves for host names. On the tree, subdomains and the hosts are members of all the domains above them on the tree.

Zones logically overlay parts of the DNS tree structure to determine the names that each DNS server supports. Your DNS server's *zones* determine the branches it covers in the name tree, its area, or which domains (plural!) it has authority for.

Figure 5.3 shows one server having a zone of authority that includes both the `mkt` and the `sales` domains. A DNS server can also have a single domain in a single zone. The `eng` domain in Figure 5.3 is an example of one zone per domain, even though it has two subdomains.

Interoperation between DNS servers and between DNS servers and DNS clients requires zones and delegations because zones determine where names are stored (that is, which DNS server has them) and delegations determine what path clients and servers will take to communicate with other DNS servers.

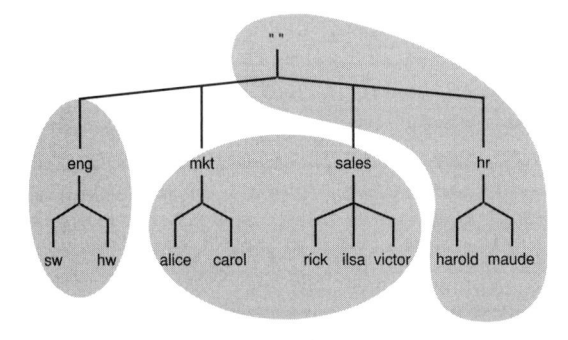

Figure 5.3 Zones determine the domain names that a DNS server will manage.

A zone can contain records for a single domain, a portion of a domain, one or more subdomains, or combinations of parent and child domains. Having records for multiple domains is especially true for the special class of reverse-address zones used for resolving numbers to names. Reverse-address zones are described in Chapter 11, "Installing and Setting Up DNS," with `in-addr.arpa`, inverse-address zones.

Zones provide the DNS server with its cut, so to speak, of the names it's supposed to manage, and delegations tell the DNS server where to look when there's a query outside its own zone. Neither zones nor delegations determine which DNS server has the authority to be the original source for a domain's records and which servers will be backups. Designating a server as a primary gives it this authority, and designating a server as secondary makes it a primary server's backup.

Primary DNS Servers

A *primary* DNS server is authoritative for names in the domain, and the one from which all information about the names in that domain is derived. When a primary server starts up, it gets its zone data from local data in files on the host where it's running. A DNS server can be the primary server for more than one domain at a time, and it can be primary for one domain and secondary for another domain at the same time. Chapter 6, "Name Server Types," will explain DNS server types in more detail. It's important to realize now, though, that domains and zones are not primary. Only DNS servers can be primary, as the term identifies a DNS server as the authoritative source of a domain's names.

If you want to set up a domain hierarchy for your organization, it's smart to first set up a primary name server for the whole domain. The zone your DNS server will manage will contain all the domain names, or you'll need one or more servers for subdomains. If you want to create organizational subdomains, say, one for each business division, each subdomain will have a primary DNS server.

Secondary DNS Servers

Secondary servers get their data from primary servers. When a secondary server starts up, it first contacts the server from which it gets zone data and compares its version with the primary's version. If needed, then, the secondary server performs a zone transfer, pulling the primary server's zone data over to itself.

Like primary DNS servers, secondary servers are an authoritative place to look up domain names. The difference is that primary servers are the origin, or source of domain names for other DNS servers needing to import zone files, whereas secondary servers are not a source of data for zone transfers. They exist to provide a backup and to support queries.

Moving Data from Primary to Secondary DNS Servers

With some understanding of domains and zones and delegation, it's now time to move to a discussion of the distributed database model that DNS is built on. Zone files are essentially database tables of DNS names, and a primary server has the source zone file(s) for its own domain(s).

Remember that subdomain name servers can take a primary role, effectively splitting a large domain's name list into smaller portions in separate zone files. If a large organization built its name servers using a single domain without subdomains, zone files would also grow large. Large, flat name spaces have another problem: An undivided DNS branch can't support two identical host names. By failing to subdivide domains, large organizations can quickly create for themselves the same problem the ARPAnet had when it decided to build the DNS architecture.

Subdividing domains also improves performance by keeping zone files smaller and easier to manage. A name server should not have to parse an enormous zone file. Although other factors also matter, it's generally true that the smaller a zone file is, the quicker the response from a name server will be. Subdomains introduce a practical problem, however. Delegations solve part of the problem by coordinating the relationship between parent and child (subdomain). But how does a secondary name server get data from an original source—its primary name server? The answer is by transferring the primary server's zone file.

When a primary name server starts up, it merely has to begin responding to name service queries. When a secondary server starts up, it is told to look at the primary for the authoritative data and is given a path and filename in which to store its local copy when the copy is received. If a secondary name server is starting up for the first time, or someone has cleaned out its data directory, the secondary server sends a request to the primary server for a copy of the zone file.

Zone transfer operates much like Window NT's directory replication, or its WINS data replication between name service partners. When a secondary name server has a copy of the primary server's zone file, then it can also begin to provide authoritative answers to name queries. What if a zone file on the primary server is changed or updated? The start-of-authority Resource Record (RR) contains fields of information instructing secondary servers how often to check back with the primary for changes. These fields set an expiration timeout and refresh frequency.

A secondary server will periodically query the primary server for the zone files it needs refreshed, checking to see if the serial number, an incremented database version indicator, has changed. If so, the secondary server knows that data in the zone has changed, and it initiates the transfer of a fresh copy. For more information about SOA RRs, see Chapter 7, "What DNS Knows."

The secondary server will perform a zone transfer only if the serial number has been incremented to a higher number. If the serial number has for any reason been decremented, the secondary server will assume that its copy of the zone is more recent, and will continue to use the local copy until the zone expires. If for some reason the serial number needs to roll over to zero, the secondary server's local zone files are erased, and the secondary server then initiates the transfer of a completely fresh zone data file from the primary.

Both Microsoft's DNS and BIND version 8 also have a notify option to trigger updates. This means that a primary server can actually notify secondary servers about changes to speed propagation of new information. The notify option increases security because a primary server can initiate all its zone transfers. Because its administrator furnishes a list of secondary servers to notify, the list of eligible secondary servers is limited to only those that have been pre-authorized. By changing who initiates data transfers from secondary servers entirely to primary servers, a domain's zone file can't easily be stolen.

Organizations that want DNS queries processed quickly in a global environment can choose to set up secondary servers in different geographical locations, maybe even locating some of their zones in servers owned by cooperating, friendly organizations. Doing this provides better local query performance and adds redundancy that'll save the day if Internet connectivity gets lost.

Secondary DNS servers can still provide resolution during a failure even though the destination host may not be reachable. For such services as sendmail, this is useful because if sendmail can resolve the host, but cannot create a session for the transfer of a message, it will simply queue the message again and try later. If sendmail cannot resolve the host, it will bounce the message and return an unknown host error.

This chapter has thus far been about the domain name space and domain name servers. It's now time to discuss clients and the queries they make. The remainder of this chapter focuses on client queries and how DNS servers cooperate to satisfy them.

Resolving Client Requests

When a client wants to communicate with a remote system, such as when a user clicks a link for a Web site, a number of steps must occur before the actual communication with the remote system can begin. The first step is to resolve the remote system's name into an IP address. Clients act as resolvers. In order to resolve the name of a remote system, the client sends a query to one of its DNS servers. At least one DNS server is designated. You can view a Windows 95 or Windows NT client's DNS server search order by selecting the *DNS* tab of the Network control panel under *Protocols, TCP/IP, Properties*. Figure 5.4 shows the dialog box you'll see.

In Figure 5.4, you can see that one or more DNS server IP addresses can be listed, indicating to the client/resolver where to ask for the addresses of all unresolved names. The client will first query the first name server in the list. If the resolver doesn't receive an acknowledgement within a specified time, it'll try the next server on the list until a name server accepts the query.

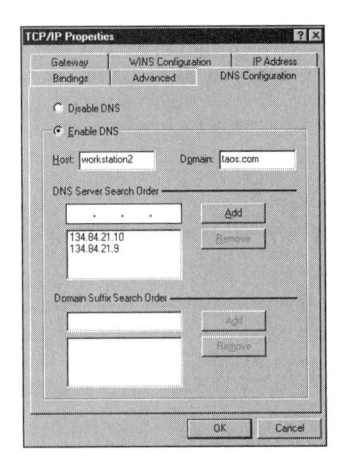

Figure 5.4 The TCP/IP properties for DNS are shown in a Windows 95 Network Control Panel.

When a name server accepts a client's query, the client usually just sits back and waits for an answer while the name server tries to find an IP address in its zone file to match the host name it received in the query. If the first DNS server accepts the query request but cannot resolve it locally or remotely, it returns a *name error* response indicating that the domain name is nonexistent. When this occurs the client will not reissue the query to a secondary DNS server.

If the host name includes the host's domain name (remember fully qualified domain names, FQDNs, from Chapter 1, "Introducing the Domain Name System"?) the DNS server will use the additional information to speed its search, possibly even referring the query directly to another DNS server or telling the client the address of another DNS server to query. If a domain name is not specified, the DNS server will just assume that the query is for a host in its own zone file.

Client Request Resolution Walkthrough

What follows is a detailed example to help you understand name resolution heuristics. You should walk through the exercise slowly enough to grasp what happens at each step because it illustrates how DNS really works.

You may recall from prior discussions (about FQDNs and the root-level domain) that a trailing period indicates that a host name is fully qualified, meaning that all necessary domain memberships are assumed to be present in its name. If the host name a client is to resolve ends with a trailing period (.), its DNS server will not make further assumptions about domain memberships. Instead, the DNS server will begin the query by sending it directly to a root-level server, from which it'll take the shortest possible path down the DNS tree to a server that's authoritative for the sought host's domain.

If the name is relative, that is, without any trailing period, the DNS server will make a series of intelligent assumptions in an attempt to reconstruct the host's fully qualified domain name.

Note
Resolvers can behave differently from one another depending on how they're designed and configured in the Network Control Panel Applet (NCPA). The examples furnished in this chapter reveal general truths about how the resolvers work. Factors specific to each resolver can change the very methods they use, but rarely do they affect final results.

Some resolvers, for example, assume that a domain name with any imbedded dots (.) is an FQDN, and pass such names unchanged to a DNS server. Others make the assumption that if there is no trailing period, the name must not be an FQDN, so the resolver appends the client's own domain name (from the NCPA) before passing it to a DNS server. Both assumptions can be wrong. Fortunately, client resolvers and DNS servers combined successfully parse and resolve most names.

The behavior of resolvers varies slightly depending on the source of the code used for the resolver libraries. It should be noted that many standard resolvers perform queries in a couple of steps based on what the resolver (client) receives from the application it's serving. If the host name www is queried, the domain name will be appended by default. If the host name www.isi.edu is queried, it will try to resolve www.isi.edu directly. If the server cannot find www.isi.edu, it would then attempt to append the domain name and try the query again.

From all indications, Microsoft resolvers seem to append the domain name to any query first, try to resolve the name, and then fall back to the original name if they can't find an answer.

The difference is that some resolvers attempt to query for the name as if there are any dots (.) in it, and if there are no dots, the resolvers automatically append the domain name. By contrast, other resolvers append the domain name regardless of whether or not dots are present before attempting to resolve the name.

For this example, let's put our client in the cnri.reston.va.us domain and say he's trying to reach the www.isi.edu Web site. If the sought host's domain name isn't fully specified (qualified), the server will try to construct the full name. Because this client initially queries his own DNS server in the cnri.reston.va.us domain and did not use a FQDN, the initial search string his DNS server tries looks like this:

    www.isi.edu.cnri.reston.va.us

Notice that the DNS server appended its own domain name, cnri.reston.va.us, to the sought host's name. DNS servers assume that a host's name is not fully qualified unless the query includes a trailing period. Only a trailing period confirms that the full domain name has been fully specified. Another way to remember this is to realize that www.isi.edu is a relative name just as www is a relative name that may or may not resolve within the current domain. As long as there's no trailing period, a name's relativity can be assumed by the resolver and is usually left up to the DNS server to sort out.

With an initial search domain of `cnri.reston.va.us`, the name server cannot resolve the host-domain name combination it received. Having failed at properly reconstructing the sought host's fully qualified domain name, the next query the DNS server tries must assume that it exists at a higher level. The second query, then, looks like the following:

`www.isi.edu.reston.va.us`

Notice that the `cnri` portion from the first query is now gone. If the name server performing the client's search is not primary for the `reston.va.us` domain and the `cnri` domain as well, it'll then send the query to another server for resolution. But if the name server is primary, and the request failed to locate the IP address on its second try, the DNS server will again reformat the query by dropping another portion of the local domain's name on the assumption that the next higher level can resolve it. This is the DNS server's third attempt.

If the third query also fails, the fourth in this case will be a little different. Because there really isn't a `us` domain (`us` is handled by the root), the fourth query actually goes to a root level server to query for `www.isi.edu`. The name server will not get an answer for the query from the root-level server for `www.isi.edu`, but will instead receive a referral pointing to the authoritative name server for `isi.edu`. The DNS server then sends a query for `www.isi.edu` directly to the `isi.edu` name server.

Because `www.isi.edu` is a valid host in the `isi.edu` domain, the name server for `isi.edu` will respond with the IP address for `www.isi.edu`. The local name server will then provide the result back to the client, allowing the client to proceed to the next step of downloading the Web page by trying to contact the Web server at the IP address that it just received. The next section clarifies the host-to-address query process in greater detail.

The preceding has been an example of a recursive query by the name server. Iterative or non-recursive name servers can also be set up, and, in fact, the result of an iterative query is like that of a name server querying a root server. The root servers do not perform queries for clients, but merely provide a best guess or a pointer showing where more information can be found.

Note

DNS servers can operate in recursive or iterative modes. In recursive mode, a DNS server becomes the client's agent, communicating with other DNS servers as necessary to retrieve the answer while the client waits. When working a query, a recursive DNS server itself becomes a resolver, or DNS client, to other DNS servers.

In iterative mode, a DNS server provides a *best guess* answer that one server that can answer with authority. Usually this answer is a referral to another DNS server that the resolver, being the original client or another DNS server, can follow. These referrals are sort of like following stepping stones that lead ever closer to the final destination. This frees an iterative DNS server from further working on the query because the client resumes working on the query by itself.

Host-to-Address Query Example

Example 5.1 is the actual detailed output from `nslookup` for a host-to-address query of www.isi.edu by the primary name server for cnri.reston.va.us. It shows what kind of communications occur between clients and servers to resolve a DNS query. Figure 5.5 is a diagram of the query in Example 5.1.

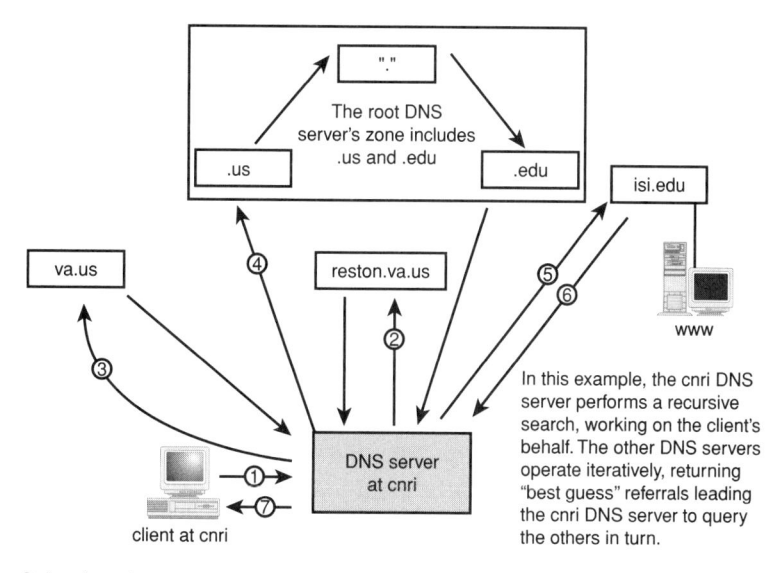

Order of events
1) Client at cnri send query for www.isi.edu to DNS server at cnri.reston.va.us.
2) DNS server at cnri queries the reston.va.us DNS server.
3) Acting on a referral, DNS server at cnri queries the va.us DNS server.
4) Acting on a referral, DNS server at cnri queries the root DNS server which is primary for the us and edu domains.
5) Acting on a referral, DNS server at cnri queries the isi.edu DNS server.
6) DNS server at isi.edu returns the address for www.isi.edu.
7) DNS server at cnri returns the address for www.isi.edu to the client.

Figure 5.5 A name query follows delegations to traverse the DNS tree.

Example 5.1 **Recursive Query Example from nslookup**

```
ns.cnri.reston.va.us:/:1$ nslookup
Default Server: localhost
Address:  127.0.0.1
> set debug

//Initial Query to CNRI Server (#1)

> www.isi.edu
Server:  ns.cnri.reston.va.us
Address:  132.151.1.1

;; res_mkquery(0, www.isi.edu.cnri.reston.va.us, 1, 255)
------------
Got answer:
    HEADER:
        opcode = QUERY, id = 4, rcode = NXDOMAIN
        header flags: response, auth. answer, want recursion, recursion avail.
        questions = 1,  answers = 0,  authority records = 1,  additional = 0
    QUESTIONS:
        www.isi.edu.cnri.reston.va.us, type = ANY, class = IN
    AUTHORITY RECORDS:
    -> cnri.reston.va.us
        ttl = 3600 (1 hour)
        origin = cnri.reston.va.us
        mail addr = action.cnri.reston.va.us
        serial = 199712220
        refresh = 3600 (1 hour)
        retry   = 300 (5 mins)
        expire  = 3600000 (41 days 16 hours)
        minimum ttl = 3600 (1 hour)

//Referral By CNRI.Reston.Va.US to Reston.Va.US (#2) which Triggers Next
➥Query

------------
;; res_mkquery(0, www.isi.edu.reston.va.us, 1, 255)
------------
Got answer:
    HEADER:
        opcode = QUERY, id = 5, rcode = NXDOMAIN
        header flags: response, auth. answer, want recursion, recursion avail.
        questions = 1,  answers = 0,  authority records = 1,  additional = 0
```

```
        QUESTIONS:
            www.isi.edu.reston.va.us, type = ANY, class = IN
        AUTHORITY RECORDS:
        -> reston.va.us
            ttl = 21600 (6 hours)
            origin = Gaia.NameTamer.com
            mail addr = hostmaster.NameTamer.com
            serial = 1997091912
            refresh = 21600 (6 hours)
            retry   = 7200 (2 hours)
            expire  = 3600000 (41 days 16 hours)
            minimum ttl = 259200 (3 days)
```

//Referral By *Reston.Va.US* to *Va.US* (#3) which Triggers Next Query
----
;; res_mkquery(0, www.isi.edu.va.us, 1, 255)

Got answer:
```
    HEADER:
        opcode = QUERY, id = 6, rcode = NXDOMAIN
        header flags:  response, auth. answer, want recursion, recursion avail.
        questions = 1,  answers = 0,  authority records = 1,  additional = 0
    QUESTIONS:
        www.isi.edu.va.us, type = ANY, class = IN
    AUTHORITY RECORDS:
    -> va.us
        ttl = 86400 (1 day)
        origin = VENERA.ISI.EDU
        mail addr = us-domain.ISI.EDU
        serial = 971219
        refresh = 43200 (12 hours)
        retry   = 3600 (1 hour)
        expire  = 1209600 (14 days)
        minimum ttl = 86400 (1 day)
```

//Referral By *Va.US* through "root" to *ISI.EDU* (#4,5) which Triggers Next
➥Query

;; res_mkquery(0, www.isi.edu, 1, 255)

Got answer:
```
    HEADER:
        opcode = QUERY, id = 7, rcode = NOERROR
        header flags:  response, want recursion, recursion avail.
        questions = 1,  answers = 1,  authority records = 3,  additional = 4
```

78 Chapter 5 How DNS Works

```
QUESTIONS:
   www.isi.edu, type = ANY, class = IN
ANSWERS:
-> www.isi.edu
   internet address = 128.9.176.20
   ttl = 25234 (7 hours 34 secs)
AUTHORITY RECORDS:
-> ISI.EDU
   nameserver = VENERA.ISI.EDU
   ttl = 130797 (1 day 12 hours 19 mins 57 secs)
-> ISI.EDU
   nameserver = NS.ISI.EDU
   ttl = 130797 (1 day 12 hours 19 mins 57 secs)
-> ISI.EDU
   nameserver = NOC.HPC.ORG
   ttl = 130797 (1 day 12 hours 19 mins 57 secs)
ADDITIONAL RECORDS:
-> VENERA.ISI.EDU
   internet address = 128.9.0.32
   ttl = 20381 (5 hours 39 mins 41 secs)
-> VENERA.ISI.EDU
   internet address = 128.9.176.32
   ttl = 20381 (5 hours 39 mins 41 secs)
-> NS.ISI.EDU
   internet address = 128.9.128.127
   ttl = 20381 (5 hours 39 mins 41 secs)
-> NOC.HPC.ORG
   internet address = 192.187.8.2
   ttl = 145775 (1 day 16 hours 29 mins 35 secs)

//Answer to Query by ISI.EDU for CNRI.Reston.Va.US (#6) which is Returned
➥to Client (#7)
-----------
Non-authoritative answer:
www.isi.edu
       internet address = 128.9.176.20
       ttl = 25234 (7 hours 34 secs)

Authoritative answers can be found from:
ISI.EDU
       nameserver = VENERA.ISI.EDU
       ttl = 130797 (1 day 12 hours 19 mins 57 secs)
ISI.EDU
       nameserver = NS.ISI.EDU
```

```
            ttl = 130797 (1 day 12 hours 19 mins 57 secs)
ISI.EDU
            nameserver = NOC.HPC.ORG
            ttl = 130797 (1 day 12 hours 19 mins 57 secs)
VENERA.ISI.EDU
            internet address = 128.9.0.32
            ttl = 20381 (5 hours 39 mins 41 secs)
VENERA.ISI.EDU
            internet address = 128.9.176.32
            ttl = 20381 (5 hours 39 mins 41 secs)
NS.ISI.EDU
            internet address = 128.9.128.127
            ttl = 20381 (5 hours 39 mins 41 secs)
NOC.HPC.ORG
            internet address = 192.187.8.2
            ttl = 145775 (1 day 16 hours 29 mins 35 secs)
>
```

In Example 5.1 and Figure 5.5, you can actually see the name server queries climb the DNS tree to the top level and then descend down another branch. You might also find it interesting that the name server VENERA.ISI.EDU shows up in several places. The reference to VENERA.ISI.EDU is at the va.us level of the query. VENERA.ISI.EDU is one of the name servers for the va.us domain. You might also notice that the server from the root cache file, VENERA.ISI.EDU, was formerly one of the DNS root-level servers. The root server maintained by ISI is currently called b.root-servers.net.

Summary

This concludes the introductory explanation of how DNS works. The next few chapters explain DNS server types, their purpose, and how the various server types work together, as well as some detailed information about DNS zone files. Chapter 8, "Dissecting Name Queries," resumes the discussion of client name resolutions with a thorough explanation of iterative and recursive queries, and an explanation of how different client configurations can affect the name resolution process.

6

Name Server Types

This chapter will review:

- **Primary name servers.** Primary name servers have authority to respond to queries for a zone, and they're the location from which all the zone's address data originates. This section describes the features that make a primary server special.

- **Secondary name servers.** Secondary name servers are backup servers. They're not where original zone data resides, but they can respond to a domain's queries with authority. Secondaries usually get their zone data from the domain's primary DNS server.

- **Caching name servers.** As the name implies, caching name servers cache address data. Caching is a behavior of most servers Caching servers are those designed to do nothing but cache queries: They don't have a zone file populated with lots of hosts, and they don't transfer zones from other DNS servers. Caching name servers answer queries, but not authoritatively. This section describes caching servers and explains what makes them valuable.

- **Passing queries: forwarders and slaves.** Forwarders and slaves are DNS servers that have a very special cooperative relationship with other DNS servers for sharing the duty of handling queries. This section explains forwarders and slaves, and explains how they give administrators service design options.

- **Determining DNS type.** If you walk up to a DNS server but don't know what role it's playing, this section can show you how to tell the difference between primary, secondary, forwarders, slaves, and caching servers.

A DOMAIN NAME SERVER can perform one role or several roles at once. This chapter provides an overview of the possible roles a server can play. It's important to note, too, that one DNS server can support multiple domains simultaneously while undertaking a different role for each. A DNS server's type, then, is determined when you choose its configuration for each domain your server will support.

In addition to explaining potential DNS server roles, this chapter will reveal and discuss several architectural options to help illustrate the differences between primary, secondary, forwarder, slave, and caching servers. It's much easier to understand them in the context of practical problems and applications. The only certainty in this regard is that you'll have one primary DNS server for each domain. The rest is up to you.

Primary Domain Servers

Primary servers are the engines of DNS, motivating the distribution and lookups of name data throughout the Internet. Primary servers are always the original sources of address data. They have the ultimate authority for the names in their domain, and because they're the sole source of zone files for zone transfers, primary servers alone have the power to publish their domain's information to any and all other servers needing it.

The publication process begins when an administrator builds a configuration boot file manually, copies one from a UNIX host's BIND DNS implementation, or, more likely, enters all the boot configuration data the server needs through the GUI during installation. MS DNS automatically puts any configuration files in the `\\<systemroot>\system32\dns` folder. Essential information includes:

- The domain's name (must be preapproved by InterNIC)
- The IP address and name of each server for which you want to provide name resolution
- The host name and address of the DNS servers themselves
- The host name and address for each other computer that will be included in the DNS server's zones

See Chapter 11, "Installing and Setting Up DNS," for instructions on building a configuration through the installation process.

Storing Windows NT DNS Boot Configuration Data

There are two ways to store the Windows NT DNS boot configuration data: via the boot file and via the Registry. By default, the service boots via the Registry. To use a boot configuration file instead of the Registry, you need to set the following key to `false/0`:

```
HKEY_LOCAL_MACHINE\SYSTEM\CurrentControlSet\Services\DNS\Parameters\Enabl
eRegistryBoot
```

The problem with switching to a boot file is that all modifications you make via the GUI may be lost. The warning MS puts in the boot file says, "Note... that ALL changes to zone information, including new zones, made through the DNS Manager will be lost."

This could be a pretty nasty problem if you try to change back and forth between the boot from file and the boot from Registry options. For most users, we recommend that you accept the default and boot from the Registry.

Synchronizing the DNS Registry and Boot Files

Microsoft realized that switching back and forth between the boot from file and boot from Registry options is a problem and now has a hotfix for the DNS service to make it write any Registry changes you make in DNS Manager back to the boot files. This keeps them synchronized. Check these files to see if they have this date or later:

```
06/10/97    06:09p    198,928 dns.exe (Alpha)
06/10/97    04:37p    119,568 dns.exe (Intel)
```

If you decide to work with synchronized Registry and boot files, apply the hotfix and also completely delete the Registry key, as it's no longer needed, because the system won't operate in an either/or mode. It'll use boot files and the Registry:

```
HKEY_LOCAL_MACHINE\SYSTEM\CurrentControlSet\Services\DNS\Parameters\
EnableRegistryBoot
```

After this, your boot file will load first when the DNS service starts, and then any secondary values (security, notify lists, forwarding timeouts, listen IP list, and so on) stored in the Registry will load.

Finally, make sure to edit the boot files manually only when the DNS Manager is not running; otherwise, you risk losing changes.

Configuration Data and Domains

MS DNS provides configuration files for compatibility with the files created on UNIX-style BIND configurations, primarily to make migration to an MS DNS server easier.

Configuration data not only specifies the directory where the server will store such data as zone files and caches; it also contains lists that name the domains the server will support, and a directive indicating what type of server the server will be for each domain: primary, secondary, or caching. If the server is primary, the boot configuration information includes the source zone for each domain thus specified. If it is secondary, the IP address of the primary server is included so the server will know where to request updates.

When a primary server is operating, changes you make to the domain are additions or deletions of hosts, subdomains, mail exchangers, name servers, and so on. If you're using a boot configuration file to get the server up and running, you make changes only to the primary server's source files. Name server boot files have a structure that looks like the following. (Comment lines, which begin with a semicolon [;], have been inserted to describe the boot file entries.)

```
; Directory where dns.exe will store backup files:
    directory            <systemroot>\system32\dns

; Directives for name server operations:
; Server Type       Domain                    Source
    primary             taos.com                  hosts.db    ; Used for forward lookups (name to IP)
    primary             46.33.207.in-addr.arpa    hosts.rev   ; Used for reverse lookups (IP to name)
    primary             0.0.127.in-addr.arpa      hosts.local ; Used for internal communications
    cache               .                         cache       ; Root cache file (names and IPs of root servers)
```

Note that files, including the cache file, have a .dns extension unless otherwise specified. Don't worry about all the configuration options at this time. Chapter 11, which covers installation, provides the information you'll need to understand the options and make decisions. Fortunately, many of the settings are selected for you automatically. MS DNS creates local host and reverse address configurations, for example, automatically.

The cache directive references the root domain (.), and the cache file contains the entries with addresses for the primary root-level servers. A root cache file comes with MS DNS, but you can always download the most current version from InterNIC using your Web browser at http://www.internic.net. The FTP site is ftp://rs.internic.net/domain/named.root. Be sure to rename the file from root.db to cache. (Also, don't confuse the root cache file with caching-only servers.) The only time the root cache file needs to be updated is when Internet authorities add a new root-level server (almost never), or your DNS server is used to support an isolated network for private use, which is not at all likely.

> **Local Host Resolutions for the Reverse Address Domain and the Cached Root Domain**
>
> Directives and the contents of files for the 0.0.127.in-addr.arpa domain and the root cache will usually be identical on every machine because every machine has a loopback port with an address of 127.0.0.1. The loopback, often labeled localhost, is used for internal communications for network services.
>
> A name server can resolve names by calling itself via the localhost address, which speeds the operations of the name server because communications do not actually go out onto the network where there's more latency.

In the previous example showing name server boot file structure, the `host.db` file contains a text table for the `taos.com` domain. The `hosts.rev` file contains a text table for the `46.33.207.in-addr.arpa` domain, the domain that contains Internet address (`in-addr`) mappings, which is the IP address to host name mappings for the `207.33.46.0` network. The directory statement tells the name server that the files are located at the `<systemroot>\system32\dns` path.

Secondary Name Servers

A secondary server contains authoritative address data for the domain, but gets it from a primary server via zone transfers. Secondaries are great for data backup, and they relieve the primary server's load by answering queries. BIND version 8 refers to secondaries as slaves.

Secondaries are authoritative because they have local copies of the zone files that are pulled from primaries during zone transfers. The function of the secondary name server is twofold:

- *Distribution of workload over several machines:* Because there are multiple machines handling queries for a domain, there is an improvement in the response time when resolving queries. Load distribution comes from the fact that resolvers keep track of what name servers they've used and what the response times were for those servers for each query.

    Depending on geographic location, routing, and so on, some servers perform better than others. The resolver uses that information to choose what name servers it will hit for different requests.

- *Redundancy:* With secondary name servers, a domain call can still be referenced, and queries resolved, even if the primary fails and becomes unavailable. It is especially useful to locate secondaries on physically different networks, even in different parts of the country.

The functionality of email is a good example with which to make the redundancy point. Assume that `xyz.com` has its primary name server in San Jose, California. The administrators decide to put the secondary on a different subnet, but in the same building. If `xyz.com` loses connectivity to the Internet, it will instantly lose the capability to answer external DNS queries in its domain. If someone tries to send email to `xyz.com`, for example, the email will bounce, probably with an "unknown host" error.

Now assume that `xyz.com` decides to put a second secondary name server on the east coast of the U.S., hosted by `abc.com`. If `xyz.com` then loses its connectivity, queries will still be answered by the secondary at `abc.com`. In addition, `xyz.com` may also have improved overall response when resolving queries to external entities because it has a distributed arrangement enabling queries to come from different parts of the country. An email message sent to `xyz.com`, for example, would in this instance simply be queued again due to delivery problems, rather than bounced.

The following example illustrates what a boot file for a secondary name server might look like:

```
; Directory where dns.exe will look for or store backup files:
    directory        <systemroot>\system32\dns

; Directives for name server operations:
; Server Type  Domain                   Source          Backup
  secondary    taos.com                 207.33.46.220   hosts.db
  secondary    46.33.207.in-addr.arpa   207.33.46.220   hosts.rev
  primary      0.0.127.in-addr.arpa     hosts.local
  cache        .                        cache
```

You will notice in the previous example that the source of the data for the domains comes from the host `207.33.46.220`, and the name server will store a backup copy of the zone file and call it `hosts.db`. The secondary name server has the same cache directive as the primary. Note that the name server is a primary for the `0.0.127.in-addr.arpa` domain because the loopback address is private to each machine, and therefore each machine will be the primary for its own loopback network.

The secondary is not required to store a backup copy of the domain information, although it is recommended. Having a local backup means that the name server will start faster because it doesn't need to contact the primary for the zone info immediately upon starting. This does not guarantee that the initial set of data is up-to-date, but the name server can at least begin to answer queries based on the data it has.

Caching Name Servers

Caching servers can be used to improve the performance of DNS servers on local networks. Where DNS queries frequently hit the same target locations, a caching name server can be installed to provide quicker responses to queries without incurring the administrative problems of a primary or secondary name server. Caching servers require little work to set up and operate, as illustrated in the following example:

```
; Directory where named will look for or store backup files:
    directory        <systemroot>\system32\dns

; Directives for name server operations:
; Server Type  Domain                 Source
  primary      0.0.127.in-addr.arpa   hosts.local
  cache        .                      cache
```

The configuration file for a caching name server requires only entries for the directory, the loopback domain (`0.0.127.in-addr.arpa`), and the cache statement itself.

The only requirement for a caching server is a valid root cache file that includes the name server itself. Because a caching server cannot be authoritative, it should not be delegated for a domain. Caching servers can be configured to forward requests and then cache the results for use when responding to future queries.

Caching servers are great for organizations that have an ISP providing their primary DNS services and that want to improve performance. To set up a caching server for MS DNS, the DNS service first must be started. The cache and loopback will be automatically generated as soon as New server is created in DNS Manager. The only action, that's required then, is to ensure that the service starts up after the Windows NT server reboots and after any other system interruptions.

Caching servers have several advantages. The main advantage is an increase in performance for many users who'd otherwise make one server too busy: The server offloads the query burden to a machine dedicated for the purpose. A disadvantage, though slight, is that caching servers may not always have accurate information. You can set its time-to-live value to control how long a caching server keeps cache data before discarding it.

Passing Queries: Forwarders and Slaves

A DNS server can designate another to be its *forwarder*, which establishes where future queries will be forwarded if it can't answer. A *slave* relationship makes a server dependent on its forwarders to answer queries by restricting its activity—that is, by preventing it from being a client to any other DNS servers. In a nutshell, the fundamental difference between a forwarder and a slave is this:

- *Forwarder:* Sends queries to a designated machine, waits for short period of time, and then begins to looks for the answer itself.
- *Slave:* Sends queries to a designated machine and waits for an answer. Slaves will not try to resolve the queries themselves.

A forwarder is a designated machine for handling queries (see Figure 6.1). Clients, including other DNS servers, wait for a short period of time after sending a query to a forwarder and then can begin to look for the answer themselves if no reply is received. Because a lot of traffic can be sent through forwarding DNS servers, they'll build up a large cache of addresses. This is useful if you want to build up a cache for many users. The process illustrated in Figure 6.1 is as follows:

1. A client sends a query to a local DNS server.
2. The local DNS server forwards the request to a forwarder and begins waiting.
3. The forwarder sends the query to a name server on the Internet and begins waiting.
4. If no reply is received, the local DNS server sends the query to a name server on the Internet.

Both the forwarder and the local DNS server will eventually get a response, building the cache on both DNS servers.

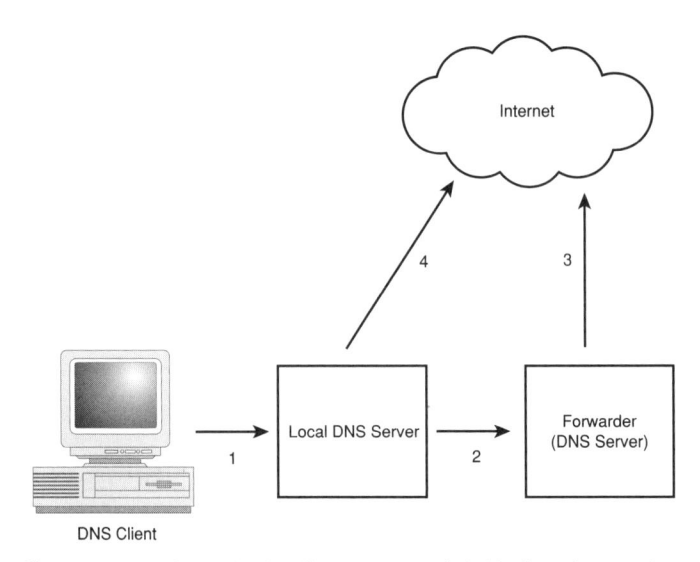

Figure 6.1 A forwarder handles queries on behalf of another DNS server.

If a client's name server has a designated forwarder and it receives a query but cannot answer the query from its local zone files or cache, the name server will not then perform a recursive search to find the answer. (Chapter 3, "How Windows Clients Use DNS and WINS," describes recursive queries.) Instead, the name server will forward the query to its designated forwarder. The designated forwarder name server will perform the search and provide an answer.

There are a couple of practical uses for forwarding. One is to forward a query to several DNS servers with the knowledge that they'll all work it, and that this will build a cache in each one of the located host's address that's useful for subsequent queries by the same or another client. The most frequent application of forwarders, however, is to use dual DNS servers to work through a firewall. Organizations connected to the Internet need to resolve Internet host names, but might not want to expose their entire network to the rest of the Internet for security reasons. In this scenario, an internal DNS server will forward all queries for names outside the organization's domain to an external DNS server for resolution.

Slave servers are those that are forced to use a forwarder (see Figure 6.2). Slaves send queries to a designated machine and wait for an answer, but they're not allowed to try to resolve queries for themselves if the forwarder doesn't answer fast enough. This option is extremely useful as a security measure because it forces all query traffic to go through one path from a slave to a forwarder. It's a great way to penetrate a firewall with authorized, predictable outgoing DNS queries and, as such, can help you implement a good security policy.

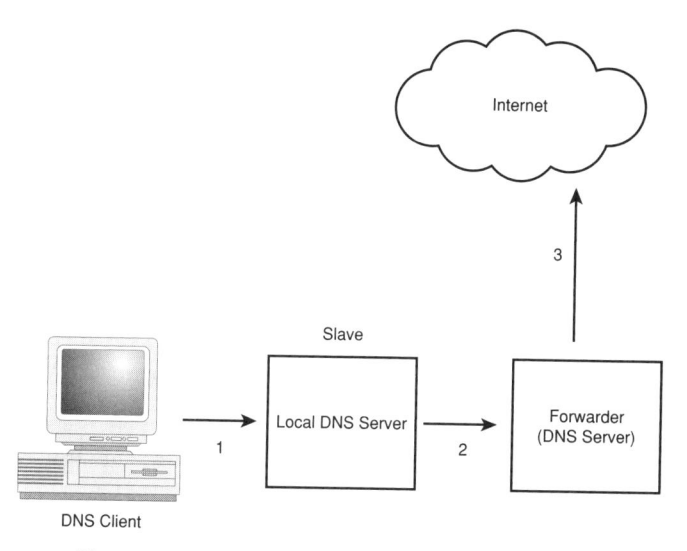

Figure 6.2 A slave must wait for the forwarder's response.

The process illustrated in Figure 6.2 is as follows:
1. A client sends a query to a local DNS server.
2. The local DNS server forwards the request to a forwarder and begins waiting.
3. The forwarder sends the query to a name server on the Internet and begins waiting.
4. If there's no reply, a slave (the local DNS server in this case) will not initiate a query on its own.

Slaves are DNS servers set up to use forwarding, with one additional restriction: Slaves will only accept responses for queries from the designated name servers to which they forward queries. This way, going back to the previously mentioned scenario, an internal DNS server provides all name resolution service for internal hosts.

An external name server provides all of the external name resolution for the protected hosts and for the organization's publicly known hosts. The rest of the internal domain should be serviced by a DNS server inside the firewall to prevent private names and addresses from becoming known. Remember: Anything in a DNS server can be discovered quite easily by using simple queries!

To set up a forwarder, the boot file must have an entry specifying the forwarder by directive, or you must make an entry in the Forwarders panel, which you display by clicking the Forwarders tab in the Server Properties dialog box, as illustrated in Figure 6.3. To open it, just select Properties on the server.

Chapter 6 Name Server Types

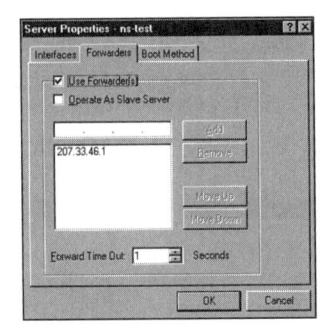

Figure 6.3 You can configure a forwarder in DNS Service Manager.

In either case, you'll have to include the IP addresses of the machines that the server will forward to. The following example shows proper boot file entries:

```
; Directory where named will store backup files:
  directory          <system root>\system32\dns

; Name servers that will serve as forwarders:
  forwarders         204.188.66.1 206.177.34.10

; Ensures that the name server will not attempt queries
; outside of itself:
  slave
; or, depending on the version:
  option forward-only

; Directives for name server operations:
; Server Type  Domain                    Source
  primary      taos.com                  hosts.db
  primary      46.33.207.in-addr.arpa    hosts.rev
  primary      0.0.127.in-addr.arpa      hosts.local
  cache        .                         cache
```

Determining DNS Type

The following list summarizes the different DNS server types and may help you to select the kind of server you need to implement:

- *Primary:* Authority for one or more zones. A zone is the data for one or more domains, and may be data for part of a domain.
- *Secondary:* Also authoritative, but functions as a backup to a primary name server. Gets all zone data from a primary server by transfer.

- *Forwarder:* A DNS designated by another to handle all its queries.
- *Slave:* A DNS server configured to use a forwarder, but which has no other options. Must use the forwarder for all queries.
- *Caching:* A server that builds up a cache of addresses by virtue of its own query activities. A caching-only server has no zone data of its own and only performs queries for clients.

You may need administrator privileges to find out what kind of server is running on an existing system; then, you can read the boot file or view the domain properties using DNS Manager. The DNS server's function is spelled out in plain English in the boot file. Statements about the operation of the name server are also listed there, starting with the purpose, or function, of the server in question. If your name server is started via the Registry (it can be started via the Registry or a boot configuration file), the boot file will contain only a statement mentioning the fact.

Using DNS Manager, right-click any of the listed domains served by the server to open the Zone Properties dialog box. Figure 6.4 shows the General tab that displays information about the domain, indicating whether the server is primary or secondary. If no domains (other than the `127.in-addr.arpa`) appear, then you'll know that the server is a caching server.

If you don't have administrative privileges for the machine, but you know its IP address, the name server can be queried to examine the SOA (start of authority) record of any of its domains. If the `source` entry in the SOA is for the same machine, then it's safe to assume that the machine is primary for the domain.

A secondary server can provide authoritative data for any of the zones it gets by transfer from a primary. Figure 6.5 shows how a secondary is configured. The IP Master(s) box shows how you specify what server is its primary. You can put a secondary server on a LAN or LAN segment to give it a dedicated query server, reducing WAN traffic and increasing security.

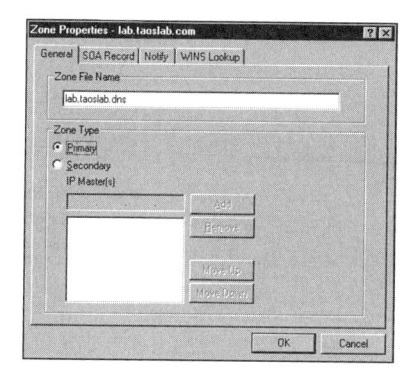

Figure 6.4 Primary servers reference a zone file where data is stored.

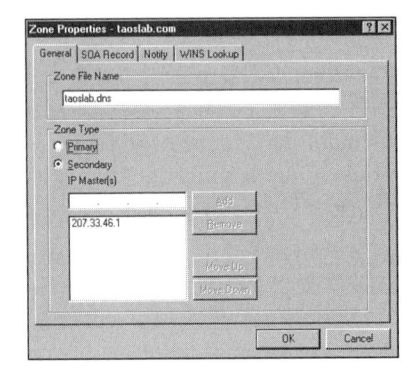

Figure 6.5 Secondary servers reference an IP address for the primary server.

If there are no NS records for the machine in question, then it could be a caching server or a secondary that has not yet been delegated for the domain (see Figure 6.6).

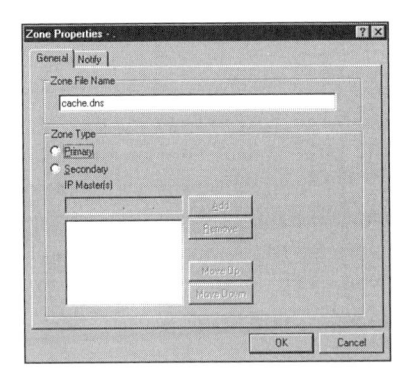

Figure 6.6 Caching servers reference only a `cache.dns` file.

Summary

The various DNS server types help you design systems to solve problems and answer name service challenges. Primaries are sources of data, secondaries are backups that help share the query load, caching servers can help relieve query workloads without adding to your administrative burdens, and forwarders and slaves can increase security and help you realize the benefits of caching.

Chapter 7, "What DNS Knows," goes into detail about how to construct DNS records, what they mean, and how to use resource records to establish relationships between DNS servers.

7

What DNS Knows

This chapter will review:

- **Database Resource Records.** Resource records (RRs) make up the contents of zone files and, as such, are at the very heart of DNS. As the name implies, each resource record contains information about a resource that's important for DNS to know about. These resources are other DNS servers and hosts. This section identifies major resource record types and explains their use.

- **The Cache File.** The cache file identifies root-level domain name servers so that any DNS server can easily find the root of the domain name system tree. This section describes the cache file, why it's needed, and how it's used.

- **Delegation.** Registering your primary DNS server with the NIC makes it accessible to clients outside your domain needing access to your domain's name list. You publish secondary servers yourself using NS resource records. This section describes the reasons why you'd publish other authoritative servers.

- **How to Distribute Zone Files.** Zone files get transferred from primary name servers to secondary name servers to distribute the domain's names. The reasons for distribution can vary. This section describes zone transfers, the reasons for them, and it explains how you can make transfers work reliably to achieve distribution goals.

IF DNS WERE A CREATURE, it would do some things by instinct, and it would develop other behaviors only after learning. This chapter describes the fundamental things DNS was designed for, those things DNS does almost instinctively, and the various resource record types you can use to make DNS perform advanced tasks to meet your specific needs.

Database Resource Records

Like any relational database, the DNS architecture is made up of tables, each containing a number of records. DNS database tables are called *zone files*. Most of the records have a special meaning because they identify the location of resources, and they may even be associated with records in other tables. Possible resource record types include the *Start-of-Authority* (SOA) record, the *Address* (A) record, and the *pointer* (PTR) record. Detailed coverage of all resource record types is provided later in the chapter.

What records you see in a zone file depends on a few things. What zone file is being examined? Forward and reverse lookup zones, for example, have very few record types in common. Another factor determining a zone file's contents is what information the DNS administrator wants, or needs, to publish. The rest of this section provides you with a thorough explanation of the most important record types. You should know about them all and how they're used.

MS DNS provides template files in the `\\winnt\system32\dns\samples` directory, where database files are stored with filenames ending with the `.dns` extension.

There are two ways to store records in MS DNS: the Registry and in BIND-compatible zone files, the sort you'd find on a UNIX machine. The examples in this chapter apply equally to BIND-compatible zone files and the MS DNS Manager configuration stored in the Registry. If anything, this chapter includes more information than you'll see in the MS DNS Manager. Where that's so, just realize that the actual storage is more complex than what you see because the server is making things more simple by selecting what it presents and by choosing intelligent default values for some configurable options.

RFC 1035, RFC 1183, and RFC 1664 (available online from `http://www.isi.edu`) are the most authoritative documents available describing how to format resource records. MS DNS formats records automatically when you use the GUI and the Registry storage option, but if you use the boot file option to move files back and forth between MS DNS and BIND, for example, you'll need to know precisely how to format records using a text editor.

Resource Record Syntax Formats

Resource record entries are parsed without case sensitivity, so that `hostname=HOSTNAME`.

Note
The underscore "_" is commonly used in Windows NT naming schemes, but it's a problem when mapping NetBIOS names to the DNS name space. *Windows NT administrators need to get used to the fact that the underscore is illegal in DNS.* Although some name servers only complain about underscores, others will return errors or refuse queries altogether.

The following excerpt from RFC 1035, written by Paul Mockapetris, explains the syntax of RR formats (pages 32–34).

The format of these files is a sequence of entries. Entries are predominantly line oriented, though parentheses can be used to continue a list of items across a line boundary, and text literals can contain CRLF within the text. Any combination of tabs and spaces act as a delimiter between the separate items that make up an entry. The end of any line in the master file can end with a comment. The comment starts with a ";" (semicolon). The following entries are defined:

```
<blank>[<comment>]
$ORIGIN <domain-name> [<comment>]
$INCLUDE <file-name> [<domain-name>] [<comment>]
<domain-name><rr> [<comment>]
<blank><rr> [<comment>]
```

Blank lines, with or without comments, are allowed anywhere in the file. Two control entries are defined: $ORIGIN and $INCLUDE. $ORIGIN is followed by a domain name, and resets the current origin for relative domain names to the stated name. $INCLUDE inserts the named file into the current file, and may optionally specify a domain name that sets the relative domain name origin for the included file. $INCLUDE may also have a comment. Note that a $INCLUDE entry never changes the relative origin of the parent file, regardless of changes to the relative origin made within the included file.

The last two forms represent RRs. If an entry for an RR begins with a blank, then the RR is assumed to be owned by the last stated owner. If an RR entry begins with a <domain-name>, then the owner name is reset. <rr> contents take one of the following forms:

```
[<TTL>] [<class>] <type> <RDATA>
[<class>] [<TTL>] <type> <RDATA>
```

The RR begins with optional TTL and class fields, followed by a type and RDATA field appropriate to the type and class. Class and type use the standard mnemonics; TTL is a decimal integer. Omitted class and TTL values are default to the last explicitly stated values. Because type and class mnemonics are disjoint, the parse is unique. (Note that this order is different from the order used in examples and the order used in the actual RRs; the given order allows easier parsing and defaulting.)

<domain-name>s make up a large share of the data in the master file.

The labels in the domain name are expressed as character strings and separated by dots. Quoting conventions allow arbitrary characters to be stored in domain names. Domain names that end in a dot are called absolute, and are taken as complete. Domain names which do not end in a dot are called relative; the actual domain name is the concatenation of the relative part with an origin specified in a $ORIGIN, $INCLUDE, or as an argument to the master file loading routine. A relative name is an error when no origin is available.

<character-string> is expressed in one or two ways: as a contiguous set of characters without interior spaces, or as a string beginning with a " and ending with a " Inside a "delimited string any character can occur, except for a " itself, which must be quoted using \ (back slash).

Because these files are text files, several special encodings are necessary to allow arbitrary data to be loaded. In particular:

.	of the root.
@	A free standing @ is used to denote the current origin.
\X	where X is any character other than a digit (0-9), is used to quote that character so that its special meaning does not apply. For example, "\." can be used to place a dot character in a label.
\DDD	where each D is a digit is the octet corresponding to the decimal number described by DDD. The resulting octet is assumed to be text and is not checked for special meaning.
( )	Parentheses are used to group data that crosses a line boundary. In effect, line terminations are not recognized within parentheses.
;	Semicolon is used to start a comment; the remainder of the line is ignored.

The syntax representations and examples describing individual RR types later in this chapter are also described in RFC 1035, RFC 1183, and RFC 1664. These documents are authoritative references for master file formats.

Start-of-Authority (SOA) Records

The Start-of-Authority (SOA) record is a required first entry in all forward and reverse (in-addr) zone files. SOA records (defined by RFC 1035) provide several key pieces of information that each domain needs. Most importantly, an SOA entry specifies what name server is authoritative for the domain. Figure 7.1 shows the Domain Name Service Manager Properties dialog box for SOA records, which appears when you double-click the zone icon in the server list.

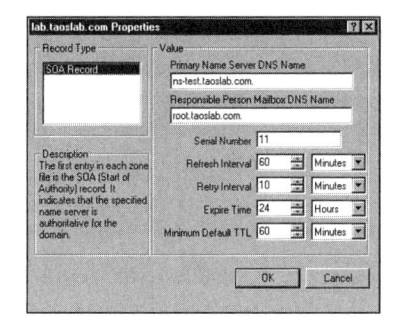

Figure 7.1 You can view SOA resource records in the DNS Manager.

SOA records are extremely important. They contain the following components. (You'll also notice some of these values in Figure 7.1. The list shows all possible options, but not exactly as they appear in the MS DNS Manager.)

- *Owner:* The SOA *owner* generally refers to the zone's origin, or what domain the zone file represents. In MS DNS Manager, owners are the domain names appearing in the server list under server names, and they're automatically entered into the database for you.
- *Class:* The *class* in the SOA defaults to type IN for *Internet*.
- *Time-to-Live:* The SOA's TTL field is not shown in the MS DNS Manager because it's rarely used. The server's default TTL is set by the minimum-time-to-live value (see the last item in this list). This TTL setting, if used, is a raw BIND-compatible data file setting you use only when overriding the server's default TTL value for an individual record.
- *Type:* The presence of the letters *SOA* in the `type` column of a resource record denotes that this is, indeed, a record indicating which DNS server has authority for the domain. In the MS DNS GUI, you just double-click the SOA record. Its type is listed in a column of the zone info records list.
- *Zone File Source:* The zone file source is the host name of the primary DNS server for the domain. In MS DNS, this entry is created automatically.
- *Responsible Person Mailbox DNS Name (mailbox):* The mailbox is an entry that typically points to the email address of the administrator for the domain. Expressed in a dot format, an example would be `action.cnri.reston.va.us`, which translates to `action@cnri.reston.va.us`. `action` would be the mail address probably pointing to the system administrator at `CNRI`.
- *Serial Number:* The serial number is used for version control. When changes are made to a zone file and the serial number is incremented, the changes will be picked up by the secondary servers. If it's not incremented, the secondary server assumes its data is already correct and will not initiate transfer of refreshed data.

- *Refresh time:* Refresh time tells a secondary how often to attempt performing a zone refresh. It's the refresh interval, or cycle. When it does, the serial number is evaluated to determine whether any changes necessitate a fresh transfer. If a change has been made and the serial number incremented, the secondaries record the new serial number while reloading the zone.

- *Retry interval:* The retry interval specifies how soon the secondaries will attempt a refresh after one has failed.

- *Expire time:* Expire time specifies how long the secondary will continue to provide authoritative answers when a refresh fails. In the event that a refresh fails due to a primary server's outage, secondaries continue to answer queries until the zone expires. If the primary server comes back online, then the secondaries will again refresh and everyone will be happy. If the zone expires and has not been successfully refreshed, secondaries will stop answering queries for that domain.

- *Minimum default TTL (M-TTL):* The minimum time-to-live (M-TTL) specifies how long an answer is good. When a client queries the DNS server, it takes the TTL information along with the response so it'll know how long it can use (cache) the answer without having to check back again for changes. If data doesn't often change, the TTL can be higher. This creates more persistent caches resulting in fewer queries. Low TTL values cause client caches to expire more quickly, resulting in more frequent queries for exactly the same records.

The SOA zone file template looks like the following prototype (refer also to Figure 7.1):

```
<owner> <ttl> IN SOA <zone file source> <mailbox> (<serial> <refresh>
↪<retry> <expire> <m-ttl>)
```

A typical SOA record might look like this:

```
taoslab.com.       IN       SOA      ns.taoslab.com     root.taoslab.com     (
        1997121201        ;serial
        10800             ;refresh
        3600                  ;retry
        604800            ;expire
        86400     )       ;m-ttl
```

The @ symbol can also indicate current origin (in this case, `taoslab.com.`), making the following SOA record equivalent to the prior example:

```
@       IN      SOA      ns.taoslab.com     root.taoslab.com     (
        1997121201        ;serial
        10800             ;refresh
        3600                  ;retry
        604800            ;expire
        86400     )       ;m-ttl
```

@ equates to the long form: `taoslab.com`. As mentioned previously, the TTL field is usually ignored because by default, the M-TTL value applies to all records in the zone.

Name Server (NS) Records

Name server (NS) records tell DNS what servers are delegated servers for the domain, or for its subdomains. Delegation gives a server authority to answer queries. Delegation is much like a manager delegating work to another person. A name server can delegate the entire responsibility for a subdomain to other servers, or a primary can delegate to secondary servers so that they'll be used for queries even though they are not the origin of address mappings. The section "Delegation" later in this chapter covers delegation in greater detail. Figure 7.2 shows the Domain Name Service Manager Properties dialog box for NS records.

NS records are used in both forward and reverse zone files, and they have the following format:

```
<owner> <ttl> IN NS <host.domain-name>
```

The first field of the record is the owner; it indicates the domain for which the name server has been delegated authority. Next is the TTL field, which is usually blank because administrators like to rely on the M-TTL value of the SOA RR instead. Next is the class field, which is almost always Internet (IN). Next is the indication that this is an NS resource record. Finally the name server's `host.domain-name` consists of a fully qualified domain name for any server that can provide answers for the domain. It has a trailing dot to ensure that resolvers understand it's a true FQDN. You can see similarities between NS and SOA records. Both contain owner, TTL, and class fields that are likely to be the same in both records.

There's an NS record for every name server delegated. You can specify additional name servers with an `A RR`, but they should only be used for internal clients—external organizations know about the name servers you've registered with the NIC and delegated in the zone. An NS record might look like the following:

```
taoslab.com.     IN      NS      ns.taoslab.com.
```

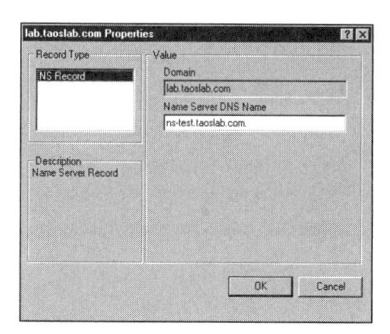

Figure 7.2 You can view NS resource records in the DNS Manager.

Other, probably more common entries, look like this:

```
IN    NS    ns.taoslab.com.
IN    NS    ns.taos.com.
```

Because the first record in a zone file is the SOA and the owner is declared in the SOA, no owner is specified in the `IN    NS    ns.taos.com` example record. It is assumed that the owner is the current origin `taos.com`.

You'll notice that the TTL is not specified in the preceding example NS records, and the FQDN of the name servers are `ns.taoslab.com.` and `ns.taos.com.` There's no requirement that a delegated name server be in the same domain, which is part of the beauty of the DNS architecture. Here, the name servers actually have different domain name suffixes. Notice that they have trailing periods to indicate that they are FQDNs.

Pointer (PTR) Records and Reverse Lookups

Pointer (PTR) resource records are keys to reverse address resolution. If you have an IP address of a host and you'd like to know what name the host goes by, then a reverse address, or simply an address, to host name resolution needs to be available. PTR resource records make up the bulk of a `[reverse network number].in-addr.arpa` domain zone file. Figure 7.3 shows the Domain Name Service Manager Properties dialog box for PTR records.

The `in-addr` zone files start off with the SOA and NS records just like any other zone file. The remainder of an `in-addr` zone file, though, is usually just PTR resource records.

The PTR template looks like this (refer also to Figure 7.3):

`<owner> <ttl> IN PTR <host.domain-name>`

If you look at the primary name server for the `46.33.207.in-addr.arpa` domain, for example, the entries in its zone file can look like the following:

```
@            IN      SOA     ns.taoslab.com      root.taoslab.com (
➥1997101501 86400 3600   608400 86400 )
             IN      NS      ns.taoslab.com.
1            IN      PTR     www.taoslab.com.
10           IN      PTR     mailhost.taoslab.com.
```

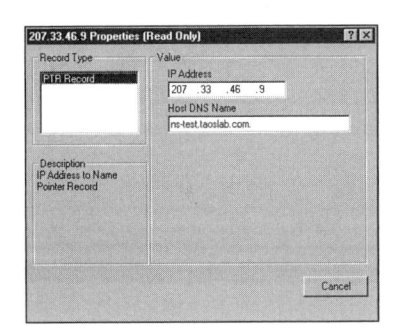

Figure 7.3 You can view PTR resource records in the DNS Manager.

First of all, notice the trailing period after host names to make sure that no additional information is ever appended to the names: These hosts are fully qualified domain names. If the trailing period is left off, the domain origin will be appended to the host names. Because the origin is `46.33.207.in-addr.arpa`, it would get pretty ugly fast.

MS Knowledge Base article #Q154555 clarifies when you should and should not enter FQDNs with trailing periods into DNS Manager. Use FQDNs with trailing periods when specifying servers as `DATA` in records (NS nameserver, CNAME canonical name, SOA primary name server, MX mail server, and so on). These fields refer to servers that may or may not be *located* in the domain, and so, must be fully qualified. They must be fully qualified literally. Otherwise, do not use FQDNs with trailing periods, such as for names located on the server (for hostname A, alias for CNAME, domain for SOA or NS). They'll be qualified by the domain where they're located by the logic of other data records.

Because this zone file represents a reverse address mapping, the numbers `46.33.207` get appended to the numbers appearing in the PTR records. Hence, the reverse address of `www.taoslab.com` is `1.46.33.207`. You can turn the numbers around and see that the real IP address is `207.33.46.1`.

This example uses the notation of class C networks. The `in-addr` zone file might look different for a class B network. Let's use the `132.10.0.0` network as an example, with a domain name of `xyz.com`. The boot file entry for such an `in-addr` zone could be represented as

```
primary      10.132.in-addr.arpa      132.10.rev
```

The zone file could be set up as follows:

```
@           IN          SOA           ns.xyz.com      root.xyz.com (
➥1997101501  86400  3600   608400 86400 )
            IN          NS            ns.xyz.com.

1.1         IN          PTR           www.xyz.com.
2.4         IN          PTR           mailhost.xyz.com.
```

Or, the zone file could be set up using the `$ORIGIN` statement to segment the file by domain, as follows:

```
@           IN          SOA           ns.xyz.com      root.xyz.com (
➥1997101501  86400  3600   608400 86400 )
            IN          NS            ns.xyz.com.
$ORIGIN 1.10.132.in-addr.arpa.
1           IN          PTR           www.xyz.com.
$ORIGIN 4.10.132.in-addr.arpa.
2           IN          PTR           mailhost.xyz.com.
```

This zone file setup can greatly simplify the management of large zone files by dividing zones into logical sections. The `$ORIGIN` statement resets the domain name for all RRs below it so that they reflect the domain name following the `$ORIGIN` statement. The `$INCLUDE` statement introduces even further simplification. `$INCLUDE` enables you to put PTR records for each origin into separate files because it includes those files in the primary zone file at the point where $INCLUDE appears. The resulting zone file using this method would look like the following:

```
@          IN        SOA          ns.xyz.com    root.xyz.com (
➥1997101501  86400 3600 608400 86400  )
           IN        NS           ns.xyz.com.
$ORIGIN 1.10.132.in-addr.arpa.
$INCLUDE sub-net1.db
$ORIGIN 4.10.132.in-addr.arpa.
$INCLUDE sub-net4.db
```

In the prior example, the two $INCLUDE files for the in-addr zones contain PTR records for their respective subnets and hosts.

Address (A) Records

Address (A) records map host names to IP addresses. These records are used in forward lookup zone files and in the root cache files. The format of an A resource record is similar to NS records. A resource record contains an owner, a class, a TTL, the A resource type itself, and finally, the host address. The order of these can vary. If you see TTL, for example, before Class, it's OK.

The A record template looks like this (see also Figure 7.4):

`<owner> <ttl> IN A <address>`

An A record might look like this:

`socrates          IN     A     206.174.16.62`

In an A resource record, the owner is the host named in the record itself. Because the origin of the SOA is taoslab.com., the entry in the prior example actually translates into socrates.taoslab.com. This is because socrates was not recorded with a trailing period. When this occurs, the default behavior of DNS is to append the domain name of the origin to the resource's name. As a result, queries to socrates.taoslab.com would reference this record, and the IP address would be returned in reply. Figure 7.4 shows the Domain Name Service Manager Properties dialog box for A records.

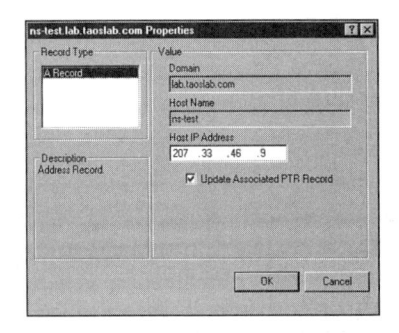

Figure 7.4 You can view A resource records in the DNS Manager.

As in previous examples, the `TTL` value is derived from the SOA's M-TTL value. `$ORIGIN` and `$INCLUDE` statements may be used with A records. If the primary name server for a domain also serves any subdomains, the `$ORIGIN` statement can be used to reset the origin for those records below it belonging to the subdomains. As with PTR records, `$INCLUDE` statements can simplify zone files by segmenting sets of records into manageable groups and sizes.

Mail Exchange (MX) Records

The Mail Exchange (MX) records provide information (as their name implies) about where mail can be routed for members of the domain. The MX record format is like the NS record. It contains fields for the owner, the TTL, the class, and the resource itself. In addition, the MX record's `preference` field enables you to set an order for each target host that can receive mail. Having an MX record point to a machine for mail does not configure that machine to receive mail!

The MX record template looks like this:

`<owner> <ttl> IN MX <preference> <exchanger.domain-name>`

An MX record might resemble the following examples (also see Figure 7.5):

```
taoslab.com    IN    MX    10    socrates.taoslab.com.
               IN    MX    10    socrates.taoslab.com.
```

The second example indicates two things. For one, if the SOA resource record is the last entry in the file to set an origin, `socrates` will automatically become the mail exchanger for mail going to the `taoslab.com` domain which was specified in that SOA. Be careful: The record order—what's immediately prior to an MX entry—has a crucial effect, so if the last entry preceding the MX record is an A type resource instead of an SOA (`fiddler IN A 206.174.16.4`, for example), `socrates` would become the mail exchanger for `fiddler` the host instead of `taoslab.com` the domain!

Figure 7.5 shows the Domain Name Service Manager Properties dialog box for MX records.

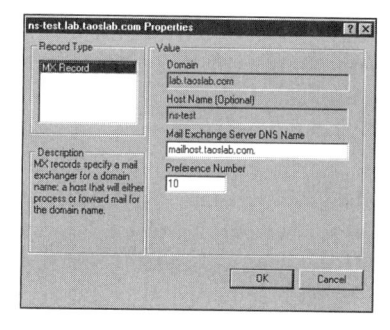

Figure 7.5 You can view MX resource records in the DNS Manager.

If no owner is specified, DNS always assumes that the owner is the last one specified in preceding records.

You can use the `preference` field to apply several MX records, each with an exchanger, to a domain. Using the `preference` field ensures that mail gets delivered as well as providing a measure of redundancy. The preference value is a number between 0 and 65535, for which the lower the number the higher the priority.

The following example demonstrates use of the `preference` field. `10`, `20`, and `30` indicate preference, in which `10` is preferred over `20`, and `20` is preferred over `30`.

```
@        IN    SOA   ns.taoslab.com       root.taoslab.com (
➥1997121201    10800     3600      604800      86400)
         IN    MX    10                   socrates.taoslab.com.
         IN    MX    20                   mailhost.taoslab.com.
         IN    MX    30                   fiddler.taoslab.com.
```

In this example, the three MX records are all for the `taoslab.com` domain. The preference settings indicate that `socrates` is the primary mail exchanger. In the event that `socrates` is unavailable or is too busy, mail might be sent to `mailhost`. If `socrates` and `mailhost` are both unable to respond, `fiddler` would be selected.

Tip

You should take precautions not to create loops with mail exchange programs, such as sendmail, because loops make mail undeliverable. Loops just send mail around in circles without making any destination final. This occurs, for example, when a mail transfer agent (MTA) sends mail to one machine, then it sends the mail to another, and the last machine sends it back again to the original machine. Some mail programs avoid mail loops by not using MX records for the local host and other machines with equal or lower preferences.

Canonical Name (CNAME) Records

The simplest way to describe a CNAME is that it creates an alias. An alias is a name that points to or references another host. You can use CNAME, for example, to run a primary DNS name server and a mailhost on one machine. Figure 7.6 shows the Domain Name Service Manager Properties dialog box for CNAME records.

The CNAME template looks like this:

`<owner> <ttl> IN CNAME <host.domain-name>`

Ponder the following scenario: An organization registers `ns.xyz.com` as the primary DNS server for its domain. The mail program, however, may require that you use a specific computer name, such as `mailhost`. To solve this problem, you can make the real name of the computer `ns.xyz.com`, and add a CNAME RR to point `mailhost` traffic to `ns.xyz.com`. This way, no one but you needs to care that two names or services actually reside at one address.

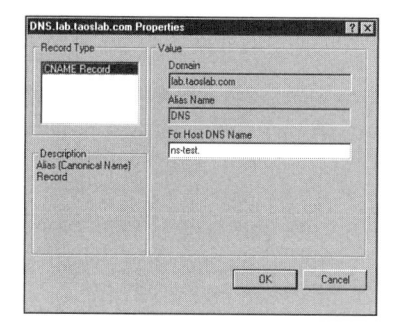

Figure 7.6 You can view CNAME resource records in the DNS Manager.

To support this example, entries in the zone file would look like this:
```
@          IN       SOA         ns.xyz.com     root.xyz.com (
➥1997101501  86400 3600 608400 86400 )
           IN       NS          ns.xyz.com.
ns         IN       A           132.165.23.1
mailhost   IN       CNAME       ns.xyz.com.
```
The name `mailhost.xyz.com` and `ns.xyz.com` will both resolve properly, resulting with the same IP address.

Here's another, simpler example, specifying addresses for FTP and WWW services:
```
Server1    IN       A           10.10.10.10
FTP                 CNAME       Server1
WWW                 CNAME       Server1
```

Warning
An NS record cannot point to a host that's not real, that is, one named only by a CNAME alias. All hosts specified in NS records must also have an A record in the same zone file for direct resolution. If you forget one of these rules, your name server won't stop operating, but it will generate error messages.

CNAME resource records can also be used for such services as FTP and HTTP. CNAMEs let you represent the hosts that these services reside on with any naming convention you like. CNAMEs can also make it easy to change physical machines while keeping services running. Practical benefits include upgrading servers without disrupting service and improving performance by employing new machines. The CNAME resource record can simply be reassigned or pointed to a new host, and the outside world is none the wiser.

Windows Internet Name Server (WINS) Records

The WINS resource record type is supported only by Microsoft's DNS server. The WINS RR format is similar to the other records with a couple of minor additions. But first, you need to know what a WINS record does. As explained in several earlier chapters, WINS is a dynamic name server that uses NetBIOS and relies on hosts to register themselves. WINS doesn't support a hierarchical namespace, and it does not communicate in the same way that DNS servers communicate. Therefore, sites with Windows networks needing Internet connectivity have a minor dilemma.

Prior to MS DNS, administrators would set up a WINS server to provide local name resolution based on the registrations it received from hosts on the network. Because WINS is dynamic, the dynamic host configuration protocol (DHCP) is often used to prevent duplicate and invalid registrations. The problem comes when Internet hosts need to be resolved, or reverse name lookups are performed on local Windows hosts by Internet clients outside the local network. DNS is not dynamic, and it's usually implemented on a UNIX host. The DNS maps are static, which means that changes routinely required by a DHCP server are just not made, and the name data gets old fast.

Microsoft's solution was to create a way for DNS to use WINS to resolve Windows network hosts. With the WINS record on a NT DNS server, the dynamic state of WINS can be captured dynamically in DNS. If a name query is made to an NT DNS server, for example, and the server does not have the information in its local database, the server can reference a local WINS server to see if the host has been registered. If so, the WINS server provides the information to the NT DNS server, which, in turn, returns an answer to the client. Now this might seem like a great way to get a dynamic DNS architecture set up, but it requires some caution: The administrator must carefully design the namespace to avoid conflicts.

The DNS server passes the host name to the WINS server to see if a computer with the same name is registered with the WINS server. If so, then the WINS server sends the IP address of that host back to the DNS server, which can then answer the client's query based on the info it got from WINS.

If all of the name servers in an organization are NT DNS on Windows NT, then there are few issues to be concerned with; however, because organizations can be large and heterogeneous, the chances for multi-level domains and a mix of NT DNS and other UNIX-hosted name servers increase. With this increase grows the risk of name conflicts.

Administrators can prevent WINS entries from propagating to select DNS servers—such as a secondary server at their ISPs, for example—by creating a single DNS subdomain where all of the Windows clients register themselves via WINS. These same clients will all be visible in DNS through a WINS resource record. This design enables the administrator to use WINS without having to worry about delegation problems in the DNS hierarchy because a delegated NT DNS server on a single-level domain can take full advantage of the WINS dynamic capabilities without the problems of transferring a WINS record to servers that can't use it. Remember, only NT DNS servers know what to do with a WINS resource record. Your ISP may not want you to send WINS records to their servers during zone transfers!

In a clean design, secondaries for the Windows domain would also run MS DNS, not a UNIX-hosted DNS, so that the WINS records would propagate properly to all servers needing them. This satisfies the design requirement that primary and secondary servers are not only authoritative, but that they can access all the same information.

The WINS record format in its most basic form looks like the following:
`<origin> <ttl> IN WINS <WINS server IP address>`

An example WINS resource record looks like this:
`@ IN WINS 10.52.120.42`

The easiest way to take advantage of the WINS lookup feature, of course, is to use the MS DNS Manager to add a WINS record to the zone files through the MS DNS GUI. To add WINS records, select the correct domain in the DNS manager window, and right-click to see the Option menu. Select Properties from the menu and a new dialog box appears. In the Zone Properties dialog box, there are several tabs for General, SOA Record, Notify, and the WINS Lookup. Selecting the WINS Lookup tab gives you an option to add the WINS record and a place to enter the IP Addresses of WINS servers, as illustrated in Figure 7.7.

What's the domain of WINS records queried by DNS? A WINS database is not only flat, it really has no domain per se. The trick is that the DNS server holds the domain name that will be applied to the WINS computer names when a match occurs. Only the DNS server with the WINS record may query the WINS server, which prevents unwanted domain memberships from popping up. Each time the DNS server receives a query that it cannot answer from its own zone data, it will query the WINS server for the host name before sending back a response. If the WINS server has a host by the requested name, then the IP address is passed back to the DNS, which is then used to answer the name server query. If the WINS server does not have that host name registered, then it responds with a standard nonexistent name error message.

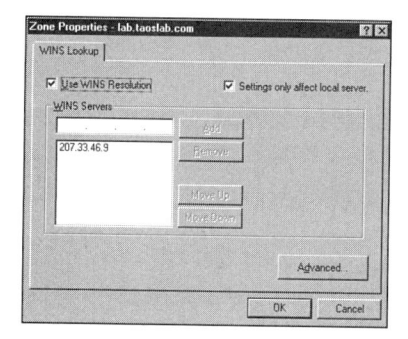

Figure 7.7 WINS Lookup tab of the DNS Manager Zone Properties dialog box.

Windows Internet Name Server-Reverse (WINS-R) Records

The other half of the Windows Internet Name Server (WINS) option is WINS-Reverse (WINS-R) records. This resource record is used in the `in-addr.arpa` domains and provides DNS with reverse lookup capability through WINS. The format of the WINS-R record is exactly like that of the WINS record; the only difference is the zone file where records get stored.

Reverse records enable users to query IP addresses instead of names, and instead of returning a number, reverse queries return the host or computer name.

In the MS DNS Manager, the WINS-R record gets enabled via the Zone Properties dialog box of an `in-addr.arpa` domain (see Figure 7.8). Choose the WINS Reverse Lookup tab to use the feature, and specify the domain name that should be appended to the host names gleaned from WINS. There's also an option to specify the WINS-R record's scope to prevent propagation to hosts that don't understand WINS record types.

Typically, the WINS-R resource record takes the following form:
```
<owner domain>  0  IN  WINS-R  <local>   <domain name to append>
```

As with the WINS record for forward lookups, the WINS-R RR usually has a TTL value of 0, which ensures that that the information will not be cached. Reverse records are not typically cached because they're infrequently used, and they could change unpredictably.

The Cache File

The cache file holds the addresses and names of root name servers. The cache file is sometimes called a *hint file* because it gives the server hints about how to resolve tough queries. The cache file does not hold previously resolved entries, as its name seems to imply. Cache file entries are static, and they give the server a last-resort outlet in the event it can't locate a host through standard delegations. Figure 7.9 shows the raw contents of the root domain's cache file. Frankly, it's not very useful as information, but it must be present for DNS to work!

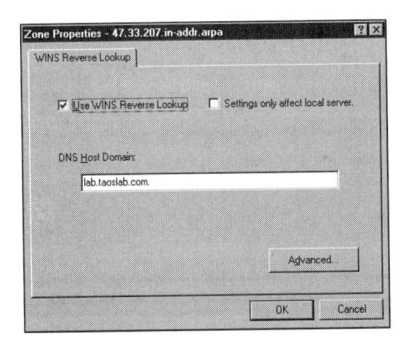

Figure 7.8 You can enable WINS reverse lookup in MS DNS Manager.

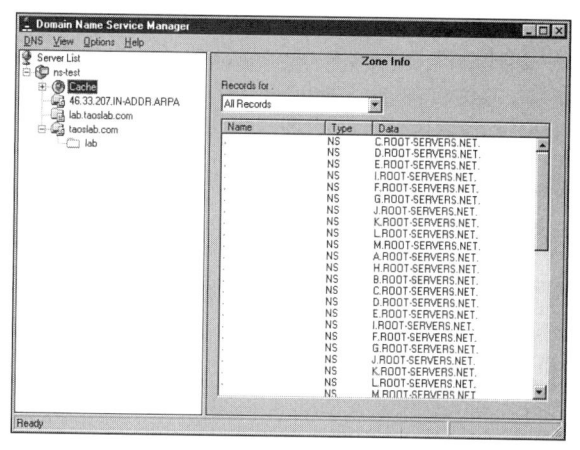

Figure 7.9 You can view the Cache file in the DNS Manager.

NT DNS server automatically loads a fully populated `cache.dns` file for you when you install it. Change your cache file only if your server doesn't connect to the Internet, or when the InterNIC root domain servers change, which is rare. You can download the root cache file directly from the InterNIC at `http://www.internic.net`. The FTP site is `ftp://rs.internic.net/domain/named.root`.

Note
The cache file and caching (which is described later in this chapter) are not the same thing. The cache file is a map of root domain servers. Caching is a dynamically created map of previously resolved hosts that enables a name server to respond quickly to two or more identical queries.

Accessing Root-Level Servers with Cache Files
Name servers must answer queries to the best of their capability, even if they don't contain local information enabling them to answer quickly and directly. Some queries require a DNS server to obtain an answer from elsewhere. If trying to climb a domain tree does not work (see Figure 5.5 in Chapter 5, "How DNS Works," which illustrates this procedure), the cache file enables a DNS server to quickly access a root-level server where it can find downward referrals in the tree, toward an authoritative DNS server for the specified host's domain.

Troubleshooting Tip
Make sure the cache file is populated. If no root level servers are defined, your DNS server can get stuck in an infinite loop. Because there's no time-out mechanism to save the day if this occurs, you won't be able to resolve any hosts.

If a machine is on a network that's not connected to the Internet and DNS is still used for host name resolution, the cache file must still refer to a root domain server. If the root domain name server happens to be at the top of the domain tree of a private network, then the cache directive in the boot configuration is replaced by a primary directive pointing to a zone file that would contain the name and IP address of the name server itself as the root domain's authority. This is legal and it works fine. The result for a query that such a machine could not itself answer is identical for a nonexistent domain. If the name server can reference a machine that it believes is a root server, the query will still be processed to a happy conclusion.

Delegation

The first, and required, way to identify an authoritative server as primary for your domain is to register it with the InterNIC. The next, optional, way to identify an authoritative server is through *delegation*. Delegation publishes primary and secondary name servers for your domain in the Internet, delegating them also as authorities. An NS record is the only mechanism you need to delegate a server.

If a name server is delegated authority for a domain, clients and other name servers outside of the domain are able to find and use it for their queries. This doesn't mean that all secondaries must be delegated. Only the name servers that you want visible from outside the domain need to be delegated.

Secondaries can also be internal to the domain so that only hosts directly configured to use them will ever send queries to secondaries. If a name server is delegated for a domain, but isn't identified by directive to be a secondary so that it can answer its queries (see the `secondary` directive in Appendix G), hosts that query the domain via that server will receive a *lame delegation* error message.

Distributing Names

Zone files residing on primary DNS servers need to be backed up. Secondary servers each need a copy of their domain's zone files. Zone transfers provide an orderly way to move maps around for these purposes. Zone transfers help, and they can hurt, too, if the names and addresses of all your computers end up in mischievous hands because they were transferred to someone you can't trust.

Zone Transfers

A primary server is always the original source of a domain's map files. Zone transfers usually send map files from primary to secondary name servers, though it's possible for a secondary to get zones from another secondary. Primary servers receive transfer requests from secondary name servers when a secondary initializes, or when a secondary's map file gets out of synch with the primary. Any DNS server from which zone files are transferred is called a Master Server. If that server happens to be a secondary, it's considered a *secondary master server*.

A complete zone file can also be obtained by any client using the interactive nslookup utility. The nslookup `ls` command gets a listing of the zone's data, which presents a security problem for administrators who don't want just anyone to get at their zone files. Servers can be set up to prevent transfers and lookups from *untrusted hosts*. More about this is in Chapter 16, "Security Issues."

A tool that can help secure your zones is the `notify` directive. With the `notify` directive, a primary server can send notifications to secondaries whenever changes have been made to a zone file. The security advantage here is that only servers specified in the notify list ask for zone transfers. The `notify` directive also propagates changes more quickly because secondaries won't then wait for the refresh timeout to initiate transfers.

Chapter 11, "Installing and Setting Up DNS," describes this option and how to use it.

Caching

All name servers perform caching. Any time a DNS client queries your DNS server for information, it'll cache the answer it gets in case it receives another query for the same target host. If, for example, a user browsing the Web follows several links on a single Web page and all of those links produce an http *get* that identifies the same Web server, the query for that one Web server is repeated several times in succession. If the answer for the first such query is cached, your local server can provide non-authoritative answers immediately to subsequent queries. The likelihood that the target host's name or address will change during such a sequence is tiny, making it safe for a client to assume that the answer is correct.

The real problem with caching comes when someone makes an error editing a zone file. If an error is not caught right away and queries are made returning bad data, the mistakes will be propagated across the network. This happens when DNS servers return a bad address they're given to the client, and the client, in turn, discovers the error when connection attempts fail. This bad cache problem can be compounded if the server issuing a bad address has a long time-to-live value, even if it's quickly corrected at the source server, because the TTL value tells other servers how long they can use the address, even if it's bad. If your domain's name server issues or receives wrong addresses, name resolution and connectivity for all hosts in the domain can become unreliable.

Summary

This chapter has described the information DNS stores, explaining in some detail the most important resource records. The remainder of Part II, "Introducing Windows NT DNS," completes the overview of the Domain Name System. Part III, "Using Windows NT DNS," goes deeply into implementation and how to administer DNS.

Dissecting Name Queries

This chapter will review:

- **Iterative and Recursive Queries.** DNS clients can use two types of query: iterative and recursive. This section describes the difference.
- **Sending the DNS Query.** This section describes what kind of messages fly back and forth between DNS clients and servers.
- **Time-to-Live.** Time-to-live tells clients how long an answer can be trusted, determining how long it can cache the result.

Iterative and Recursive Queries

Iterative and recursive queries are the two types of requests that can be sent to a name server. Recursive queries are the most common type sent to local name servers. When a local name server accepts a client's query, the local name server itself will attempt to find the answer on its client's behalf, and the client waits while the name server does all the work. If the local name server does not already have the answer, it will perform a recursive search for the answer, working its way up and down the branches of the domain tree. See Chapter 5, "How DNS Works," for an example of an `nslookup` trace.

For a recursive name query, the DNS server will continue to search until it receives an answer. The answer may be the IP address for a host, or it may be that the host does not exist. Either way, the recursive name server will report an answer back to the client.

A name server set up to use a forwarder will send a *recursive* query to the designated forwarder host. The host that receives the forwarded query will operate in recursive mode to answer the query. If a local name server is set up to be a *slave* to a *forwarder*, things work a little differently. The client can send a recursive query to the local name server, but if the name server is a slave, it can't perform a recursive query. It essentially becomes the client to the forwarder server and waits for it to reply. Chapter 6, "Name Server Types," has a thorough description of forwarders and slaves.

Iterative queries are slightly different. The best example of an iterative query is a local name server sending a request to a root-level server. When the local name server for an organization makes a query to a root server, the root server doesn't necessarily take responsibility for answering the query on behalf of the local name server. In fact, the root server can only perform one step to resolve the request—pointing the local name server to another place to query for the answer. This is commonly called a *referral*. For example, if a root server is queried for www.isi.edu, it will not go to the ISI name server and ask for the address of the host www. Instead, the root server answers back with a hint, telling the local name server to go and query the name server at ISI instead.

An iterative query is answered by the name server with an "educated guess" based on what it knows. For more information on iterative and recursive queries, see Chapter 3, "How Windows Clients Use DNS and WINS."

Sending the DNS Query

Users start name service queries by trying to access resources on the network. The resource the user is trying to reach might be on another host on the local network or on one halfway around the world. Typically, the user will enter the remote host name either by typing it on the command line or going through some application like Netscape or WS-FTP. An entry made in this way then must be converted into an IP address.

Depending on the configuration of the user's local machine, the name may be resolved in a number of ways. One way of resolving a host name is to look at a local host's file. The local host's file does not scale very well, which is why DNS was created in the first place. If DNS is the method chosen to resolve the remote host name, then the local host references its *resolver library* to determine if a default domain has been chosen, a search path has been set up, and what the IP addresses of the name servers are. In Windows NT, this information is configured and can be found on the DNS tab of the TCP/IP Properties dialog box (choose Network Control Panel, Protocols), as illustrated in Figure 8.1.

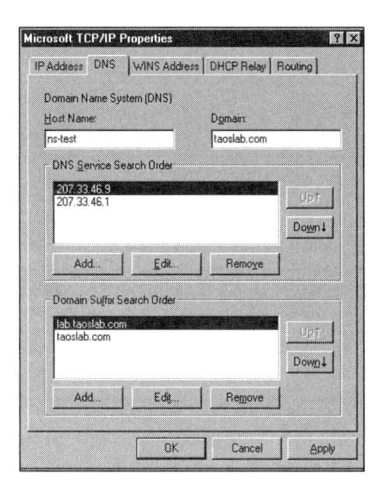

Figure 8.1 The DNS Tab of the TCP/IP Properties dialog box.

Once this information has been properly entered, the host can use DNS for hostname resolution. After obtaining the IP address of the name server, the local host can send a query to the name server for the remote host's IP address. The format of the IP packet that is sent to the name server contains five sections, as illustrated in Figure 8.2.

DNS messages (whether queries or answers) contain specific bits of information. The header section, always present, contains information about the packet, including which of these sections are included in the packet, whether this is a query or answer, the type of query (standard, inverse, server status, and so on) and if the packet is an answer, whether the answer is authoritative or not. Figure 8.3 illustrates the header format.

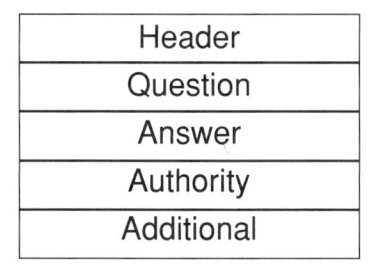

Header
Question
Answer
Authority
Additional

- The question for the named server
- RRs answering the question
- RRs pointing toward the authority
- RRs holding additional information

Figure 8.2 Contents of an IP packet sent to the name server.

Chapter 8 Dissecting Name Queries

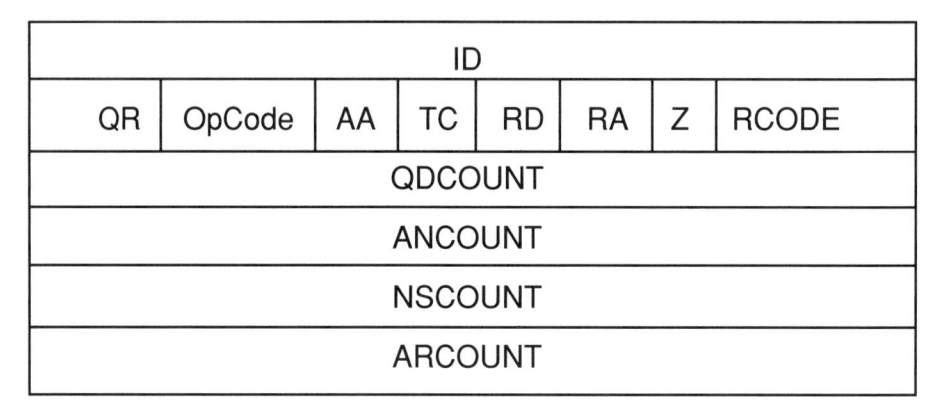

ID								
QR	OpCode	AA	TC	RD	RA	Z	RCODE	
QDCOUNT								
ANCOUNT								
NSCOUNT								
ARCOUNT								

Figure 8.3 Header format of a packet.

Note
RFC 1035 contains more detailed information about the contents of DNS messages and how they're encoded.

The Question section of the packet illustrated in Figure 8.2 contains three pieces of information: the domain name that is being inquired about, the type of inquiry, and the class of the query. The domain name might actually be a host, but that depends on the type of query that is being sent. If the user is trying to get to www.isi.edu via a Web browser, then the query will be an address query. The packet would contain the host name www.isi.edu in the query section, the type of query would be represented by a code that symbolizes an address or A record, and the class would be a code that represents the Internet or IN class. Figure 8.4 illustrates the format of the Question section of the packet.

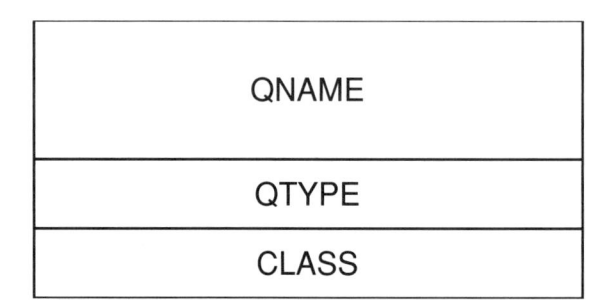

QNAME
QTYPE
CLASS

Figure 8.4 The Question field of a DNS message.

The Answer, Authority, and Additional Information section of the packet, as illustrated in Figure 8.2, are all identical in format. The fields included in these sections of the packet include a name, type, class, ttl, length field that specifies how long the resource data field is, and the resource data itself. The name, class, and type fields of the answer should be identical to the question. The ttl field contains the time-to-live for the record data that is being received, and the Rdata will be the actual answer.

In the preceding example, the name field would contain www.isi.edu, and the Rdata section would contain the IP address of the host. Figure 8.5 illustrates the format of the Answer, Authority, and Additional Information fields, all of which are identical.

Now, in the big picture, the client sends the request to its local name server. The name server accepts the query and begins looking for the answer. If the name server has the information in its cache and the ttl has not expired, the name server will provide the information to the client directly. In this case, the answer returned is not authoritative (so the AA flag is not set in the header), but the response time is greatly diminished.

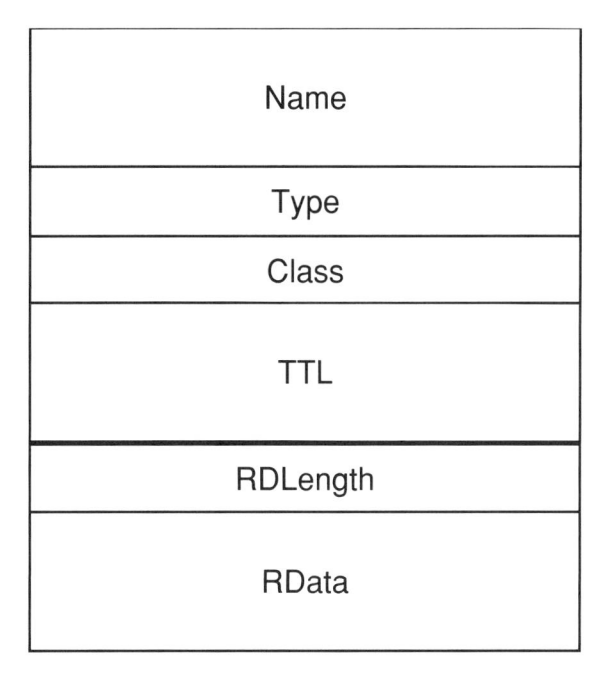

Name
Type
Class
TTL
RDLength
RData

Figure 8.5 The Answer, Authority, and Additional Information fields of a DNS message.

If the answer is not in the name server's cache, then the local name server will begin querying other name servers, climbing up the domain name tree to the root, and back down another branch to find the answer. In this case, when the local name server does finally get an answer for the client, the AA flag is set, acknowledging that the answer came from an authoritative server. With the information in hand, the client can proceed to establish a connection to the remote host.

When receiving the response from the name server, the client is normally concerned with the authority status of the answer, that is, if there is a problem reaching the *resolved* host. A problem occurs if a name server answers non-authoritatively for a domain for which it is an authority. This usually indicates that someone made a typo or some other error in the zone data.

The following sections, "Cache Hits" and "Cache Misses," illustrate and describe the process of caching results in more detail.

Cache Hits

In a transaction between a client and a name server, if the answer the client is querying for resides in the name server's local cache, the sequence illustrated in Figure 8.6 occurs.

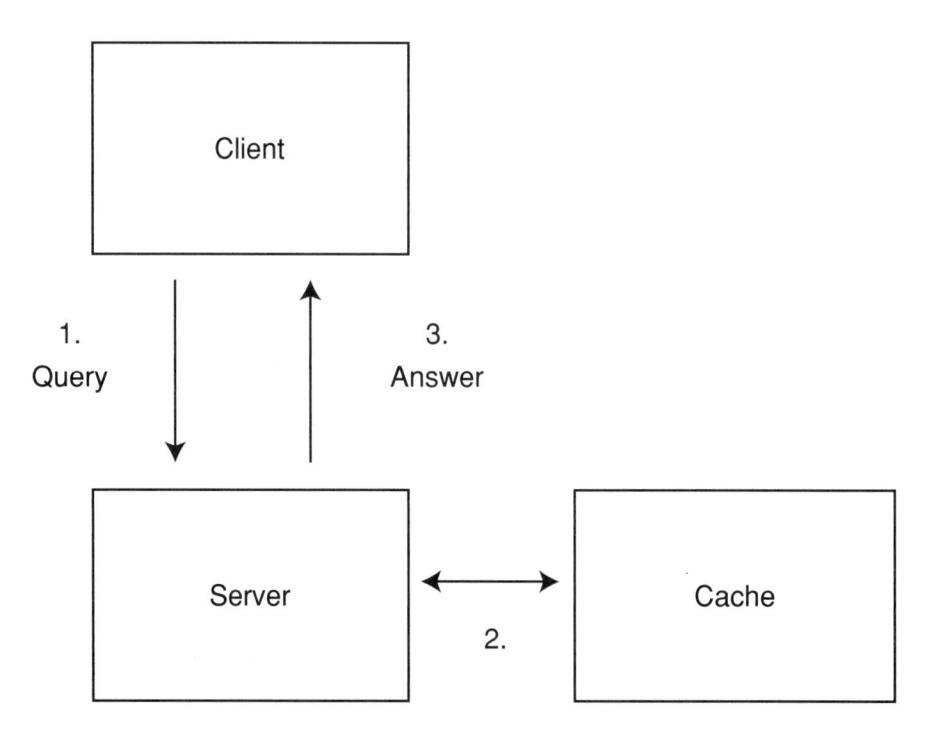

Figure 8.6 Answering a client query from the name server's local cache.

The numbered sequence in Figure 8.6 is as follows:
1. The client sends the query to the name server.
2. The name server checks its local cache.
3. If the name server has the answer in its local cache, the name server returns the answer to the client directly.

Cache Misses

In a transaction between a client and a name server, if the answer the client is querying for does not reside in the name server's local cache, the sequence illustrated in Figure 8.7 occurs.

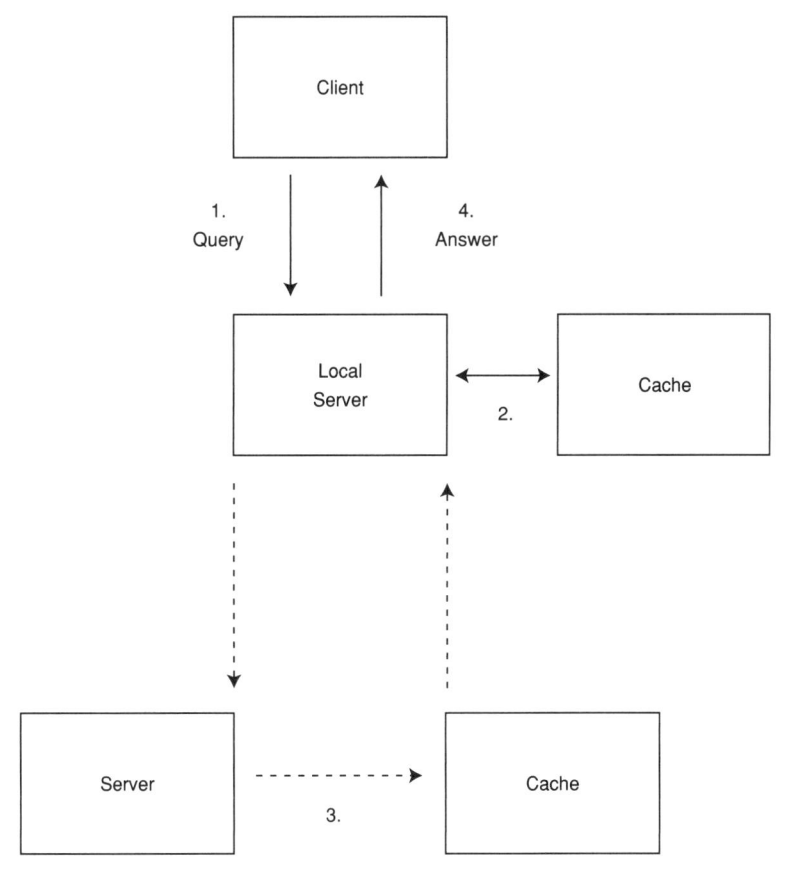

Figure 8.7 Answering a client query from an authoritative server.

The numbered sequence in Figure 8.7 is as follows:
1. The client sends the query to the name server.
2. The name server checks its local cache. If the answer is not in the local cache, the name server must look elsewhere for the information.
3. The name server may send a query to a root-level server, and get a referral to an authoritative server for the domain in question.
4. Once the local server receives the answer from an authoritative server, then it will place the answer in its cache and provide the answer to the client.

Time-to-Live

The *time-to-live* (TTL) is a timer that tells a name server how long an answer is good for, once it has contacted an authoritative server. As described in Chapter 7, "What DNS Knows," the TTL can be set on a per-record basis, or it can be set to a default value as specified by the minimum time-to-live (m-ttl) in the SOA record for a domain. If the TTL of a single record is set to something other than the default m-ttl, every record following that one will have the same TTL until another record is implicitly set back to the m-ttl. If TTL is set to zero, the client knows that it cannot cache the result.

How the TTL is used is quite simple. When a user's local name server receives a query for information that it does not already have, the local name server must acquire the answer from an authoritative name server for the particular domain through some sequence of steps. Once the local name server receives an answer, it caches the answer in the event that some other local host queries for the same information. The TTL specifies how long the local name server will keep the answer it has received in its cache. Once the TTL has expired, the local name server flushes the information from the cache and must contact an authoritative name server again if another query is received. If the TTL is set to zero, the answer will not be cached, and the data is only valid for the transaction in progress.

Summary

This chapter described how standard DNS queries work. The query process is also described in other places in the book, Chapters 5 and 6, for example, but not as simply as presented here. For more information about how DNS servers work together, see Chapter 9, "How MS DNS Works with Other Servers."

How MS DNS Works with Other Servers

This chapter will review:

- **Communication Between MS DNS and Other Name Servers.** Although compliant with most other name servers, Microsoft's DNS Server encounters some problems when communicating with early BIND-based name servers. This section provides some precautionary measures for communication between these two types of name servers.
- **Migrating from BIND to MS DNS.** This section covers the required operations necessary when integrating or replacing BIND-based name servers with MS DNS.
- **Boot Files and Other Differences.** Migration, configuration, and integration with MS DNS require an understanding of the effects on the Registry and the boot file for the name server. This section provides this required information.

Communication Between MS DNS and Other Name Servers

Microsoft's DNS is RFC-compliant in terms of how it talks to other name servers. The message format and query packets have the same structure and bit alignment. The MS DNS will accept and respond appropriately to both iterative and recursive queries. The one thing to watch out for with the MS DNS server, in regard to versions of name server binaries based on BIND 4.9.x or earlier, is the messages that are sent during zone transfers. Although written into the RFC, the older versions of BIND and its derivatives can have problems with messages that contain multiple resource records. If this situation should occur, the administrator should take care to set the MS DNS server to send only single-resource record messages to other servers during zone transfers. This is accomplished by uncommenting the `BindSecondaries` line in the boot file, or editing the value of the `BindSecondaries` key in the Registry.

If the administrator wants to affect the change by editing the boot file, and name server system is running from the Registry, the administrator will have to do the following:

1. Change the Registry keys to boot from a file instead of the Registry.
2. Create a boot file that matches the current configuration.
3. Reset the name server so it boots from the file.
4. Start the DNS manager and perform an "Update Server Data Files" from the DNS menu. This will eliminate a number of problems related to the zone transfers themselves, as well as protect the health and well-being of the other name servers in the network.

In contrast, the key in the Registry that affects this operation contains a binary operator. The value of the `BindSecondaries` key is simply set to one or zero. The binary value of one represents a true state, implying that BIND secondaries will be used, and zero represents a false state.

One of the drawbacks to the MS DNS is the lack of a tool that provides the capability to generate a boot file that matches the Registry settings. Switching back and forth between boot files and the Registry can cause problems in and of itself by the sheer fact that configuration settings may be lost in transitions. The administrator needs to pay very close attention to every detail when making these changes or, for that matter, any others.

Migrating from BIND to MS DNS

An administrator already running BIND who wants to implement the MS DNS solution must answer a couple of questions first:

- Will the MS DNS be used in conjunction with BIND? If so, will it be the primary or the secondary?
- Will the MS DNS be used to replace the BIND server outright, or will it function for only a delegated portion (subdomain) of the domain?

If the MS DNS server will be used in conjunction with BIND, you will need to know which version of BIND is being used. If BIND 8 and MS DNS are to be used together, the issues of building the MS DNS are minimal if the MS DNS will be a secondary. The administrator will need to set up the MS DNS for the secondary domains only. There is little else to do unless the MS DNS machine will also be a secondary master, meaning that other secondaries will pull their zones from it. For a primary, the issues really relate only to the setup of the server. BIND 8 configuration files will not load on an MS DNS server. This means that the configuration of the MS DNS will need to be performed manually. For more information about manual configuration, see Chapter 11, "Installing and Setting Up DNS."

BIND 4, on the other hand, requires that certain features are turned off in MS DNS. On the bright side, the BIND 4 boot file can be modified slightly to set the initial configuration of the MS DNS. The issues here are related to the fact that the MS DNS does not support the XFRNETS directive and cannot be used in transferring the configuration from another machine. Another change that the administrator needs to pay attention to, is the `directory` directive. The proper syntax needs to be included for the path name of the directory used to store the database files.

Another factor is whether BIND servers will run as secondaries to the MS DNS servers. If BIND 4.x servers are going to be used as secondaries for the MS DNS, a switch (called `BindSecondaries`) must be set in the configuration file to specify this because most older versions of BIND will not transfer zones correctly if there are more than one resource record per message. BIND 8 has resolved this problem.

If the MS DNS server is going to be a primary, the sources for the zone files will also be needed. The zone files, if coming from an existing server, can simply be copied over via FTP for nfs/cifs. As they are simply formatted text files, no special warnings need be given. The only potential problem might be a resource record that is not supported by the MS DNS, like the SRV or LOC records that have been added recently. This isn't likely to occur, as most servers are not currently making use of these resource records.

Boot Files and Other Differences

The main thing to remember in configuring the MS DNS server is the WINS integration. Because WINS is not supported as part of the RFCs for DNS, and there are other Dynamic DNS implementations being worked out, it is doubtful, in the author's opinion, that WINS will appear in the ISC BIND. Chapter 2, "Introducing NetBIOS," Chapter 3, "How Windows Clients Use DNS and WINS," Chapter 4, "WINS and DNS: Making the Most of Both Services," and Chapter 12, "Integrating DNS with WINS," have more information about this subject.

Another difference in the boot and configuration of the MS DNS is where the configuration information is stored. MS uses its Registry for the key components of the DNS configuration. A boot file can be used to initially set up the DNS, but once the DNS Manager is used to make any changes, the system will automatically switch to the Registry for booting and configuring the name server. Attempts to revert back to the boot file method will frustrate the administrator, as changes made in the boot file will likely be lost when the DNS Manager is opened again. The configuration usually reverts back to the last set of keys that were built in the hive. Copies of the boot file should also be made because the DNS Manager replaces the file *boot* with a generic text file explaining that the DNS server is set to use the Registry.

For some issues, however, the administrator must either use the boot file, or become intimate with the Registry. In the example at the beginning of the chapter, a BIND secondary is going to be used with an MS DNS primary. Here, the option that sets the message format for zone transfers can only be set by editing the boot file or modifying the Registry directly. No other option or property box can be used to set the mode of operation. Chapter 11, "Installing and Setting Up DNS," has more information about boot files and the Registry.

The last difference that's worth mentioning is the `BIND XFRNETS` directive. Essentially, this directive is not supported under the MS DNS, and it will generate an error message in the event log, but will not hinder the operation of the name server. It simply remarks on the invalid directive, and moves on.

III

Using Windows NT DNS

10 Designing Your DNS Service(s)

11 Installing and Setting Up DNS

12 Integrating DNS with WINS

13 Configuring Clients

14 Working with Service Providers

15 Maintenance Tasks

16 Security Issues

17 Troubleshooting Tools and Utilities

18 Dynamic Host Configuration Protocol (DHCP)

10

Designing Your DNS Service(s)

This chapter will review:

- **DNS server capacities.** This section explains some of the factors that determine the capacity of a DNS server.
- **Deciding how many domains to have.** This section will help you think through the issues you'll face when you consider how many domains to have.
- **Deciding how many DNS servers to have.** This section describes the role DNS servers play serving multiple and single domains to help you decide how many DNS servers you'll need for your application.
- **Practical design examples.** This section provides several illustrative DNS design examples to give you ideas you can copy for your own DNS installation.

THIS CHAPTER PROVIDES INFORMATION that you can use to make key decisions, such as deciding how many DNS servers and how many domains you will need. The last section provides design illustrations to help you see clearly what the issues are and how various design alternatives can affect the results of the decisions you make.

DNS Server Capacities

The capacity of a server to handle the queries it receives (both internal and external) will vary depending on the following factors:

- The number of domains that the server is expected to host
- How many subnets to which the server is directly attached
- How many client requests the server will actually serve

The best way to determine the capacity of the servers at a given site is to use Performance Monitor in conjunction with the statistics reports from the DNS Manager. Performance Monitor will provide a record of the overall performance of the server in question. The most important things to look at are network performance, disk performance, memory allocation, and CPU utilization.

Although the DNS service itself is not a heavily taxing process, the number of requests that come in that generate a load on a DNS server can take a toll. If the server is used for other services as well, you should be concerned about the response times of the DNS service. In general, a single DNS server can handle a fair number of domains and keep up with the flow of requests.

A DNS server with 65,553 Resource Records in each of 1,000 zones can support more than 65 million records! There are limits however: DNS Manager will hang if there's more than 65,553 records in one zone or more than 1,000 zones. These limits are documented in Microsoft Knowledge Base articles Q172477 and Q1700518, respectively.

The next issue is managing the zone information on a single server. For ISPs that offer domain hosting, the servers should be fairly hefty in terms of processor performance. They should be loaded with as much memory as possible, and have a modest amount of disk space. The disk capacity needs to accommodate only the OS that the system runs on, and the zone files for the domains. Again, since the zone files are text, the size of the individual zones is generally not large.

Memory is a big factor, as the caching operations of the name servers use the system memory. Having plenty of memory will ensure a snappy performance from the name server, and enable some fairly large caches. For an average organization that will need to serve only its own domain information, very modest machines can go quite far. For most implementations, having enough memory in the system is probably the biggest issue and the key to improving name server performance.

Here are some guidelines to help you build a system based on recommended DNS Manager resource requirements: Use a Pentium with 64MB of RAM, and then add 8MB of RAM for every 64k (65,536) entries that will be published including domain and host records. This assumes that no other services will be running on the same computer to compete for resources. If additional services are going to run on the system, then increase resources to meet requirements of the additional software. Also consider the speed of the network interface and the bandwidth available for queries and answers. The speed of the hard disk is not terribly important if there's enough RAM to keep the server from paging.

Deciding How Many Domains to Have

The number of domains that will be established in a single server is really just a matter of management. The typical name server can, theoretically, handle an almost infinite number of domains, but who would want to manage such a beast? Having the sole responsibility for thousands (or hundreds of thousands) of domains, would not be a task to take lightly. Remember, too, that one DNS server can handle many domains, and one domain can be managed by multiple DNS servers.

Organizations with several thousand computers in only one location, or in a single metropolitan area network, can easily use only one domain. Organizations that are geographically dispersed can have one domain to top their tree, with one subdomain under it for each city or region.

ISPs that provide domain hosting have a lot of responsibility for commercial clients that rely on email and Web presence for their livelihood. If the ISP fails to provide quality name service for even one day, the results could be catastrophic for a business waiting for an all-important email to close a deal, or losing business through customers being unable to reach their Web site and make purchases.

For the average DNS administrator or IS manager, decisions about the number of domains are usually matters of company politics or geographic limitations. For many technology-oriented companies, the engineering departments usually have their own domains for the simple reason that they can't wait for a corporate bureaucracy to get around to making changes. Engineers often need to move more quickly than that for testing new products. The responsibility for maintaining these domains is dispersed among different departments so they won't impede each other with conflicting requests based on their respective missions.

In terms of geographic limitations, many companies have a global presence in the physical location of their offices. It's generally easier for local administrators to be responsible for subdomains that they can touch and feel, rather than having to email another person halfway around the world to make a host record change. Much of this is decided on the basis of efficiency, and it can significantly affect email delivery as well.

Because email addresses are associated with domain names, it's a good idea to make your mail services match the domain structure. DNS domains can be broken up along political, organizational or geographical boundaries, often mirroring the IT support structure.

Problems may arise when a potential mail recipient works for a company in the United States, but lives and works out of an office on another side of the world. Rather than having email go to a single large company server, subdomains and mail aliases are usually set up to redirect mail to servers that are distributed around the company (and, often, the world) to provide better access to the recipient, and decrease the load on a single machine.

Deciding How Many DNS Servers to Have

The number of name servers that an organization may need is a judgment call. There are no rules of thumb that cover all cases and recommendations are advisory at best. Still, you'll find some general rules of thumb a little later in this chapter to provide a modicum of guidance.

If you want to set up a number of subdomains to match the hierarchy of your organization, you'll surely need a primary and a secondary server for each domain. It's not that two machines couldn't handle everything; they can. But there are always issues of accessibility, reliability, and redundancy to consider.

Accessibility, Reliability, and Redundancy

Accessibility refers to two issues: Is the machine accessible by the administrator for maintenance? Is the machine accessible by the clients who need the service? The machine (especially in the case of Windows NT) needs to be where the administrator can physically access the keyboard. Making changes to a zone can be rather difficult otherwise. Access from the clients really means network connectivity. A single server, set up to handle queries for a domain, could easily be saturated by a high request load. This saturation could easily result in a denial of service—names not getting resolved before a timeout occurs.

Having multiple machines for a single domain at least means that some of the requests will be serviced by other hosts. The issues of redundancy and reliability are pretty straightforward. What happens if a name server crashes (or the hard disk fails, or memory error occurs, and so on)? The loss of a host supporting a domain by itself essentially means the loss of the domain until the service is restored. With multiple machines serving the domain, the administrator can be assured that at least some portion of the queries for the domain are being answered.

Having multiple machines means that the query load will be spread among the machines, and if one goes down, there can be problems getting names resolved such as delays or timeouts. Aged cached information pointing to a downed machine can also cause some short-term resolution failures.

Another redundancy issue is location. If all the name servers are in one location and your ISP connection is lost, the domain becomes inaccessible. By default, the greater the number of servers providing name service and the better geographic distribution, the better the reliability of the name service.

General considerations to take into account when deciding on a name server architecture include: the number of locations that need support, the type of network communications that will be established among the locations, the number of clients at each location, and the nature and type of connectivity the organization has to the Internet.

Rules of Thumb for Selecting the Number of DNS Servers

All organizations need two DNS servers. If an ISP handles name service for you, though, neither of these need to be yours to set up or manage. Small organizations often let the ISP manage the whole thing, and some have only one DNS server—either the primary or secondary—letting the ISP keep the other. For reasons discussed earlier, this is a good, safe practice.

Mid-sized organizations need only two DNS servers, and they can add one site server for every geographical location to facilitate outbound queries (these would be caching only). Alternatively, they could turn geographically dispersed DNS servers into secondaries in order to add redundancy for inbound queries.

Large organizations can have very complex DNS setups involving multiple domains and subdomains. The next section, "Practical Design Examples," illustrates some of the many options that can make large systems complex, as well as necessary. Trade-offs between capacity, responsiveness, and reliability make simple rules of thumb useless for designing DNS services for a large organization.

Practical Design Examples

This section provides several illustrations you can use to help you determine what kind of design is best for your installation.

Setting Up a Domain with One or More Subdomains

Engineering organizations are often very dynamic environments where experiments occur, so it's a good idea to separate them from the main corporate domain. The goal is to give an engineering department control over its own subdomain and the ability to handle changes independent of the rest of the company. Figure 10.1 shows a DNS setup that could be used for a domain named xyz.com.

xyz.com, the main corporate domain, delegates authority for the engineering subdomain to the DNS servers in eng.xyz.com. In this scenario, changes made in eng.xyz.com won't affect the corporate domain, xyz.com., and engineering can make changes themselves for all their own hosts without having to bother corporate system administrators.

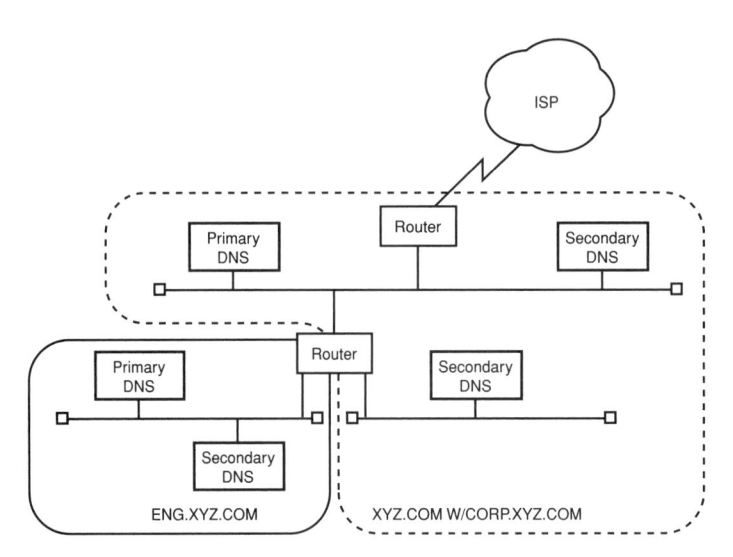

Figure 10.1 A corporate domain with primary and secondary DNS servers, delegating to a subdomain.

Using an ISP to Provide Primary DNS Service

In very small organizations or even homes, it is often advisable to have the ISP provide the primary DNS service, as illustrated in Figure 10.2.

You can have your own caching server to improve performance, or secondary server for redundancy. If you don't have a secondary server, the ISP can easily provide one. In this scenario, DNS is managed by the ISP and your organization doesn't need to bother except to initiate changes with the ISP. Every change requires communication with the ISP and they'll have to edit the zone file for you.

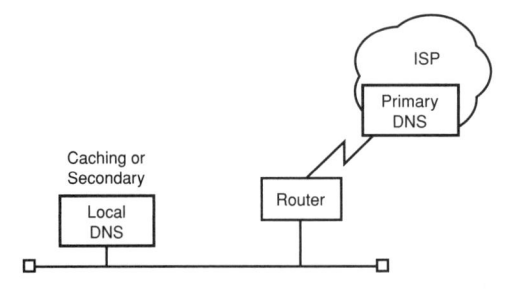

Figure 10.2 The ISP provides primary DNS services for this domain.

If the connection to your ISP is persistent, a caching-only server is fine. If the link is a dial-up or an on-demand line of some kind, installing a secondary DNS server might be better because you can then do local lookups without having to connect to the ISP for each query. Having a secondary also means that you can easily verify changes by examining the local copy of the zone file which is periodically updated by transfer from the ISP's primary server.

Using an ISP to Provide Secondary DNS Service

In Figure 10.3, the organization is hosting its own primary DNS server, but the ISP or some other external organization is hosting the secondary. Remember, two servers—one primary and one secondary, or two secondaries—must be registered with InterNIC.

This scenario can help the performance of the whole system by distributing DNS query processing to several machines in different places. It also provides redundancy. If xyz.com loses connectivity, for example, a timeout would occur trying to connect, but its hosts could still be resolved by external systems. It is important to always have DNS for your domain, which is one reason why you shouldn't ever put all primary and secondary DNS servers for a domain on a non-dedicated link (such as a dial-up).

Protecting a Primary DNS Server from Unauthorized Access

You can improve security by registering two secondaries with the InterNIC instead of a primary, as shown in Figure 10.4.

This setup hides the machine hosting the zone data files from hackers. While the primary provides the zone data for the domain, it feeds the secondaries with authoritative data by transfers. Although all the servers can answer with authority, then, only the secondaries will respond to requests from external sources.

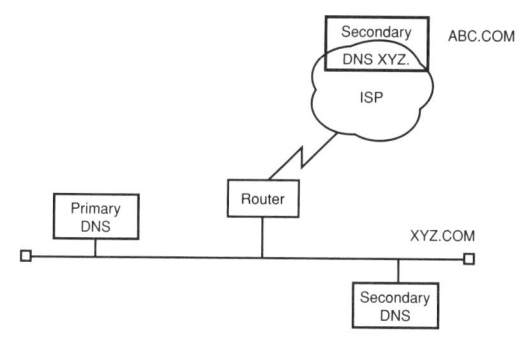

Figure 10.3 The ISP provides secondary DNS service for this domain.

134   Chapter 10 Designing Your DNS Service(s)

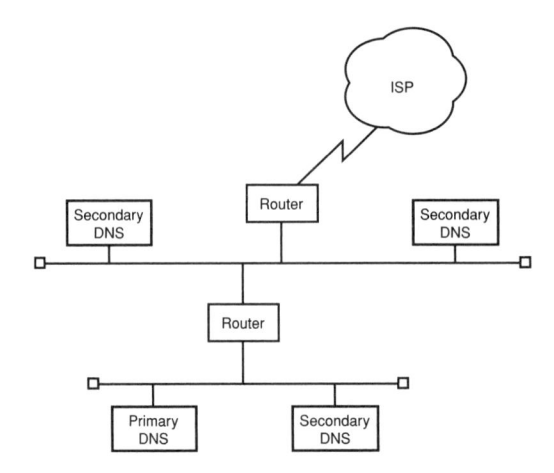

Figure 10.4   Secondaries serve outside queries into the domain, hiding the primary name server.

Additionally, the option to allow only secondaries in the notify list to perform zone transfers can prevent unscrupulous people from dumping the contents of the zones. This setup prevents hackers from accessing a machine with the zone source. Routers can also be used to block access to the primary from outside the organization.

How a Large Site Can Create a Large Cache of Queries

If you want to reduce the number of name queries that must be resolved outside your organization, such as by ISP DNS servers, you can create a site-wide cache, as illustrated in Figure 10.5.

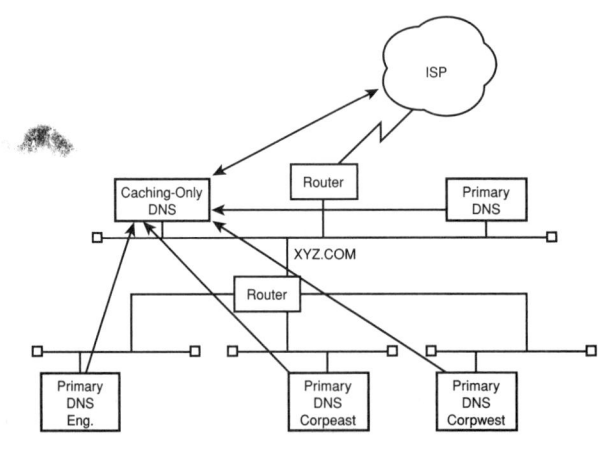

Figure 10.5   A site-wide caching-only DNS server can respond more quickly than individual queries going to outside servers.

You install a site-wide caching-only server by having all the name servers forward queries to one or more caching servers. This way all requests and answers get cached on a single machine that will be queried by all other name servers in the company. This eliminates the need for the corpwest name server to go outside for any queries that have already been cached by any clients anywhere in the company.

Establishing an Organization-Only DNS That's Coordinated with External DNS

Split-brain DNS, as it is sometimes called, uses multiple primaries to increase security for a domain (see Figure 10.6). The practical value of this setup for large organizations is profound. Split-brain DNS enables you to provide DNS service to internal clients for internal addresses, without having to post all addresses where outside DNS clients can see them. Administrators can decide precisely which internal hosts will be listed in outside DNS servers and which ones will be listed only in internal DNS servers.

The primary external server only contains entries in its zone file that you want the outside world to know about, while the internal primary contains entries for all hosts in the domain. The internal name servers are set up to forward to the external primary name server all requests that they cannot answer directly, where they can be cached. The internals are also slaves to the externals, so they cannot attempt resolutions on their own. This keeps the internal servers hidden from the outside world, giving hackers fewer targets.

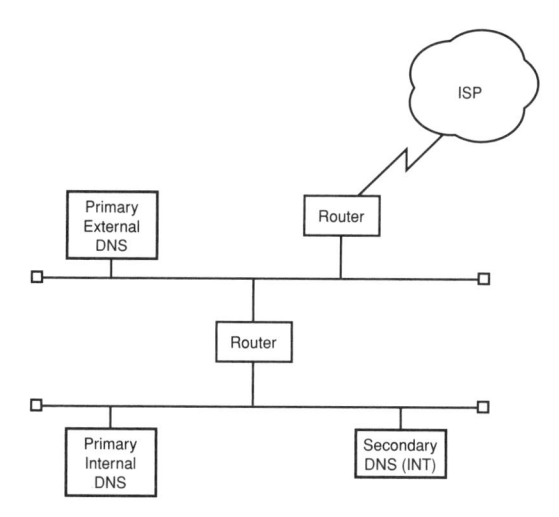

Figure 10.6 Split-Brain DNS provides a measured degree of security for zone data.

Security is a big concern of large corporations, and DNS servers contain significant data: knowledge of every machine in your domain! For this reason, it's a good idea to employ some scheme that prevents access to primary DNS servers because they're designed to transfer authoritative data to secondary servers. Hackers know this and they know how to exploit this feature for their own purposes.

Summary

This chapter provided practical information you can use to help design your own DNS installation. Chapter 11, "Installing and Setting Up DNS," takes you to the next step, getting your DNS server up and running.

11

Installing and Setting Up DNS

This chapter will review:

- **Installing the DNS Service.** Provides steps to follow to install the DNS service on a Windows NT server.
- **Configuring the DNS Server.** Shows how to use DNS Manager to create zones, add and change Resource Records, perform load balancing, update the network efficiently, and create multihomed servers.
- **Creating Virtual Servers.** Shows how to enter Resource Records for servers with more than one IP number assigned to one interface.

THE DESIGN OF YOUR DNS SERVICE needs to be decided upon before installing and configuring DNS. Every domain requires at least one primary DNS server. More than one primary is necessary to delegate to a subdomain because subdomains require their own primary server. Each primary needs a secondary for backup purposes, and to share the query load. The number of secondaries you need is based on your redundancy requirements and how many queries your domain will process during heavy periods. If you have not already read it, Chapter 10, "Designing Your DNS Service(s)," can help you make these decisions.

Before actually installing the Windows NT DNS service, we can check off a list of things that are needed:

1. Verify that your domain name is registered and active with the InterNIC.
2. Know where each server will reside physically, what subnetwork the server will connect to, and what the server's IP address and host name will be.
3. Obtain administrative privileges on the computer you're configuring by logging on as a member of the Administrators local group or the Domain Administrators global group. Let's assume that to begin with, you'll be logged on locally to the DNS server.

If you haven't completed these steps, stop and do so now.

You'll need access to the distribution files from the Windows NT Server CD-ROM, either by inserting the CD-ROM in the machine you'll be installing onto, or else knowing the path to the files if they've been copied to another location such as on a fixed disk or network server.

Finally, you'll need to verify the TCP/IP stack configuration:

1. From the Start menu, select Settings and then select Control Panel.
2. Double-click Network. (Another way to open the Network Control Panel Applet (NCPA) is to right-click Network Neighborhood and select Properties.)
3. Click the Protocols tab.
4. Double-click TCP/IP Protocol and then click the DNS tab. Make sure there's a correct Host Name and Domain filled in. (Fill in the DNS domain that this computer will be a part of, such as `taoslab.com`, not the Windows NT domain.)

Installing the DNS Service

Installing the DNS service on Windows NT Server is quite simple if you perform the following steps:

1. Open the Network Control Panel.
2. Select the Services tab and click Add.
3. Select Microsoft DNS Server, as shown in Figure 11.1, and click OK. You'll be prompted to insert the CD or other media containing the DNS Server programs. If necessary, enter the full path to the distribution files on your CD or elsewhere (for example, `E:\i386`) and click Continue. The DNS Server service will load, appearing in the list of Network Services (see Figure 11.2).
4. Click Close to close the NCPA. The system will then review the network services and prompt you to restart the computer. Click Yes to restart. After restarting, installation will be complete. The installation will put files into the `\<systemroot>\system 32\dns` directory.

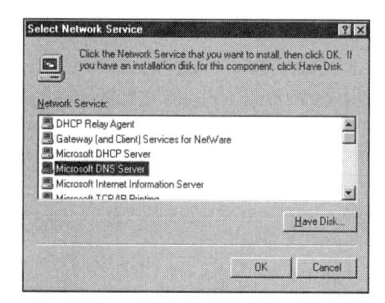

Figure 11.1 Add the DNS Server network service using the Select Network Service dialog box.

After installing the DNS service, it is strongly recommended to apply or reapply the latest Windows NT Service Pack and any patches that Microsoft has shipped for DNS Manager. You'll also need to restart the computer after this.

Configuring the DNS Server

After the server is installed, the next step is to configure the server. You can configure the MS DNS server two ways: through DNS Manager or by putting BIND configuration files in the DNS directory. WordPad, Notepad, and other text editors work fine if you opt to edit and supply BIND-style configuration files, but it's not a good idea unless you've already got experience with text-configured DNS servers. Chapter 9, "How MS DNS Works with Other Servers," explains how to migrate from BIND to Windows NT DNS.

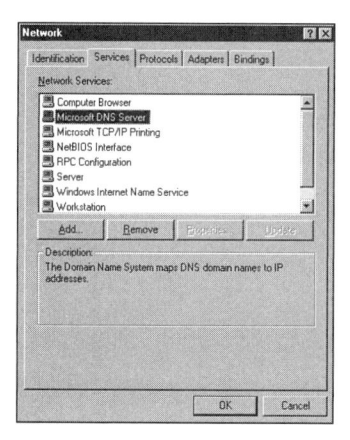

Figure 11.2 After loading, the DNS Service appears in the list of network services.

Note

If you start the MS DNS server for the first time without any BIND data files in the `<systemroot>`\system32\dns directory, it will automatically initialize to be a caching-only server because a root cache.dns file is present by default in a new installation. At that point, the Registry would have to be edited to use the BIND files again.

The remainder of this chapter assumes that you'll interactively configure the server using the built-in DNS Manager. All configuration and management can be done through the DNS Manager, which is in the Administrative Tools group. To run DNS Manager, click the Start button, point to Programs, and Administrative Tools. Finally, click DNS Manager. The display should look like Figure 11.3.

Using the DNS Manager, the first thing you'll do is add a DNS server to configure. In the DNS menu, click New Server, enter the host name or IP address of the DNS server, as shown in Figure 11.4 (usually the local machine), and click OK. When you're done, the server will appear like the illustration in Figure 11.5.

To save any changes you make to the configuration from this point onward in the server's data files, right-click the server's hostname or IP address under Server List, and click Update Server Data Files, or select the same option under the DNS menu.

Navigating DNS Manager

DNS Manager has a fairly simple and straightforward interface. There are only four menus, and three of those have only one or two options.

- *DNS menu:* Contains all the main commands for configuring the DNS server; however, most of these can also be accessed by right-clicking an object in the left pane of DNS Manager.

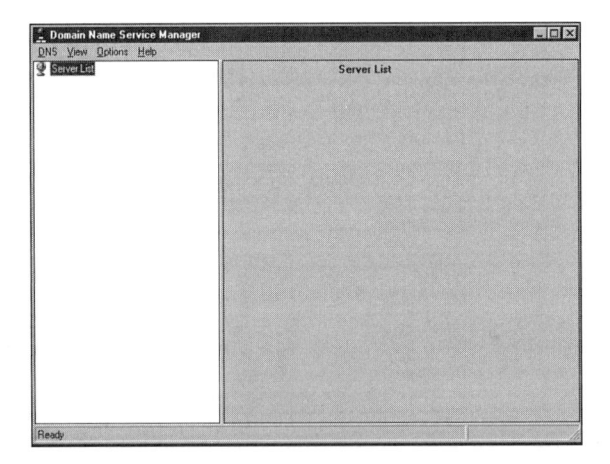

Figure 11.3   DNS Manager before configuration.

Configuring the DNS Server   141

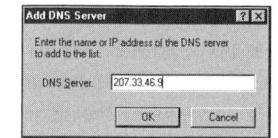

Figure 11.4   Adding a DNS Server.

- *View menu:* Contains the Split command, which moves the split between the left and right panes, and the Refresh command, which refreshes the server statistics.
- *Options menu:* Contains the Preferences command. Inside here are three settings: Auto Refresh Statistics, which species the interval at which the server statistics are updated, Show Automatically Created Zones, which was discussed earlier in this chapter, and Expose TTL, which adds a time-to-live field for each Resource Record, so that the default can be overridden.
- *Help menu:* Enables you to access online help through Contents, and you can also check the version info in the About window.

Creating Zones

Without configuration, a new server is already able to handle queries for hosts in external domains because it can locate root-level DNS servers through the `cache.dns` file, and it'll even cache the results. The limitation in this state, however, is that the server can't automatically handle queries for hosts in your own domain! By configuring the server, you can enable clients to resolve their names using your new server as easily as they can resolve names belonging to external domains. The first step is to create a zone for hosts belonging to your own domain.

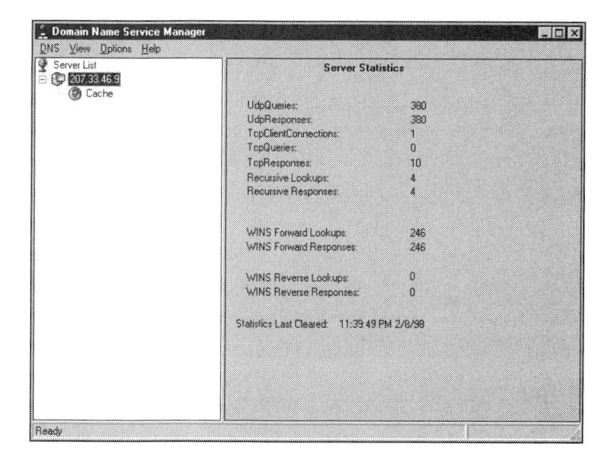

Figure 11.5   Viewing DNS Server statistics.

142   Chapter 11 Installing and Setting Up DNS

Some predefined data exists that won't show up in DNS Manager unless you go to the Options menu, choose Preferences, and check Show Automatically Created Zones. Some domains, such as `0.in-addr.arpa`, `127.in-addr.arpa`, and `255.in-addr.arpa` are created automatically for primarily performance reasons. `127.in-addr.arpa` is a local loopback domain present on all DNS servers. Don't alter or delete predefined domains: They're standard fare and should remain as they are. Figure 11.6 shows what the contents of an in-addr zone look like.

DNS Manager needs to be closed and restarted, or you can click the refresh (F5) key to pull this data forward and make it always visible. Then, double-click the server to show the predefined domains.

To establish a new primary domain, right-click the server and select New Zone. The next dialog box that appears presents the options of creating a zone for a primary or a secondary name server, as illustrated in Figure 11.7.

Select primary, and click Next. The next screen prompts for the name of the zone and the name of the local zone file that will be used. If after filling in the Zone Name field you press the tab key, the Zone File field will automatically be filled in for you, by simply appending the extension `.dns` onto the zone name. Click Next and then Finish. Figure 11.8 shows the zone creation dialog box in DNS Manager.

The same process is used for both forward and reverse lookup zones, only the names are changed.

Note
Remember: A primary DNS server's address and the name of the domain it's for both need to be registered with the InterNIC beforehand. You cannot just add domains without following the administrative process. The process is described in Appendix D, "Registering Addresses on the Internet."

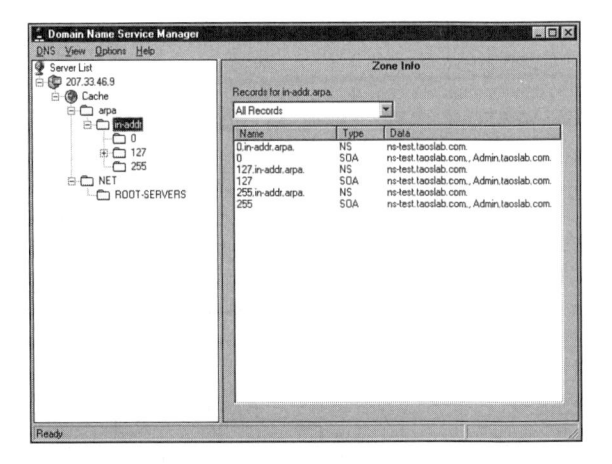

Figure 11.6   Inverse address (in-addr) zone information.

Configuring the DNS Server   143

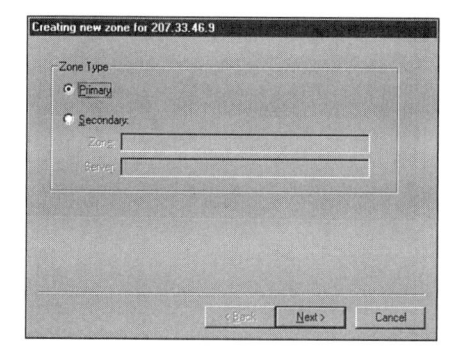

Figure 11.7   Initial dialog box for creating a new zone.

Primary and secondary zones have to do with the zone data's source server. A *primary* is the source, a *secondary* is a replica. Figure 11.9 shows how a secondary server's reverse (in-addr) zone is specified. Note that it provides an address for the primary server so that the zone can be transferred.

Figure 11.10 shows how a primary server's reverse (in-addr) zone is specified. The zone information provides a filename because zone data physically resides on the primary server.

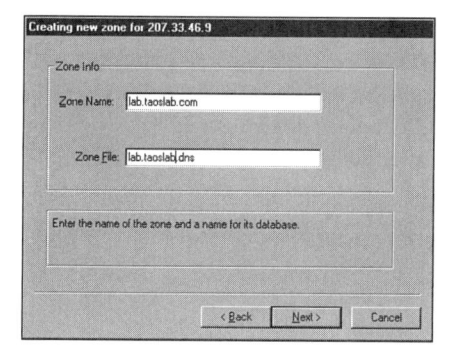

Figure 11.8   Zone information for a new zone.

144 Chapter 11 Installing and Setting Up DNS

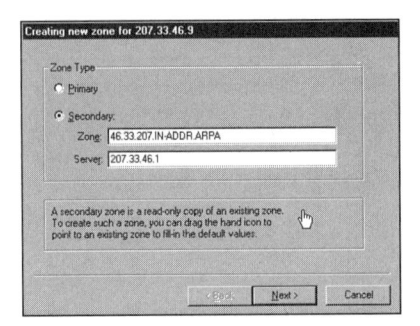

Figure 11.9 Creating a secondary zone.

You may recall that forward and reverse lookup zones contain the same data, but they satisfy different queries. Most queries are forward: They seek an IP address in return for a host name sent to the DNS server. Reverse queries, by contrast, seek a host name in return for an IP address sent to the DNS server.

If the name server is a secondary, then the IP address of the primary name server for that zone needs to be specified. Figure 11.11 shows the DNS Manager dialog box where you can specify the primary server's address. If the primary name server is also being managed through DNS Manager (by using the Add Server command), you can use the little hand icon to point to the zone on the primary server, and this will automatically fill in the needed values for you.

After the zones are established, they must be populated with the Resource Records for the domain. If the name server is a secondary, this will occur automatically when the name server requests a zone transfer from its master. For primary name servers, the zones must be populated locally by the administrator.

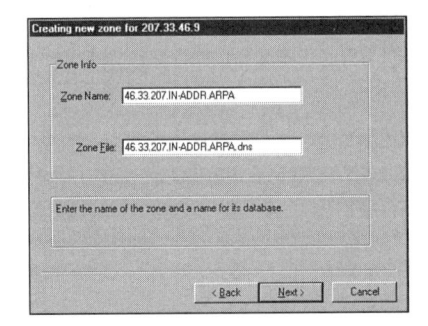

Figure 11.10 Zone information for a reverse lookup zone.

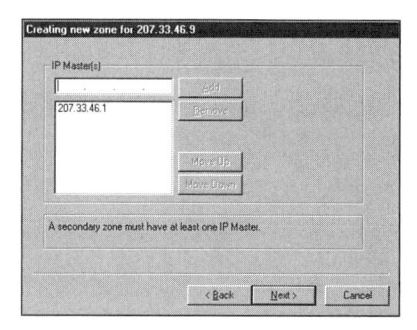

Figure 11.11   Defining the master servers for a secondary zone.

Adding DNS Resource Records

Using the DNS Manager, right-click the domain name that the records will be added to. (*Hint:* For hosts, start with the forward lookup domains.) Select the New Host item to get started. In the dialog box that appears, enter the name of the host (this name will not be an FQDN) and the IP address. Figure 11.12 depicts how to add an A record.

If the domains for forward and reverse lookups have been created ahead of time, the administrator can now select the Create Associated PTR Record check box, and the entry for the reverse lookup zone will be created automatically.

Click Add Host to place this entry into the zone file. Continue until all the necessary entries have been added, then click Done. For entries that are not related to A or PTR records, select the New Record item, as illustrated in Figure 11.13.

This dialog box gives the option of selecting a specific record type. Chapter 7, "What DNS Knows," lists all the record types you're likely to need, and Appendix F, "Resource Records and the InterNIC Cache File," provides information on others that are not as commonly used.

The rest of the dialog box will change according to the record type that is selected. For MX records, the dialog box presents the domain that the MX record is being established for, the preference that will be set for the MX record, and the host that will be used for the mail exchanger itself. Name Server (NS) records are added by simply adding the NS record with the name of the machine that will provide name service for the domain. Remember that NS hosts must be resolvable by A records.

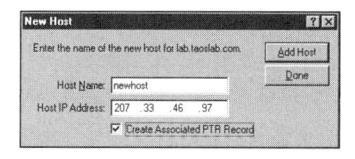

Figure 11.12   Adding an A type Resource Record using the New Host command.

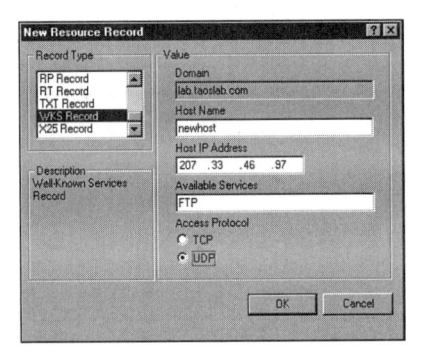

Figure 11.13 Adding other Resource Records using the New Record command.

Changing DNS Resource Records

Making changes to the Resource Records is as simple as adding new records. If the location of the record that needs to be changed is known ahead of time, a dialog box for the properties of the individual records can be opened by double-clicking the record itself. Depending on the type of record that is being edited, the dialog box will be presented with the changeable fields in white. The fields that cannot be changed will be the same color as the dialog box field. Figure 11.14 illustrates the property sheet when creating an MX record.

An MX record, for example, presents the name and domain for a host, and the IP address is the only editable field. For an A record, the mail exchanger name and the preference can be changed.

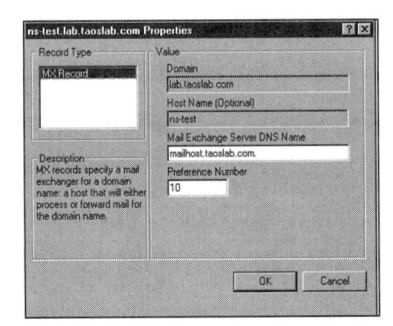

Figure 11.14 Creating an MX record.

Load Balancing with DNS Round Robin

Microsoft DNS provides a method of doing load balancing through a technique called *round robin*. DNS does not really load balance because it does not interact with systems to determine system or network loads. What DNS does is reply to name queries for a particular host with different IP addresses in a round robin fashion. For example, if a company has three Web servers that all contain the same info (or the data for the Web server comes from some kind of shared directory), but the company wants everyone to access the servers through the host name www, the zone file can be configured with multiple A records, as illustrated in Figure 11.15.

In the following example zone file, the host name www.xyz.com can be resolved to any of the IP addresses listed.

```
; Web servers for xyz.com
www          IN      A       207.33.46.100
             IN      A       207.33.46.101
             IN      A       207.33.46.102
```

The first query the name server receives, it will respond with the 207.33.46.100 address. The next query the name server receives will be answered with 207.33.46.101, and the third with 207.33.46.102. The fourth query that the name server receives will be answered with 207.33.46.100 again, and so on. This round robin resolution can be fairly effective in distributing the requests across the servers, but says nothing about the load placed on the machines. If a single machine happens to be getting hit with persistent connections, then its load could be much higher than the other machines, even though it may be handling the same number of requests.

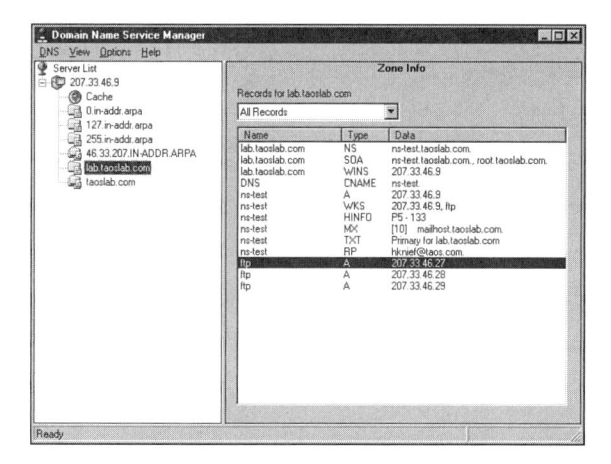

Figure 11.15 Creating multiple A records for use in a round robin system.

The problem that arises from this kind of arrangement is when one of the machines is not available. If the host with the IP address `207.33.46.100` crashes, then clients whose name queries are answered with that address will not be able to reach the site, although the other servers are operating fine. Because the name server that made the request caches the response for the client, the client would not be able to reach this Web site until the time-to-live expired and the name server tries to resolve the address again (hopefully getting a different answer), or the machine becomes a backup.

In some applications, hosts can be configured for a fail-over operation, so if a machine goes down, its IP address can be assumed by another machine. (That is a whole other book by itself.) The thing to remember here is that you can assign multiple addresses to a single name to distribute the requests to hosts, but it is not a complete solution.

The Notify Option

The Notify option provides a way to more efficiently and quickly distribute DNS changes around the network. Notify informs secondary name servers that changes have been made to the zone files, and that new copies of the zone need to be transferred by the secondaries. When the notification that a zone has changed is sent out, the secondaries then check the serial number of the source zone file to verify that the zone has indeed been updated. If the notification was valid, a request for a zone transfer is sent to the master. The check is still performed on the serial number to try and ensure that bogus information in the zones is not introduced by individuals sending invalid notifications.

To set up Notify, right-click a zone and select Properties; then, click the Notify tab (see Figure 11.16). Notify options are set up on a per-zone and per-server basis.

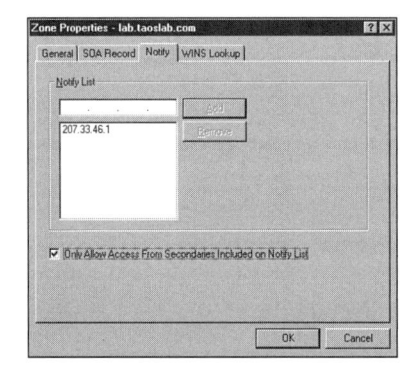

Figure 11.16 Configuring the Notify option.

The other part of the Notify option that adds a little bit of integrity to the zones being transferred is the check box for Only Allow Access from Secondaries Included on Notify List. By checking the box, this little feature will ensure that only the secondaries that the administrator has set up can perform the zone transfers, thus preventing others from attempting to set up their own secondaries and possibly contaminating the zone.

Note
After changes are made to a zone file, the Primary DNS server will *not* automatically send change notification messages to secondaries on the Notify list. To trigger an immediate update following your edits, select the DNS menu and then select Update Server Data Files.

Supporting Multihomed Servers

Multihomed servers are those that have multiple network adapters connecting to different networks. The MS DNS has the feature/capability to answer requests only on the IP addresses it is configured to receive requests for. An administrator may have a server with two or more interfaces, but only want the machine to answer requests on a specific interface. The administrator has the option to define which interfaces will answer requests, based on IP addresses. A *multihomed* computer is defined as *one with two or more network interfaces.* Figure 11.17 shows how multihomed computers appear in the Network Control Panel.

Assume that a machine has two interfaces, but the administrator only wants the first interface to answer requests. By setting up the DNS Manager to use only one IP address for its name server, the administrator can reserve the second interface for other purposes. Figure 11.18 shows a server with only one address.

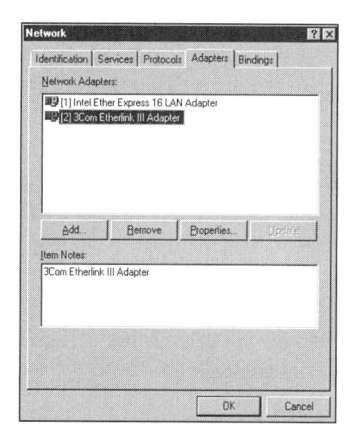

Figure 11.17   Network Control Panel showing multiple network interface cards.

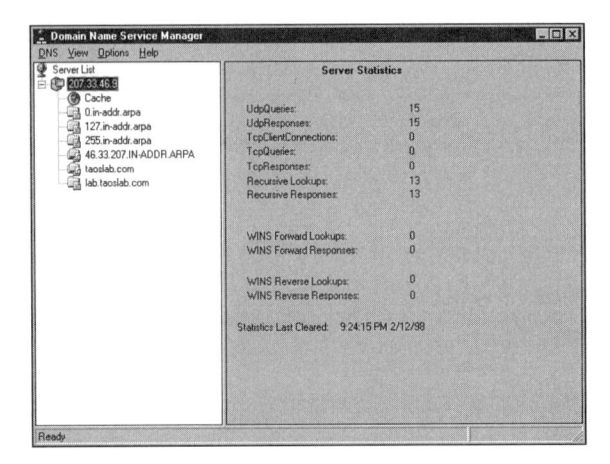

Figure 11.18 DNS has been set up so far on only one interface.

If the administrator wants to use both interfaces for name service, the administrator needs only to add the second interface by creating a new server. The domains serviced by the server that is already set up will be echoed by the second server. The downside to the MS DNS in this respect is that both interfaces will serve the same information. The administrator cannot serve different domain information through each different interface.

Creating Virtual Servers

Virtual servers are created by assigning multiple addresses to a single interface. The act of assigning multiple addresses to an interface is performed through the Network Control Panel by selecting the Protocols tab and editing the properties for TCP/IP. When the TCP/IP properties dialog box is open, an Advanced Settings button is available in the lower-right corner of the pane. Selecting Advanced presents the dialog box illustrated in Figure 11.19 to add additional address information to the selected interface.

Providing additional interfaces to the configuration of the interface is really quite simple; however, the machine will need to be rebooted for the changes to take effect. When the secondary addresses (or IP aliases) have been set up, the DNS Manager can be used to create name server entities that will service the new network address, as illustrated in Figure 11.20.

Again, the MS DNS will serve the same domains for any additional name servers that are set up as the first one configured.

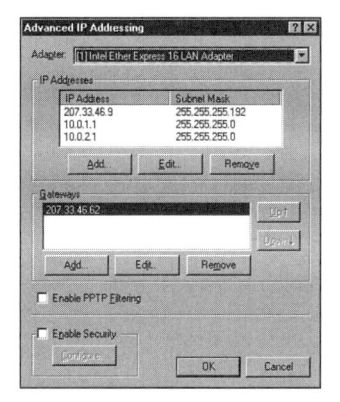

Figure 11.19 Configuring IP addresses for the adapters.

Summary

This chapter covered the installation and configuration of the Microsoft DNS Server service running on Windows NT. The graphical interface called DNS Manager was used to set up either primary or secondary name servers. We created zones and domains and then added Resource Records to the configuration. To create a caching-only name server only requires installing the service without defining any zones. Chapter 12, "Integrating DNS with WINS," can help you use WINS with DNS to resolve NetBIOS computer names, and Chapter 13, "Configuring Clients," can help you set up clients properly to take advantage of these services.

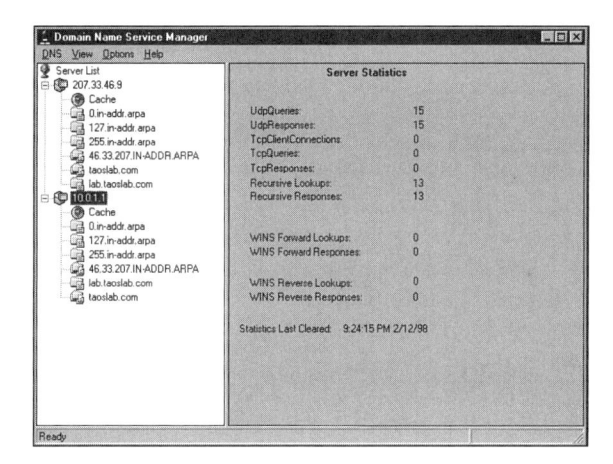

Figure 11.20 DNS set up with a virtual server on a second IP address.

12

Integrating DNS with WINS

This chapter will review:

- **How Integration Works.** This section explains why it's a good idea to make WINS and DNS cooperate. Multiple-platform networks can benefit by providing several kinds of name resolution to various clients with different client configurations.
- **Enabling WINS Lookups.** This section shows how to establish WINS lookups through a DNS server.
- **Testing WINS Lookups.** This section shows how to be sure that WINS lookups through DNS are working properly.
- **Reverse Lookups with WINS.** This section shows how to establish reverse lookups through DNS for clients that register to a WINS server.
- **Multihomed Servers.** WINS typically does a good job of handling multihomed computers. This section shows how to provide multihomed resolutions through DNS for WINS-registered computers.

MIXED NETWORKING ENVIRONMENTS are today's norm. A multiple-platform network can have a UNIX-based server to handle DNS requests and a Windows NT-based server to handle WINS requests, but this means you'd spend a lot of time administering two separate name resolution methods. Windows NT 4.0 cuts this administrative overhead by integrating both name resolution methods.

DNS and WINS both participate in resolving host names and computer (NetBIOS) names to IP addresses in a typical Windows environment. They help you resolve names so you can connect to remote computers across the LAN and across the Internet. WINS resolves computer names that are flat names, such as \\EARTH, and DNS resolves FQDNs, such as `earth.paradise.com`.

Table 12.1 shows some noteworthy comparisons illustrating key differences between WINS and DNS:

Table 12.1 **WINS Versus DNS**

WINS	DNS
The purpose is to resolve NetBIOS names to IP addresses.	The purpose is to resolve host names to IP addresses.
Names are flat and 15 characters long.	Names are hierarchical in nature.
Name registration is dynamic and happens automatically.	Name registration is static and has to be done manually.
Supports incremental replication of the data, which means that only changes in the database are replicated between WINS servers.	Doesn't support incremental replication of data between DNS servers. This means the whole database has to be replicated every time.
Supports DHCP.	Doesn't support DHCP.
Doesn't support email routing or additional TCP/IP application services.	Supports other TCP/IP application services such as email routing.

These differences create a challenge for anyone designing name resolution in a mixed naming environment. WINS also supports dynamic name registration, which makes name resolution possible in a DHCP environment. By contrast, DNS depends on static files for host name resolution. Only dynamic DNS using the latest versions of BIND for UNIX can support dynamic updates.

How Integration Works

For ideal integration, NetBIOS and DNS hosts should support both name resolution and reverse address lookups. Name resolution is a process in which a NetBIOS or DNS host name is resolved to an IP address. It simply means that such a name as `Host.taos.Com` (the DNS name) or Host (the NetBIOS name) should uniquely resolve to an IP address such as `198.25.40.31`. Reverse address lookups resolve IP addresses to a unique NetBIOS or DNS host names. It simply means that an IP address, such as `198.25.40.31`, should uniquely resolve to such a name as `Host.Company.Com` or Host.

This section discusses how to integrate name resolution methods and identifies issues you may face when implementing support for reverse address lookups. When dealing with name resolution, the part that involves more effort is the process to ensure that DNS hosts can resolve dynamic NetBIOS names. The opposite is trivial because NetBIOS hosts can use a DNS resolver to resolve any static DNS host names. Depending on the amount of interaction between the DNS hosts and NetBIOS hosts, the whole name resolution issue brings some interesting scenarios.

One scenario is where the clients connect to the servers and no interaction is necessary between clients. If the connectivity involves NetBIOS hosts (such as Microsoft hosts) and DNS hosts (such as UNIX hosts), then the integration can be done without many problems simply because

- The NetBIOS hosts have the capability to query a DNS server for DNS host name resolution. This ensures that the UNIX servers can be accessed from the NetBIOS clients.
- The NetBIOS hosts (such as a Windows NT server used to run FTP, Telnet, or other TCP/IP-based server services) can be assigned static IP addresses that can be mapped in the DNS database. UNIX clients will be able to use DNS to resolve these important NetBIOS hosts.
- The WINS clients continue to use WINS servers for resolving dynamic NetBIOS host names to IP addresses.

The second scenario is where every host may need to connect to every other host, such as in a workgroup setting. The integration becomes more challenging if you want peer-to-peer connectivity between NetBIOS-based hosts and UNIX hosts. Windows NT DNS Server can accomplish this integration.

Microsoft's Windows NT-based DNS Server offers connectivity between DNS and WINS. In addition to being a regular DNS server, the Windows NT DNS Server helps in checking the WINS database for a given host name that can't be found in the DNS database. For example, if a UNIX client is querying for a dynamic host, the DNS resolver software on the UNIX box can be configured to point to the Windows NT machine running the DNS service. The Windows NT machine will go through the DNS part of the resolution and then use the WINS database (located either on the same machine or on a remote machine) to resolve the dynamic name.

In Windows NT 4.0, Microsoft's implementation of DNS is tightly integrated with WINS. This enables non-WINS clients to resolve NetBIOS names by querying a DNS server.

Administrators can now remove any static entries for Microsoft-based clients in legacy DNS server zone files in favor of the dynamic WINS/DNS integration. For example, if a non-Microsoft-based client wants to get to a Web page on an HTTP server that is DHCP/WINS enabled, the client can query the DNS server, the DNS server can query WINS, and the name can be resolved and returned to the client. Previous to the WINS integration, there was no way to reliably resolve the name because of the dynamic IP addressing.

For more information, refer to Chapter 18, "Dynamic Host Configuration Protocol (DHCP)."

Analyzing Name Registration in WINS Systems

In a WINS system, all names are registered with a WINS server. The names are stored in a database on the WINS server which answers requests for name-to-IP address resolution based on the entries in this database. Redundancy and load balancing are maintained by allowing more than one WINS server in the WINS system. These servers replicate their database entries among one another periodically in order to maintain a consistent view of the name space.

Each name has an entry in the database. The name is owned by the WINS server it registered with and is a replica on all other WINS servers. Each entry has a state associated with it—the entry may be in the active, released, or extinct (also known as tombstone) state. Entries are also assigned a version ID. This number is used in the replication process.

The WINS system also allows the registration of static names. This enables the administrator to register names for servers running operating systems that are not capable of dynamic name registration. WINS distinguishes between dynamic and static entries. Static names are treated somewhat differently than dynamic names. If you register non-WINS computers as static entries, WINS clients will not register that name.

Resolving WINS/DNS Integration Problems

Some critics like to point out that the arrangement with WINS and DNS can lead to problems involving static DNS name registration and Dynamic Host Configuration Protocol (DHCP)-assigned IP addresses. Integrating WINS and DNS in Windows NT 4.0 helps a lot to solve these problems.

The first problem involves clients trying to reach a server in a network where the DNS administrator is far behind schedule on updating the DNS. Consider the network shown in Figure 12.1.

Suppose Terri tries to ping a new host recently installed (`frenchy.paradise.com`) on the corporate side of the network.

After checking its WINS server, Terri's computer (`terri.paradise.com`) checks its lmhosts and hosts files for a `frenchy.paradise.com` entry. If Terri has no entries in her LMHOSTS or HOSTS files and doesn't know the host's IP address, she queries her DNS server, `earth.paradise.com`. Terri's request will then reach `mars.paradise.com`, called the authoritative DNS server for the `paradise.com` domain.

If the DNS administrator hasn't yet manually updated the configuration files for `paradise.com`, Terri's DNS request fails. If Terri is a Windows client, however, she has another option: She can query her WINS server on `wins1.paradise.com`. If this WINS server has a mapping for `\\FRENCHY`, Terri can ping `frenchy.paradise.com`.

How Integration Works   157

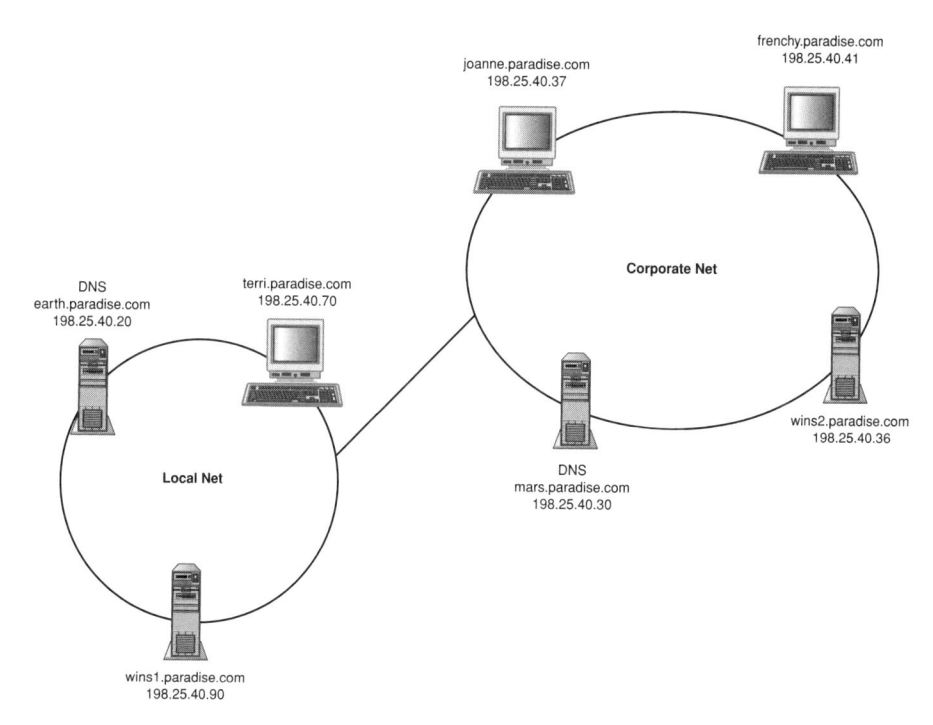

Figure 12.1   A typical LAN setup.

Another problem you can face when integrating WINS and DNS involves networks that manage IP addresses with DHCP. If frenchy.paradise.com has a static IP address of 199.103.10.41 and the DNS administrator manually creates an address (A) record in the configuration file to reflect that address, Terri can ping frenchy.paradise.com. If \\FRENCHY uses DHCP, however, the IP address is dynamic and can therefore change. So, when you are using DHCP, make sure your host is not also registered in DNS because the static DNS name registration of an IP address relies exclusively on manual updates.

In order to query a WINS database by DNS hosts (using Windows NT DNS Server), you must decide the zone of the DNS name space in an organization that will have dynamic (WINS-enabled) hosts. For example, if an organization has an Internet domain called taos.com assigned to it, then it should allocate a zone, say, interactive.taos.com, where the zone interactive will contain all the dynamic DHCP (WINS-enabled) clients.

The Windows NT-based DNS server can be designated as the primary DNS server for the `interactive` zone. The primary Windows NT DNS machine for the dynamic zone can also be a WINS server or can point to another WINS server on the network. The UNIX hosts can be configured to query the Windows NT DNS Server for all host names to be resolved in the `interactive.taos.com` part of the DNS name space. The Windows NT DNS Server will in turn use the WINS database (local or remote) to resolve the names in the dynamic zone.

Now consider another situation, with the same company, but with the dynamic NetBIOS hosts split among two zones, such as, `interactive1.taos.com` and `interactive2.taos.com`. In this situation, having one Windows NT-based DNS server as the primary host for both the `interactive1` and `interactive2` zones will help resolve dynamic NetBIOS host names by UNIX hosts following the process described in the previous section. Also, having a separate Windows NT DNS Server as primary for each dynamic zone will achieve the same result.

The Windows NT DNS Server, while using WINS to resolve dynamic names, won't know that a given dynamic NetBIOS host truly belongs to the `interactive1` or `interactive2` zone from a DNS perspective (because WINS is just a database of flat names). This granularity of difference becomes important while doing reverse address lookup, as discussed in a later section in this chapter, "Reverse Lookups with WINS."

Note
Although DNS dynamic update is not yet an IETF standard, some implementations already exist. Microsoft has chosen to wait until this is standardized in order to minimize impact on customers if changes are made before the standard is released.

Although WINS is actually based on IETF standards (RFC 1001, 1002), its NetBIOS roots have very limited acceptance by IETF and the UNIX community.

Enabling WINS Lookups

In addition to the basic Resource Records (A, PTR, NS, SOA, CNAME, MX, MB, MR, MG, HINFO, TXT, MINFO, RT, RP, X25, ISDN, WKS, AFSDB) that the DNS configuration files support, Windows NT 4.0 DNS includes a WINS lookup record. The lookup record is specific to Windows NT and solves the problems previously described by letting DNS query WINS (see a sample of WINS lookup record in the "Testing WINS Lookups" section).

As the `PLACE.DOM` sample file that Microsoft provides in the \SYSTEM32\DNS directory states, "the presence of a WINS record at the zone root instructs the name server to use WINS to look up any request for A records for names which are direct children of zone root, and which do not have A records in the zone file."

You can configure non-NetBIOS hosts to query Windows NT DNS Server for names in the zones that use WINS lookups. If the dynamic portion of the network exists in several zones, you can give each of those different zones its own DNS Server, or you can even set up one Domain Name Server as the primary master name server for each one of them.

WINS lookup can be enabled for a zone through the DNS Manager instead of requiring manual entry of the WINS record. This is accomplished by first selecting the zone with the secondary mouse button and clicking Properties. Then click the WINS Lookup tab. Check the Use WINS Resolution check box and type in the IP address of the WINS server that you want to use and click Add.

You can also add the WINS record to the BIND file and then import it as demonstrated in the following code:

```
<domain> IN WINS <IP address of WINS server>
```

A WINS lookup record might resemble the following:
```
PARADISE.DOM    File
@                         IN WINS            earth.paradise.com
earth.paradise.com.       IN A               198.25.40.20
mars.paradise.com.        IN A               198.25.40.30
```

Notice that you can add multiple WINS server addresses, as shown in Figure 12.2.

You probably only need to use WINS lookup if you have non-Microsoft-based TCP/IP clients (UNIX clients) that need to resolve host name to IP addresses, for example, if there is a need in your organization to be able to use FTP or HTTP on your servers running Windows NT from non-Microsoft-based clients.

If you have a zone configured to do WINS lookup, then all DNS servers that are authoritative for that zone need to be able to do WINS lookup or you will have intermittent behavior.

In order to easily add the Microsoft WINS/DNS lookup to a legacy DNS architecture, you have to create a new DNS subdomain in your company and have the Windows NT-based primary and secondary servers enabled to do WINS lookups in this domain. For example, there is a `paradise.com` domain and a `mydomain.paradise.com` domain in Figure 12.3. All of the Microsoft-based clients will register with the WINS server in the `mydomain.paradise.com` domain.

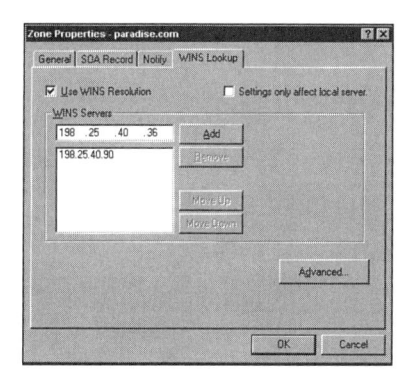

Figure 12.2 Adding WINS lookup to a DNS zone.

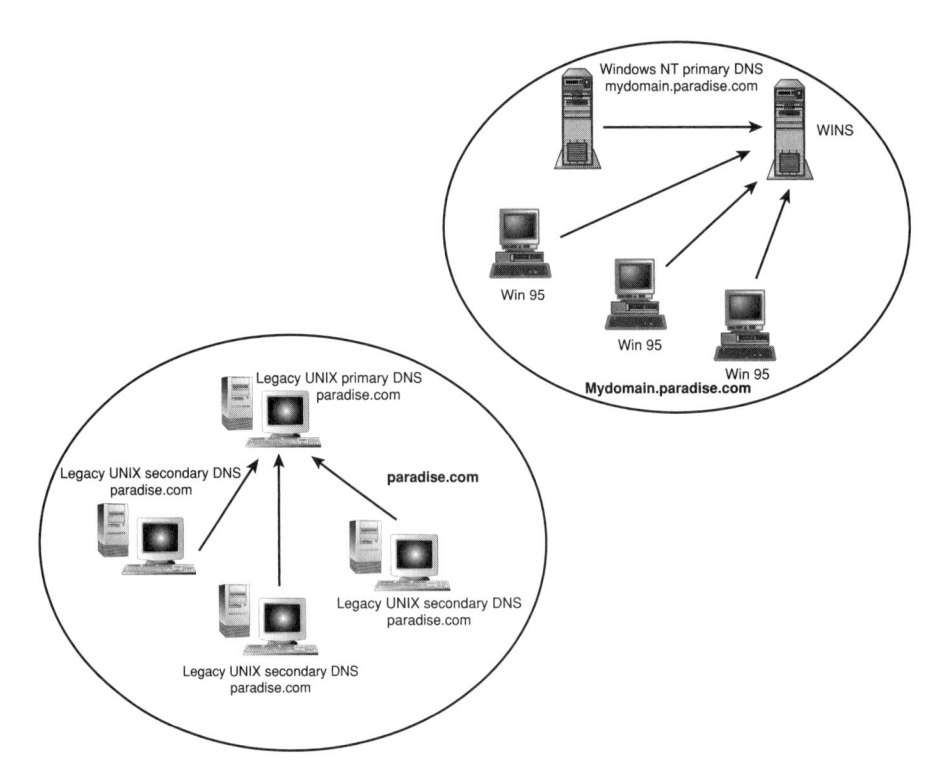

Figure 12.3 A domain with a subdomain just for WINS.

WINS lookup is always done on a DNS-zone basis. A query to a DNS server for ericr.taos.com would go to the WINS server if the DNS server that had the WINS lookup record was authoritative for zone taos.com. But a query for ericr.france.taos.com would not go to that same WINS server.

Setting the Time-to-Live for WINS

If you are using a WINS record, the time-to-live (TTL) in the SOA record doesn't affect WINS. The WINS TTL is configured, as shown in Figure 12.4, in the Advanced Zone Properties dialog box under the WINS Lookup tab. To get to the Advanced Zone Properties dialog box, select the zone with the secondary mouse button and click Properties. Then click the WINS Lookup tab. Check the Use WINS Resolution check box and then click the Advanced Button.

When an IP address or host name gets resolved via WINS, the address is cached for the WINS Cache Timeout Value. If this address is ever forwarded to another DNS server, the WINS Cache Timeout Value TTL is sent.

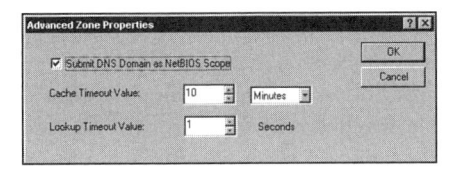

Figure 12.4 Configuring the WINS time-to-live (TTL) value.

If your data doesn't change much, then you will want to set your TTL high. Keep in mind that you can set the TTL on individual records as well.

If the TTL on an individual Resource Record's address is lower or higher than the TTL in the SOA record, the individual RR's TTL takes precedence.

Testing WINS Lookups

Considering the network and the computers shown in Figure 12.1, imagine that Terri tries to reach `joanne.paradise.com`. If she doesn't find a listing for `joanne.paradise.com` in her LMHOSTS or HOSTS files, she queries her DNS server, `earth.paradise.com`, which queries Joanne's DNS server `mars.paradise.com`. So far, she can reach only the DNS at `mars.paradise.com` looking for an A record for `joanne.paradise.com`. If that A record is not there, Judy's request fails.

If the DNS administrator of `mars.paradise.com` adds a WINS lookup record for `wins2.paradise.com` to the configuration files, DNS can query the WINS database for `joanne.paradise.com` and respond to Terri's request. If `joanne.paradise.com` is registered in the corporate WINS database on `wins2.paradise.com`, Terri can ping `joanne.paradise.com` successfully.

Notice with host name resolution, if DNS doesn't have an A record for `joanne.paradise.com`, Terri tries her WINS server, `wins1.paradise.com`, which doesn't know anything about this. Now, consider if DNS on \\MARS doesn't have an A record for `joanne.paradise.com`, \\MARS tries its registered WINS server, `wins2.paradise.com`. This redirection takes the burden off Terri's WINS server and puts the load on the `paradise.com` corporate network WINS server where it belongs.

This DNS/WINS integration solves the first big problem of the busy DNS administrator not updating the name registration. By removing most A records from the DNS server and it to the local WINS Server, you can make the DNS server work as if it were dynamically updated.

The same approach also solves the problem associated with DHCP-assigned IP addresses. Because in this particular case, the WINS server updates the WINS database when the DHCP-enabled client's IP address changes. Then, the system picks up this change when someone sends a query to the Domain Name Server for a name not in the DNS database.

The Microsoft DNS server works hand in hand with the Microsoft WINS server and provides a great deal of interoperability. To provide this interoperability, a new record was defined as part of the zone database file. The WINS record is specific to Windows NT and may be attached only to the zone root domain. The presence of a WINS record instructs the name server to use WINS to look up any requests for hosts in the zone root that do not have static addresses in the IP database. This functionality is particularly useful for UNIX-based clients that need to contact DHCP/WINS-enabled clients via Internet Protocol.

Reverse Lookups with WINS

Although WINS was not constructed to provide reverse lookup capabilities, this functionality can still be accomplished for DHCP/WINS-enabled clients when using Microsoft's DNS server. The presence of a WINS-R record at the zone root instructs the name server to use a NetBIOS node adapter status lookup for any reverse lookup requests for IP addresses in the zone root that are not statically defined with PTR records. The following is a sample of a WINS-R record:

```
<domain> IN WINS-R <domain to append to returned NetBIOS names>
```

Using a real-world domain, this would appear as

```
@                        IN WINS-R           taos.com.
```

You use reverse address lookups—the process of obtaining the DNS domain name of a host, given its IP address—for login, printing, and firewall applications. The process tends to complicate WINS and DNS integration. Because the WINS database contains flat names, reverse lookup functionality needs a mechanism for associating a dynamic NetBIOS name to a DNS domain name.

Consider the example where you have two dynamic zones (`paradise1` and `paradise2`) in a DNS name space with WINS-enabled clients. The WINS system in this case will be completely replicated and synchronized. It is impossible to associate the dynamic NetBIOS hosts to a specific DNS zone by looking at the WINS database.

If all the dynamic hosts are located in a single DNS zone in a company, it's easier to devise a method to append the result of a reverse address lookup of a WINS database with a default DNS domain name (this helps to achieve reverse lookup functionality with dynamic hosts). It is recommended to restrict the dynamic NetBIOS hosts to a single DNS zone in a company to achieve complete DNS/WINS integration with the current tools available.

Name resolution integration between WINS and DNS can be done with the proper design.

You need to know that having a single dynamic zone (a zone with dynamic NetBIOS hosts) in an organization's DNS name space ensures almost complete DNS-to-WINS integration (taking into consideration that reverse address lookup is slated to be added to the Windows NT DNS Server for WINS hosts). This may change if any modifications are done to the WINS replication process in order for DNS-WINS integration to have multiple dynamic zones.

It remains a challenge, however, to achieve reverse address lookups of dynamic NetBIOS hosts (belonging to multiple DNS zones) to map to a unique DNS domain name.

WINS reverse lookups can be enabled for a zone through the DNS Manager instead of requiring manual entry of the WINS-R record. This is accomplished by selecting the appropriate in-addr.arpa zone with the mouse button and clicking Properties. Then click the WINS Reverse Lookup tab. Check the Use WINS Reverse Lookup check box, as shown in Figure 12.5, and type in the DNS Host Domain to be appended to the NetBIOS name before returning a response to the resolver.

The Microsoft DNS server can be configured to not send WINS records to secondary servers. This is necessary if you have a mixture of Microsoft- and UNIX-based DNS servers because UNIX-based DNS servers do not have the capability to do WINS lookups.

However, there are other things you need to know. DNS and WINS integration does not establish an efficient DNS reverse lookup. Both the DNS server and the host being located are involved when a reverse lookup is requested for a WINS client because the DNS server does a NetBIOS node adapter status lookup to resolve the IP address to a name. DNS-only reverse lookups are more efficient.

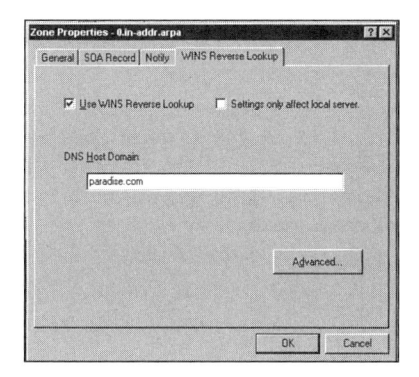

Figure 12.5   Establishing a reverse WINS lookup.

Chapter 12 Integrating DNS with WINS

The following is a sample of tracing a reverse name lookup using the PING -a [IP address] command:

```
Ping -a 198.25.40.20
DNS: 0x1:Std Qry for 20.40.25.198. in-addr.arpa of type Dom. name ptr on
➥class INET addr.
DNS: Query Identifier = 1 (0x1)
DNS: DNS Flags = Query, OpCode-Std Qry, RD Bits Set, RCode-No error
DNS: Question Entry Count = 1 (0x1)
DNS: Answer Entry Count = 0 (0x0)
DNS: Name Server Count = 0 (0x0)
DNS: Additional Records Count = 0 (0x0)

DNS: Question Section: 20.40.25.198.in-addr.arpa of type Dom. name ptr on
➥class INET addr.
DNS: Question Name: 20.40.25.198.in-addr.arpa
DNS: Question Type = Domain name pointer
DNS: Question Class = Internet address class
You can notice that the Question name is the IP address backwards
➥20.40.25.198.in-addr.arpa of type PTR.


*****************************************************************
DNS: 0x1:Std Qry Resp. for 20.40.25.198.in-addr.arpa of type Dom. name
➥ptr on class INET addr.
DNS: Query Identifier = 1 (0x1)
DNS: DNS Flags = Response, OpCode-Std Qry, AA RD RA Bits Set, RCode-No
➥error
DNS: Question Entry Count = 1 (0x1)
DNS: Answer Entry Count = 1 (0x1)
DNS: Name Server Count = 0 (0x0)
DNS: Additional Records Count = 0 (0x0)

DNS: Question Section: 20.40.25.198.in-addr.arpa of type Dom. name ptr on
➥class INET addr.
DNS: Question Name: 20.40.25.198.in-addr.arpa
DNS: Question Type = Domain name pointer
DNS: Question Class = Internet address class

DNS: Answer section: 20.40.25.198.in-addr.arpa of type Dom. name ptr on
➥class INET addr.
DNS: Resource Name: 20.40.25.198.in-addr.arpa
DNS: Resource Type = Domain name pointer
DNS: Resource Class = Internet address class
DNS: Time To Live = 86400 (0x15180)
DNS: Resource Data Length = 23 (0x17)
DNS: Pointer: frenchy.paradise.com
```

This sends the IP address to the DNS server and asks for the host name associated with the NetBIOS name. Remember that if the DNS server didn't have this name in its table, the DNS server will actually do an Adapter Status on the IP address rather than going to WINS. However, that's only if you have the Use Wins Reverse Lookup check box checked in the properties of the *in-addr.arpa zone.

Multihomed Servers

This is similar to a unique name in that it is the WINS Client's computer name; however it can have up to 25 addresses and is for use by multihomed systems. A multihomed system is a system with more than one network card and more than one IP address.

Warning
Be aware that extending network bandwidth in your server has some trade-offs. Extra overhead and I/O processing (such as interrupt handling) come into play when you add cards.

Each PCI network interface card you add is another interrupt that the CPU must handle to service I/O requests. More CPU interruptions result in slower processing. Adding bandwidth increases the amount of information the system must process and consumes extra resources such as memory and CPU time. You may need to augment these resources to maintain your desired performance level.

A multihomed server is a server with multiple network interface cards (NICs). A multihomed server can be defined by a single, unique name with which multiple IP addresses are associated.

Mapping IP Addresses for Multihomed Servers

You can provide multihomed name-to-IP-address mappings in the LMHOSTS file by creating entries that are specified by using the keyword #MH (MultiHomed). An #MH entry associates a single, unique NetBIOS computer name to an IP address. You can create multiple entries for the same NetBIOS computer name for each NIC in the multihomed server, up to a maximum of 25 different IP addresses for the same name. That means the administrator will need 5 NICs (maximum) for a multihomed server.

The format of the LMHOSTS entry that is used to specify name-to-IP-address mappings for multihomed servers is the same as the other keyword entries. For example, the entries required to map a name to IP address for a multihomed server with two NICs are as follows:

```
38.168.20.106   Sales                   #sales server NIC 1
38.168.20.107   Sales                   #sales server NIC 2
```

You can set up to five IP addresses for each installed NIC. From the Control Panel, double-click the Network icon, then click the Protocols tab; from the Protocols tab select TCP/IP Protocols, then click the Properties button; on the IP Address tab, click Advanced, and add the IP addresses and subnet mask, as shown in Figure 12.6.

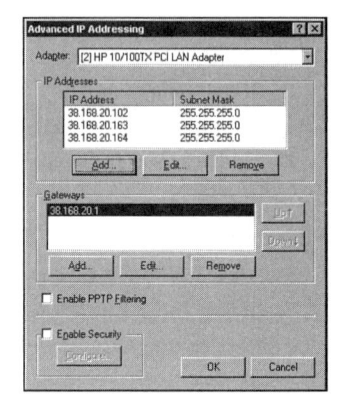

Figure 12.6 Advanced IP Addressing.

You can also add those IP addresses to a network card by modifying the Registry. This method of adding IP addresses through the Registry is a way around the limit of 5 IP addresses in the control panel.

Use the Registry Editor (REGEDT32.EXE) to add your IP addresses and subnet masks, as follows:

1. Start REGEDT32.EXE and locate the following Registry subkey:
   HKEY_LOCAL_MACHINE\SYSTEM\CurrentControlSet\Services\<Adapter Name>\Parameters\Tcpip

2. Find the IP Address value and double-click it.

3. The Multi-String Editor dialog box should appear with the IP address selected. Type each additional IP address on a new line within the dialog box, then click OK. For example:

   38.168.20.106

   38.168.20.107

   38.168.20.108

4. Find the SubnetMask value and double-click it.

5. The Multi-String Editor dialog box should appear with the Subnet Mask selected. Enter each additional subnet mask on a new line within the dialog box, then click OK. For example:

   255.255.255.0

   255.255.255.0

   255.255.255.0

   IMPORTANT: The order of the IP addresses and subnet masks must correspond.

6. Exit REGEDT32.EXE.

7. Exit Windows NT and reboot your computer.

Make sure to have all of the IP addresses specified in the Registry bound to your network interface cards.

Warning
Be aware of using the Registry Editor very carefully. Any incorrect use of the Registry can cause serious problems that may require you to reinstall your operating system!

Directing Queries in Multihomed Server Systems

DNS can operate on all the NICs of a mutihomed server if you don't specify any particular IP addresses. Actually, this could be the first reason to install multiple network cards in a DNS server. But it could just as well be because you want to specify which NICs will accept DNS queries.

To do so, in the Server List, right-click the Server icon. Choose Properties, and select Interfaces tab. In the DNS Server IP Addresses field (see Figure 12.7), type the IP addresses for each NIC that you want to enable for DNS traffic.

NetBIOS over TCP (NetBT) only binds to one IP address per physical network interface. From the NetBT viewpoint, a computer is multihomed only when it has more than one NIC installed. When a name registration packet is sent from a multihomed computer, it is flagged as a multihomed name registration so that it will not conflict with the same name being registered by another interface in the same computer.

If a broadcast name query is received by a multihomed computer, all NetBT/interface bindings receiving the query will respond with their addresses, and by default the client will choose the first response and connect to the address supplied by it. This behavior can be controlled by the RandomAdapter Registry parameter.

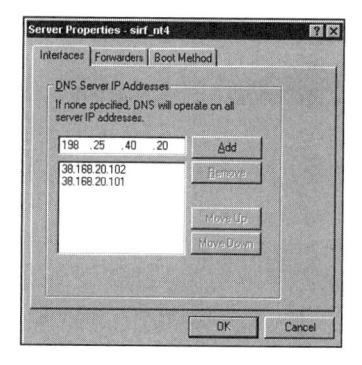

Figure 12.7 IP addresses for a multihomed DNS server.

When a directed name query is sent to a WINS server, the WINS server responds with a list of all IP addresses that were registered with WINS by the multihomed computer.

Choosing the best IP address to connect to on a multihomed computer is a client function. The following algorithm is employed, in the order listed:

1. If one of the IP addresses in the name query response list is on the same logical subnet as the calling binding of NetBT on the local computer, then that address is selected. If more than one of the addresses meet this criteria, one is picked at random from those that match.

2. If one of the IP addresses in the list is on the same logical subnet as any binding of NetBT on the local computer, then that address is selected. If more than one of the addresses meet this criteria, one of these is picked at random.

3. If none of the IP addresses in the list is on the same subnet as any binding of NetBT on the local computer, then an address is selected at random from the list.

This algorithm provides a reasonably good way of balancing connections to a server across multiple NICs, while still favoring direct connections when they are available.

Warning
Keep in mind, however, that you need to have computers running at least Windows NT 4.0 Service Pack 2; otherwise some problems can occur. If the IP address chosen from the list does not respond, the connection attempt will fail. In some cases, another attempt to connect the resource may succeed; however, the user or application may receive an error and the retries may need to be done manually.

Connecting to Multihomed Server IP Addresses by Preference

Service Pack 2 includes an enhancement to NetBT. NetBT still uses the algorithm previously outlined to choose a "best" IP address to connect to on a multihomed computer; however, now NetBT retains the list of addresses and orders them by preference. NetBT attempts to *ping* each of the addresses in the list in order, until one of them responds. Two ping attempts are made for each address, with a two-second wait for a response after each attempt. If there is a successful response to one of the pings, then a TCP connection and NetBIOS session are established to that address.

If none of the addresses respond to the ping attempts, then NetBT will revert to the old behavior, and attempt to establish a TCP connection to the best address in the list.

In addition, if a session is already in existence and the network interface responsible for the session on the multihomed computer fails, the failure will be detected and a new session will be established over one of the working interfaces, provided that one exists. The status of open files may not be preserved because file handles will be invalidated when the old session is deleted.

This feature is only specific to NetBT sessions, and does not apply to TCP connections used by other protocols or interfaces, such as Windows Sockets.

Connecting to Multihomed Servers with Disabled NICs

Service Pack 2 also includes an enhancement to NetBT that improves the capability to connect to multihomed computers even when one or more of the NICs are disabled. There are currently no plans to *port* this enhancement back to prior versions of Windows NT.

On a computer running Windows NT with multiple IP addresses assigned to the same network interface card, resolving the computer's host or NetBIOS name will return the last IP address listed in the Network Control Panel, Advanced TCP/IP Properties sheet, rather than the first address listed. All other computers on the network that resolve this name will correctly get the first IP address listed.

This can cause problems with applications that are running on a computer that performs a lookup of its own host name (such as Web servers).

If you are using DNS for name resolution, however, you can add an additional A record for the same computer, with a different name. For example, if your computer name is listed in DNS as `SIRF_NT4`, you may also want to add an entry in DNS for WWW that refers to the same IP address. In this case, when you type `ping WWW`, the name is not resolved locally, but rather at the DNS server, and the correct IP address will be indicated in the reply.

The following is an example of this configuration:
```
HOST name = SIRF_NT4
Assigned IP Addresses #1= 38.168.20.106
Assigned IP Addresses #2= 38.168.20.107
Assigned IP Addresses #3= 38.168.20.108
```

If you are at `SIRF_NT4` and type `ping SIRF_NT4`, your reply will indicate the `38.168.20.108` address.

If you are at another computer on the network and type `ping SIRF_NT4`, your reply will indicate the `38.168.20.106` address.

Fortunately, this problem has been corrected in the latest Microsoft Windows NT 4.0 U.S. Service Pack. (Check the Microsoft Web site at `http://support.microsoft.com/support/downloads/`.)

Summary

This chapter explained how to integrate WINS and DNS to support environments with mixed name types. You also learned how to test lookups and how to establish reverse lookups for clients that are registered via WINS and not directly via DNS. Chapter 13, "Configuring Clients," goes the next step to show you how to set up clients to properly take advantage of the name resolution features in WINS and DNS as separate services, and as an advanced integrated service, as this chapter illustrated.

13

Configuring Clients

This chapter will review:

- **Configuring the client to use WINS.** This chapter describes the options used to configure clients to use WINS. It also explains configuration using the Network Control Panel and the Registry.
- **Configuring the client to use DNS.** This chapter briefly explains the differences between IP host names and NetBIOS computer names, and shows you how to configure Windows clients to use DNS.

A WINDOWS COMPUTER CAN RESOLVE NAMES in several ways, depending entirely on how it's configured. This chapter shows how to configure clients to perform NetBIOS name lookups on WINS servers and host name lookups on DNS servers. Under special circumstances also described in this chapter, you can also get clients to look up NetBIOS computer names via DNS.

Configuring the Client to Use WINS

The WINS-enabled client communicates with the WINS server to register the client names in the WINS database—as well as to get mappings for user names, NetBIOS names, DNS names, and IP addresses from the WINS database. WINS clients are configured with the IP address of one or two WINS servers: a primary and secondary. At

Chapter 13 Configuring Clients

startup, WINS clients communicate directly with a WINS server to register their computer name and corresponding IP address.

When a WINS client needs to resolve a computer name to an IP address—such as when a `net use \\server\share` is performed—the WINS client sends a request to the WINS server for the IP address of the computer name being used. WINS clients—referred to as WINS-enabled clients—are configured to use the services of a WINS server.

The following operating systems can currently act as WINS clients when using Windows NT Server version 4.0 as a WINS server:

- Windows NT Workstation version 3.5x or version 4.0
- Windows NT Server version 3.5x or version 4.0
- Windows 95
- Windows for Workgroups 3.11 (WFWG), with the Microsoft 32-bit TCP/IP stack installed
- Microsoft Network Client for MS-DOS, with real-mode TCP/IP driver (which is one of the clients included on the Windows NT Server CD)
- LAN Manager for MS-DOS 2.2c, included on the Windows NT Server CD

When Microsoft TCP/IP is installed under Windows 95, WINS client software is installed automatically.

Windows 95 and Windows NT-based clients are configured with the IP address of one or two WINS servers by using the WINS Address tab on the Microsoft TCP/IP properties sheet in the Control Panel.

Figure 13.1 illustrates the process of enabling WINS in a Windows NT 3.51 environment.

Figure 13.2 illustrates the process of enabling WINS in a Windows NT 4.0 environment.

Figure 13.3 illustrates the process of enabling WINS in a Windows 95 environment.

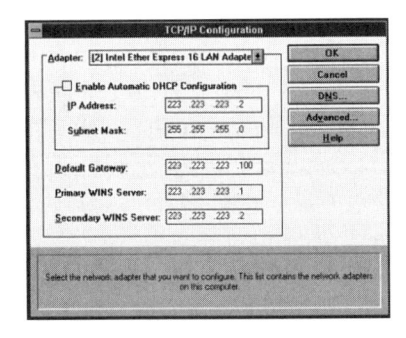

Figure 13.1 Enabling the WINS Service on a WINS client (Windows NT 3.51).

Configuring the Client to Use WINS 173

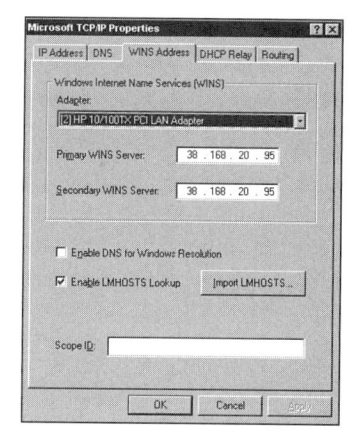

Figure 13.2 Enabling the WINS Service on a WINS client (Window NT 4.0).

To configure a computer running Windows 95 to use WINS for name resolution, follow these steps:

1. In the Microsoft TCP/IP properties sheet, click the WINS Configuration tab.
2. If a DHCP server is available that is configured to provide information on available WINS servers, select Use DHCP For WINS Resolution. If a WINS server is available but a DHCP server isn't, select Enable WINS Resolution and type the IP addresses of the primary and secondary WINS servers. These values should be provided by the network administrator and should be based on the IP addresses assigned to these Windows NT Server computers.
3. If WINS is enabled, in the Scope ID box, type the computer's scope identifier, if required on an internetwork that uses NetBIOS over TCP/IP (usually this value is left blank).

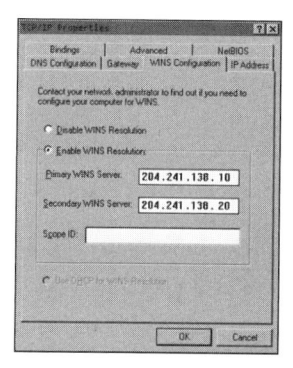

Figure 13.3 Enabling the WINS Service on a WINS client (Windows 95).

To configure a computer running Windows NT 4.0 to use WINS for name resolution, use the following steps:

1. In the Microsoft TCP/IP properties sheet, click the WINS Configuration tab.
2. Type the IP addresses of the primary and secondary WINS servers. These values should be provided by the network administrator and should be based on the IP addresses assigned to these Windows NT Server computers.
3. In the Scope ID box, type the computer's scope identifier, if required on an internetwork that uses NetBIOS over TCP/IP (usually this value is left blank).

NetBIOS Scope

To segment the NetBIOS Namespace, we use the NetBIOS Scope. The NetBIOS scope enables interoperation with other NetBIOS implementations that use the NetBIOS scope ID. Before any packets that contain a NetBIOS name are transmitted, the NetBIOS scope ID is appended to the name. This includes packets such as name queries, name registrations, and session requests. On the receiving end, the NetBIOS scope in a packet must match the locally configured NetBIOS scope; otherwise, the packet is ignored. Therefore, only computers that have the same scope can communicate with each other using NetBIOS. Additionally, the Scope ID is case sensitive, so computers configured with the Scope ID "scope" that attempt to communicate with computers with Scope ID "SCOPE" will be unable to communicate via NetBIOS over TCP/IP.

For Microsoft Windows 95, the Scope ID configuration can be found on the WINS Configuration tab in the properties for TCP/IP in the Network section of the Control Panel. In Windows for Workgroups and Windows NT, the Scope ID can be configured from the Advanced options in the TCP/IP configuration dialog box in the Network section of the Control Panel.

In the Network option in the Windows 95 Control Panel, you must first enable WINS name resolution so that you can manually configure the NetBIOS scope ID in the TCP/IP properties. Therefore, you must also enter at least one IP address for a WINS server, even though a WINS server might not be present on the network. If you install Windows 95 using a setup script and define the NetBIOS scope ID in the setup script, you do not also have to specify wins=1 plus a WINS server IP address.

Notice that because NetBIOS scope IDs are used to segment network traffic, you must be very careful about assigning NetBIOS scope IDs. With a faulty scope ID configuration, users may not be able to connect to other computers.

You can modify the TCP/IP NetBIOS Scope ID through the Control Panel only if WINS Resolution is enabled. If WINS is not enabled, the TCP/IP NetBIOS Scope ID can be changed only manually, by editing the Registry as follows:

1. Run Registry Editor (`REGEDIT.EXE`).
2. From the `HKEY_LOCAL_MACHINE` subtree, go to the following key:
   `System\CurrentControlSet\Services\VXD\MSTCP`
3. Add the new ScopeID by clicking Edit, then clicking New, and then selecting `String Value`. Type `ScopeID`, and press Enter. Double-click the value. A window appears for Edit String. Enter your Scope ID under Value data.

Warning

Using Registry Editor incorrectly can cause serious systemwide problems that may require you to reinstall Windows 95 to correct them.

Configuring DHCP Servers to Supply WINS Configuration Information

When TCP/IP is installed on a Windows 95 or Windows NT Workstation, it can be configured to use a WINS server to resolve computer names to IP addresses by supplying the IP addresses of a primary and secondary WINS server.

If a DHCP server is used to supply an IP address and other configuration information to DHCP clients, the DHCP server can also be configured to supply WINS configuration information. To supply the necessary WINS configuration information to DHCP clients, the DHCP server must have the following DHCP options enabled:

- 044 WINS/NBNS Servers configured with the IP address of one or more WINS servers.
- 046 WINS/NBT Node Type set to 0x1 (b-node), 0x2 (p-node), 0x4 (m-node), or 0x8 (h-node). For more information on the node types, see Chapter 3, "How Windows Clients Use DNS and WINS."

Refer to Chapter 18, "Dynamic Host Configuration Protocol (DHCP)," for more information on setting up DHCP.

Name Registration

When a WINS-enabled computer is started, the WINS client service attempts to directly contact the WINS server (by using point-to-point communication) to register the client names and corresponding IP address. The type of message the client sends is referred to as a *name registration request*. The WINS client sends one name registration request (which includes the computer IP address) for the computer, logged-on user, and networking services running on the computer.

A DHCP server dynamically assigns the IP address if the client is DHCP-enabled. If DHCP is not used, the IP address is a statically assigned number, which you must obtain from a network administrator and manually configure on the computer.

When the WINS server receives a name registration request, it checks the WINS database to ensure that the name in the request is unique and that it does not exist in the WINS database. The WINS server responds with either a positive or negative *name registration response*.

WINS clients must renew their name registrations before the time-to-live (TTL) value expires. The TTL value indicates how long the client can own that name.

When a WINS client renews its name registration, it sends a *name refresh request* directly (point-to-point) to the WINS server. The name refresh request includes the WINS client's IP address and the name that the client is requesting to have refreshed. The WINS server responds to the name refresh request with a *name refresh response* that includes a new TTL for the name.

A WINS client first attempts to refresh its name registrations at one-eighth of the TTL, and in equal TTL increments until half the TTL is reached.

If the WINS client does not receive a name refresh response from the WINS server, it sends name refresh requests every two minutes until half the TTL is expired.

If the WINS client does not receive a name refresh response and half the TTL is expired, the WINS client begins sending name refresh requests to a secondary WINS server if the computer is configured with an IP address for a secondary WINS server. The WINS client attempts to refresh its registrations with the secondary WINS server as if it were the first refresh attempt—in time increments equal to one-eighth of the TTL. The WINS client sends the name refresh requests until it successfully receives a name refresh response, or until half the TTL is expired. If the WINS client cannot contact the secondary WINS server by the time half the TTL has expired, it reverts back to the primary WINS server. After a WINS client has successfully refreshed its name registrations, it does not start subsequent name registration requests until half the TTL is expired.

When a WINS-enabled computer gracefully shuts down, the WINS client sends a *name release request* to the WINS server. A name release request is sent for each name associated with the computer, logged-on user, and network client service registered with the WINS server. The name release request includes the computer IP address and the name that should be released (deleted) from the WINS server database.

Because the WINS-enabled client is configured with the IP address of the WINS server, the name release requests are sent directly to the WINS server. When the WINS server receives a name release request, the WINS server checks the WINS database for the specified name.

Based on the results of the database check, the WINS server sends a positive or negative *name release response* to the WINS client and removes the specified name from the WINS database. The name release response contains the name released and a TTL of zero.

Computer Name-to-IP Address Mapping Resolution

WINS clients perform NetBIOS computer name-to-IP-address mapping resolution by using the NetBIOS over TCP/IP (NetBT) component. A Windows NT-based computer is automatically configured to use one of four different NetBT name resolution modes (methods), based on how TCP/IP is configured on the computer.

From a Windows NT Workstation, at a DOS command prompt, use the `ipconfig/all` command to display the TCP/IP configuration (including node type) of your computer. From a Windows 95 client, at a DOS command prompt use the `winipcfg/all` command. For example, on a computer that is configured as a WINS client, the node type Hybrid appears when the `ipconfig /all` (for Windows NT, see Figure 13.4) or `winipcfg /all` command (for Win95, see Figure 13.5) is entered.

Windows-based networking clients (WINS-enabled Windows NT or Windows for Workgroups 3.11 computers) can use WINS directly. Non-WINS computers on the internetwork that are b-node compatible (as described in RFCs 1001 and 1002) can access WINS through proxies, which are WINS-enabled computers that listen to name query broadcasts and then respond to names that are not on the local subnet or that are p-node computers.

Browsing in Windows NT Networks

On a Windows NT network, users can browse transparently across routers. To enable browsing without WINS, the network administrator must ensure that the users' primary domain has Windows NT Server or Windows NT Workstation computers on both sides of the router to act as master browsers. These computers need correctly configured LMHOSTS files with entries for the domain controllers across the subnet.

With WINS, such strategies are not necessary because the WINS servers and proxies transparently provide the support necessary for browsing across routers where domains span the routers.

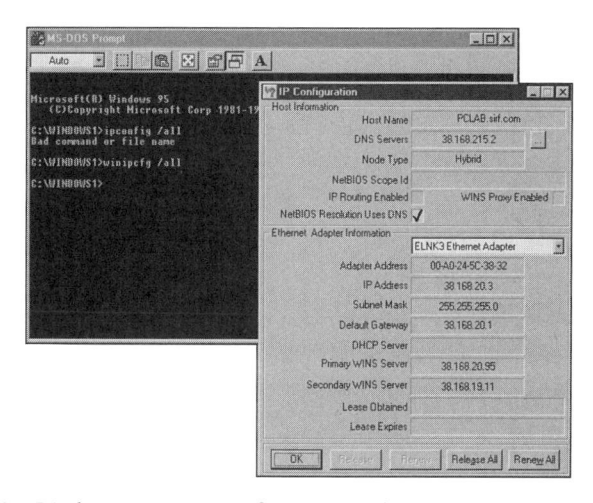

Figure 13.4 Displaying TCP/IP configuration with `ipconfig /all` (Windows NT).

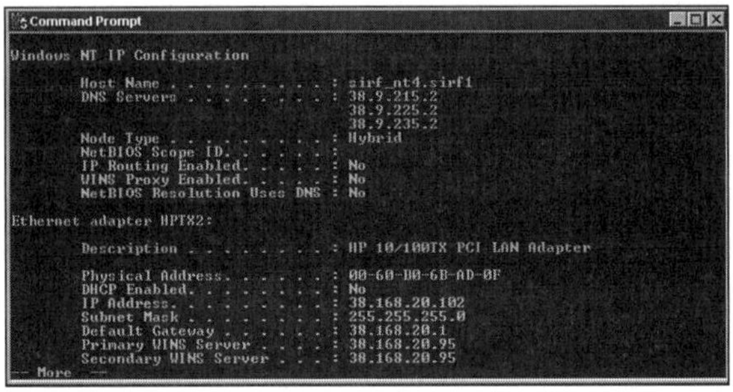

Figure 13.5 Displaying TCP/IP configuration with `winipcfg /all` (Windows 95).

The proxy communicates with the WINS server to resolve names (rather than maintaining its own database) and then caches the names for a certain time. The proxy serves as an intermediary, by either communicating with the WINS server or supplying a name-to-IP address mapping from its cache.

To enable WINS name resolution for a computer that does not use DHCP, specify WINS server addresses in the TCP/IP Configuration dialog box.

With a Windows NT 3.5*x* platform, to designate a proxy you check the Enable WINS Proxy Agent option in the Advanced Microsoft TCP/IP Configuration dialog box.

With a Windows NT 4.0 platform, to designate a proxy you must use the Registry Editor (regedt32.exe) and add an entry, as follows:

HKEY_LOCAL_MACHINE\System\CurrentControlSet\Services\Netbt\Parameters\
,set EnableProxy=1.

With WINS servers in place on the internetwork, names are resolved using two basic methods, depending on whether WINS resolution is available and enabled on the particular computer. Whatever name resolution method is used, the process is transparent to the user after the system is configured.

WINS provides a distributed database for registering and querying dynamic computer name-to-IP address mappings in a routed network environment. If you are administering a routed network that includes computers running Windows NT Server, WINS is your best choice for name resolution because it is designed to solve the problems that occur with name resolution in more complex internetworks.

WINS reduces the use of local broadcasts for name resolution and enables users to locate computers on remote networks automatically. Furthermore, when dynamic addressing through DHCP results in new IP addresses for computers that move between subnetworks, the changes are updated automatically in the WINS database. Neither the user nor the network administrator needs to make manual accommodations for name resolution in such a case.

Windows networking clients that are WINS-enabled can use WINS directly. Non-WINS computers on the internetwork that are b-node-compatible (as described in RFCs 1001 and 1002) can access WINS through proxies, which are WINS-enabled computers that listen to name query broadcasts and then respond to names that are not on the local subnet or that are h-nodes.

On a Windows network, users can browse transparently across routers. To enable browsing without WINS, you must ensure that the user's primary domain has Windows NT Server computers on both sides of the router to act as master browsers. These computers must contain correctly configured LMHOSTS files with entries for the domain controllers across the subnet.

With WINS, such strategies are not necessary because the WINS servers and proxies provide the support necessary for browsing Windows NT domains across routers.

If WINS servers are installed on your network, you can use WINS in combination with broadcast name queries to resolve NetBIOS computer names to IP addresses. If you do not use this option, Windows 95 can use name query broadcasts (b-node mode of NetBIOS over TCP/IP) plus the local LMHOSTS file to resolve computer names to IP addresses. Broadcast resolution is limited to the local network.

The MS-DOS TCP/IP implementation for Microsoft Network Client version 3.0 for MS-DOS supports the following:

- An MS-DOS–based interface
- Domain name resolver (DNR) to resolve host-name-to-IP address mappings if your network has a Domain Name System (DNS) server
- The Dynamic Host Configuration Protocol (DHCP)
- Windows Internet Name Service (WINS) resolution
- Windows Sockets

MS-DOS–based clients do not support the following features, which are provided by TCP/IP-32 for Windows for Workgroups version 3.11, TCP/IP for Windows 95, and Windows NT Workstation and Windows NT Server versions 3.5, 3.51, and 4.0:

- Support for DNS resolution using WINS
- Support for WINS resolution using DNS
- Name registration with the WINS database. Note that MS-DOS–based computers are clients, not servers, so they generally do not need registration.
- Capability to act as a WINS proxy node
- Support for multiple network adapters
- Support for Internet Group Management Protocol (IGMP)

Windows 95 requires both the primary and secondary entries for the WINS server setting. If you enter only the primary WINS server's IP address, the setting is not retained. If only one WINS server exists for the network, enter the IP address for the server in both the primary and secondary WINS server setting boxes.

IP Address and NetBIOS Computer Names

In an Internet Protocol (IP) internetwork, every host is uniquely identified by its IP address. The TCP/IP suite of protocols uses the IP address for communication. Users, of course, find it easier to remember host names (such as `Santaclara-Server.taos.Com` for an office in Santa Clara) than IP addresses (such as `184.216.2.15`).

A naming standard provides a fairly straightforward way to give users friendly names for communicating with IP hosts, thereby alleviating the need to remember the IP addresses. Enforcing a host naming standard throughout your company may require one of two things: either the creation of a host file (a static file found on every IP host that contains a map of host names to IP addresses) or the use of a DNS server.

In the NetBIOS networking world, every host is uniquely identified by its NetBIOS name (the computer name). The communication between hosts in a traditional NetBIOS environment is achieved by broadcasting on the network to resolve a name. In an internetwork (a collection of networks connected by intermediate system devices such as routers), broadcasts aren't forwarded across a router, so the concept of the LMHOSTS file was created. LMHOSTS is a static file that maps a NetBIOS name to an IP address and helps in communication between two NetBIOS hosts across a router in an internetwork.

Microsoft networking components, such as Windows NT Workstation and Windows NT Server services, enable the first 15 characters of a NetBIOS name to be specified by the user or administrator, but they reserve the 16th character of the NetBIOS name (00-FF hex) to indicate a resource type. Following are some examples of NetBIOS names used by Microsoft components:

- `\\computer_name[00h]`. Registered by the Workstation Service on the WINS client.

- `\\computer_name[03h]`. Registered by the Messenger Service on the WINS client.

- `\\computer_name[06h]`. Registered by the Remote Access Service (RAS), when started on a RAS Server.

- `\\computer_name[1Fh]`. Registered by the Network Dynamic Data Exchange (NetDDE) services, and only appears if the NetDDE services are started on the computer. By default under Windows NT 3.51, the NetDDE services are not automatically started.

- `\\computer_name[20h]`. Registered by the Server Service on the WINS client.

- `\\computer_name[21h]`. Registered by the RAS Client Service, when started on a RAS Client.

- **\\computer_name[BEh]**. Registered by the Network Monitoring Agent Service, and only appears if the service is started on the computer. If the computer name is not a full 15 characters, the name is padded with plus (+) symbols.
- **\\computer_name[BFh]**. Registered by the Network Monitoring Utility (included with Microsoft Systems Management Server). If the computer name is not a full 15 characters, the name is padded with plus (+) symbols.
- **\\username[03h]**. Usernames for the users currently logged on are registered in the WINS database. The username is registered by the Server component so that the user can receive any `net send` commands sent to his username. If more than one user is logged on with the same username, only the first computer at which a user logged on with that username registers the name.
- **\\domain_name[1Bh]**. Registered by the Windows NT Server primary domain controller (PDC) that is running as the domain master browser and that is enabling the remote browsing of domains. When a WINS server is queried for this name, a WINS server returns the IP address of the computer that registered this name.
- **\\domain_name[1Dh]**. Registered only by the master browser, of which only one can exist for each subnet. This name is used by the Backup Browsers to communicate with the master browser to retrieve the list of available servers.

  WINS servers always return a positive registration response for domain_name[1D], even though the WINS server does not "register" this name in its database. Therefore, when a WINS server is queried for the domain_name[1D], the WINS server returns a negative response and causes the client to broadcast to resolve the name.
- **\\domain_name[00h]**. Registered by the Workstation Service so that it can receive browser broadcasts from LAN Manager-based computers.
- **\\domain_name[1Ch]**. Registered for use by the domain controllers within the domain; can contain up to 25 IP addresses. One IP address will be that of the Primary Domain Controller (PDC), and the other 24 will be the IP addresses of Backup Domain Controllers (BDCs).
- **\\domain_name[1Eh]**. Registered for browsing purposes and used by the browsers to elect a master browser (this is how a statically mapped group name registers itself). When a WINS server receives a name query for a name ending with [1E], the WINS server always returns the network broadcast address for the requesting client's local network.
- **\\--__MSBROWSE__[01h]**. Registered by the master browser for each subnet. When a WINS server receives a name query for this name, the WINS server always returns the network broadcast address for the requesting client's local network.

Configuring NetBT (NetBIOS over TCP/IP) Parameters

All the NetBT parameters are Registry values located under one of two different subkeys of `HKEY_LOCAL_MACHINE\SYSTEM\CurrentControlSet\Services`:

- `Netbt\Parameters`
- `Netbt\Adapters\<Adapter Name>` (where `<Adapter Name>` refers to the subkey for a network adapter to which NetBT is bound, such as `Lance01`)

Values under the latter key(s) are specific to each adapter. If the system is configured via DHCP, a change in parameters takes effect if the command `ipconfig /renew` is issued in a command shell. Otherwise, a reboot of the system is required for a change in any of these parameters to take effect.

TIP
To make sure to enable a full registration, the server should be rebooted to regenerate WINS address entries.

During the installation of the TCP/IP components, the Network Control Panel installs the parameters covered in the following sections with default values. These parameters may also be modified using the Registry Editor (`regedt32.exe`).

NameServerPort Parameter

The `NameServerPort` parameter determines the destination port number to which NetBT sends name service-related packets, such as name queries and name registrations, to WINS. The Microsoft WINS listens on port 0x89. NetBIOS name servers from other vendors may listen on different ports. The attributes of this parameter are as follows:

- **Key:** `Netbt\Parameters`
- **Value type:** `REG_DWORD` (UDP port number)
- **Valid range:** 0–0xFFFF
- **Default:** 0x89

NameSrvQueryCount Parameter

The `NameSrvQueryCount` parameter determines the number of times NetBT sends a query to a WINS server for a given name without receiving a response. The attributes of this parameter are as follows:

- **Key:** `Netbt\Parameters`
- **Value type:** `REG_DWORD` (Count)
- **Valid range:** 0–0xFFFF
- **Default:** 3

NameSrvQueryTimeout **Parameter**

This parameter determines the time interval between successive name queries to WINS for a given name. The attributes for this parameter are as follows:

- **Key:** Netbt\Parameters
- **Value type:** REG_DWORD (time in milliseconds)
- **Valid range:** 100–0xFFFFFFFF
- **Default:** 1,500 (1.5 seconds)

BroadcastAddress **Parameter**

The BroadcastAddress parameter can be used to force NetBT to use a specific address for all broadcast name-related packets. By default, NetBT uses the ones-broadcast address appropriate for each net (that is, for a network of 11.101.0.0 with a subnet mask of 255.255.0.0, the subnet broadcast address would be 11.101.255.255). This parameter would be set, for example, if the network uses the zeros-broadcast address (set using the UseZeroBroadcast TCP/IP parameter). The appropriate subnet broadcast address would then be 11.101.0.0 in the example given, and this parameter would be set to 0x0b650000. Note that this parameter is global and is used on all subnets to which NetBT is bound. This parameter normally does not exist in the Registry, but it may be created to modify the default behavior of the NetBT protocol driver. The attributes for this parameter are as follows:

- **Key:** Netbt\Parameters
- **Value type:** REG_DWORD (little-endian encoded IP address consisting of 4 bytes)
- **Valid range:** 0–0xFFFFFFFF
- **Default:** The ones-broadcast address for each network

EnableDns **Parameter**

If the value of the EnableDns parameter is set to 1 (True), then NetBT queries the DNS for names that cannot be resolved by WINS, broadcast, or the LMHOSTS file. This parameter can be set via the Network Control Panel; you should not have to configure this parameter directly. The attributes of this parameter are as follows:

- **Key:** Netbt\Parameters
- **Value type:** REG_DWORD (Boolean)
- **Valid range:** 0 or 1 (False or True)
- **Default:** 0 (False)

EnableLmhosts Parameter

If the value of the `EnableLmhosts` parameter is set to 1 (True), then NetBT searches the LMHOSTS file, if it exists, for names that cannot be resolved by WINS or broadcast. By default, no LMHOSTS file database directory (specified by `Tcpip\Parameters\DatabasePath`) exists, so no action is taken. This value is written by the Advanced TCP/IP configuration dialog of the NCPA. This parameter can be set via the Network Control Panel; you should not have to configure this parameter directly. The attributes of this parameter are as follows:

- **Key:** `Netbt\Parameters`
- **Value type:** `REG_DWORD` (Boolean)
- **Valid range:** 0 or 1 (False or True)
- **Default:** 1 (True)

NameServer Parameter

The NameServer parameter specifies the IP address of the primary WINS server. If this parameter contains a valid value, it overrides the DHCP parameter of the same name. This parameter can be set via the Network Control Panel; you should not have to configure this parameter directly. The attributes for this parameter are as follows:

- **Key:** `Netbt\Adapters\<Adapter Name>`
- **Value type:** `REG_SZ` (dotted decimal IP address, such as `11.101.1.200`)
- **Valid range:** Any valid IP address
- **Default:** Blank (no address)

NameServerBackup Parameter

The `NameServerBackup` parameter specifies the IP address of the backup WINS server. If this parameter contains a valid value, it overrides the DHCP parameter of the same name. This parameter can be set via the Network Control Panel; you should not have to configure this parameter directly. The attributes for this parameter are as follows:

- **Key:** `Netbt\Adapters\<Adapter Name>`
- **Value type:** `REG_SZ` (dotted decimal IP address, such as `11.101.1.200`)
- **Valid Range:** Any valid IP address
- **Default:** Blank (no address)

ScopeId Parameter

The `ScopeId` parameter specifies the NetBIOS name scope for the node. This value must not begin with a period. If this parameter contains a valid value, it overrides the DHCP parameter of the same name. A blank value (empty string) will be ignored. Setting this parameter to the value "*" indicates a null scope and overrides the DHCP parameter. This parameter can be set via the Network Control Panel; you should not have to configure this parameter directly. The attributes for this parameter are as follows:

- **Key:** `Netbt\Parameters`
- **Value type:** `REG_SZ` (character string)
- **Valid range:** Any valid DNS domain name consisting of two dot-separated parts, or a "*"
- **Default:** None

DhcpNameServer Parameter

This parameter specifies the IP address of the primary WINS server. It is written by the DHCP client service, if enabled, and is created and used internally by the NetBT components. A valid NameServer value overrides this parameter. This parameter should never be modified using the Registry Editor and is listed here for reference only. The attributes for this parameter are as follows:

- **Key:** `Netbt\Adapters\<Adapter Name>`
- **Value type:** `REG_SZ` (dotted decimal IP address, such as `11.101.1.200`)
- **Valid range:** Any valid IP address
- **Default:** None

Configuring the Client to Use DNS

As you know from previous chapters, DNS provides a distributed database that contains a hierarchical naming system for identifying hosts on the Internet. The specifications for DNS are defined in RFCs 1034 and 1035.

Although DNS may seem similar to WINS, one major difference exists: DNS requires static configuration of IP addresses for name-to-address mapping. WINS can provide name-to-address mapping dynamically and requires far less administration.

The DNS database is a tree structure called the domain name space, where each node or domain is named and can contain subdomains. The domain name identifies the domain's position in the database in relation to its parent domain, with a period (.) separating each part of the name for the network nodes of the DNS domain.

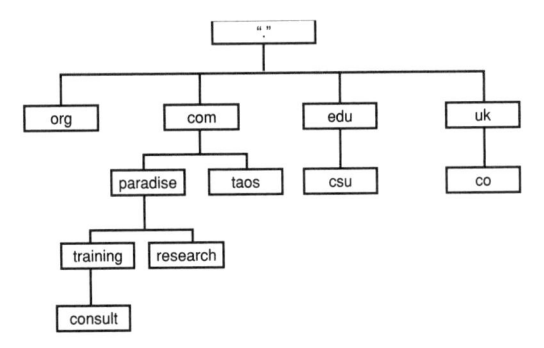

Figure 13.6 A portion of a DNS database.

As illustrated in Figure 13.6, the root node of the DNS database is unnamed (null and is referenced in DNS names with a trailing period (.). For example, in the name `research.paradise.com.`, the period after `com` denotes the DNS root node.

The root of the DNS database is managed by the Internet Network Information Center (InterNIC). The top-level domains were assigned organizationally and by country. These domain names follow the International Standard 3166. Two-letter and three-letter abbreviations are used for countries, and various abbreviations are reserved for use by organizations, as shown in Table 13.1.

Table 13.1 **InterNIC Domain Names**

Domain name	Type of Organization
com	Commercial (for example, `taos.com`)
edu	Educational (for example, `mit.edu` for Massachusetts Institute of Technology)
gov	Government (for example, `nsf.gov` for the National Science Foundation)
org	Noncommercial organizations (for example, `Petnet.org` for PetNet)
net	Networking organizations (for example, `bte.net` for BTENET)

For more complete information about domain names, see Appendix C, "Top-Level Internet Domains."

DNS uses a client-server model, in which the DNS servers contain information about a portion of the DNS database and make this information available to clients, called *resolvers*, that query the name server across the network. DNS *name servers* are programs that store information about parts of the domain namespace, called *zones*. The administrator for a domain sets up name servers that contain the database files with all the Resource Records describing all hosts in their zones. DNS resolvers are clients trying to use name servers to gain information about the domain namespace.

Note
All the resolver software necessary for using DNS on the Internet is installed with Microsoft TCP/IP. Microsoft TCP/IP includes the DNS resolver functionality used by NetBIOS over TCP/IP and Windows Sockets connectivity applications such as FTP and Telnet to query the name server and interpret the responses.

The key task for DNS is to present friendly names for users and then resolve those names to IP addresses, as required by the internetwork. If a local name server doesn't contain the data requested in a query, it sends back names and addresses of other name servers that could contain the information. The resolver then queries the other name servers until it finds the specific name and address needed. This process is made faster because name servers continuously cache the information learned about the domain namespace as the result of queries.

TCP/IP utilities, such as FTP and Telnet, can also use DNS in addition to the HOSTS file to find computers when connecting to foreign hosts or computers on your network.

Enabling DNS

You must determine whether users should configure their computers to use DNS. Usually, you will use DNS if you are using TCP/IP to communicate over the Internet or if your private internetwork uses DNS to distribute host information.

Microsoft TCP/IP provides a DNS client for resolving Internet or UNIX system names. Windows networking provides dynamic name resolution for NetBIOS computer names using WINS servers and NetBIOS over TCP/IP. If you choose to use DNS, you must configure the way in which the computer will use DNS and the HOSTS file. DNS configuration is global for all network adapters installed on a computer. If DHCP is used for automatic configuration, these parameters can be provided by the DHCP server.

To configure a computer running Windows 95 to use DNS for name resolution, follow these steps:

1. In the Microsoft TCP/IP properties, click the DNS Configuration tab.
2. If a DNS server is available, click Enable DNS. Then specify a host name and complete the other configuration information as described in the following procedure.

To configure a computer running Windows NT 4.0 to use DNS for name resolution, you enable the DNS resolution tab via the WINS address tab.

The host name is used to identify the local computer for authentication by some utilities. Other TCP/IP-based utilities can use this value to learn the name of the local computer. Host names are stored on DNS servers in a table that maps names to IP addresses for use by DNS.

The HOSTS file can be used as a local DNS equivalent; the LMHOSTS file can be used as a local WINS equivalent.

Note

Sample versions of LMHOSTS and HOSTS files are added to the Windows NT `systemroot\SYSTEM32\DRIVERS\ETC` directory when you install Microsoft TCP/IP.

Figure 13.7 illustrates the process of enabling DNS in a Windows NT 3.51 environment.

Figure 13.8 illustrates the process of enabling DNS in a Windows NT 4.0 environment.

Figure 13.9 illustrates the process of enabling DNS in a Windows 95 environment.

Setting the Host Name for DNS

To set the host name for DNS, type a name in the Host Name box. The name can be any combination of the letters A through Z, the numerals 0–9, and the hyphen (-), plus the period (.) character used as a separator. By default, this value is the Microsoft networking computer name, but the network administrator can assign another host name without affecting the computer name.

However, it's a good idea to make both names the same to avoid any name resolution problems.

Some characters that can be used in computer names, especially the underscore, cannot be used in host names.

Setting the Domain Name for DNS

The DNS domain name is used with the host name to create a fully qualified domain name (FQDN) for the computer. The FQDN is the host name followed by a period (.), followed by the domain name. For example, this could be `frenchy.taos.com`, where `frenchy` is the host name and `taos.com` is the domain name.

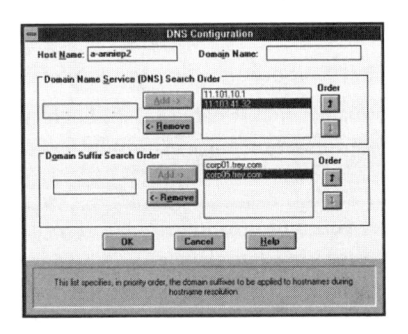

Figure 13.7 Configuring client Windows NT 3.51 to use DNS.

Configuring the Client to Use DNS

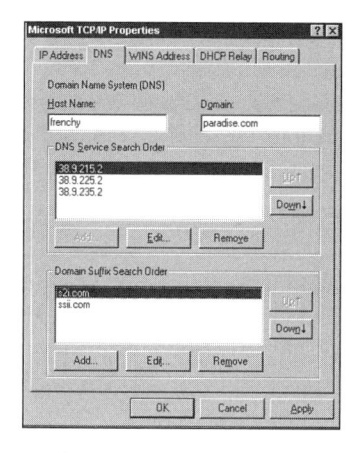

Figure 13.8 Configuring client Windows NT 4.0 to use DNS.

During DNS queries, the local domain name is appended to short names. A short name consists of only a host name, such as `frenchy`. When querying the DNS server for the IP address of `frenchy`, the domain name is appended to the short name, and the DNS server is actually asked to resolve the FQDN of `frenchy.taos.com`. Notice that the FQDN of frenchy at Taos (`frenchy.taos.com`) is not the same as his Internet electronic mail address of `frenchy@taos.com`.

To set the DNS domain name, optionally, type a name in the Domain Name box. This is usually an organization name followed by a period and an extension that indicates the type of organization, such as `microsoft.com`. The name can be any combination of the letters A through Z, the numerals 0–9, and the hyphen (-), plus the period (.) character used as a separator.

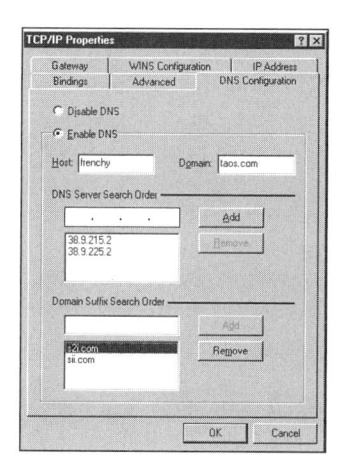

Figure 13.9 Configuring Windows 95 client to use DNS.

A DNS domain is not the same as a Windows NT or LAN Manager domain. A DNS domain is a hierarchical structure for organizing TCP/IP hosts that provides a naming scheme used in UNIX environments. A Windows NT or LAN Manager domain is a grouping of computers for security and administrative purposes.

Specifying DNS Servers

You can add up to three IP addresses for DNS servers. For a given DNS query, Windows 95 attempts to obtain DNS information from the first IP address in the list. If no response is received, Windows 95 goes to the second server in the list, and so on. To change the order of the IP addresses, you must remove them and retype them in the order that you want the servers to be searched.

Although TCP/IP uses IP addresses to identify and reach computers, users typically prefer to use computer names. DNS is a naming service generally used in the UNIX networking community to provide standard naming conventions for IP workstations. Windows Sockets applications and TCP/IP utilities, such as FTP and Telnet, can also use DNS in addition to the HOSTS file to find systems when connecting to foreign hosts or systems on your network.

Contact the network administrator to find out whether you should configure your computer to use DNS. Usually, you can use DNS if you are using TCP/IP to communicate over the Internet or if your private internetwork uses DNS to distribute host information. Microsoft TCP/IP includes DNS client software for resolving Internet or UNIX system names. Microsoft Windows networking provides dynamic name resolution for NetBIOS computer names via WINS servers and NetBIOS over TCP/IP. DNS configuration is global for all network adapters installed on a computer.

For Windows NT 3.51, to set the search order for a DNS server, type the IP address of the DNS server that will provide name resolution in the Domain Name System (DNS) Search Order box. Then choose the Add button to move the IP address to the list on the right (refer to Figure 13.7).

For Windows NT 4.0 or Windows 95, to set the search order for a DNS Server, type the IP address of the DNS server that will provide name resolution in the Domain Name System (DNS) Search Order box, and then choose the Add button to move the IP address to the list (refer to Figure 13.8 and Figure 13.9).

The network administrator should provide the correct values for this parameter, based on the IP address assigned to the DNS server used at your site.

The servers running DNS are queried in the order listed. To change the order of the IP addresses, select an IP address to move, and then use the up- and down-arrow buttons. To remove an IP address, select the IP address and then choose the Remove button.

In the Domain Suffix Search Order box, type the domain suffixes to add to your domain suffix search list, and then choose the Add button.

Configuring the Client to Use DNS

This list specifies the DNS domain suffixes to be appended to host names during name resolution. You can add up to six domain suffixes. To change the search order of the domain suffixes, select a domain name to move, and then use the up- and down-arrow buttons. To remove a domain name, select the domain name and then choose the Remove button.

If you have two servers listed in this dialog box, Windows 95 checks the second server only if no response is received from the first server. If Windows 95 attempts to check a host name with the first server and receives a message that the host name is not recognized, the system does not try the second DNS server.

When you are done setting DNS options, choose the OK button.

When the TCP/IP Configuration dialog box reappears, choose the OK button. When the Network Settings dialog box reappears, choose the OK button. The settings take effect after you restart the computer.

Using Suffix Search Order to Qualify Names

The DNS server Domain Suffix Search Order specifies the DNS domain suffixes to be appended to host names during name resolution. You can add up to five domain suffixes. Domain suffixes are placed in the list in alphabetic order.

To set the Domain Suffix Search Order through the Control Panel, follow these steps:

1. In the Domain Suffix Search Order box, type the domain suffixes to add to your domain suffix search list, and then click the Add button.

2. To remove a domain name from the list, select it and then click the Remove button.

When attempting to resolve a fully qualified domain name (FQDN) from a short name, Windows 95 first appends the local domain name. If this is not successful, Windows 95 uses the Domain Suffix list to create additional FQDNs and query DNS servers in the order listed, as illustrated in Figure 13.10.

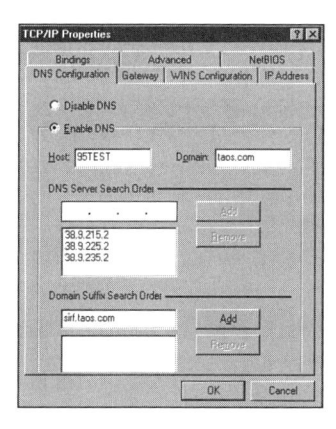

Figure 13.10 Configuring Windows 95 domain suffix search.

The DNS Domain Suffix Search Order can also be set during an unattended install of Windows NT Workstation or Windows NT Server 4.0. To do so, you must use the Registry Editor because the unattended setup mode of Windows NT does not offer a way to specify the domain suffix order.

Setting the DNS Domain Suffix Search Order via Text File

Create a text file with the following two lines of text, and save it as `Suffix.txt`. The spacing must appear exactly as shown below, where "xxxxxxxx.xxx" signifies a domain suffix. Up to six domain suffixes can be specified. The search order works left to right.

    \\HKEY_LOCAL_MACHINE\System\CurrentControlSet\Services\TCPIP
    \Parameters
    "SearchList=textxxxx.com test2xxxx.net test 3xxxx.gov"

Note
The preceding Registry key is one path; it has been wrapped for readability.

Copy `Regini.exe` and `Suffix.txt` to the `$OEM$` subdirectory at the installation Sharepoint. `Regini.exe` is a Windows NT Resource Kit utility.

If one does not exist, create a `Cmdlines.txt` file in the `$OEM$` subdirectory, and add the following line (including the quotation marks):

    [Commands]
    ".\REGINI SUFFIX.TXT"

Only one instance of the `[Commands]` heading should exist in the `Cmdlines.txt` file.

Make sure the entry `OEMPREINSTALL = Yes` exists in the `[UNATTEND]` section of your `Unattended.txt` file.

Setting the DNS Domain Suffix Search Order via Registry

Create a Registry file with the following two lines of text, and save it as `Suffix.reg`. The spacing must be exactly as shown in the example that follows, where xxxxxxxx.xxx signifies a domain suffix. Up to six domain suffixes can be specified. The search order works left to right.

    \\HKEY_LOCAL_MACHINE\System\CurrentControlSet\Services\TCPIP
    \Parameters
    "SearchList=textxxxx.com test2xxxx.net test 3xxxx.gov"

Note
The preceding Registry key is one path; it has been wrapped for readability.

Copy `Regedit.exe` and `Suffix.reg` to the `$OEM$` subdirectory at the installation Sharepoint. `Regedit.exe` is part of Windows NT.

If one does not exist, create a `Cmdlines.txt` file in the `$OEM$` subdirectory, and add the following line (including the quotation marks):

`[Commands]`
`".\REGEDIT /s SUFFIX.REG"`

Only one instance of the `[Commands]` heading should exist in the `Cmdlines.txt` file.

Make sure the entry `OEMPREINSTALL = Yes` exists in the `[UNATTEND]` section of your `Unattended.txt` file.

Warning
Once again, I cannot stress enough the importance of using the Registry Editor carefully. Any incorrect use of the Registry can cause serious problems that may require you to reinstall your operating system!

Summary

This chapter described in some detail how to configure clients to use WINS and DNS name services. The chapters remaining in this section on using Windows NT DNS cover server issues such as maintenance, security, and how to troubleshoot your installation. Chapter 18, "Dynamic Host Configuration Protocol (DHCP)," shows how you can use a central DHCP server to automatically assign an IP number and other configuration information to clients when they start up.

14

Working with Service Providers

This chapter will review:

- **Domain name registrations.** This section explains how to research the status of domain names and how to secure a domain name for yourself, your company, or on behalf of other parties.
- **Internal and external servers: primary, secondary, and caching.** This section describes the relationship of primary, secondary, and caching name servers to assist you in deciding where servers should reside. For example, should your ISP have a primary, a secondary, or both?
- **Zone transfers: which way?** This section reminds you of the direction that name data flows between DNS servers, which is an important consideration for setting up reliable service.
- **Interpreting the event log.** The Windows NT Event Viewer provides valuable information for DNS administrators seeking to ensure that DNS data is moving between servers as planned. This section describes what to look for and what it means.
- **What to expect in the DNS database.** This section describes the contents you'll find in a DNS database. This section also provides helpful information for new administrators trying to understand where data goes and how to tell if everything is in its place, which is crucial when sharing DNS data and duties with an ISP.

Domain Name Registrations

The first thing an organization that's looking to connect to the Internet needs to consider is how it will be known or found. Good domain names that have meaning are those that are easily found by targeted audiences. Many organizations choose to abbreviate their name to make up a domain name—and it's a real trick to find a domain name that someone else has not already registered. Recently, some relief has come from the addition of seven new generic top-level domains (gTLDs). The new gTLDs are: .arts, .firm, .nom, .info, .rec, .web, and .shop. These gTLDs provide some breathing and growing room as additions to the existing .gov, .edu, .org, .com, and .net, making available many more names for the choosing.

Querying for Existing Domain Names

To verify whether a domain name is in use, the whois command can be used. On most UNIX machines, whois can be performed from the command line: whois <domain name>. This returns the information about the domain if the name is in use. A version available on the Web is accessible to Windows users at http://www.internic.net/cgi-bin/whois. If you want an equivalent of the UNIX whois to use on a Windows computer, WinFinger32 is a good option. You can download a copy using a Web browser by visiting its author's home page at http://eb-p5.eb.uah.edu/~adanil/. In any case, the information obtained is the same.

For example, if whois taoslab.com is searched, the result looks like Listing 14.1.

Listing 14.1 **Verifying domain names with** whois

```
>whois taoslab.com

Taos Mountain (TAOSLAB-DOM)
   3970 Freedom Circle
   Santa Clara, CA 95054

   Domain Name: TAOSLAB.COM

   Administrative Contact:
     Tech Services Group (TS326-ORG) TSG@TAOS.COM
     408.588.1200
   Fax- 408.588.1296
     Technical Contact, Zone Contact:
     Knief, Herman (HK1392) hknief@TAOS.COM
     408.588.1200 (FAX) 408.588.1296
     Billing Contact:
     Tech Services Group (TS326-ORG) TSG@TAOS.COM
     408.588.1200
   Fax- 408.588.1296
```

```
    Record last updated on 18-Feb-98.
    Record created on 04-Mar-96.
    Database last updated on 24-Feb-98 04:08:59 EST.

    Domain servers in listed order:

    SOCRATES.TAOSLAB.COM    207.33.46.1
    LAGUNA.TAOS.COM         204.188.112.62

The InterNIC Registration Services Host contains ONLY Internet
➥Information
(Networks, ASNs, Domains, and POCs).
Please use the whois server at nic.ddn.mil for MILNET Information.
```

The response in Listing 14.1 indicates that the domain name is already registered and that it belongs to the organization listed in the response. If a whois is tried for a domain name that doesn't exist, the result would look like Listing 14.2.

Listing 14.2 **Verifying that a domain name doesn't exist with** whois

```
>whois justjoking.com

No match for "JUSTJOKING.COM".

The InterNIC Registration Services Host contains ONLY Internet
Information
(Networks, ASNs, Domains, and POCs).

Please use the whois server at nic.ddn.mil for MILNET Information.
```

Registering Domain Names: An Overview

After a name has been selected and it has been verified that the name is not in use, the registration process can begin. Appendix D, "Registering Addresses on the Internet," provides templates for the registration forms. Network Solutions, Inc. is chartered with the task of providing domain name registration services for the InterNIC (Internet Network Information Center). The InterNIC basically handles domain registrations through email, although templates for the forms can be retrieved in several ways.

For the inexperienced, two Web browser forms can be used to complete the registration forms. The first Web form is a step-by-step process that guides the administrator through the questions. The second Web form is simply the registration template displayed through a browser interface. Another way to complete the template is to download the text form and complete the registration with a text editor. The forms are available from a number of sources, although the author recommends using the InterNIC site `http://www.internic.net` just to make sure that the latest version is being used.

The next action is to email the completed form to `mailto:hostmaster@internic.net`. In the case of the Web form, the completed form is emailed to the administrator who completed the template; that administrator then must return the form to the same email address listed previously. Remember that this process works for domain names only. If an organization needs to register a network number, autonomous system, or an `in-addr.arpa` domain (for reverse DNS lookups), the templates for these must be completed and submitted as well. These go not to InterNIC but to ARIN (the American Registry for Internet Numbers). (To refresh your memory, reverse lookups are those that map IP addresses back to host names.)

Domain names do represent a cart and horse issue, however. To register a domain, an organization must set up the servers that will act as primary and secondary before the registration template goes to the InterNIC. If the machines do not exist, InterNIC will not process the request. The process usually requires completion of several steps.

First, the organization must have at least one registered and routable IP address. With a valid IP address, the organization can at least set up the primary name server and domain information (and, it is hoped, get someone else to host the secondary). So, typically, the template for ARIN must be completed first, unless the ISP is providing the network numbers from its supply (which leads into the next section).

Second, the templates for the domain name registration are sent to InterNIC, which usually takes three to five days to process. After a domain has been registered and the NIC has responded with a confirmation that the domain name is active, it is generally a good idea to have someone test the domain from outside the organization. Testing the lookups from outside the domain ensures that the names and addresses are properly mapped and that the hosts (by name) are reachable by the outside world.

Internal and External Servers: Primary, Secondary, and Caching

Determining Company Requirements

The first step in determining company requirements is to determine how many name servers the organization should have, where they should be located, and what type of name servers should be used in which locations. The questions of how many and where may also be complicated by the network topology and security policies put in place. Does the name server need to work through a firewall? How many routers or WAN links will be used in the network? What are the speeds of the WAN links that will be used? Also, how big is the organization and how many subdomains should be established?

For a small company just starting out, a single domain may be perfectly suitable—and would certainly be easier to manage. If an organization is larger and geographically diverse, then subdomains should probably be set up, either departmentally or by region. Sites with firewalls must consider design issues. Should there be a "hole" punched in the firewall to allow the name server traffic to pass directly through? Should two separate name servers be set up and maintained, or should the external name server be a secondary for the domain? With split-brain DNS (so-called because primary name servers exist on both sides of the firewall), the external primary server publishes only the hosts that the organization wants the public to see. The internal primary server has mappings for all the hosts in the domain but is configured to forward to the external DNS server for hosts external to the name server's zones. The internal primary can also be configured to slave to the external primary, thereby remaining hidden from the rest of the Internet.

Analyzing Network Traffic to Determine the Need for Internal Secondary Name Servers

Organizations that are geographically diverse will often have multiple routed connections to different offices. It is often wise to place at least a caching name server in these remote offices. The traffic patterns for the organization should be examined to determine what percentage of network traffic is bound for internal hosts as opposed to external hosts. If the majority of the traffic is bound for internal hosts, then secondaries are a wise choice for the remote offices. With secondaries in each remote office, most of the name service queries can be localized to the servers located in the office.

General Considerations for Name Service with ISPs

Internet service providers (ISPs) are the means by which most organizations connect to the Internet. For small organizations, those without an MIS staff, or those unable to afford an MIS staff, ISPs will generally provide name server service (for a fee). In situations where the ISP will host the DNS server, an organization may choose to implement a secondary locally. This provides authoritative information and gives the organization the assurance (because the secondary will have a copy of the zone) that the ISP is publishing the correct information and making changes in a timely manner.

The organization may also choose to simply implement a caching-only name server to improve performance in answering common name queries by building a local cache. This relieves the organization of some of the administrative problems and overhead, but it leaves the organization at the mercy of the ISP when it comes time to make changes. Without a tremendous amount of work, an organization could run its own primary name server and have the ISP provide the secondary. This offers a couple of nice benefits. For one, the organization is free to make and implement changes at will instead of when the ISP gets around to it.

If the ISP hosts the secondary, some level of redundancy arises in the event that the circuit to the ISP goes down for some reason.

In an ideal scenario, the ISP would assign and delegate the authority for a block of network addresses to the organization. The term "delegate" here refers to the delegation of the IN-ADDR domain for the block of addresses. In this instance, the organization now has the freedom to set up its network, build its name servers, and publish the domain names it wishes to register. If the organization is large enough, it may need to receive a network number assignment from ARIN and to complete the IN-ADDR domain registration without the involvement of the ISP.

Zone Transfers: Which Way, and Why?

Zone transfers occur from a primary to a secondary, or from a master secondary to another secondary. That is to say, one secondary can request a zone transfer from another secondary. The secondary that provides the map is said to be a master secondary. More detailed information about zone transfers can be found in Chapter 5, "How DNS Works," and Chapter 6, "Name Server Types."

The question for the administrator is twofold: Just which servers should be configured to provide zones to other servers? And what kind of distribution pattern should be utilized to speed the propagation of changes and make zone transfers more efficient? Organizations that rely on ISPs for some part of their name service, or those that have multiple offices connected by slow WAN links, may choose to have multiple remote master secondaries that pull the zones from the primary at the local office. These remote secondaries, in turn, act as the master servers for other name servers at the remote locations, including the ISP. If the ISP hosts multiple name servers for an organization's domain and the organization maintains the primary, it makes sense to instruct only one name server at the ISP to request the zone transfer from the primary. Then the ISP name server that receives the zone data can redistribute the data to other name servers for the domain that resides at the ISP. This conserves some of the organization's bandwidth because it's necessary to provide only one zone transfer to an external name server rather than multiple transfers.

Interpreting the Event Log

It's one thing to plan and execute a plan to share DNS data and duties with an ISP. Yet it's another thing altogether to make sure everything is working properly. The event log provides valuable clues you can use to verify that transfers are happening as they should.

Event logs are records of all system messages written to Windows NT. Event logs generally have the following format:

`<SYMBOL/DATE> <TIME> <SOURCE> <CATEGORY> <EVENT> <USER> <COMPUTER>`

Access to the event logs is available through the Event Viewer, which resides in the Administrative Tools program group. The Event Viewer displays three different logs: SYSTEM, SECURITY, and APPLICATION. For monitoring the DNS service, the SYSTEM log is the appropriate view (see Figure 14.1).

Figure 14.1 Event Viewer, showing the System log.

Figure 14.1 shows the format of the typical event log. Notice the left-most column, which displays the date. The symbol just to the left of the date provides some general information about the type of event. The blue dot with the "i" denotes that this is an informational message and that no error condition exists. The yellow dot with the "!" denotes that this is a warning message. Some condition requiring the administrator's attention has been noted, but the system continues to function. The third symbol, a small stop sign, tells the administrator that a fatal error has occurred and that a service or device will not be available. This could have resulted from a simple driver conflict or from a failed piece of hardware. Double-clicking on an item of interest brings up a window with further details, as illustrated in Figure 14.2.

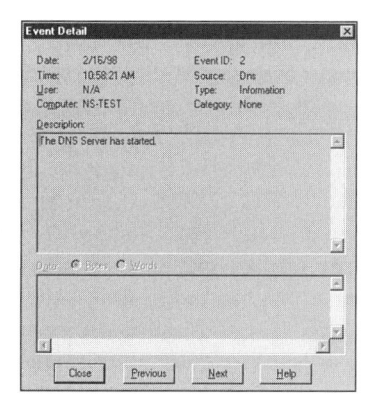

Figure 14.2 Event showing successful startup of the DNS server.

The event log shown in Figure 14.2 indicates that the DNS service has started. This message should occur any time the DNS service is started, either by the administrator manually starting it from the services control panel, or by the system starting it during a reboot. Other messages will be displayed when zone transfers occur or if the service stops. If any other messages appear in the event log regarding DNS, they should be evaluated to see what has happened. Warnings occur if the administrator has started the service via a boot file and then issued an unsupported directive (as is the case with the warning that was issued in Figure 14.1). Generally, warnings indicate a problem, but they do not stop the DNS server from answering queries. If a fatal error has occurred and the stop sign appears in the event log, the DNS server is not functioning and the administrator must correct some problem.

What to Expect in the DNS Database

The contents of the DNS database on a local name server depend largely on the type of name server that is configured. Primary name servers should contain only entries that have been placed in the zone files by the administrator. Secondary name servers should contain only the entries they have transferred from their masters. Cache files that are used for the root server hints should be identical for any name server that is attached to the Internet. A difference exists between the cache file for the root servers and the contents of a cache dump: The reason is simply that the cache dump contains all the entries for the local zones and the hosts from any name lookups the name server has successfully answered that have not exceeded the time-to-live (ttl). Microsoft's DNS does not provide a cache dump per se, but the contents of the cache can be viewed via the DNS Manager. Looking into the cache provides a glimpse of the queries the name server has answered (see Figure 14.3).

From Figure 14.3, it is obvious that the name server has handled queries for a number of different domains, including .edu, .mil, and .org. Drilling into any of these top-level domains gives a better overview of the requests that have been made. Here, the .edu domain shows that a request was made for the Web server at ISI. Hence, the ISI subheading appears under the .edu domain, with the contents of the name server and the Web server. If the name server is operating properly, the administrator should be able to compare the name server statistics to the cache entries. Cache entries should appear for every external lookup that's completed and should match the statistics for the server. The server statistics provide information about the number of queries and responses the server has handled, as well as the number of recursive queries the server has performed. The total number of queries accepted will normally be greater than the number of recursive queries. This indicates how many queries were answered by the name server directly, and how many queries the name server had to look for (see Figure 14.4).

What to Expect in the DNS Database   203

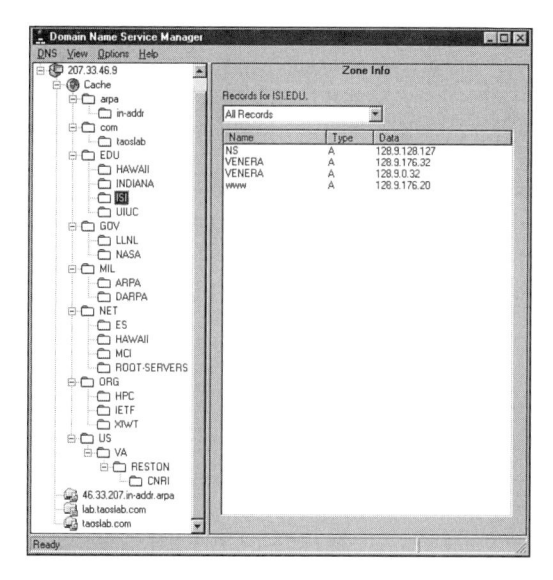

Figure 14.3   Viewing the contents of the DNS cache.

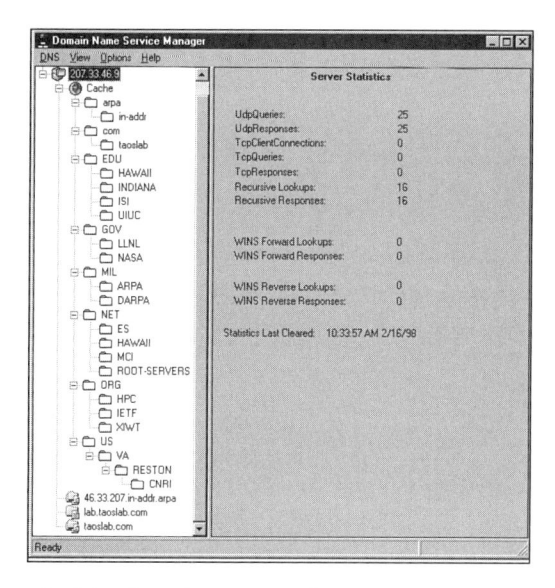

Figure 14.4   Server Statistics show the amount of query activity since the last time the server was started.

Summary

This chapter showed once again that planning plays an important part in the success of a DNS installation. By working with an ISP, you can assure that everyone on the Internet will be able to access your domain, and that zone transfers are done in the most efficient manner possible. The Windows NT Event Viewer and the DNS Manager are the two places to gather information about the operation of a DNS server and to verify that the DNS servers, though separated by distance, are working together as they should.

15

Maintenance Tasks

This chapter will review:

- **Moving zone files between servers.** This section explains how you can maintain an accurate database of DNS servers by transferring an entire zone's information via a TCP connection.
- **Managing multiple zones.** You generally must maintain two zones: one to find IP addresses and the other (IN-ADDR zone) to find host names in reverse.
- **Changing a DNS server's IP address.** This section helps you consider some important aspects when changing a DNS server's IP address.

Moving Zone Files Between Servers

A zone is authoritative for all the DNS information within that zone. One zone may contain one or several domains, and the same given zone can also contain subdomains. To enhance performance and availability, each zone must have more than one authoritative name server. This can create the common data maintenance problems that arise when more than one master database must be kept accurate and timely. A master name server can initialize the database for each zone it maintains from either a local data file or from another master name server. In the latter case, the secondary master asks the primary master where the database is maintained to transfer an entire zone's information via a TCP connection. The information is recorded and stored locally in a data file, to be used later in case a zone transfer cannot be completed.

Regardless of which DNS strategy is adopted for the primary DNS, the secondary DNS should be arranged with a remote site. Such arrangements can usually be made with Internet Service Providers (ISPs), other groups within a large organization, or other sites willing to arrange a secondary DNS swap (that is, to handle each other's secondary DNS servers).

Zones are typically moved between name servers via a process called a zone transfer. A zone transfer is initiated by a secondary, either upon startup (especially the first time around, or if the secondary does not have a backup copy of the zone) or after the secondary detects a change in the serial number of its master. One way to decrease the time it takes to propagate changes is by implementing the Notify option (as shown in Figure 15.1) so that the primary or master tells the secondaries that a change has been made. Using the Notify option prompts the secondaries to verify that the serial number has been incremented, and it requests a zone transfer if this is the case.

Zone Transfers in DNS/WINS Integrated Environments OK

If Microsoft's DNS server is integrated with WINS, it must be explicitly configured to interoperate with non-Microsoft name servers (UNIX servers). Microsoft represents WINS information in the DNS using a nonstandard Resource Record type. All the Resource Records are commonly used by DNS name servers on the Internet *except* for the WINS and WINS_R Resource Records. These records are specifically implemented for interoperability between Microsoft DNS servers and Microsoft WINS servers.

This can cause a name server to fail when attempting a zone transfer from a Microsoft server. Older BIND servers may actually terminate when receiving such Resource Records in a zone transfer.

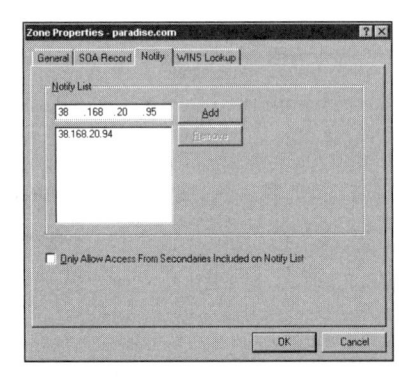

Figure 15.1 The Notify list in the Zone Properties dialog box.

Because these records are unique to Microsoft DNS servers, when transferring primary zone files to a secondary zone, these records should not be copied to a DNS name server running non-Microsoft DNS server software.

If you are using WINS lookup or WINS reverse lookup with a non-Microsoft DNS server, you must prevent users from copying WINS or WINS_R records to a non-Microsoft DNS server.

To correct the problem, ensure that the Zone Properties; WINS Lookup; Settings only affect local server option is set for each such zone on the Microsoft server. To do so, you will need to follow these steps:

1. Start DNS Manager.
2. Right-click the folder for the appropriate zone.
3. Click Properties.
4. Click the WINS Lookup or WINS Reverse Lookup tab (see Figure 15.2).
5. Select the Settings only affect local server check box.
6. Click OK.

Between UNIX name servers and Windows NT name servers, you can perform zone transfers by using nslookup, which comes with Windows NT Server. Start nslookup, then type "server servername," where "servername" is a name server authoritative for the zone you want to transfer. Then type "ls zonename". Effectively, this transfers zone information from a Windows NT name server to a UNIX name server.

Zone Transfers Between NT DNS Servers

When you use the Microsoft DNS server to move one or more zones from one Windows NT DNS server to a new Windows NT DNS server, you have the option of starting the service using a boot file or using information that is stored in the Registry.

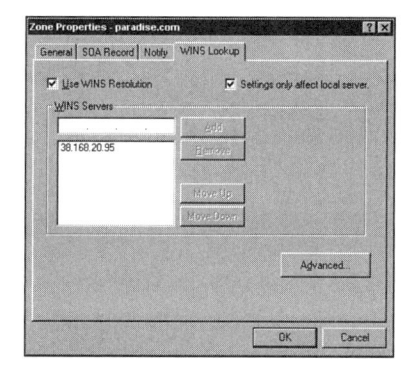

Figure 15.2   Ensuring WINS and WINS-R records are copied only to MS-DNS servers.

DNS Servers with Boot File Startup

If you are starting DNS using a boot file, follow these steps to move your zone file(s). These steps, of course, assume that you have installed the Microsoft DNS server service on the new Windows NT-based server and that you have not configured any information for it.

1. From Services in Control Panel, stop the Microsoft DNS server on both Windows NT DNS servers.
2. Manually copy the entire contents (subfolders included) of the %Systemroot%\System32\DNS folder from the source server to the destination server.
3. Restart the Microsoft DNS server on the new Windows NT DNS server.

DNS Servers with Registry Startup

If you are starting DNS using the Registry, you must follow these steps when you are moving a single zone file:

1. From Services in the Control Panel, stop the Microsoft DNS server on both Windows NT DNS servers.
2. From the source DNS server, copy the desired zone file, <zone name>.dns, from the %Systemroot%\System32\DNS folder to the same folder on the destination Windows NT DNS server.
3. Create the new zone (see Chapter 11, "Installing and Setting Up DNS") on the destination server using the DNS Service Manager. Configure the zone as it was configured on the source server, either as a primary or secondary zone. The new zone must be created using the same zone filename as the original file.

   For example, if paradise.com.dns was the original file copied from the source server to the destination server, paradise.com.dns must be the name of the new file.
4. Restart the Microsoft DNS Server on the new Windows NT DNS server.

The procedure that follows guides you through the process of moving multiple zones if you are starting DNS using the Registry. Perform steps 1–2 on the destination Windows NT DNS server only. Perform steps 5–8 on the source server only. Perform steps 9–14 on the destination server only.

1. Using the DNS Manager, create a sample primary zone called Sample.com. Creating the sample zone ensures that the DNS server boot file information has been written to the registry and that the DNS server knows where the cache information is located.

2. Using DNS Manager, delete the sample zone that you just created in step 1.
3. From Services in Control Panel, stop the Microsoft DNS server service on both Windows NT DNS servers.
4. From the source DNS server, copy the desired zone file, `<zone name>.dns`, from the `%Systemroot%\System32\DNS` folder to the same folder on the destination Windows NT DNS server.
5. Start Registry Editor (`Regedt32.exe`).
6. Go to the following subkey:
   `HKEY_LOCAL_MACHINE\SYSTEM\CurrentControlSet\Services\DNS`
7. Click Zones, click Registry, and click Save Key.
8. Save this key to a location from which you can restore it to the destination server and close Registry Editor.
9. Start Registry Editor (`Regedt32.exe`).
10. Go to the following subkey:
    `HKEY_LOCAL_MACHINE\SYSTEM\CurrentControlSet\Services\DNS`
11. Click Zones to verify that it is selected, click Registry, and click Restore.
12. Locate the Registry key file that you exported on the destination server.
13. Click Yes in the confirmation dialog box, and close Registry Editor.
14. Restart the Microsoft DNS Server service on the new NT DNS server.

The information transferred in the Registry key maintains the names of the zones and keeps you from re-creating the zone names in the DNS Manager for every zone file that was copied.

Be aware, however, that using the Registry Editor incorrectly can cause serious systemwide problems that may require you to reinstall Windows NT to correct them. Make sure to backup your Registry before using this tool.

Note

Microsoft DNS seems to be unable to manually push zones for testing purposes. An administrator must wait for the zone to transfer and then personally check the results. The nslookup utility can be used to view the contents of a zone and copy it to a file if the machine from which it is run has the authority to perform a zone transfer. One tool the administrator does have is the Event Viewer, which captures zone transfer requests and the zone transfers themselves. The Event Viewer reports on the status of the transfer, the date and time it occurred, the domain that was affected, and the name of the zone file that was written. Both nslookup and Event Viewer are the best troubleshooting tools for Windows NT if your DNS does not run.

Zone Issues When Manipulating Primary and Secondary Servers

If the purpose of moving the zones is a precursor to replacing the primary name server, an easy way to transfer a lot of the information is to set up the new machine as a secondary. After the zones have been transferred, the DNS service can be altered to change the host from a secondary to a primary. The new host can now be put on the network in place of the old host and can begin serving the DNS information. See Chapter 11 for setting up and modifying the name server properties.

The process of manipulating zones, however, may not be so smooth in some cases. For example, if you create a secondary zone and then change that zone to primary, the Registry is not updated to reflect the change. The next time you restart the DNS server, you receive an error message stating that the primary DNS address is missing. In this instance, the DNS server does not start. Also, the `Cache.dns` file may be overwritten with a blank file, causing you to lose name resolution outside your zone of authority.

The Microsoft DNS server has been modified to correctly write back the Zone Type key to reflect the correct role of the zone. You can obtain the following hotfix from the Internet, or you can wait for the next Windows NT service pack.

`ftp://ftp.microsoft.com/bussys/winnt/winnt-public/fixes/usa/NT40/hotfixes-postSP3/dns-fix`

Some other problems may occur: In particular, when a zone file contains a large number (approximately 100) of "A" records for a single host name (each mapped to a different IP address), the user interface appears to stop responding (hang) when trying to display the zone information.

During this time, the amount of memory used by `Dnsadmin.exe` progressively increases until the system displays a dialog box that says the system is running low on virtual memory and that instructs the user to increase the size of the paging file.

Several minutes later, the system displays another dialog box stating there is not enough memory to get all the records. An "out of memory" message is also displayed in the lower-right corner of DNS Manager, followed by another message stating that the system is running low on virtual memory.

The DNS Admin tool hangs when there are a lot of records for a particular node because it is running out of the RPC buffer space.

To resolve this problem, you will need to edit the Registry to increase the default RPC Buffer size for the DNS Admin (refer to the following procedure).

1. Run Registry Editor (`Regedt32.exe`).

2. Go to the following key:
   `HKEY_LOCAL_MACHINE\Software\Microsoft\DNS Administrator`

3. On the Edit menu, click Add Value and use the following entry:
   `Value name: RpcBufferAlloc`
   `Data type: REG_Dword`

```
Data: 0-FFFFFFFF
Default: 800(2048)
Description: This parameter determines the Size of the RPC Buffer
Allocation used by the DNS Administrator.
```

4. Repeat steps 2 and 3 for the following key:
   ```
   HKEY_CURRENT_USER\Software\Microsoft\DNS Administrator
   ```

5. Increase the value of RpcBufferAlloc to 16384.

6. Close Registry Editor.

If one or more of your zones contain more than 65,553 records, you may face another problem: When you view your DNS zones with DNS Manager, it may stop responding.

If you check Performance Monitor or Task Manager, you may notice that DNS Manager is using up to 90 percent of the CPU utilization.

Currently, no resolution exists for this issue. The DNS server will start and continue to function correctly, but DNS Manager stops responding. If you have zones with more than 65,553 records, you will need to edit these files using a text editor, such as WordPad or Edit.

Note
Remember to stop the DNS server service before editing the zone files, and restart the DNS server service after you have saved the changes to the zone files.

When you attempt to create any zone in DNS Manager, you may receive the following error:
```
The new zone could not be created because there is already a zone by this
name.
```
Event Viewer on your DNS server may also log one or more of the following event messages in the System event log:
```
Event ID    : 100
Source      : DNS
Description: DNS server could not open the file 'zone name'.
```
or
```
Event ID    : 104
Source      : DNS
Description: Could not open Database 'zone name' for DNS.
```
or
```
Event ID    : 150
Source      : DNS
Description: Could not create 'zone name'.
```
or
```
Event ID    : 242
Source      : DNS
Description: Encountered invalid Domain username.domainname.
```

The preceding event messages may be caused by either of the following:

- The user account that you are using to create the new zones contains one or more spaces in its name.
- The built-in SYSTEM account does not have FULL CONTROL permissions on `<NT_Root>\System32\DNS\`.

You can resolve these issues by doing one of the following:

- Rename the current user account, removing any spaces.
- If you have an NTFS partition, verify that the built-in SYSTEM account has FULL CONTROL permissions on the `%SystemRoot%\System32\DNS` folder:

```
Keywords      : ntnetserv NTSrv kberrmsg kbnetwork
Version       : WinNT:4.0
Platform      : winnt
Issue type    : kbprb
```

Managing Multiple Zones

Managing multiple zones takes a little skill and a lot of attention to keeping the databases organized and easy to read. The administrator must be concerned with IP address allocations and must have a scheme for assigning addresses to hosts. Typically, an administrator will have two zones to maintain: one for the forward lookups of domain names to find IP addresses, and an IN-ADDR zone for the lookups of IP addresses to find host names in reverse.

With DNS Manager, you can add or change Microsoft DNS servers and the zones managed by those servers. It is important to note that when creating the primary and secondary servers required for Internet connectivity, you must first define and configure a server by using DNS Manager. You then define one or more zones managed by that server. No fixed limit exists for the maximum number of zones you can manage.

The generally used reference to primary and secondary DNS servers is actually misleading when applied to the actual configuration and operation of DNS name servers. Because each DNS server manages its portion of the domain name space using the administrative grouping of a zone, data on the server is stored in zone files.

When data is transferred between primary and secondary servers, it is actually the zone files that are transferred. Microsoft DNS server is designed to incorporate this operational characteristic by assigning the primary or secondary characteristic to the zone file. In other words, the designation of the primary or secondary data source is configured on a zone-by-zone basis, not a server-by-server basis. You configure zone properties to create the primary or secondary data files.

Administrators who are fortunate enough to get experience with DNS from an ISP—especially one that performs domain hosting—may have to deal with thousands of zones on a single server. While the number of IN-ADDR domains may be relatively few, the zones for the standard domains can become a jumble of files that may or may not be easily identifiable by name alone. Careful management of zones and domains must be followed so that IP addresses don't get cross-referenced or, worse, assigned to the wrong domain altogether.

An administrator thinking of restructuring the network of his company might run across this type of question: Is it possible to have two primary domain name servers, each serving a zone and having a domain such as `taos.com` with the following nodes?

```
consult.taos.com
training.taos.com
advisory.taos.com
communication.taos.com
```

The administrator would like, for example, to assign one name server consult and training and the other name server advisory and communication.

No problem. You can do this, but you have to create five or three zones, depending on your preference:

```
primary: taos.com
primary: consult.taos.com
primary: training.taos.com
```

and

```
primary: advisory.taos.com
primary: communication.taos.com
```

Here, `taos.com` includes delegation to all subdomains of `taos.com`.

You could also leave two of the subdomains in the same zone as `taos.com`. That would leave you with the following configuration:

```
primary: taos.com
```

with `consult.taos.com` and `training.taos.com` in the taos.com zone and

```
primary: advisory.taos.com
primary: communication.taos.com
```

Adding the DNS Server, Primary, and Secondary Zones

The following procedures provide an example of how to add a Microsoft DNS server, primary zones, and secondary zones. This example assumes that the server managing the primary zone is configured on the local computer and that the server managing the secondary zone is located on a remote computer in the same network configured with Microsoft DNS server. In addition, this example illustrates that you can manage multiple computers configured with Microsoft DNS server from one central computer running DNS Manager.

Adding a DNS Server

Adding a DNS server involves two procedures, as follows:

- Adding the Microsoft DNS server that will manage the primary zone
- Adding a server on the local computer that represents a remote computer configured with Microsoft DNS server

To add the Microsoft DNS server that will manage the primary zone, follow these steps:

1. In DNS Manager, double-click the Server List icon.
2. On the DNS menu, click New Server. In the Add DNS Server dialog box, enter either the DNS server host name or the IP address (see Figure 15.3).
3. Click OK.

DNS Manager automatically creates the new server icon in the left pane of the DNS Manager window. To configure server properties, follow these steps:

1. Right-click the server icon, and click Properties.
2. Click the Interfaces tab (see Figure 15.4).
3. Type an IP address, and click Add.
4. Repeat the above steps until all IP addresses configured on the server are entered. You can enter a maximum of 15 IP addresses, even if the computer is a multihomed computer configured to support more than 15 IP addresses. If you do not specify IP addresses on the Interfaces tab and the computer is a multihomed computer configured with more than 15 IP addresses, you might encounter Event 410 or 520 errors. These errors occur in part because, if no IP addresses are specified, Microsoft DNS Manager by default attempts to monitor all IP addresses configured on the server computer.
5. If you are using a DNS forwarder to control access to the Internet, click the Forwarders tab and enter the IP address of the Microsoft DNS server that is designated as the forwarder (see Figure 15.5).
6. Click OK.

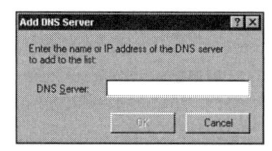

Figure 15.3 Adding a DNS server to manage the primary zone.

Managing Multiple Zones 215

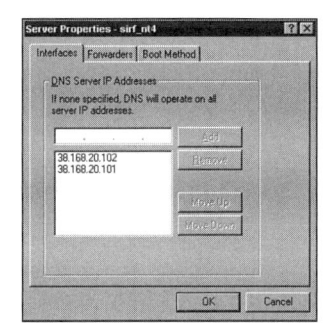

Figure 15.4 Specifying IP addresses for a DNS server.

To add a server on the local computer that represents a remote computer configured with Microsoft DNS server, follow these steps:

1. In DNS Manager, double-click the Server List icon.
2. Click New Server. In the Add DNS Server dialog box, enter either the DNS server host name for the remote computer or its IP address.
3. Click OK.

DNS Manager automatically adds a new server icon that represents the remote server in the left pane of the DNS Manager window.

If you follow the preceding procedures for a local and a remote server, the servers are added to DNS Manager on the local computer. Then you can configure the remote server properties.

Note
Before creating a zone, make sure you have correctly configured TCP/IP Properties by entering the correct host name and domain name for the local computer on the DNS page in the Microsoft TCP/IP Properties dialog box. To reach this dialog box, click the Start button, point to Settings, and click Control Panel. Double-click the Network icon, click the Protocols tab, click TCP/IP Protocol in the Network Protocols list, and then click Properties (see Figure 15.6).

Figure 15.5 Designating an MS-DNS server as a forwarder.

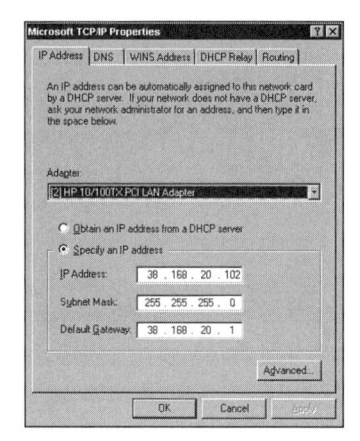

Figure 15.6 Ensuring proper TCP/IP configuration.

Adding a Primary Zone

To add a primary zone, follow these steps:

1. Right-click the local server icon, and click New Zone to start the zone wizard.
2. Click Primary, and then click Next (see Figure 15.7).

    The zone wizard indicates that all information has been entered (see Figure 15.8). The wizard then automatically creates the zone and zone file and adds SOA and NS records to the zone file.

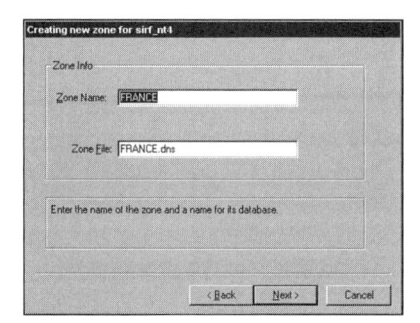

Figure 15.7 Adding a new zone.

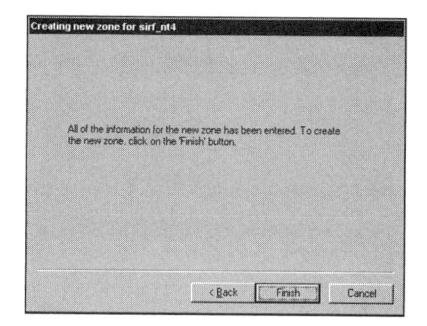

Figure 15.8 Confirming that a new zone has been created.

TIP

To create a reverse-lookup zone, use the preceding procedure and use a zone name that complies with the reverse-lookup name format (nnn.nnn.nnn.in-addr.arpa). For example, the reverse-lookup zone to contain PTR records for IP addresses 38.168.20.94 through 38.168.20.254 would be named .168.38.in-addr.arpa.

Whenever possible, create a reverse-lookup zone for each zone before adding A records for computers contained in that zone. By doing so, you can use the automatic Create PTR Record option in the Add Host dialog box.

Adding a Secondary Zone

To add a secondary zone, follow these steps:

1. Right-click the remote server icon, and click New Zone to start the zone wizard.
2. Click Secondary, and enter the requested information.
3. Click Next. The zone wizard indicates that all information has been entered and then automatically creates the zone. The zone wizard doesn't add records to the zone file because it's a secondary zone. The secondary zone appears blank until there's a zone transfer.

Changing Zone Properties

After you have successfully added a zone, you can perform additional configuration by changing the zone properties. Figure 15.9 illustrates the Zone Properties dialog box for a normal zone.

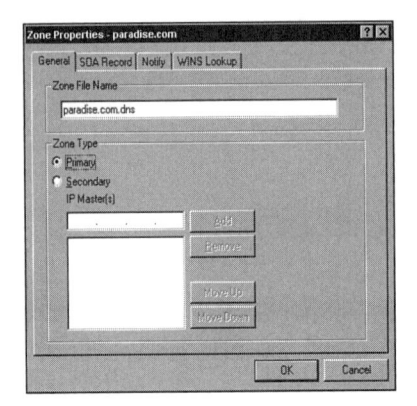

Figure 15.9 Zone Properties and general information.

After you create a zone, you can add A, PTR, and other Resource Records for computers logically contained within the zone. To display a menu of actions that you can perform on the zone, point to the zone folder and right-click.

The two menu commands you can use to add information about the computers in the zone are New Host and New Record.

You can use the New Host command to add A and PTR records for the zone computers that have statically assigned IP addresses. The A Resource Record provides the name-to-IP address mapping used in name resolution. The PTR Resource Record contains the reverse-lookup (IP address-to-name) mapping that is needed by some programs.

You can use the New Record command to add other types of DNS Resource Records, such as CNAME (alias), MX (mail exchange), or ISDN records.

Note

As with any server of importance, the administrator must be sure to make backups routinely. If the server handles many different domains, the importance of good backups is intensified. No precautions are required in performing backups, as the zone files themselves are merely text files, and the configuration information will either reside in a text file or the Registry. To back up the Registry, the administrator should use the REG-BACK.EXE utility from the Windows NT Resource Kit. If the Registry is too large to fit on a floppy, archiving the information to another hard disk or tape is advisable. Also included in the Resource Kit is the REGREST.EXE utility for restoring the hive.

The Registry subtree is divided into parts, called *hives*. A hive is a discrete body of keys, subkeys, and values that are rooted at the top of the Registry hierarchy. By default, most hive files (Default, Sam, Security, Software, and System) are stored in the *SystemRoot*%\system32\config folder.

When making changes to the zones with the DNS Manager, the administrator should be aware of the Update Server Data Files... selection under the DNS menu.

Selecting this menu item writes the new data to the appropriate database immediately. The data will also be written out upon termination of the DNS Manager or, if configured to do so, at specified time intervals.

Changing a DNS Server's IP Address

An administrator should not have to change the IP address of a server very often. Once in a while, however, it might be necessary. The act of changing the IP address itself is relatively straightforward and simple. The loss of service that might occur if proper planning does not precede such a change, however, can be distressing. First, verify whether this name server is registered with InterNIC (InterNIC registration services are provided by Network Solutions, Inc.). Second, if the name server is registered with the InterNIC, is it a primary or a secondary server? If the machine is registered with the InterNIC, the registration information must be entered on a modification template, which is then submitted to InterNIC. If the name server is a primary, the modification template becomes that much more important.

Changing the Registration

The modification template is called the Host Template and should be used to update the IP address and/or the host name of a name server. Version 3.5 of the Domain Name Registration Agreement does not allow changes to the IP address or name of a host. The Domain Name Registration Agreement does, however, allow the appropriate party to replace the current name server for a domain with a different existing name server. In other words, the Domain Name Registration Agreement can be used to switch a domain to a new service provider, but it cannot be used by an Internet Service Provider or a server administrator to alter the IP address or name of a host.

The Host Template is used to register, delete, and modify information associated with a name server. To see information currently associated with a name server, search WHOIS for the NIC handle. If you have a name server already associated with certain domain names but don't know that name server's NIC handle, search WHOIS for that server's domain name or IP address.

The WHOIS program verifies that the domain is available. To use WHOIS, connect to http://www.internic.net/ through a Web browser.

Fortunately, if the IP address or host name of a name server must be changed, all the domain records associated with the host do not need to be updated. When the IP address or host name of a server is updated, all domain records associated with the host are automatically updated. This occurs because both the name and the IP address of a name server are associated with a NIC Handle, and all domain records are associated with the host by its NIC Handle.

A NIC Handle is a unique identifier, which can be up to 10 alphanumeric characters, that is assigned to each domain name record, contact record, and network record in Network Solutions' domain name database. NIC Handles should be used on registration forms whenever possible, as they save time and help to ensure accuracy in the records.

The registration forms are used to submit and process registration requests. These forms, which include the Domain Name Registration Agreement, are used to register new domain names, new contacts for domain names, and new hosts (name servers) as well as to update domain name, contact, and host records. Both Web versions and Plaintext (ASCII) versions of the forms exist.

Before actually submitting the modification request, make sure that the name server is configured to answer on the new address, and make sure that a new server has been built to take the place of the old one. InterNIC will not process requests that it cannot verify. If the machine claimed as primary does not answer requests, InterNIC will not make the changes. If the change is simply a new IP address, make sure that a secondary address is configured and accessible. If the change entails building a new server, the machine should be built and should run the DNS server with a complete set of maps. If the name server to be changed is the primary or a master secondary, the other consideration involves making sure that the secondaries that perform zone transfers from this host are updated as well. If not, the administrator will be in for quite a surprise when all the secondaries' zones expire and they stop answering queries.

The final thing to remember is the clients. Any clients that were pointed to the changing name server will need to have their resolver maps changed as well. For hosts that are using DHCP, this may be a trivial matter of making the changes in the DHCP data and setting a lease time that is appropriate. The key to changing any active service is to plan the changes and ensure attention to all the details.

Changing the IP Configuration

Figure 15.10 shows the Network Control Panel TCP/IP properties where you'll need to make a change of address for the computer itself.

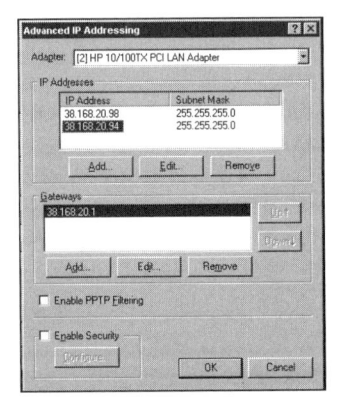

Figure 15.10 Changing a computer's IP address.

If you have not already changed the computer's IP address, you'll need to perform the following steps:

1. Add a second IP address to the network adapter.
2. Run DNS Manager.
3. Update the DNS server information.
4. Remove the second IP address.

The steps involved for carrying out these four processes are summarized in the text that follows.

Adding a Second IP Address to the Network Adapter

To add a second IP address to the network adapter, follow these steps:

1. Open the Network Control Panel and select the Protocol tab.
2. Select TCP/IP, and click on the Properties tab.
3. Click Advanced, and then click Add.
4. Enter the old IP address, and click Add.
5. Close the Control Panel, and reboot the computer.

Running DNS Manager

The next thing you need to do is run DNS Manager, as follows:

1. Right-click the Server List, and select New Server.
2. Enter the new IP address, and click OK.
3. Select the old IP address and right-click, then select Delete Server from the menu and confirm.

Updating DNS Server Information

After running DNS Manager, you must update the DNS server information, as follows:

1. Select the new IP address in the left pane.
2. In the menu, select DNS option, and then click Update Server Data Files....

Removing the Second IP Address

Finally, you must remove the second IP address, as follows:

1. In the Network Control Panel, click the Protocol tab.
2. Select TCP/IP, and click Properties.

3. Click Advanced, and select the old address; then click Remove.
4. Close the Control Panel, and reboot the computer.

Viewing DNS Server Registry Entries

If you want to take a look in the Registry, the entries for the DNS servers are stored in the location `HKEY_LOCAL_MACHINE\SYSTEM\CurrentControlSet\Services\Tcpip\Parameters` under the `NameServer` value. Each entry should be separated by a space. Using the Resource Kit utility (`REG.EXE`), the command to change would be as follows:

```
reg update HKLM\System\CurrentControlSet\Services\Tcpip\Parameters\
NameServer="38.168.20.89 38.168.20.90" \\<machine name>
```

Here, `38.168.20.89` and `38.168.20.90` are the addresses of the DNS servers you wanted to configure. Note that this command sets the value (it does not append), so make sure that you enter the existing DNS servers as well as the new ones.

This may be useful for granting users access to the Internet by remotely updating their Registry with the correct DNS servers to use.

16

Security Issues

This chapter will review:

- **Spoofing Name Queries.** Spoofing can make your DNS server trust an untrustworthy host that's impersonating a valid secondary server. Unscrupulous hackers use this technique to get copies of zone files, and when your internal computer addresses are known, they're vulnerable to direct attacks.
- **Firewalls.** Firewalls are dedicated devices or computers running special software to limit what can pass through them in order to protect one or more networks from unwanted access. Most firewalls use two or more network cards where at least one is connected to the Internet and one to an internal network.
- **WWW Security.** As Web servers and browsers become more powerful and popular, they also become more capable of creating holes that can breach security. This section describes some Web security issues and techniques you can use for protection.
- **FTP Security.** FTP servers are useful for posting software and electronic documents for download, and they can even be accessed through Web browsers. They present some security problems that this section describes.
- **Mail Security: SMTP, POP, and IMAP.** Mail servers are subject to a variety of attacks. This section describes a few potential security holes and suggests how you can use DNS MX records and mail relays to reduce exposure.

Spoofing Name Queries

THIS CHAPTER DOESN'T COVER ALL THE SECURITY ISSUES you should consider when setting up a network connected to the Internet. The intention here is to help you understand those issues most closely related to DNS services. Last in the chapter are a few references to books and Web sites you can use to help you establish a secure network for DNS and other services.

Spoofing Name Queries

DNS Spoofing—the process by which hackers penetrate the system and alter the host IP mappings to point to bogus servers—is possible, but fairly difficult to accomplish. The biggest issue with an attack on the DNS server is the integrity of the zone information, and the possible redirection of requests to alternate hosts. The bright side is that this sort of attack is fairly easy to detect and correct.

Nslookup, ping, and traceroute can identify machines that have been altered (especially to an IP address that does not belong to the site or domain). If there seems to be a problem, query other authoritative servers and check the results. If the attack happened some time ago, the information may be cached around the net, but will expire and return to normal operation.

The difficulty lies in determining how and where the hacker gained access to the system to make changes in the first place. Intrusion detection packages and auditing can aid in tracking down a suspected hacker. There are a number of other books and resources that are available that deal specifically with these topics.

The benefit to a hacker manipulating zones is that he can use redirections to point users to machines under his own control. The hacker can then use this setup to capture information from unsuspecting users regarding logins or mail accounts, and even gain access to other hosts on the remote network.

One way to reduce the risk of this sort of attack is to use reverse lookups as validation. If a host is impersonating another server, the reverse lookup can be used to make sure that the IP address maps back to the same hostname. This is actually done by some FTP servers before they allow downloads.

The best policy for setting up a name server is to try to make it as secure as possible. Don't use a machine that has a lot of user login activity or provides other interactive services.

A hacker can pose a false machine as an authoritative server for a domain and pollute the cache for other name servers on the Internet by intercepting and answering queries.

Another concern is a hacker performing a zone transfer from your name server to get addresses. The best way to reduce the risk of transferring data to any illegitimate secondary server is to list the legitimate DNS servers in the DNS Manager Notify list, and then to select the Only Allow Access From Secondaries Included on Notify List check box, as shown in Figure 16.1.

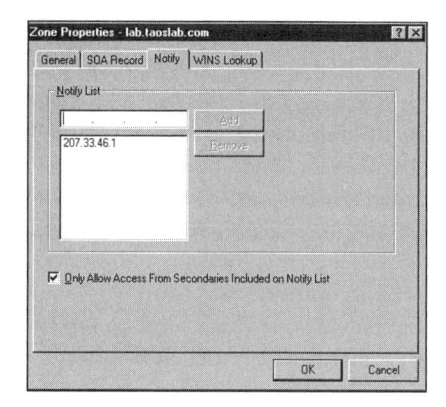

Figure 16.1   Identifying legitimate secondary servers in the Notify List.

Firewalls

When using DNS with or through firewalls, you must consider two things: the security policies of the site or organization and the type of firewall that is going to be used. You must examine the security policies to determine what traffic will be allowed to go through the firewall. Also, the type of firewall being used will determine how data is handled between the private network, the DMZ (demilitarized zone), and the Internet.

Firewalls can have several capabilities, including packet filtering and proxies, with caveats concerning *stateful inspection*. Stateful inspection is a mechanism that stores information on packets going in and out of the firewall to determine the state of a session. The state is used by the inspection agent to determine whether packets should be allowed through the firewall.

Combinations of authentication, encryption, and high levels of auditing give you several powerful tools. Many firewall solutions provide DNS support directly, or have templates for easily setting up a configuration to pass, or proxy name service requests from one side to another. For the administrator who has to design the security policy for a site, there are at least two schools of thought:

- Make everything accessible and be sure that there are good backups.
- Restrict access to every machine, and allow only that traffic into your network that is absolutely necessary.

In the first scenario, a site may not even use basic filters on the router that acts as their gateway to the Internet. In the second situation, only certain ports and protocols are allowed, and then, for only a few specifically named machines, and these machines would be further protected from each other on the same network.

Protecting machines from each other necessitates, at minimum, that you set up separate administrator accounts with different passwords on each. The goal is to make the machines as independent as possible so that a hacker who's managed to gain access to one machine cannot use its accounts to also access other systems in the DMZ. By analogy, this is like separating airplanes and volatile fuels on a military airfield to minimize the damage caused when any one target is destroyed. Using separate accounts makes it much harder to exploit many machines at once.

DNS can be handled in as many different ways as firewalls can be configured. The key thing to remember is that an authoritative name server must be reachable for the outside world to resolve any public hosts at the local site, and external name servers must be reachable (through some mechanism, such as forwarders and proxies) by internal hosts for lookups on other domains.

The best protection for the name server is to make sure that you back up the zone and configuration information regularly. You should also ensure that this information is accessible in the event that the files need to be recovered. The concept of hiding a domain from the outside world is certainly good protection, but it offers little to the users inside the network who want to reach the outside world.

You can set up a domain such that the primary name server is kept inside the firewall (where it is safe) and a secondary is put outside to handle lookups by external hosts. This is a good solution if the administrator doesn't mind letting the outside world see the entire domain. Then there is the concept of the split-brain DNS, with two versions of a domain, one for public consumption and the other for the organization's internal use.

In most organizations today, the users of hosts in the domain need Internet access for the Web and email, at the very minimum. In these situations, the idea of hiding a domain is not a viable solution. If security is needed, and the administrator wants to limit what the outside world sees of the domain, a split-brain DNS, or some other method of limiting the hosts that are published to the world, is probably the best solution. Chapter 10, "Designing Your DNS Service(s)," has a description and drawing depicting a split-brain setup.

A traditional split-brain DNS uses two primary servers: one inside the firewall and the other outside. The external primary name server that resides outside the firewall will be furnished with a minimum number of entries for its zone files, typically the MX records for the domain, WWW and FTP hosts, and, depending on the type of firewall, some entries may be used for reverse lookups by outside hosts to sessions that are established from inside the firewall.

Some firewalls use address translation to reassign a predetermined list of IP addresses. In order for these IP addresses to be useful for certain transactions, a reverse lookup that maps to a valid host name may be required. These host names would be handled by the external primary name server, as there could be no resolution by the internal name server. The internal primary DNS server would be populated with the entries for every host in the domain (including the external hosts). The internal DNS would also be set up to forward to the external DNS, as well as slave from the external DNS. See Figure 10.6 in Chapter 10 for an example of a split-brain DNS server installation.

This will result in a name server which, when queried for information by a client resolver that it cannot answer, forwards the query to the external name server. Because the internal name server is configured to slave from the external, the internal name server will not attempt to resolve the query itself, but must wait for the external server to provide an answer. The firewall, configured to allow name server queries to be passed only between these hosts, would then prevent queries from outside hosts from reaching the internal name server.

Because both the internal and external name servers are primaries, no zone transfers need to go through the firewall. The difficulty with this arrangement is that the administrator has to maintain two separate sets of zone files, not to mention the additional maintenance that's needed if there are also secondary servers on each side of the firewall.

The key steps to remember when setting up a DNS server to work through a firewall are as follows:

1. Build Primary internal DNS and secondaries.
2. Build Primary external DNS and secondaries.
3. Decide which hosts to publish in zones.
4. Register the external hosts with the InterNIC (as these are the ones that will be "seen").
5. Allow name service through the firewall for designated hosts only.
6. Test the design and make sure it works as expected.

The last step should be obvious, but it's always wise to make sure that the design works, especially from an external site, to make sure that only the information that the administrator wants published is available. Also, testing from the inside is required to make sure that the firewall is properly configured and external domains are resolvable by users inside the firewall.

WWW Security

When it comes to the World Wide Web, just about everyone seems to have a Web site these days. The trick is to make the Web server secure and protect its content. The problem is that having a Web presence means hanging a machine out for everyone to see. (After all, if they can't see the machine, there's not much point in having a Web server on it, is there?) The exception to that rule is the intranet site targeted to the internal staff of an organization.

A number of products and technologies are available to help secure the information on your machines. The solution that has been around probably the longest is packet filtering. An administrator can protect the Web server by putting a filter in front of the machine that allows only Web traffic to hit the server, and nothing else. Blocking access to such things as Telnet, FTP, and mail from this machine will limit the types of attacks that can be made on it.

Proxies also can be valuable for protecting a Web site because the remote users never actually get to the real Web server. Remote user requests are intercepted by the proxy servers, which then query the Web server. The proxy servers then pass the information back to the remote user, requesting the data.

A number of redirection schemes also can be employed, where the Web server's name resolves to a virtual IP through DNS. When http requests come to the virtual IP, the requests can be redirected to the actual server. In this situation, the remote user does get the information from the actual Web server, but the real IP address of the Web server is hidden from the requestor. These redirection schemes can also provide a great deal of flexibility for load balancing and high-availability solutions.

FTP Security

FTP servers have their own vulnerabilities, but one way to help secure the FTP server is through the use of reverse lookups. Many FTP servers log connections that are made by remote hosts, capturing the host name and IP address. Reverse lookups are used to verify that the host name and IP address that were used to establish the connection match. Although this may not seem like much in terms of security, the logs will at least indicate a true IP address and host name, should a break-in occur via the FTP server.

The purpose of the reverse lookup is to make sure that the IP address and the host name match either way. If the host name and IP address do not match, the connection is refused by the FTP server when the download is attempted. Along with the use of reverse lookups, filters can also be applied to prevent other types of traffic from reaching the FTP host.

One mistake administrators often make when setting up an anonymous FTP site is allowing anonymous users to write to directories. This can create vulnerability to problems such as hackers attempting to fill a file system and create instability in the system, or generating numerous login requests that can lead to high levels of CPU and memory utilization. This sort of attack can create a denial of service for both the server and the network segment that the server is attached to.

Having anonymous FTP is very useful and, in some situations, a necessity; however, putting limits on the number of connections that the FTP server will allow and disallowing anonymous writes can prevent a lot of hardship for the administrator. Anonymous FTP also presents the problem of passwords passing in clear, readable text that anyone with a network-traffic snooping or tracing tool can capture.

Mail Security: SMTP, POP, and IMAP

The security advisories are full of warnings about exploits against sendmail, Exchange, IMAP servers, and so on. How mail is handled by a domain can largely depend on the setup of the name servers and firewalls. In general, POP and IMAP services should be kept behind the firewall to protect the users' mail, directories, and especially passwords from external entities that could use this information to invade the site.

Generally speaking, you should use some host in the DMZ as a relay for both inbound and outbound mail. Using the relay for inbound mail, the actual mail spool can be placed on the inside of the firewall, which would be configured to allow mail connections from the DMZ host only. In the same manner, the relay would be used for outbound mail to hide the internal machines, and could include special rules for the addressing to have all outbound mail addressed simply by the user@the.domain. This simplifies the ability of recipients to be able to respond to mail addressed to a domain, and helps protect the identity of the originating machine.

Of course, a display of the full headers will reveal the path that a mail message has traversed, but if the originating host is hidden behind a firewall and is not resolvable through the external DNS server for an organization, this is not an issue.

MX records on the internal name servers can be used to direct mail from internal hosts to the relay for any addresses that are not local. The relay, upon receiving the mail messages, would perform another lookup (using the external name servers) to send the mail on to its Internet destination. The relay would also be set up to forward any inbound mail for the domain to a specific host inside the firewall, which would then be responsible for distributing mail to internal users and subdomains via mail aliases. Again, MX records would be used for distribution to hosts inside the domain.

Summary

This chapter did not cover all the security issues you'll consider when setting up a network connected to the Internet. It only describes those most closely related to DNS services. The following are a few good books on security you can consult to help you establish a secure site for DNS and other services:

- *Firewalls Complete*, Marcus Goncalves, McGraw-Hill. ISBN 0-07-024645-9.
- *Guide to Windows NT Security*, Charles B. Rutstein, McGraw-Hill. ISBN 0-07-057833-8.
- *Internet Firewalls and Network Security*, Karanjit S. Siyan and Chris Hare, New Riders Publishing. ISBN 1-56205-437-6.
- *Internet Security: Professional Reference, Second Edition*, Derek Atkins, et. al., New Riders. ISBN 1-56205-760-X.
- *Windows NT Security Guide*, Stephen A. Sutton, Addison-Wesley. ISBN 0-201-41969-6.

- *Windows NT Security Handbook*, Tom Sheldon, Osborne McGraw-Hill. ISBN 0-07-882240-8.
- *Maximum Security: A Hacker's Guide to Protecting your Internet Site and Network*, Anonymous (an experienced hacker), Sams Net. ISBN 1-57521-268-4.

Troubleshooting Tools and Utilities

This chapter will review:

- **nslookup.** The nslookup tool is included with Windows NT and always comes with the BIND software package. This powerful diagnostic tool offers many options and provides a way to trace DNS queries from start to finish. This section explains how to use it.
- **dig.** The dig tool is less intimidating than nslookup. It comes with BIND and provides much of the same information.
- **ping.** The ping tool provides the simplest method to find out if another host can be reached over the network. This is probably the most-used diagnostic tool for TCP/IP.
- **tracert.** As its name implies, the tracert tool indicates what route through the network a packet will take to go from one computer to another.
- **Netlab.** Netlab is a Swiss army knife of network tools. This shareware product you can download at no cost provides some of the same functionality of several standalone tools in a simple, friendly, graphical user interface.
- **ipconfig.** A built-in command-line tool for Windows NT, ipconfig provides basic information about how each TCP/IP network interface is configured.
- **winipcfg.** A built-in GUI tool for Windows 95, winipcfg provides basic information about how each TCP/IP network interface is configured.

- **netstat.** A built-in command-line tool for Windows 95 and Windows NT, netstat reveals more than basic configuration about each TCP/IP interface; it shows routes, connections, ports, and connection statistics.
- **nbtstat.** A built-in command-line tool for Windows 95 and Windows NT, nbtstat reveals NetBIOS information, including connections and statistics.

nslookup

The nslookup tool is one of the most commonly used tools for manually performing DNS queries. This particular tool is somewhat unique in that it can emulate both a standard client resolver and a server. Used as a client resolver, nslookup can directly query a server for information. Used as a server, nslookup can perform zone transfers from a primary or master server. This tool can be used in two modes: noninteractive (which is typically typed from the command line as `nslookup www.taos.com`), and interactive (which is entered by typing `nslookup` and pressing Enter with no arguments). Options can be passed to nslookup in either mode, but interactive mode is more often used in times of trouble with the name server. Windows NT does have a version of nslookup that is installed with TCP/IP networking that can be used on Windows NT Workstation and Windows NT Server alike. In interactive mode, you can obtain help by typing `help` or `?` at the > prompt. Doing so provides basic information on the commands covered in the sections that follow.

help (?) Command

The `help` or `?` command displays the help information with a very brief summary of the commands. The syntax for this command is as follows:

```
> help
```

or

```
> ?
```

exit Command

The `exit` command enables you to quit nslookup. If you type `quit`, nslookup treats it as a host name and tries to resolve it, as it will any other string that is not a valid command. The syntax for the `exit` command is as follows:

```
> exit
```

finger Command

The standard `finger` command applies to the current host. The term "current" refers to the most recent successful lookup performed. If the last command was for an "A" record query for `www.taos.com` (which returned an IP address in which the `finger`

<username> command was entered), this would basically be the same as entering a finger command for the <username>@hostname. While in nslookup, standard redirects can be used to capture the information in a file. The syntax for the finger command is as follows:
> finger <username> [> filename]

lserver Command

The lserver command first uses a local name server to perform a lookup on another name server and then sets the name server that was just resolved as the default. This operation can be useful when you have reset the default server to a host that is not responding or that has failed to respond. Using the lserver command, the default name server can be reset without having to rely on the current default name server. The syntax for this command is as follows:
> lserver <host name>

server Command

The server command is very similar to the lserver command in that it resolves another name server and sets that server as the default. The difference is that the server command uses the current default server to resolve the new server. The syntax for the server command is as follows:
> server <host name>

root Command

The root command enables the user to change the default name server for a given session to the root server listed by the set all command. The default root server is a.root-servers.net. The default name server is set to a.root-servers.net. by issuing the root command. The syntax for this command is as follows:
> root??

ls Command

The ls command, with its associated options, enables the user to view the contents of zone files for DNS domains. With no options specified, the default displays the host names and IP addresses for a domain. Other options can be specified to vary the scope of the listing. Again, standard redirects are available to capture information. In fact, using the ls command is one way of performing a manual zone transfer to a client or secondary name server. The syntax for this command is as follows:
> ls [option] <domain name> [> filename]

The options available for the ls command are as follows:

- `-t <RR>`. Lists all records of the specified type
- `-a`. Lists all aliases of computers in the domain (same as `-t CNAME`)
- `-d`. Lists ALL records for the domain (same as `-t ANY`)
- `-h`. Lists the CPU and OS information about the hosts in the domain (same as `-t HINFO`)
- `-s`. Lists the well-known services of hosts in the domain (same as `-t WKS`)

set Command

The `set` command modifies operating parameters for nslookup and essentially consists of a prefix used to offset a number of other subcommands. The first subcommand to become familiar with is the `set all` command, which will display the current operating parameters with which the queries will be executed. The `set` commands can be entered in such a way that each command is unique, so completing the command is not necessary. The commands will be illustrated using brackets to indicate the point of completion. Some versions of the commands include an implicit `[no]` to turn off a feature as well. Example syntax for the `set all` command is as follows:

```
> set all
Default Server:  socrates.taoslab.com
Address:  207.33.46.1
```

The options in this example syntax for the `set all` command are as follows:

- nodebug
- defname
- search
- recurse
- nod2
- novc
- noignoretc
- port=53
- querytype=A
- class=IN
- timeout=5
- retry=4
- root=a.root-servers.net.
- domain=taoslab.com
- srchlist=taoslab.com

Other subcommands that fall under the `set` command are as follows:

- `set class` or `set cl`
- `set [no]debug` or `set [no]deb`
- `set [no]d2`
- `set [no]defname` or `set [no]def`
- `set domain` or `set do`
- `set [no]ignore` or `set [no]ig`
- `set port` or `set po`
- `set querytype` or `set q`
- `set [no]rec[urse]` or `set [no]rec`
- `set ret[ry]` or `set ret`
- `set ro[ot]` or `set ro`
- `set [no]sea[rch]` or `set [no]sea`
- `set srch[list]` or `set srch`
- `set ti[meout]` or `set ti`
- `set ty[pe]` or `set ty`
- `set [no]v[c]` or `set [no]v`

Using the `set` commands can require some experimentation to obtain the desired effect. The sections that follow provide some hints as to the functional purpose of each option.

set class Command Option

The `set class` option is used to set the appropriate protocol for the class of the query. The default is the Internet class; other options are Chaos, Hesiod, and ANY. The syntax for this command option is as follows:

```
>set class=<class name>
```

set [no]debug Command Option

The `set [no]debug` option turns on (or off) standard debugging. In debug mode, information about the query sent to the server and the answer is printed in a formatted text display. Default operation is `nodebug`. The syntax for this command option is as follows:

```
> set debug
> set nodebug
```

set [no]d2 Command Option

The `set [no]d2` option turns on (or off) the exhaustive debugging, in which every packet for the query and answer that are sent to or received from the server are printed. The default mode of operation is `nod2`. The syntax for this command option is as follows:
```
>set d2
>set nod2
```

set [no]defname Command Option

Setting the `defname` option assigns the default domain name to be appended to any query for a name that does not contain dots (.) in the name. The `defname` command is the default mode of operation, though it can be disabled. No arguments exist, as the default domain name is set elsewhere. The syntax for this command option is as follows:
```
set defname
set nodefname
```

set domain Command Option

The `set domain` command option actually sets the default domain name that will be used by `defname`. The default is the local host domain, if one is assigned, but it can be changed to match any domain. The syntax for this command option is as follows:
```
set domain=<domain name>
```

set [no]ignore Command Option

The `set [no]ignore` option enables nslookup to ignore received packets with the truncation errors flag set during a query, although the default is `noignore`. When nslookup receives a truncated packet (usually a UDP packet), it means that all the information could not be put into the packet. With `noignore`, nslookup retries the query using TCP. TCP responses can be larger, thereby allowing more information to be received and hopefully completing the answer. The syntax for this command option is as follows:
```
>set ignore
>set noignore
```

set port Command Option

The default port number assignment for DNS is 53 (TCP and UDP). Using the `set port` option, a DNS server can be configured to use another port. This is generally done when debugging. The syntax for this command option is as follows:
```
set port=<number>
```

set querytype Command Option

The `set querytype` (or `set type`) command option changes the type of information for which the query looks. Changing the query type modifies the question asked of the name server to reflect the information required. For example, if the user wants to see the mail exchange (MX) records for a given domain, the query type would be set to MX. By default, the query would look for an A record to match a host/domain name. If the query is sent with an IP address in the question, then the resolver reverses the address, and adds the `in-addr.arpa.` domain, and looks for a PTR record. The syntax for this command option is as follows:
   >set querytype=<value>

The values that you can set for this option are as follows:

- **A**. Finds an IP address for the host/domain
- **ANY**. Finds all information about the host/domain
- **CNAME**. Finds canonical name for an alias
- **GID**. Finds a group identifier for a group name
- **HINFO**. Finds host CPU and OS type
- **MB**. Finds mailbox domain name
- **MG**. Finds mail group member
- **MINFO**. Finds mailbox information
- **MR**. Finds mail rename information
- **MX**. Finds mail exchange information
- **NS**. Finds name servers for the host/domain
- **PTR**. Finds a host name that matches the IP address
- **SOA**. Displays the domain's start-of-authority
- **TXT**. Displays any text information about the host/domain
- **UID**. Finds a user ID for the host/domain
- **UINFO.** Finds the user's information
- **WKS**. Displays well-known services information

set [no]recurse Command Option

The `set [no]recurse` option enables nslookup to send recursive or iterative queries to another host. The default mode is `recurse`, which means that a name server that accepts the query should query other name servers if it does not have the answer. By setting `norecurse`, nslookup can emulate another name server sending an interactive query looking for hints about a domain. The syntax for this command option is as follows:
   >set recurse
   >set norecurse

set retry Command Option

The `set retry` option specifies the number of times a query will be sent before giving up the search. Typically, when a query is made, the client sends the query to the name server. If no response is received, the client resends the query up to the number of retries set. Each time the query is sent on a retry, the timeout value is doubled. This grants the name server a longer window in which to find the answer. The default value is typically 4. The syntax for this command option is as follows:

```
>set retry=<number>
```

set root Command Option

The `set root` option enables the default root server to be changed to another root server. The default root server is `a.root-servers.net` but could be changed to `e.root-servers.net`. The syntax for this command option is as follows:

```
>set root=<server name>
```

set [no]search Command Option

The `set [no]search` option provides for a search of the entries in the domain search list. If a query is received that contains at least one dot (.) in the name but that is not terminated with a dot, the domain names listed in the search are appended to the query until an answer can be found. One caveat here is that `defname` is disabled if `search` is on. Because `search` is the default, `defname` is not used unless the `set nosearch` command is given. The syntax for this command option is as follows:

```
>set search
>set nosearch
```

set srchlist Command Option

The `set srchlist` option permits a list of domain names to be specified that will be used with the search option. The domain names are added to any query that is not terminated with a dot. Unless otherwise set, the default search list contains the local host's domain name. This command also overrides the `set domain` command. The search list can contain up to six different domain names, separated by slashes. The syntax for this command option is as follows:

```
set srchlist=<domain 1>/<domain 2>/.../<domain 6>
```

set timeout Command Option

The `set timeout` option specifies the initial timeout period that the resolver will wait for a reply. If no reply is received before the timeout, the request is sent again and the timeout is doubled. Each time a reply is not received, the request is re-sent, up to the

number of retries, and the timeout period is doubled. The default timeout is five seconds. The syntax for this command option is as follows:
    set timeout=<number of seconds>

set [no]vc Command Option

The set vc, or virtual circuit, option enables the user to specify whether UDP (novc) or TCP (vc) should be used for the query. This could be used in conjunction with the ignore option. If the user wanted all the queries to be handled with TCP, then the ignore option could be set. The syntax for this command option is as follows:
    >set vc
    >set novc

Error Messages

The user should pay attention to a couple of error messages when using nslookup. The error messages (as described in the list that follows) can provide insight into the nature of a problem on the server.

- **Timed out.** This typically means that the server did not respond in the allocated time. Check to see that the server is alive and well, and review the event logs to see if any errors have occurred that may be affecting the service.

- **No response from server.** This means that DNS is not accepting queries at all. Check the service and event log for errors.

- **No records.** This would typically occur if, for example, the user requested an HINFO record for a domain, but no HINFO records are published in the domain.

- **Format error.** The name server is rejecting the query because of the format. This could be caused by an old version of some name server binary, or it might indicate corruption of the data on the network.

- **Server failure.** This typically occurs when there is a problem in a zone file. A misplaced semicolon or some other typo is usually the cause of this kind of failure. Check the event log for more detail, or contact the mailbox listing in the SOA if this error is coming from a remote machine.

- **Connection refused, or Network unreachable.** This could mean a couple of things. First, make sure that the name server can be pinged. If not, some kind of network failure has occurred. If the name server can be pinged, the error may be caused by the type of query you are sending. If you try to do an ls on a domain using some level of security (for example, if the option to allow transfers to hosts in the notify list only is set), the error may indicate that the user does not have permission to get a copy of the zone.

- **Refused.** This could be very similar to the last case, or it may mean that the query went to an interface that is not configured to answer name service queries. Check the configuration of the name server.

dig

The dig tool is another utility that can be used for querying name servers for information. This tool isn't built into Windows NT, but it does come free with the BIND distribution, and there's also an online interface to dig run by one of the computing centers at Berkeley (see Appendix A). The dig tool does not offer an interactive mode, but it has a number of options that can be specified from the command line. Typically, the syntax used with dig is as follows:

```
> dig [@server][domain][q-type][q-class]{q-opt}{d-opt}[%comment]
```

The options for the dig utility are defined in the following list.

- **[@server].** The name server at which the query is pointed. This enables the user to change the name server just as the server <name> option does with nslookup. The default value for this option is the first name server in resolver list.

- **[domain].** A name in the Domain Name System. Essentially, this is what the user is seeking.

- **[q-class] or [query-class].** Sets the class for the query; is one of (in, any, hs,...). The default value for this option is in.

- **[q-type] or [query-type].** Sets the type of Resource Record that the query is requesting. Just as nslookup uses the set querytype=<type>, the type will be one of (a, any, mx, ns, soa, hinfo, axfr, txt,...). The default value for this option is a.

- **{q-opt} or {query-option}.** Defined as one of the following values:
  - -x dot-notation-address. For resolution of dot notation addresses without having to specify PTR query-type.
  - -f file. For batch operations to resolve multiple addresses.
  - -T time. To specify a time interval between queries when operating in batch mode.
  - -p port. To specify an alternate port. The default value for this option is 53.
  - -Pping-string. After a successful query returns; also performs a ping for response time comparisons, and may specify a string to send in the ping packet.
  - -t query-type. Same as the q-type.
  - -c query-class. Same as q-class.
  - -envsav, -envset. Allows for modifying or setting environment variables. The dig tool can use a dig.env file for preset parameters.

- -[no]stick. Determines whether environment settings stick or not between successive queries. The default value is nostick.

- **{d-opt} or {dig-option}.** Is of the form +keyword=value, where the keyword is defined by the options in Table 17.1.

Table 17.1 **Keywords for the {d-opt} and {dig-option} Options**

[no]debug	[no]d2	[no]recurse
retry=#	time=#	[no]ko
[no]vc	[no]defname	[no]search
domain=NAME	[no]ignore	[no]primary
[no]aaonly	[no]sort	[no]cmd
[no]stats	[no]Header	[no]header
[no]ttlid	[no]cl	[no]qr
[no]reply	[no]ques	[no]answer
[no]author	[no]addit	pfdef
pfmin	pfset=#	pfand=#
pfor=#		

Most of these dig options are quite similar to the nslookup options, but these options are activated by a + if the option takes a value as part of its operation. Detailed help files are available with the distribution.

The defname and search options for the resolver don't work with dig, so the user should remember to use fully qualified domain names for queries.

The dig utility can be a very useful tool for testing and troubleshooting a name server. One very effective use of dig is obtaining a current copy of the root cache. By simply typing "dig > cache" at the command prompt, one can capture a complete root cache that can be compared to the existing file to see whether changes or updates need to be made. If dig is being used to test the local system, typing "dig domain.name" dumps the entire message from the server with the appropriate labels for the fields. The following example shows a typical implementation of the dig utility.

```
C:\> dig taos.com

; <<>> DiG 2.2 <<>> taos.com
;; res options: init recurs defnam dnsrch
;; got answer:
;; ->>HEADER<<- opcode: QUERY, status: NOERROR, id: 6
;; flags: qr aa rd ra; Ques: 1, Ans: 1, Auth: 1, Addit: 1
;; QUESTIONS:
;;      taos.com, type = A, class = IN

;; ANSWERS:
taos.com.       36000    A     204.188.112.62
```

```
;; AUTHORITY RECORDS:
taos.com.        36000      NS      laguna.taos.com.

;; ADDITIONAL RECORDS:
laguna.taos.com.      36000      A      204.188.112.62

;; Total query time: 10 msec
;; FROM: ws-hknief to SERVER: default -- 206.14.194.74
;; WHEN: Mon Apr 27 13:12:07 1998
;; MSG SIZE  sent: 26  rcvd: 79
```

ping

The ping utility is not really a DNS tool but rather a TCP/IP tool for determining whether a host is connected to a network. This tool also provides some level of functionality for answering network requests. The ping tool actually uses the Internet Control Message Protocol (ICMP) to send an echo request message to the remote host, and then it waits for a reply. If the reply is received before the timeout period (which can be set by the user), the round-trip time for the message and reply is displayed for the user. With the ping utility provided with Windows NT, a series of four requests is sent to the remote host by default. A variety of command-line options can be used with ping, providing a general syntax that resembles the following:

```
ping [-taf] [-n count] [-l length] [-i ttl] [-v tos] [-r count] [-s
count] [-j host-list] [-k host-list] [[-w timeout] destination
```

In this syntax, the following holds true:

- -t sets ping to work continuously until interrupted.
- -a is used to resolve addresses to host names.
- -f tells ping not to fragment packets. (If -l is set to a value that requires fragmentation, the message is not sent and a message is displayed concerning the DF [Don't Fragment] flag.)
- -n specifies a count for the number of ping requests to send.
- -l specifies a length for the echo request.
- -i specifies a time-to-live. (Values from 1 to 255 are accepted.)
- -v enables the user to change the type of service (TOS) field in the IP datagram.
- -r records the route for the requests and replies. A minimum of one and maximum of nine hosts can be recorded as specified by the value.
- -s produces timestamps for the number of hops that are specified by the value.
- -j specifies loose source route hosts with a maximum of nine host names. (Loose source routes provide for intermediate routers between hosts.)

- `-k` specifies strict source route hosts with a maximum of nine hosts. (Strict source routes do not allow for intermediate routers between hosts.)
- `-w` enables the user to specify a timeout interval for the replies, in milliseconds.
- `destination` can be a host name or an IP address.

traceroute *(tracert)*

The traceroute utility or `tracert` (the command on the Windows NT platform) establishes the relative path that packets must travel to get to the destination. A series of ICMP packets (note: most UNIX varieties of traceroute actually send UDP packets) is sent to the destination, but the ttl is set to 1 for the first three packets and is incremented by 1 on each subsequent set of three packets. Because routers are required to decrement the ttl by 1, the first packet will make it only to the first router. The router then sends an ICMP reply to the originator that the ttl has expired. This allows the `tracert` command to log the IP address of the first router. Hence, the second set of packets with a ttl of 2 will make it to the second router in the path when the ttl expires. Then another ICMP reply is sent to the originator. This process of incrementing the ttl continues until the destination answers, or until the max ttl (255) is reached. Command-line syntax and options for `tracert` are as follows:

    tracert [-d] [-h maxhops] [-j hostlist] [-w timeout] destination

In this syntax, the following holds true:

- `-d` tells `tracert` not to resolve IP addresses to host names.
- `-h` specifies the maximum number of hops to try (this essentially sets the max ttl).
- `-j` enables the user to specify loose source route hosts. (Again the maximum number is nine, just as with ping.)
- `-w` specifies the timeout interval, in milliseconds.
- `destination` can be a host name or an IP address.

Netlab

Netlab (current version is 1.3.6) is a freeware utility written by Alexander Danileiko (contact info: `adanil@ebs330.eb.uah.edu` or `http://www.eb.uah.edu/~adanil/`) that can be downloaded from a number of mirror sites. The easiest way to find a good download site is by searching on `http://www.shareware.com`. Although Netlab does not offer the broadest choice of configuration options, it does combine a nice set of tools in a single graphical user interface. The basic tool set that Netlab provides includes: finger, whois, Time, Quote, ping, traceroute, DNS, and a Port Scan. Netlab doesn't take a lot of disk space and seems to be fairly efficient in terms of memory use. This tool can be configured to work through a firewall and gives rudimentary info about the Winsock. The downside to this tool for DNS queries is its inability to set a query type. Netlab performs A record and PTR record queries, but there is no way to select an MX record—or anything else, for that matter. Maybe in the next release?

ipconfig

The ipconfig utility is a diagnostic command-line tool for Windows NT that shows how the computer's IP stack is configured. The syntax for the ipconfig tool is as follows:

```
ipconfig
ipconfig /all
ipconfig /release [adapter]
ipconfig /renew [adapter]
```

If you use ipconfig without arguments, it reveals the basic network configuration, as shown in the following example:

```
C:\> ipconfig

Windows NT IP Configuration

Ethernet adapter E100B1:

        IP Address. . . . . . . . . : 216.114.94.50
        Subnet Mask . . . . . . . . : 255.255.255.0
        Default Gateway . . . . . . : 216.114.94.1
```

If you use the optional /all switch, ipconfig reveals a good bit more than basic configuration information. It shows the IP host domain name, the DNS and WINS servers, the NetBIOS node type, the NetBIOS scope ID (if any), and other things. The tool also shows information for every network adapter, if more than one is installed.

If the client is configured to use a WINS server, Node Type is automatically set to Hybrid. Chapter 3, "How Windows Clients Use DNS and WINS," explains how the node type affects name resolution. The following example shows a typical implementation of the ipconfig tool using the /all switch.

```
C:\> ipconfig /all

Windows NT IP Configuration

        Host Name . . . . . . . . . : superdude.taos.com
        DNS Servers . . . . . . . . : 214.88.12.62
                                      216.14.14.254
        Node Type . . . . . . . . . : Hybrid
        NetBIOS Scope ID. . . . . . :
        IP Routing Enabled. . . . . : No
        WINS Proxy Enabled. . . . . : No
        NetBIOS Resolution Uses DNS : No
```

```
Ethernet adapter E100B1:

    Description . . . . . . . . : Intel EtherExpress PRO/100B PCI LAN
Adapter
    Physical Address. . . . . . : 00-A0-B9-68-B1-60
    DHCP Enabled. . . . . . . . : No
    IP Address. . . . . . . . . : 216.14.94.50
    Subnet Mask . . . . . . . . : 255.255.255.0
    Default Gateway . . . . . . : 216.14.94.1
    Primary WINS Server . . . . : 216.14.94.24
    Secondary WINS Server . . . : 216.14.94.25
```

If DHCP is enabled, you can use the optional /release switch with ipconfig to release the configuration. Likewise, the /renew switch reconfigures the IP stack directly from the DHCP server. The /release and /renew switches can also be used with an optional adapter name so that you can specify the adapter to change. This is important when the computer is multihomed.

winipcfg

The winipcfg utility is a graphical diagnostic tool for Windows 95 that, like ipconfig, shows how the computer's IP stack is configured. You can invoke winipcfg from a command window or from the RUN menu, or you can create a shortcut for the winipcfg.exe program itself. The syntax for the winipcfg tool is as follows:
```
winipcfg
winipcfg /all
```

Figure 17.1 shows the dialog box that appears when you type winipcfg. OK closes the tool, and Release releases the current adapter's configuration information. Renew renews the current adapter's configuration information.

The More Info button expands the dialog box to reveal additional information, as shown in Figure 17.2. If you type winipcfg /all, the same expanded dialog box appears immediately.

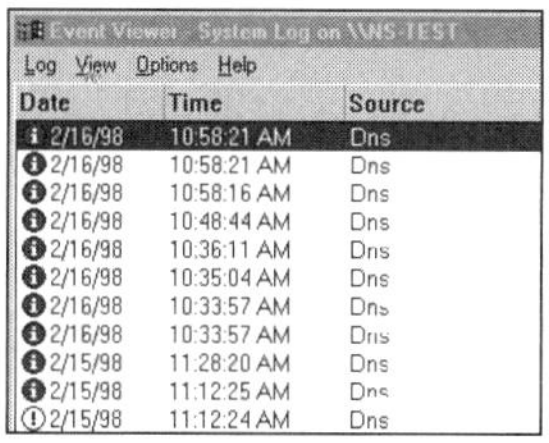

Figure 17.1 IP Configuration information revealed by the winipcfg utility.

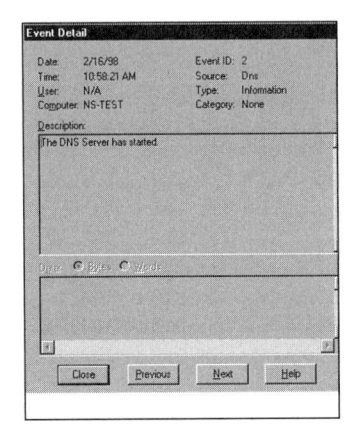

Figure 17.2 The /all option for winipcfg shows more information.

netstat

The netstat tool displays protocol statistics and the state of current TCP/IP connections. Note the difference: Netstat works for TCP/IP connections, and nbtstat works for NetBIOS connections. The syntax for the netstat utility is as follows:

```
C:\>netstat /?

Displays protocol statistics and current TCP/IP network connections.

NETSTAT [-a] [-e] [-n] [-s] [-p proto] [-r] [interval]

  -a        Displays all connections and listening ports. (Server-side
            connections are normally not shown).
  -e        Displays Ethernet statistics. This may be combined with the -s
            option.
  -n        Displays addresses and port numbers in numerical form.
  -p proto  Shows connections for the protocol specified by proto; proto
            may be tcp or udp. If used with the -s option to display
            per-protocol statistics, proto may be tcp, udp, or ip.
  -r        Displays the contents of the routing table.
  -s        Displays per-protocol statistics. By default, statistics are
            shown for TCP, UDP and IP; the -p option may be used to specify
            a subset of the default.
  interval  Redisplays selected statistics, pausing interval seconds
```

between each display. Press CTRL+C to stop redisplaying
statistics. If omitted, netstat will print the current
configuration information once.

nbtstat

The nbtstat tool checks the state of NetBIOS over TCP/IP connections and also returns NetBIOS session and name resolution statistics. In addition, this tool can be used to force an update of the local NetBIOS name cache. The syntax for the nbtstat utility is as follows:

```
C:\>nbtstat /?

Displays protocol statistics and current TCP/IP connections using
NBT(NetBIOS
over TCP/IP).
NBTSTAT [-a RemoteName] [-A IP address] [-c] [-n]
        [-r] [-R] [-s] [S] [interval] ]
  -a   (adapter status) Lists the remote machine's name table, given its
                        name.
  -A   (Adapter status) Lists the remote machine's name table, given its
                        IP address.
  -c   (cache)          Lists the remote name cache, including the IP
                        addresses.
  -n   (names)          Lists local NetBIOS names.
  -r   (resolved)       Lists names resolved by broadcast and via WINS.
  -R   (Reload)         Purges and reloads the remote cache name table.
  -S   (Sessions)       Lists sessions table with the destination IP
                        addresses.
  -s   (sessions)       Lists sessions table converting destination IP
                        addresses to host names via the hosts file.

     RemoteName   Remote host machine name.
     IP address   Dotted decimal representation of the IP address.
     interval     Redisplays selected statistics, pausing interval seconds
                  between each display. Press Ctrl+C to stop redisplaying
                  statistics
```

18

Dynamic Host Configuration Protocol (DHCP)

This chapter will review:

- **It's Not Dynamic DNS.** This section explains the problem of dynamically allocated IP addresses and the solution that DHCP is not.
- **What is DHCP?** This section gives the history of DHCP. DHCPs work hand-in-hand to register clients with Windows NT DNS.
- **How DHCP configures a client.** This section shows what transpires when the client and server interact.
- **Installing a DHCP server.** This section shows how to install the DHCP service on a Windows NT server.
- **Configuring a DHCP server.** Learn how to create and configure scopes.
- **Configuring clients to use DHCP.** Part of the beauty of DHCP is the minimal amount of configuration required on the client end. Presented in this section are a few things to keep in mind.
- **Checking the registration in WINS and DNS.** This section presents ways of checking that the whole DHCP-to-WINS-to-DNS registration is working.

So far, setting up DNS as a database of host names to IP address mappings has been fairly straightforward. Hosts on your network are assigned IP addresses, and then A records are created for each host. But every time you need to change the IP address of a host, you need to manually edit the DNS database. What if there were a way to automatically hand out IP addresses? What if there were a way to automatically update the DNS database with those addresses? DHCP, when used in conjunction with WINS and Microsoft DNS, provides that sort of functionality.

It's Not Dynamic DNS

Dynamic DNS (DDNS) is essentially an implementation of DNS binaries that allows zones to be dynamically updated whenever changes are made to the domain. Whether hosts are being added or removed, CNAMEs changed, or MX record preferences modified, Dynamic DNS is leading to a method of simpler administration for the name server. DDNS is being implemented with "hooks" in such a way that the name server can be updated by a DHCP server when hosts register and receive their leases, or through some other interface like a SQL database.

It appears that future versions of BIND will offer a series of API setups, and that administrators will be given a choice of back-end types for controlling zone manipulation. Although Microsoft DNS can use a WINS server to query for hosts that are not in the DNS databases, which gives it the appearance of being dynamic, it really is not a DDNS. The simple fact is, when MS DNS receives a query for a name it does not know, if configured to do so, it queries the WINS server much in the same way it would query another name server for additional information. The main differences are the format of the query sent to the WINS server, and the fact that the DNS server was queried as the authority for the information. The MS DNS databases are not actually updated with the information, although the MS DNS may cache the WINS data for a short time.

Dynamic DNS is a complex alternative. DDNS is not as easy to set up and maintain as WINS with Microsoft's DNS Server, which this book describes, but it is useful, especially for anyone who runs DNS on a UNIX server.

A DDNS server can automatically register clients through updates from a DHCP server. Dynamic DNS is not yet a standard, but it is an RFC in the Internet standards track at the time of this book's writing. You can view the DDNS RFC document at http://www.ds.internic.net/rfc/rfc2136.txt. Also, a pre-standard Dynamic DNS product for UNIX and Windows NT is available for download at http://www.isc.org/bind.html.

What is DHCP?

The Dynamic Host Configuration Protocol (DHCP) is used to automatically assign TCP/IP settings to clients. Upon startup, a DHCP-enabled client requests an IP address and other information (such as a default gateway address or a WINS server address) from a DHCP server. IP addresses come from a pool that is defined in the DHCP server's database called a scope. The server offers the IP address for a specified period of time called a lease.

This means users no longer have to obtain IP information from an administrator, or have to manually configure computers for these settings. Common problems stemming from manual TCP/IP configuration include duplicate IP addresses, mistyped information leading to no network connectivity, and administrative overhead from hosts moving to different subnets. DHCP was designed to alleviate these problems. To complete the introduction to DHCP, you should understand where it fits in with DNS, and its relation to BOOTP—another protocol designed to assign IP addresses.

DHCP is defined in RFCs 1533, 1534, 1541, and 1542.

The DHCP/DNS Problem and the Solution

What does DHCP have to do with DNS? Picture a scenario involving a PC that is running an HTTP (Web) server service. The PC has been configured with a static IP address and a corresponding A record in the DNS database. When a UNIX computer attempts to connect to the PC's Web server using a host name, it does a DNS lookup and is able to resolve the PC's IP address and connect.

If you were to make that PC a DHCP client, it may end up with a different IP address than what its DNS Resource Record says. The DHCP client may also get a different IP address depending on the length of the DHCP lease, if the client is moved, or its network adapter is replaced. Without manually updating the DNS database every time the PC gets a new IP address, other computers will not be able to resolve the PC's IP address.

With Microsoft DNS, WINS, and DHCP, there is a solution to this problem, while lessening the amount of client configuration and DNS administration. Figure 18.1 illustrates the method that the UNIX host would use to be able to connect to the PC's Web server.

The steps of the procedure illustrated in Figure 18.1 are as follows:

1. The DHCP client sends an IP lease request to a DHCP server.
2. The DHCP server gives the client IP configuration information including the address of a WINS server (this is discussed in detail earlier in this chapter).
3. The client registers its name and IP with the WINS server.
4. The UNIX host queries the DNS server for the IP address of the PC.
5. After not finding an A type Resource Record for the PC, the DNS server uses the WINS type Resource Record to query the WINS server.
6. The WINS server returns the IP address of the PC to the DNS server.
7. The DNS returns the IP address to the UNIX host.
8. The UNIX host can now establish a connection to the PC.

The DHCP server, WINS server, and DNS server may all be the same physical computer, but are separated here for clarity.

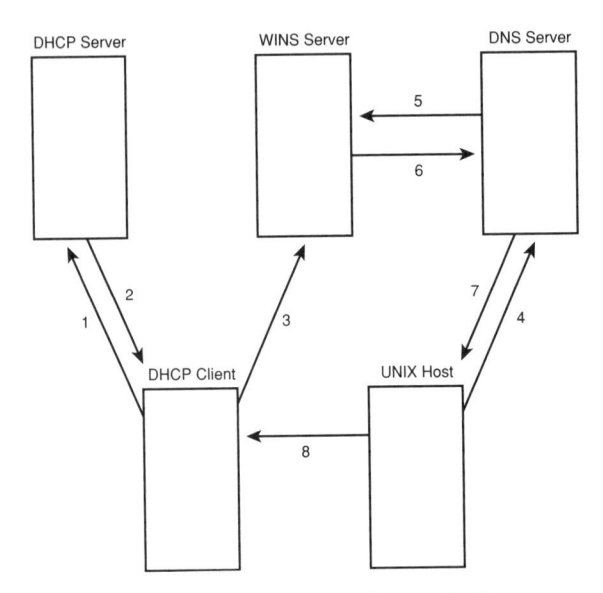

Figure 18.1 Steps for DNS resolution of a DHCP client computer.

DHCP Versus BOOTP

DHCP is an extension of BOOTSTRAP PROTOCOL (BOOTP). BOOTP (defined in RFC 1532) was designed for two purposes: so that clients could request an IP address and other TCP/IP settings, and for diskless workstations to request the location of boot file information from which the client is to boot. BOOTP does not support the concept of leases, however, and each client's hardware address must be associated with a particular IP address.

DHCP requires less administration, and because Windows computers support DHCP but not BOOTP, there's really no reason to use BOOTP in a PC environment. But since Windows NT provides DHCP services, and DHCP is based on BOOTP, support for BOOTP clients was offered in Windows NT 4.0, Service Pack 2. This means that a DHCP server can respond to DHCP requests as well as BOOTP requests from UNIX clients and/or diskless workstations.

To configure your Microsoft Windows NT DHCP Server to assign IP address information to BOOTP clients, you must add a *reservation* (a specific IP address for a specific client) for each BOOTP client. For information about how to add a reservation, view the "Managing Client Reservations" Help topic in DHCP Manager. You then use DHCP options to provide the other TCP/IP settings. DHCP Manager and DHCP options are covered in the upcoming section called "Configuring a DHCP Server." Remember though that unless a BOOTP client can register itself with WINS, it cannot participate in the MS DNS WINS lookup, and therefore still needs to have a static A record in the DNS database.

To configure your Microsoft Windows NT DHCP Server to provide boot file information for BOOTP clients, you must add a reservation for each client, and then edit the BOOTP Table in DHCP Manager. Under DHCP Servers, double-click *Local Machine*, then from the Server menu, select Properties. Click the BOOTP Table tab, and add entries for each BOOTP client. Figure 18.2 shows the BOOTP Table configuration screen.

How DHCP Configures a Client

DHCP uses a four-phase process to configure a DHCP client. If a client is multi-homed, the process takes place separately for each adapter, with each adapter getting a unique IP address.

In the first phase, the client initializes a limited version of TCP/IP and broadcasts a request for an IP address. This phase is called the *IP lease request phase*.

In the second phase, all (one or more) DHCP servers that receive the request broadcast an answer. This broadcast contains the requestor's hardware address, an offered IP address, subnet mask, length of lease, and the IP address of the offering server. This phase is known as the *IP lease offer phase*.

In the third phase, the client accepts the first offer that reaches it, and broadcasts that it has accepted the offer. This lets the offering server know to "close the deal" and lets the other DHCP servers know to retract their offers. This phase is called the *IP lease selection phase*.

In the fourth phase, the DHCP server with the accepted offer broadcasts an acknowledgement to the client. This message contains the valid IP address and other configuration information if the server is set up to provide it. This phase is the *IP lease acknowledgment phase*.

Figure 18.3 illustrates the four phases of the DHCP client-configuration process.

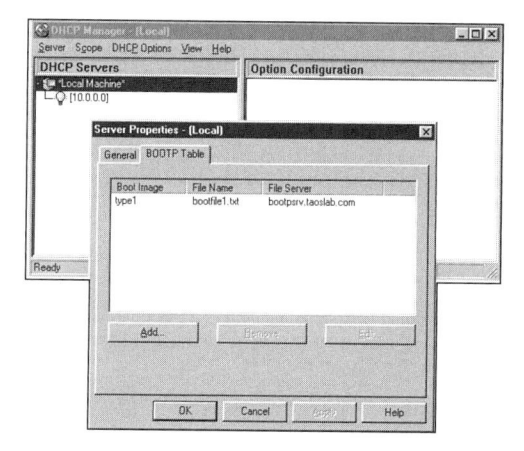

Figure 18.2 The BOOTP Table in DHCP Manager.

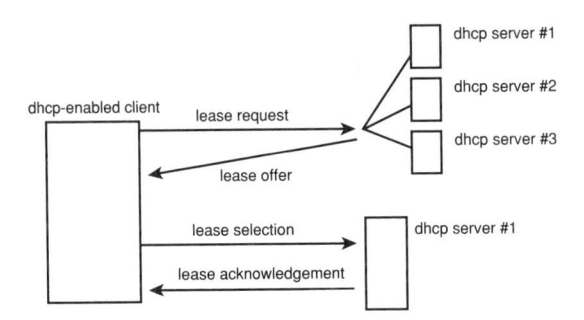

Figure 18.3 Four-phase process to configure a DHCP-enabled client.

After a DHCP client has a leased IP address, it attempts to renew its lease after 1/2 of the lease duration has expired. The default lease is three days, so in this case after a day and a half the client sends out a message to the DHCP server. If the client's IP address is still valid, the server responds with an acknowledgment and any updated information. The messages are similar to Phases three and four in the initial configuration process.

Installing a DHCP Server

Before installing a DHCP server, you need to consider your network configuration so you can properly match your server configuration to it in the most efficient manner. In small- to medium-sized networks, the DHCP Server service can be run on the same computer that other services, such as WINS, DNS, or domain controllers, are running. In networks with thousands of DHCP clients, you must take into account the network bandwidth and processor power required by the DHCP server.

If there are multiple subnets with DHCP clients, the simplest solution is to have DHCP servers on each subnet. If you don't have a DHCP server on each subnet, then you must use a relay agent, discussed later in this section.

Each DHCP server must have at least one pool of IP addresses for leasing to clients called a scope. A DHCP server can have scopes for more than one subnet, assuming client broadcasts can reach the server from each of those subnets. In this case, the DHCP server would have to be multihomed or relay agents must be used.

On each particular DHCP server, only one scope can be assigned to a specific subnet, but a subnet can be split between two or more DHCP servers for redundancy. Just make sure that the same IP address isn't available from each server. DHCP servers don't share information with each other so there can be no overlap in address pools.

Consider DHCP server A on subnet 1, and DHCP server B on subnet 2. Server A and server B would have 75 percent of the IP address pool for subnet 1 and subnet 2, respectively configured in their scope. Then another scope would be defined for the other 25 percent of the IP address pool in the remote subnet. Server A would in theory handle all client requests on its own subnet because it would respond faster than server B who's farther away, but if server A is down, server B would take over. Figure 18.4 gives a pictorial representation of this 75/25 configuration.

Installing a DHCP Server 255

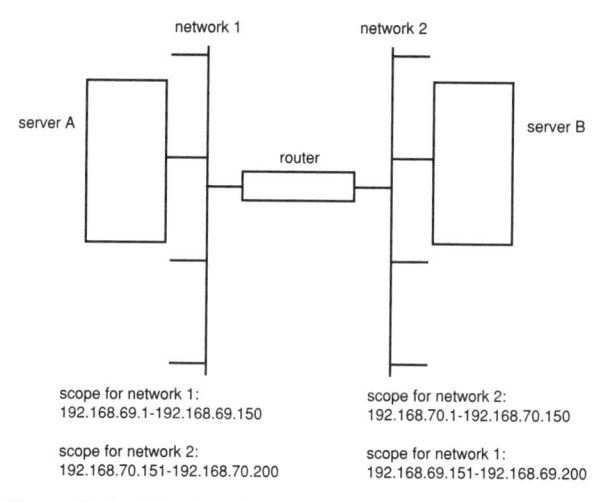

Figure 18.4 Distributed scopes among multiple DHCP servers.

Although there are third-party DHCP server software packages available, this book assumes that you will be using the Microsoft DHCP Server included with Windows NT Server. Microsoft DHCP Server will not run on Windows NT Workstation. The prerequisites are the same as for installing WINS or DNS—you need the NT Server distribution files, either on CD-ROM or a disk share, and the TCP/IP protocol installed and configured. You also need to be logged in to Windows NT with administrator privileges.

Warning
Any Windows NT computer running the DHCP Server service MUST have a statically assigned IP address. In other words, the Windows NT computer cannot be a DHCP client itself.

The installation process for DHCP Server is the same as for DNS Server or WINS Server. First, as shown in Figure 18.5, open the Control Panel by clicking the Start button, select Settings, then select Control Panel.

Double-click the Network icon (highlighted in Figure 18.6).

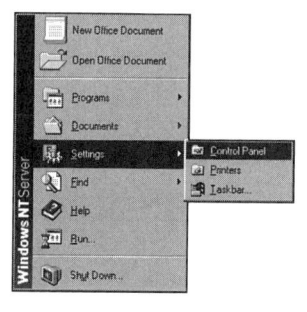

Figure 18.5 Getting to the Control Panel.

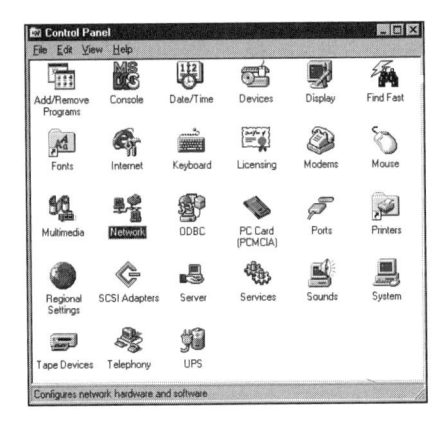

256   Chapter 18   Dynamic Host Configuration Protocol (DHCP)

Figure 18.6   The Control Panel showing the Network Control Panel.

Selecting the Network Control Panel brings up the Network Settings dialog box. Click the Services tab, and then click the Add button. The Select Network Service dialog box appears, as shown in Figure 18.7.

Select Microsoft DHCP Server, and then click OK. You'll be prompted for the path to the distribution files. Type in the full path and click Continue. Files will be copied to your computer, and then a warning message will appear stating you must have a static IP address. Click OK, then when you are back to the Network Settings dialog box, click Close and restart the computer.

It is suggested at this time to install the latest Windows NT Service Pack, which includes bug fixes and enhancements over the original version. Even if you previously installed the Service Pack, you need to reinstall it every time you install a component from the original distribution files.

Now you have one DHCP server set up. If you have more than one subnet, you'll need to find a way to handle clients that are on a different subnet than your server. Because DHCP is broadcast-based, and broadcasts normally don't pass through routers, you must use a *relay agent*.

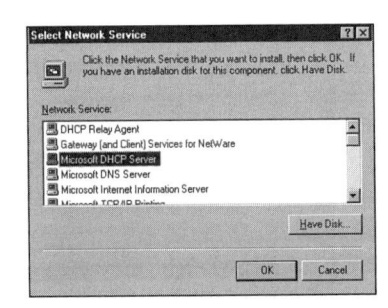

Figure 18.7   The Select Network Service dialog box.

DHCP Relay Agents

A Windows NT DHCP server can provide IP addresses to clients across multiple subnets if the router that separates them can act as an RFC 1542 (BOOTP) relay agent. If the router cannot function as a relay agent, each subnet that has DHCP clients must have a DHCP server, or a service called DHCP Relay Agent can be installed on a Windows NT computer.

Windows NT does not support configuring routers for DHCP/BOOTP relay; however, a Windows NT computer can be configured to serve as a DHCP relay agent, to intercept DHCP (and BOOTP) broadcast messages, and to send packets directly to the DHCP server. These directed messages can cross IP routers; thus the DHCP relay agent acts as a local proxy for the remote DHCP Servers. The DHCP Relay Agent is installed as a network service, using the same steps as installing the DHCP Server service. The relay agent is configured in the TCP/IP Properties sheet, as shown in Figure 18.8. Simply enter the IP addresses of DHCP servers you want this computer to forward DHCP requests to.

Warning
A DHCP server does not need to have the DHCP Relay Agent installed on it. The relay agent is installed on computers that are on subnets with no DHCP servers.

Configuring a DHCP Server

The Windows application for configuring a DHCP server is called DHCP Manager. Just like WINS Manager and DNS Manager, you can use DHCP Manager to manage multiple servers enterprisewide. DHCP Manager is accessible through the Windows taskbar. Click the Start button, then select Programs, then Administrative Tools, then DHCP Manager. The first time you open DHCP Manager, it will look like Figure 18.9.

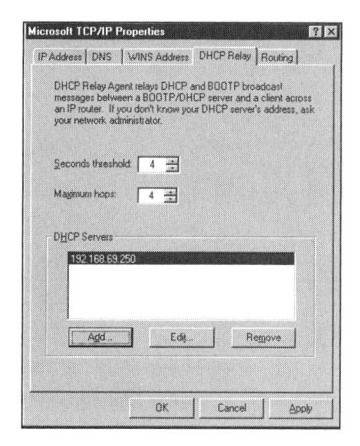

Figure 18.8   The DHCP Relay Agent configuration screen.

258   Chapter 18   Dynamic Host Configuration Protocol (DHCP)

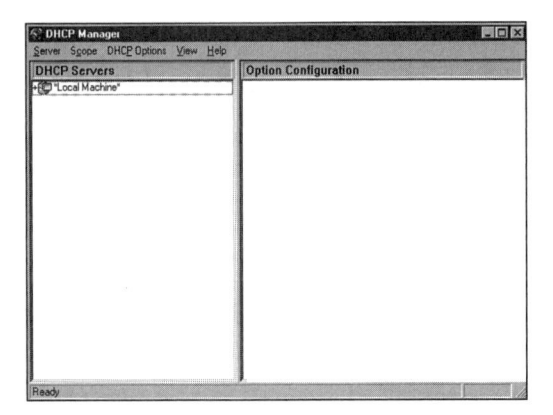

Figure 18.9   The DHCP Manager interface.

Creating Scopes

Under DHCP Servers (illustrated in Figure 18.9), double-click *Local Machine*. Local Machine indicates that you are configuring the local DHCP server, and not a remote DHCP server. From the Scope menu, choose Create. The Scope Properties dialog box (shown in Figure 18.10) appears. Complete the scope configuration. Click OK when done. Click Yes to activate the scope.

The scope must be activated before it is available for lease assignments. You can also simply deactivate a scope for maintenance or troubleshooting, instead of deleting it and having to re-create it.

The DHCP Manager window appears with the new scope added. The yellow light bulb next to the IP address indicates an active scope.

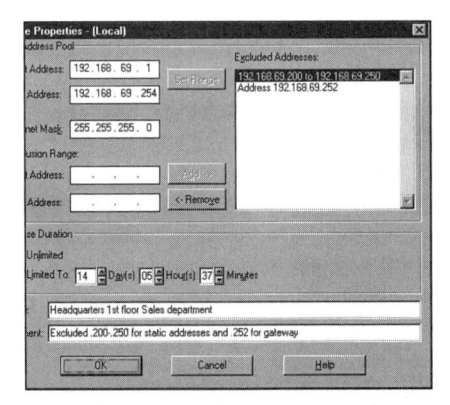

Figure 18.10   The Create Scope dialog box, with a sample configuration.

Note
You may receive an error message after creating your first scope saying "No more data available..." Simply exit DHCP Manager and restart it.

You can configure DHCP so that a DHCP server will always give the same IP address to a particular client. This is called a *client reservation*. To configure a client reservation, click the light bulb icon for the scope, then from the Scope menu, select Add reservations. Fill in the IP address and Ethernet address (or MAC address) in the Unique Identifier field, and fill in a Client Name and, optionally, the Client Comment field. Click Add, then Close when finished.

DHCP Options

Now clients can get IP addresses from the server, but what about other TCP/IP configuration information? The DHCP server can provide a list of options that can be sent to the DHCP client. Options can be on three levels—Global, Scope, and Client. Global options are available to all DHCP clients on the server. Scope options are available to all clients in a particular scope and override any Global options. Client options are created for a specific client and override the Global and Scope options.

Although the RFC defines many options, Microsoft DHCP clients can only accept six of them:

- Default gateway (router) addresses
- DNS server addresses
- DNS domain name
- WINS server addresses
- NetBIOS node (name resolution) type
- NetBIOS Scope ID

To configure DHCP options, perform the following steps:

1. Click the light bulb icon for the scope you created.
2. From the DHCP Options menu, select Scope or Global.
3. Scroll down the list of Unused Options, highlight the one you want, then click the Add button.
4. Now click the Value>>> button, then click the Edit Array button to add the values for a particular option. Some options will not have an array editor but another type of input depending on the option.

Figure 18.11 shows a Router option being added for a scope.

For the least amount of administration in the DHCP/WINS/DNS relationship, define all of the listed options (although NetBIOS Scope is normally not used—NetBIOS scopes are covered in Chapter 2, "Introducing NetBIOS").

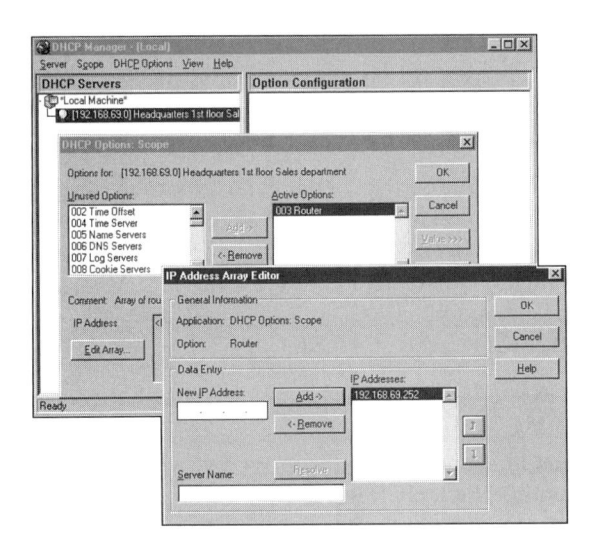

260 Chapter 18 Dynamic Host Configuration Protocol (DHCP)

Figure 18.11   Adding values for a DHCP scope option.

To configure a Client option, the client must have a *client reservation* as described earlier in this section. To add Client options, double-click the scope icon. Double-click a client with a reservation, then click the Options button, as shown in Figure 18.12. Add the options the same way you would for Global or Scope options.

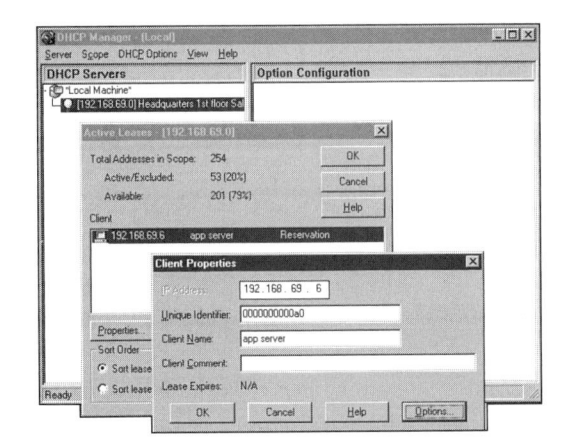

Figure 18.12   Configuring Client options.

Configuring Clients to Use DHCP

The only requirement that a DHCP client must meet to use DHCP is that the client computer have a DHCP supported operating system. The following operating systems allow DHCP to be enabled for the client:

- Windows NT Server 3.5, 3.51, and 4.0
- Windows NT Workstation 3.5, 3.51, and 4.0
- Windows 95
- Windows for Workgroups 3.11 with the Microsoft TCP/IP-32 for Windows for Workgroups installed
- MS Network Client 3.0 for MS-DOS with the real-mode TCP/IP driver installed
- LAN Manager 2.2c

To enable a Windows NT DHCP client, you must log on with administrator privileges at the client. Normally, you enable DHCP as part of the installation procedure for Microsoft TCP/IP, however, you can use the following procedure if you have previously manually configured TCP/IP:

1. Run Control Panel and choose Network. The Network Settings dialog box appears.
2. Under Installed Network Software, select TCP/IP Protocol and then choose Configure. The TCP/IP Configuration dialog box appears.
3. Select Enable Automatic DHCP Configuration. A Microsoft (MS) TCP/IP message appears, indicating that the DHCP Protocol attempts to configure the server automatically during system initialization.
4. Choose Yes. An MS TCP/IP Configuration dialog box appears, displaying current TCP/IP configuration parameters. The IP Address and Subnet Mask boxes are not available (grayed out) and the manually configured values are no longer displayed.
5. Choose OK to return to the Network Settings dialog box.
6. Choose OK again.
7. Shut down and restart the computer.

Checking the Registration in WINS and DNS

Several different utilities are available to check that your DHCP clients are working with WINS and DNS. After a client is configured to use DHCP, the TCP/IP configuration parameters do not show up in the Network Control Panel anymore (unless you have entered in values to manually override DHCP). From a Windows NT client, you can open a command prompt and run the command `IPCONFIG /all`. Running this command should provide the IP address, gateway, and other information given from the DHCP server.

If the IP address is 0.0.0.0, the client has not gotten its IP address from the DHCP server. The `WINIPCFG` command provides the same function from a Windows 95 client. To check that a DHCP client can be resolved through DNS, use the `NSLOOKUP` command. These commands are covered in detail in Chapter 17, "Troubleshooting Tools and Utilities."

You can also use the WINS Manager application to see if DHCP clients are properly registered in the database. From the Mappings menu, select the Show Database command and browse through the Mappings list for DHCP clients. If you want to look up a particular client, click the Set Filter button, and enter the computer name or IP address on which to filter your mappings.

Summary

Many people have been unable or hesitant to use DHCP because it does not normally integrate with DNS. This chapter illustrates that by using a combination of DHCP, WINS, and Microsoft DNS, network computers can get dynamically assigned IP addresses and are still able to participate in DNS without a lot of administration. To use DHCP, thought is given to the number and placement of DHCP servers, the DHCP Server service is set up, scopes are defined, and clients are configured to become DHCP clients.

IV

Appendices

A Third Party Utilities and DNS Servers
B RFCs on DNS, BIND, and NetBIOS
C Top-Level Internet Domains
D Registering Addresses on the Internet
E Sample Network Traces for DNS Resolutions
F Resource Records and the InterNIC Cache File

Third Party Utilities and DNS Servers

THIS APPENDIX OFFERS INFORMATION about several useful utilities and some alternative DNS servers. Read the description of each utility to see if it's valuable to you in a given situation. This appendix also provides information about alternative DNS servers that run on Windows NT.

Utilities

The following list describes the various available utilities for use with Windows NT that can help you understand system behavior and troubleshoot problems. Most of these tools are bundled with MS software or are accessible online.

- *nslookup:* This utility is installed automatically on all Windows NT systems. nslookup provides detailed information about the path a query takes to get resolved, and it's particularly useful to troubleshoot name-resolution problems when DNS data or DNS servers themselves are suspected.

- *Network Monitor:* This utility is included on the MS-SMS installation CD-ROM. Network Monitor can be installed with SMS, or as a separate package. This packet capture and analysis tool is useful for "sniffing" the net to see what the packets look like.

- *Cisco DNS/DHCP Manager:* Cisco's DNS/DHCP Manager is a commercial product that provides a consolidated management tool for DNS and DHCP services. Evaluation software is available at
  http://www.cisco.com/warp/public/751/dnsmg/dnsmg_pa.htm

- *dig:* dig is available as part of the BIND for NT distribution, which is available for download from http://www.software.com. dig is an alternative to the nslookup utility, judged by many to be more reliable.

- *NETINFO:* NETINFO is a menu-driven online (Telnet) interface to dig that is supported by the University of California at Berkeley. To use the tool, simply Telnet nak.berkeley.edu on port 117 or telnet:nak.berkeley.edu:117. This tool includes a handy way to perform lookups of Internet Hosts and BITnet hosts, and perform whois queries.

- *DNS Resolver:* A 32-bit utility designed to resolve DNS/Reverse DNS lookups. This comprehensive tool provides an easy, interactive way to run test queries. Available at http://www6.zdnet.com.

- *DNS Workshop:* DNS Workshop enables conversions between IP addresses and Internet host names. It's simple and has a good interface. It is available at http://www6.zdnet.com.

- *dnscmd:* dnscmd comes with MS DNS and provides all the statistics you can see in the DNS Manager window. Unfortunately, there is no readme file or printed documentation. You can, however, run dnscmd /? to view an onscreen listing of usage options.

- *nslookup4WWW:* This is a Web-based interface to the nslookup utility. Connect to http://jos.net/projects/nslookup4WWW/nslookup4WWW.html.

DNS Server Software

Microsoft's DNS Server is an excellent choice, especially because it can support WINS integration; however, system administrators who are more comfortable working in a UNIX environment or who know BIND can select from alternatives that'll also run on NT. This section provides some information about those alternatives, not to dissuade you from using Microsoft's excellent DNS Server, but so you'll be better informed about what's out there.

UNIX Versus Windows NT: Is MS DNS Real DNS?

There's an old adage that, "If it looks like a duck, walks like a duck, and sounds like a duck, it must be a duck." Unless Microsoft starts giving out source code (figure the odds), the service must be judged by its behavior in a live environment. It speaks like DNS (accepts and answers queries, publishes zone info, performs zone transfers) and looks like DNS (the boot file, if used, and the zone files basically have the same format as standard version 4.9.x BIND), so it must be DNS. With the noted exceptions to "standard" DNS binaries, namely WINS integration, options to specify single- or multi-resource record messages in zone transfers, and lack of support for an XFR-NETS directive, MS DNS is almost indistinguishable in operation from any other DNS server based on BIND 4.9.x.

Berkeley Internet Name Daemon (BIND) Version 8.x

Version 8.1.1 is the latest version of BIND from the Internet Software Consortium (ISC). The jump from version 4.x to version 8.x of BIND marks a number of major advancements in the code. BIND version 8 incorporates a number of the new features outlined by the Internet Engineering Task Force (IETF) DNSIND enhancements.

DNSIND stands for *Domain Name System incremental zone transfers, notify and dynamic update*. With these enhancements come a number of improvements for efficiency, reliability, and security. Incremental zone transfers provide a mechanism through which only the changes in a zone file need to be transferred during zone updates by secondaries. Rather than having to download an entire zone file every time a single record is added or changed, only the changes need to be transferred, thereby conserving bandwidth and improving the efficiency of the name servers' capability to propagate changes.

BIND's Notify option, as in the MS DNS, provides a mechanism to trigger zone transfers when changes have been made to a zone. The primary can now signal the secondaries that changes have been made, thus speeding the propagation process, rather than having to wait until a refresh occurs. Also, some security can be added, allowing only the name servers listed in the notify list to perform zone transfers (analogous to the XFRSNETS directive of deprecated versions of BIND). Dynamic updates are being enabled to consolidate management of DNS servers with other services like DHCP.

BIND v8 can be configured so that the primary DNS has its source zone files updated via a DHCP server. Additions, modifications, and deletions can be performed, providing greater flexibility and simplifying management. BIND v8 also incorporates a new management application called Name Daemon Controller (NDC), which provides a handy way to deal with the name service daemon for killing, restarting, reloading, dumping the cache, and so on. BIND, being the source on which virtually all other DNS servers are based, will in all likelihood be the most interoperable among different vendor-specific applications.

Non-Microsoft Versions of DNS

Currently, you can get four versions of non-Microsoft DNS for NT. One is freeware and the other three are commercial versions of DNS. The non-Microsoft versions of DNS that you can run on Windows NT are as follows:

- *Bind for NT:* A free port of 4.9.x available from Software.com at
  http://www.software.com/prod/bindnt/bindnt.html.
- *Meta IP DNS 3.1:* A commercial port based on BIND 8.1.1. A demo is available for download free of charge at
  http://www.metainfo.com/products/metaip/dns.htm.
- *DNS Pro 5.6:* A commercial product based on BIND 4.9.6, and is available from PortaSoft at http://www.portasoft.com.

- *QIP Enterprise 5.0:* A commercial product available from Quadritek. Information and demo software can be found at `http://www.qtek.com/Products/Ent5_0`.

BIND for NT

The BIND for NT name server implementation is currently based on the Berkeley Internet Name Daemon (BIND), version 4.9.6. To get NT BIND, send email to `access@drcoffsite.com`, which will generate an automated reply with instructions about how and where to get the latest versions. Software.com also has BIND for NT on its Web site, although it is slightly older, based on BIND version 4.9.5.

This implementation of DNS does not contain the WINS integration of MS DNS, as it is basically a port to the NT platform. It is a stable implementation, provides a management tool that appears under the Control Panels once installed, and is fully compatible with all standard BIND directives supported by the 4.9.x series binaries. Support is limited, but the Software.com site includes some information about the product and hyperlinks for additional information and configuration samples.

MetaIP DNS 3.1

The MetaInfo version of DNS, called MetaIP, is based on the BIND version 8.1.1 from the ISC. This version has support for such features as Dynamic DNS, Secure DNS, real-time secondary updates, IPv6, and does include WINS integration support. MetaIP includes a graphical management tool that allows management of NT and UNIX name servers running BIND 4.9.x or later. You can also purchase a load balancing module as an add-on.

MetaIP runs as a service under Windows NT, and works on Windows NT Workstation as well as Windows NT Server. Configuration information can be stored in any ODBC compliant database. The load balancer option uses the Windows NT performance monitor to intelligently distribute incoming DNS requests and provides a *failover* in the event of a server outage. The MetaIP Web page also provides a number of useful hyperlinks to other resources and information.

DNS Pro 5.6

DNS Pro 5.6 from PortaSoft is another port based on BIND 4.9.6, which runs on Windows NT Workstation or Windows NT Server. DNS Pro provides a Control Panel tool for management of the server, secure zone transfers, and dynamic load balancing, but does not provide WINS integration support. DNS Pro does provide a very nice set of help utilities and statistics report generation. The PortaSoft site also includes a FAQ, intranet setup documentation, discussion lists, mailing lists, and links to the InterNIC for domain registrations and whois utilities.

QIP Enterprise 5.0

QIP is a little different than the other products listed in this appendix, in that QIP provides a complete IP management solution. QIP supports full compatibility with both BIND versions 4.x and 8.x simultaneously. QIP includes support for DNS, Dynamic DNS, Secure DNS, DHCP, RADIUS, LDAP Gateway, M-SQL option, multi-directional database replication, bootp, and NIS (Sun's Network Information Service).

QIP does not have native support for WINS integration, although it is modular, offering an extensible architecture. If WINS integration is of great importance along with the other features offered by QIP, it could probably be added. QIP also offers a wide choice of interfaces, including PC client (95, NT), UNIX clients, X clients, command-line interfaces, and HTTP (both secure and through a customizable API). QIP operates across many platforms, including Windows NT, Solaris, HP/UX, and AIX.

DNS and IP Version 6 (IPv6)

The Internet Protocol version 6 (IPv6) is the new version of the Internet's standard protocol suite. There are a number of changes that improve security and expand the network address space by changing from a 32-bit address to a 128-bit address. What does this mean to DNS? Well, if there were no DNS, in order to connect to another host or site, the IP address would have to be used.

With IPv4 (the current version), an IP address typically looks like 207.33.46.123. With IPv6, a typical IP address could look like 46df:3856:a46c:18a9:0543:a51f:96fb:11dc. As far as reverse lookups go, instead of the .IN-ADDR.ARPA domains, the IPv6 designation would be represented with an .IP6.INT. The 46df:3856:a46c:18a9:0543:a51f:96fb:11dc address would be represented by
c.d.1.1.b.f.6.9.f.1.5.a.3.4.5.0.9.a.8.1.c.6.4.a.6.5.8.3.f.d.6.4.IP6.INT.

It would be hard enough to remember the IP address of the local machine, let alone any other hosts on the network. This would make DNS even more important, and, subsequently, would only add more stress to the usually overburdened administrators. The changes to DNS to support IPv6 have included an AAAA record, which is the IPv6 equivalent of the A record for IPv4 addresses.

The other difference, as evidenced by the reverse lookup record, is that IPv6 addresses do not have natural boundaries. That is, subnets do not end on 32-bit, 16-bit, or 8-bit boundaries. This is why the reverse lookup key for the IPv6 address has a dot separating every digit. This is so IPv6 addresses can be resolved a *nibble* at a time. For more information about IPv6, refer to the following sites:

http://www.whatis.com/ipv6.htm

http://sunsite.auc.dk/RFC/rfc/rfc1881.html

http://www.cs.duke.edu/~narten/ipng.html

http://www.3com.com/nsc/ipv6.html

http://www.openvms.digital.com/openvms/products/ipv6/index.html

B

RFCs on DNS, BIND, and NetBIOS

RFC (REQUEST FOR COMMENT) DOCUMENTS serve several purposes. Some RFCs describe how the Internet works, defining standards. Others are informational, and others, yet, are for discussion, providing suggestions that may lead to future standards. At the top of every RFC is a statement of its status, indicating what kind of document it is.

The RFCs are maintained by the RFC editor at the Information Sciences Institute (ISI) who is responsible for publishing the documents in their final form. RFCs can be found by visiting a number of sites; the most direct is http://www.isi.edu/rfc-editor/RFC.html. For an overview of what RFCs are and how the RFC process works, visit http://www.isi.edu/rfc-editor/overview.html. The rest of the appendix provides the RFC numbers for RFCs concerned with RFCs for DNS/BIND, NetBIOS, and directory services.

RFC 819: The Domain Naming Convention for Internet User Applications
RFC 920: Domain Requirements
RFC 974: Mail Routing and the Domain System
RFC 1001: Protocol standard for a NetBIOS service on a TCP/UDP transport: Concepts and methods
RFC 1002: Protocol standard for a NetBIOS service on a TCP/UDP transport: Detailed specifications
RFC 1032: Domain Administrators Guide

RFC 1033: Domain Administrators Operations Guide
RFC 1034: Domain Names: Concepts and Facilities
RFC 1035: Domain Names: Implementation and Specification
RFC 1101: DNS Encoding of Network Names and Other Types
RFC 1122: Requirements for Internet Hosts—Communication Layers
RFC 1123: Requirements for Internet Hosts—Application and Support
RFC 1183: New DNS RR Definitions
RFC 1535: A Security Problem and Proposed Correction With Widely Deployed DNS Software
RFC 1536: Common DNS Implementation Errors and Suggested Fixes
RFC 1537: Common DNS Data File Configuration Errors
RFC 1591: Domain Name System Structure and Delegation
RFC 1597: Address Allocation for Private Internets
RFC 1627: Network 10 Considered Harmful (Some Practices Shouldn't be Codified)
RFC 1632: A Revised Catalog of Available X.500 Implementations
RFC 1637: DNS NSAP Resource Records
RFC 1700: Assigned numbers
RFC 1713: Tools for DNS debugging
RFC 1794: DNS Support for Load Balancing
RFC 1876: A Means for Expressing Location Information in the Domain Name System
RFC 1884: IP Version 6 Addressing Architecture
RFC 1886: DNS Extensions to support IP version 6
RFC 1912: Common DNS Operational and Configuration Errors
RFC 1995: Incremental Zone Transfer in DNS
RFC 1996: A Mechanism for Prompt Notification of Zone Changes (DNS **NOTIFY**)
RFC 2010: Operational Criteria for Root Name Servers
RFC 2052: A DNS RR for specifying the location of services (DNS **SRV**)
RFC 2065: Domain Name System Security Extensions
RFC 2097: The PPP NetBIOS Frames Control Protocol (NBFCP)
RFC 2116: X.500 Implementations Catalog-96
RFC 2132: DHCP Options and BOOTP Vendor Extensions
RFC 2136: Dynamic Updates in the Domain Name System (DNS **UPDATE**)
RFC 2137: Secure Domain Name System Dynamic Update
RFC 2148: Deployment of the Internet White Pages Service
RFC 2156: MIXER (Mime Internet X.400 Enhanced Relay): Mapping between X.400 and RFC 822/MIME
RFC 2164: Use of an X.500/LDAP directory to support MIXER address mapping
RFC 2200: Internet Official Protocol Standards
RFC 2218: A Common Schema for the Internet White Pages Service
RFC 2219: Use of DNS Aliases for Network Services

RFC 2247: Using Domains in LDAP/X.500 Distinguished Names
RFC 2251: Lightweight Directory Access Protocol (v3)
RFC 2252: Lightweight Directory Access Protocol (v3): Attribute Syntax Definitions
RFC 2253: Lightweight Directory Access Protocol (v3): UTF-8 String Representation of Distinguished Names
RFC 2254: The String Representation of LDAP Search Filters
RFC 2255: The LDAP URL Format
RFC 2256: A Summary of the X.500(96) User Schema for use with LDAPv3

C

Top-Level Internet Domains

THIS APPENDIX PROVIDES A LIST OF FIRST-LEVEL DOMAINS. You can use Table C.1 to see where your domain attaches to the tree at root level and what other domains appear at the highest level.

In the domain name system, all DNS Servers and computer hosts belong to one country or one type of organization. You've probably seen some of these top-level domains. They frequently appear, for example, at the end of web server names: com is for commercial organizations, edu is for educational organizations, net is for network support centers, and so on. There's also a top-level domain for each of the world's countries: au, for Australia, ca for Canada, uk for the United Kingdom, and de for Germany, to name just a few.

Top-level domains can contain many computer host names, but the DNS servers that service top-level domains don't usually store the names of all those hosts. This is important. There would simply be too many names for one server to manage. Instead, top-level DNS servers have delegation entries that refer to lower-level DNS servers.

Low-level domain names in the DNS name hierarchy can change frequently and without many consequences, just as the leaves and branches of a real tree can change by season or by trimming. Top-level domain names, though, are like large tree branches. While not necessarily permanent, top-level domains can't change easily or frequently because they support all the names below.

Some top-level domains have their own DNS servers. Others are managed by root DNS servers, such as the us and edu domains illustrated in Figure 5.5 in Chapter 5, "How DNS Works."

Appendix C Top-Level Internet Domains

Table C.1 **Top-level Internet domains**

Domain name	Scope
AD	Andorra
AE	United Arab Emirates
AG	Antiqua and Barbuda
AI	Anguilla
AL	Albania
AM	Armenia
AN	Netherlands Antilles
AO	Angola
AQ	Antarctica
AR	Argentina
ARPA	Advanced Research Projects Agency
AT	Austria
AU	Australia
AW	Aruba
AZ	Azerbaijan
BA	Bosnia-Herzegovina
BB	Barbados
BE	Belgium
BF	Burkina Faso
BG	Bulgaria
BH	Bahrain
BI	Burundi
BJ	Benin
BM	Bermuda
BN	Brunei
BO	Bolivia
BR	Brazil
BS	Bahamas
BW	Botswana
BY	Belarus
BZ	Belize
CA	Canada
CF	Central African Republic
CH	Switzerland
CI	Cote d'Ivoire
CK	Cook Islands
CL	Chile
CM	Cameroon
CN	China

Domain name	Scope
CO	Colombia
COM	COMMERCIAL
CR	Costa Rica
CU	Cuba
CV	Cape Verde
CY	Cyprus
CZ	Czech Republic
DE	Germany
DJ	Djibouti
DK	Denmark
DM	Dominica
DO	Dominican Republic
DZ	Algeria
EC	Equador
EDU	EDUCATION
EE	Estonia
EG	Egypt
ER	Eritrea
ES	Centro de Communicaciones CSIC RedIRIS (ESNIC)
ET	Ethiopia
FI	EUnet Finland Oy
FJ	Fiji
FM	Micronesia
FO	Faroe Islands
FR	France
GB	Great Britain
GD	Grenada
GE	Georgia (Republic of)
GF	French Guyana
GG	Guernsey (Channel Islands)
GH	Ghana
GI	Gibraltar
GL	Greenland
GN	Guinea
GOV	GOVERNMENT
GP	Guadeloupe
GR	Greece
GT	Guatemala
GU	Guam

continues

Table C.1 **Continued**

Domain name	Scope
GY	Guyana
HK	Hong Kong
HN	Honduras
HR	Croatia/Hrvatska
HU	Hungary
ID	Indonesia
IE	Ireland
IL	Israel
IM	Isle of Man
IN	India
INT	International
IR	Iran
IS	Iceland
IT	Italy
JE	Jersey (Channel Islands)
JM	Jamaica
JO	Jordan
JP	Japan
KE	Kenya
KH	Cambodia
KI	Kiribati
KN	Saint Kitts & Nevis
KR	Korea
KW	Kuwait
KY	Cayman Islands
KZ	Kazakhstan
LA	Lao People's Democratic Republic
LB	Lebanon
LC	Saint Lucia
LI	Liechtenstein
LK	Sri Lanka
LS	Lesotho
LT	Lithuania
LU	Luxembourg
LV	Latvia
MA	Morocco
MC	Monaco
MD	Moldova
MG	Madagascar
MH	Marshall Islands

Domain name	Scope
ML	MILITARY
MK	Macedonia
ML	Mali
MN	Mongolia
MO	Macau
MP	Northern Mariana Islands
MR	Mauritania
MT	Malta
MU	Mauritius
MV	Maldives
MX	Mexico
MY	Malaysia
MZ	Mozambique
NA	Namibia
NC	New Caledonia
NE	Niger
NET	NETWORK
NF	Norfolk Island
NG	Nigeria
NI	Nicaragua
NL	Netherlands
NO	Norway
NP	Nepal
NZ	New Zealand
OM	Oman
ORG	ORGANIZATION
PA	Panama
PE	Peru
PF	French Polynesia
PG	Papua New Guinea
PH	Philippines
PK	Pakistan
PL	Poland
PR	Puerto Rico
PT	Portugal
PY	Paraguay
QA	Qatar
RO	Romania
RU	Russia
RW	Rwanda
SA	Saudi Arabia
SB	Solomon Islands

continues

Table C.1 **Continued**

Domain name	Scope
SE	Sweden
SG	Singapore
SK	Slovakia
SM	San Marino
SN	Senegal
SR	Telesur
SU	Soviet Union
SV	El Salvador
SY	Syria
SZ	Swaziland
TG	Togo
TH	Thailand
TN	Tunisia
TO	Tonga
TR	Turkey
TT	Trinidad and Tobago
TV	Tuvalu
TW	Taiwan
TZ	Tanzania
UA	Ukraine
UG	Uganda
UK	United Kingdom (Great Britain)
US	United States of America
UY	Uruguay
UZ	Uzbekistan
VA	Vatican City State
VC	Saint Vincent and the Grenadines
VE	Venezuela
VI	Virgin Islands
VN	Vietnam
VU	Vanuatu
WS	Samoa
YE	Yemen
YU	Yugoslavia
ZA	South Africa
ZM	Zambia
ZR	Zaire
ZW	Zimbabwe

D

Registering Addresses on the Internet

INTERNET REGISTRATIONS ARE HANDLED by the InterNIC (the Internet Network Information Center) which is managed by Network Solutions, Inc. Any network entity that an individual or organization wants to use on the Internet must be registered with InterNIC in order to be seen by others. This includes registrations for domain names and network numbers (in-addr.arpa.).

The process is relatively painless and the cost is minimal. There are organizations on the Net that will perform the service of registering domains, but they often charge an additional fee. InterNIC's standard charge for registering a domain is $50 US per year, but the amount you'll be invoiced after registering a domain is $100 to cover the first two years. After two years, a new invoice will be issued to you for $50 each year for renewal. For a complete overview of the process, you can view a flow diagram by visiting http://rs.internic.net/domain-info/domflow.html.

For an organization that's new to the Internet, there are a couple of issues to address before registering. You must have a valid IP network address. That is to say, the numbers used for the IP addresses of your hosts must be assigned (numbers cannot be randomly chosen), and the network portion of the IP address must be routable. Both issues are usually handled by the Internet service provider you'll use to provide your connection to the Internet.

The next thing to do is decide on a domain name. In reality, having several names in mind is wise because your first and second choices might already be registered by someone else. You can check to see if the name you want is already registered with the whois <domain name> command, or by using the Web interface that the InterNIC offers at http://rs.internic.net/cgi-bin/whois. Once you select a good domain name, complete the registration forms and submit them to the InterNIC.

InterNIC provides a few ways to register a domain name. The first and easiest is to follow the step-by-step Web form at http://rs.internic.net/cgi-bin/itts/domain. There's also a single page version at http://rs.internic.net/cgi-bin/domain. Finally, you can download the text version from ftp://rs.internic.net/templates/domain-template.txt, complete the form, and email it back to the InterNIC. The rest of this appendix provides a copy of the text form for your reference and convenience.

[URL ftp://rs.internic.net/templates/domain-template.txt] [01/98]

*************** Please DO NOT REMOVE Version Number **************

Domain Version Number: 3.5

********** Please see attached detailed instructions **************

NETWORK SOLUTIONS, INC.

DOMAIN NAME REGISTRATION AGREEMENT

A. Introduction. This domain name registration agreement ("Registration Agreement") is submitted to NETWORK SOLUTIONS, INC. ("NSI") for the purpose of applying for and registering a domain name on the Internet. If this Registration Agreement is accepted by NSI, and a domain name is registered in NSI's domain name database and assigned to the Registrant, Registrant ("Registrant") agrees to be bound by the terms of this Registration Agreement and the terms of NSI's Domain Name Dispute Policy ("Dispute Policy") which is incorporated herein by reference and made a part of this Registration Agreement. This Registration Agreement shall be accepted at the offices of NSI.

B. Fees and Payments. Registrant agrees to pay a registration fee of One Hundred United States Dollars (US$100) as consideration for the registration of each new domain name or Fifty United States Dollars (US$50) to renew an existing registration. The payment may be made payable either directly to "Network Solutions, Inc.," or indirectly to NSI through the Registrant's Internet Service Provider ("ISP"). Payment is due within thirty (30) days from the date of the invoice. The non-refundable fee covers a period of two (2) years for each new registration, and one (1) year for each renewal, and includes any permitted modification(s) to the domain name's record during the covered period.

C. Dispute Policy. Registrant agrees, as a condition to submitting this Registration Agreement, and if the Registration Agreement is accepted by NSI, that the Registrant shall be bound by NSI's current Dispute Policy. The current version of the Dispute Policy may be found at the InterNIC Registration Services web site: "http://rs.internic.net/dispute.html."

D. Dispute Policy Changes or Modifications. Registrant agrees that NSI, in its sole discretion, may change or modify the Dispute Policy, incorporated by reference herein, at any time. Registrant agrees that Registrant's maintaining the registration of a domain name after changes or modifications to the Dispute Policy become effective constitutes Registrant's continued acceptance of these changes or modifications. Registrant agrees that if Registrant considers any such changes or modifications to be unacceptable, Registrant may request that the domain name be deleted from the domain name database.

E.   Disputes. Registrant agrees that, if the registration of its domain name is challenged by any third party, the Registrant will be subject to the provisions specified in the Dispute Policy.

F.   Agents. Registrant agrees that if this Registration Agreement is completed by an agent for the Registrant, such as an ISP or Administrative Contact/Agent, the Registrant is nonetheless bound as a principal by all terms and conditions herein, including the Dispute Policy.

G.   Limitation of Liability. Registrant agrees that NSI shall have no liability to the Registrant for any loss Registrant may incur in connection with NSI's processing of this Registration Agreement, in connection with NSI's processing of any authorized modification to the domain name's record during the covered period, as a result of the Registrant's ISP's failure to pay either the initial registration fee or renewal fee, or as a result of the application of the provisions of the Dispute Policy. Registrant agrees that in no event shall the maximum liability of NSI under this Agreement for any matter exceed Five Hundred United States Dollars (US$500).

H.   Indemnity. Registrant agrees, in the event the Registration Agreement is accepted by NSI and a subsequent dispute arises with any third party, to indemnify and hold NSI harmless pursuant to the terms and conditions contained in the Dispute Policy.

I.   Breach. Registrant agrees that failure to abide by any provision of this Registration Agreement or the Dispute Policy may be considered by NSI to be a material breach and that NSI may provide a written notice, describing the breach, to the Registrant. If, within thirty (30) days of the date of mailing such notice, the Registrant fails to provide evidence, which is reasonably satisfactory to NSI, that it has not breached its obligations, then NSI may delete Registrant's registration of the domain name. Any such breach by a Registrant shall not be deemed to be excused simply because NSI did not act earlier in response to that, or any other, breach by the Registrant.

J.   No Guaranty. Registrant agrees that, by registration of a domain name, such registration does not confer immunity from objection to either the registration or use of the domain name.

K.   Warranty. Registrant warrants by submitting this Registration Agreement that, to the best of Registrant's knowledge and belief, the information submitted herein is true and correct, and that any future changes to this information will be provided to NSI in a timely manner according to the domain name modification procedures in place at that time. Breach of this warranty will constitute a material breach.

L. *Revocation.* Registrant agrees that NSI may delete a Registrant's domain name if this Registration Agreement, or subsequent modification(s) thereto, contains false or misleading information, or conceals or omits any information NSI would likely consider material to its decision to approve this Registration Agreement.

M. *Right of Refusal.* NSI, in its sole discretion, reserves the right to refuse to approve the Registration Agreement for any Registrant. Registrant agrees that the submission of this Registration Agreement does not obligate NSI to accept this Registration Agreement. Registrant agrees that NSI shall not be liable for loss or damages that may result from NSI's refusal to accept this Registration Agreement.

N. *Severability.* Registrant agrees that the terms of this Registration Agreement are severable. If any term or provision is declared invalid, it shall not affect the remaining terms or provisions which shall continue to be binding.

O. *Entirety.* Registrant agrees that this Registration Agreement and the Dispute Policy is the complete and exclusive agreement between Registrant and NSI regarding the registration of Registrant's domain name. This Registration Agreement and the Dispute Policy supersede all prior agreements and understandings, whether established by custom, practice, policy, or precedent.

P. *Governing Law.* Registrant agrees that this Registration Agreement shall be governed in all respects by and construed in accordance with the laws of the Commonwealth of Virginia, United States of America. By submitting this Registration Agreement, Registrant consents to the exclusive jurisdiction and venue of the United States District Court for the Eastern District of Virginia, Alexandria Division. If there is no jurisdiction in the United States District Court for the Eastern District of Virginia, Alexandria Division, then jurisdiction shall be in the Circuit Court of Fairfax County, Fairfax, Virginia.

Q. *This is Domain Name Registration Agreement Version Number 3.5. This Registration Agreement is only for registrations under top-level domains: COM, ORG, NET, and EDU. By completing and submitting this Registration Agreement for consideration and acceptance by NSI, the Registrant agrees that he/she has read and agrees to be bound by A through P above.*

Authorization

0a. (N)ew (M)odify (D)elete..........:

0b. Auth Scheme.....................:

0c. Auth Info......................:

1. Purpose/Description.............:

2. Complete Domain Name............:

Organization Using Domain Name

3a. Organization Name (Registrant)...:

3b. Street Address...................:

3c. City............................:

3d. State..........................:

3e. Postal Code.....................:

3f. Country Code (2 letter).........:

Administrative Contact/Agent

4a. NIC Handle (if known)...........:

4b. (I)ndividual or (R)ole?.........:

4c. Name............................:

4d. Organization Name...............:

4e. Street Address..................:

4f. City............................:

4g. State...........................:

4h. Postal Code.....................:

4i. Country Code (2 letter).........:

4j. Phone Number....................:

4k. Fax Number......................:

4l. Email Address...................:

Technical Contact

5a. NIC Handle (if known)...........:

5b. (I)ndividual or (R)ole?.........:

5c. Name............................:

5d. Organization Name...............:

5e. Street Address..................:

5f. City...........................:
5g. State..........................:
5h. Postal Code....................:
5i. Country Code (2 letter).........:
5j. Phone Number...................:
5k. Fax Number.....................:
5l. Email Address..................:

Billing Contact
6a. NIC Handle (if known)..........:
6b. (I)ndividual or (R)ole?........:
6c. Name..........................:
6d. Organization Name..............:
6e. Street Address.................:
6f. City...........................:
6g. State..........................:
6h. Postal Code....................:
6i. Country Code (2 letter).........:
6j. Phone Number...................:
6k. Fax Number.....................:
6l. Email Address..................:

Primary Name Server
7a. Primary Server Hostname........:
7b. Primary Server Netaddress......:

Secondary Name Server(s)

8a. Secondary Server Hostname........:

8b. Secondary Server Netaddress......:

END OF AGREEMENT

-----INSTRUCTIONS-----

I. This Registration Agreement must be submitted to NSI for any of the following actions:

a. Registering a New Domain Name.

b. Modifying a Domain Name Record.

c. Deleting a Domain Name.

d. Transferring a Domain Name.

Specific Instructions for completing each action can be found under the appropriate heading for each section. To ensure your agreement is promptly processed, please read and follow the instructions carefully.

II.   The Registration Agreement must be submitted for acceptance to NSI via Email at: "HOSTMASTER@INTERNIC.NET."

III.   Upon receipt of the Registration Agreement, NSI will acknowledge receipt by Email. The Email will include a tracking number in the form "NIC-YYMMDD.#" (#=Sequential number from 1 to 5 digits). Use the tracking number in the Subject of any Email you send regarding that particular Registration Agreement.

IV.   Upon initial acceptance and processing of the Registration Agreement, NSI will send an Email notice that the domain name registration is completed.

V.   Do not modify the Registration Agreement or remove the Registration Agreement version number.

VI.   Before completing the Registration Agreement, check to see if the domain name has already been registered by accessing the "whois" database at the World Wide Web location: "http://rs.internic.net/cgi-bin/whois." Use the information in the database where appropriate and as required. This will minimize the possibility of your Registration Agreement being returned.

REGISTERING A NEW DOMAIN NAME

Section 0 - Registration Type and Security

*Item 0a: Following the colon, type the character "N" or the word "New" to indicate a new domain name registration.

*The purpose of security (Items 0b and 0c) is to protect the Registrant's domain name information from unauthorized modifications. For more information about security, refer to the InterNIC homepage at "http://rs. internic.net/guardian/."

*If Item 0a is marked (N)ew, Items 0b and 0c will be ignored.

(Items 0b and 0c can only be used to (M)odify and (D)elete names.)

Section 1 - Purpose of Registration

*Briefly describe the domain name Registrant and the purpose for which this domain name is being applied. The description should support the choice of the top-level domain described below in Section 2.

Section 2 - Complete Domain Name

*For second-level domain names under .COM, .ORG, .NET, or .EDU, insert the name of the domain you wish to register as in, "EXAMPLE.COM." The total length of the two-part (second level.top level) name may be up to 26 characters (including the 4 characters .com). The only characters allowed in a domain name are letters, digits and the dash (-). A domain name cannot begin or end with a dash. The top-level domains registered by NSI are .COM, .ORG, .NET, and .EDU.

*Registrant is responsible for the accuracy of name submission; names will be registered as submitted; any changes will entail an additional registration fee.

Section 3 - Domain Name Registrant

*The domain name is considered to be registered to a "legal entity," even if the legal entity is an individual (e.g., Lee Smith). Do not list a "dba" or acronym as the registrant. In this section, it is important to list the legal name and address of the Registrant, not the Internet Service Provider ("ISP").

*If Items 3d or 3e are not applicable for your country, leave that Item blank. Items 3a, 3b, 3c and 3f must be completed or the Agreement will not be accepted.

*Item 3f may be either the country name or two-letter country code. A list of country codes is available at "http://www.isi.edu/div7/iana/domain-names.html."

Sections 4, 5 & 6 - Contacts

*The Administrative Contact/Agent is the person or organization authorized by the domain name Registrant to act on behalf of the legal entity listed in Item 3a. The Administrative Contact/Agent should be able to answer non-technical questions about the legal entity's plans for using the domain name and the procedures for establishing sub-domains.

*Generally, the Technical Contact is the person or organization who maintains the domain name Registrant's primary name server, resolver software, and database files. The Technical Contact person keeps the name server running and interacts with technical people in other domains to solve problems that affect the domain name. An ISP often performs this role.

*The Billing Contact will be invoiced for registrations and renewals.

*If the Technical or Billing Contact information is missing from the Registration Agreement, it will be presumed that the domain name Registrant has authorized the Administrative Contact/Agent to perform those roles.

*If the contact has never been registered or the handle is unknown, leave Item "a" (NIC Handle) blank. The registration software will check for matches with existing contact records. If a contact record is found in the database that matches the information on the Registration Agreement in a significant way (name, organization, phone, Email Address), the database information will override the information you supply in the Registration Agreement. (A contact record cannot be updated by using the Registration Agreement.)

*Each contact in NSI's database is assigned a "handle" - a unique tag to differentiate him/her from all other contacts in the database. Only one handle should exist for each Individual or Role. If the contact handle is already in the database, insert it in Item "a" and leave the rest of the section blank. If the contact handle is inserted and additional information is also provided, only the contact handle will be used. Any additional information will be ignored. Use contact handles whenever possible.

*Item b - indicate the type of contact you are registering. If the contact is a person, insert "I" for "Individual." If it is a group or an organization where several individuals may be acting in that role, insert "R" for "Role."

*Item c - place the name of the Individual or Role being registered. For Individuals, supply the full name (last, first and middle initial). Do not use titles. If suffixes are used, such as "Jr." or "III", separate the name from the suffix with a comma. For example, "Public, John Q., III" will result in a handle in the form of "JQP123." For Role contacts, provide the full name, for example, "Customer Service Support Center" would generate a handle of CSSC-ORG. The maximum length of a handle is 10 characters.

*Item e - Street Address.

*Multiple entries in Items j, k, and l must be separated by a comma.

*For each contact, if a NIC handle is not entered in a, Items b, c, d, e, f, i, j, and l must be completed. Agreements that do not have this information will be returned.

Sections 7 & 8 - Name Servers

*Items a and b must be completed in full. Incomplete information in Sections 7 and 8 will result in the Agreement being returned.

* Most ISPs can provide one or more name servers if you do not have your own. Do not list name servers without the explicit approval of their owners. The owners of the servers listed must configure the servers before your domain name will function.

* If possible, name servers should be in physically separate locations and on different networks.

* Provide the fully qualified name of the machine that is to be the name server. For example, use "machinename.domainname.com" not just "machinename."

* If several secondary servers are desired, copy and complete Section 8 as many times as necessary. Do not renumber or change the copied section.

* A new domain name registration Agreement will not change either the hostname (i.e., the name of the name server) or the netaddress (i.e., the IP number) of a name server registered in the database. (To change a hostname or netaddress, submit a Host Template. For more information about a Host Template refer to "ftp://rs.internic.net/template/host-template.txt.")

MODIFYING A DOMAIN NAME RECORD

* Modifying an existing domain name record is done by "replacement." This means the contents of various fields in the database are replaced with new information from the Registration Agreement. Use the "whois" database at "http://rs.internic.net/cgi-bin/whois" if you are unsure about the current information for a domain name, name server or contact.

* If you want to transfer a domain name from one organization (Registrant) to another organization (Registrant), see the Registrant Name Change Agreement at http://rs.internic.net/reg-change/agreement.html.

* The spelling of a domain name cannot be changed by submitting a modification Agreement. If you want a domain name with different spelling, you must file a New Registration Agreement for the new domain name and a Delete Registration Agreement when you are ready to have the old name removed. A new registration fee will be charged; payments will not be transferred.

* If you want to change a contact record, use the Contact Template at "ftp://rs.internic.net/templates/contact-template.txt."

* If you want to change a Name Server record, use the Host Template at "ftp://rs.internic.net/templates/host-template.txt."

Section 0 - Registration Type and Security

* Item 0a - type the character "M" or the word "Modify" to indicate a modification to an existing domain name registration.

*Modifications will be made according to the security parameters established by the contacts for the domain name registrant. If the contacts have not chosen any level of security, the change will be made if the Registration Agreement is submitted by the domain name Registrant or the Administrative Contact/Agent. - Items 0b and 0c depend on the level of security chosen by the contact submitting the modification.

   - If Item 0b is blank, Item 0c will be ignored.

   - If Item 0b is M or Mail-From, Item 0c will be ignored. This is the default.

   - If Item 0b is C or Crypt-PW, enter your cleartext password (i.e., the plain text of the encrypted password) in Item 0c.

   - If Item 0b is P or PGP, Item 0c is ignored. The sender should sign the entire Modification Registration Agreement with the PGP key and send it in cleartext.

*Notification of pending or finished modifications will be made according to the security parameters chosen by the contacts. If no security parameter has been chosen, the notification of the modification and the approximate time the modification will take effect will be sent to:

   - the requester

   - if contacts are changing, both old and new contacts

   - if name servers are changing, the Technical Contacts for the domains in which the old and new primary name servers reside

*This dissemination of modification information is to ensure that all parties involved are aware and are given an opportunity to agree or disagree with the modification.

*For more information on the levels of security available and how to generate passwords, see "http://rs.internic.net/guardian."

*Complete Sections 0 through 2, then complete only the Sections being modified. The completed Registration Agreement should be sent to "HOSTMASTER@INTERNIC.NET."

Section 1 - Purpose of Modification

*Briefly describe the purpose of the modification in Item 1. If the request for modification is not from a currently listed contact, the request will be forwarded to the listed contacts for approval before being processed.

Section 2 - Complete Domain Name

*Insert the domain name of the domain name to be modified (e.g., "EXAMPLE.COM"). This section is required.

Section 3 - Organization Using the Domain Name

*The domain name is considered to be registered to a "legal entity" even if the legal entity is an individual (e.g., Julie Smith). (Transfer of a domain name from one legal entity to another is not considered to be a modification. Please see the Registrant Name Change Agreement at http://rs.internic.net/reg-change/agreement.html.)

Sections 4, 5 & 6 - Contacts

*A contact can be changed only by supplying another Individual or Role contact. If the new contact's information is already in the database, enter the handle in Item a. To register a new contact, complete Items b through 1. If you want to change the information associated with a previously registered contact (e.g., Email address, Telephone number, etc.), you must submit a Contact Template.

Sections 7 & 8 - Primary and Secondary Name Servers

*To change the primary and secondary name servers, complete Items a and b. A complete list of name servers must be provided even if only one name server is being replaced.

DELETING A DOMAIN NAME

*A request that comes from the Registrant or the Administrative Contact/Agent will be honored, providing any security constraints are met.

*Notification of a completed deletion request will be sent to:

- the requester

- the contacts currently listed

- the Technical Contact for the domain in which the primary name server resides

*A request that comes from an ISP currently providing name service for the domain name may result in the name being placed on hold.

*If the request comes from none of the above, and does not meet any security established for the contacts, it will be returned for further explanation of the relationship between the requester and Registrant. The Administrative Contact/Agent and the Technical Contact will be notified.

*If an ISP removes name service, the domain name may be placed on "hold." "Hold" means that the domain name will be visible via "whois" at "http://rs.internic.net/cgi-bin/whois", but cannot be used.

*The completed Registration Agreement requesting the deletion should be sent to "HOSTMASTER@INTERNIC.NET."

Section 0 - Registration Type and Security

*Item 0a - type the character "D" or the word "Delete" to designate the deletion of an existing domain name registration.

*Deletions will be made according to the security parameters established for the contacts for the domain name Registrant.

*Items 0b and 0c depend on the level of security chosen by the contact submitting the modification.

*If Item 0b is blank, Item 0c will be ignored.

*If Item 0b is M or Mail-From, Item 0c will be ignored. This is the default.

*If Item 0b is C or Crypt-PW, enter your cleartext password (i.e. the plain text of the encrypted password) in Item 0c.

*If Item 0b is P or PGP, Item 0c is ignored. The sender should sign the entire Modification Registration Agreement with the PGP key and send it in cleartext.

*Notification of pending deletions will also be made according to the security parameters chosen by the contacts. If no security parameter has been chosen, the notification of the modification will be sent to:

    - the requester

    - contacts

*This dissemination of deletion information is to ensure that all parties involved are aware and are given an opportunity to concur or disagree with the deletion.

Section 1 - Purpose of Deletion

*If the request for deletion is not from a currently listed contact, the request will be forwarded to the listed contacts for approval before being processed.

*If additional records, such as the point(s) of contact or name servers should also be deleted, use the appropriate Contact Template or Host Template referred to above.

Section 2 - Complete Domain Name

*Insert the domain name of the domain name to be deleted (e.g., "EXAMPLE.COM").

Section 3 through Section 8

*These sections should be left blank.

-----END OF INSTRUCTIONS-----

REGISTERING IN-ADDR DOMAINS FOR IP NETWORKS

Network numbers (for an organization that needs a new IP address network assignment) are assigned and registered through the American Registry for Internet Numbers (ARIN). This was previously handled by Network Solutions, but changed to ARIN as of December 22, 1997. ARIN handles registration of Networks, ISP CIDR Blocks, Autonomous System Numbers and IN-ADDR Domains. More information on any of these items can be found at <http://www.arin.net/regserv.html>. It is quite common for the ISP to assign network numbers, however, an organization may elect (with the authorization of the ISP) to provide their own IN-ADDR domain service. In this case, the ISP may require the completion of the IN-ADDR template for their records. The registration template for the IN-ADDR registration can be found at <http://www.arin.net/templates/inaddrtemplate.txt> and must be emailed to the DNS administrator of the ISP. In the event that the network number is assigned directly by ARIN, the template must be emailed to hostmaster@arin.net. The fee schedule for ARIN's services can be found at <http://www.arin.net/feeschedule.html>. Below is the text copy of the IN-ADDR domain template.

*************** Please DO NOT REMOVE Version Number ****************

IN-ADDR Version Number: 1.0

************* Please see attached detailed instructions **************

Registration Action Type

0. (N)ew (M)odify (D)elete:

Network Information

1a. Network Name...................:

1b. Start of Network Block.........:

1c. End of Network Block...........:

2a. Name of Organization...........:

2b. Postal address of Organization:

Technical Contact

3a. NIC Handle (if known).........:

3b. Name (Last, First)............:

3c. Organization..................:

3d. Postal Address................:

3e. Phone Number..................:

3f. E-Mail Address................:

Primary Name Server

4a. Primary Server Hostname........:

4b. Primary Server Netaddress......:

Secondary Name Server(s)

5a. Secondary Server Hostname......:

5b. Secondary Server Netaddress....:

6. Comments......................:

–––––––––––––––––––- cut here –––––––––––––––––––

GENERAL INSTRUCTIONS: REGISTERING INVERSE ADDRESSING (NAME MAPPING) WITH ARIN

The Internet uses a special domain to support gateway location and Internet address to host mapping called In-ADDR.ARPA. The intent of this domain is to provide a guaranteed method to perform host address to host name mapping, and to facilitate queries to locate all gateways on a particular network in the Internet. Whenever an application is used that requires user identification, i.e., ftp, or remote login, the domain must be registered in the IN-ADDR.ARPA zone or the application will be unable to determine the origin of the IP.

IN-ADDR domains are represented using the network number in reverse.

EXAMPLE: The IN-ADDR domain for network 123.45.67.0 is represented as

67.45.123.IN-ADDR.ARPA.

NOTE: Please do not list your network number in reverse on your template.

Use the above template for registering new IN-ADDR entries, making changes to existing IN-ADDR records, and removing inverse-address mapping from the ARIN database and root servers.

The IN-ADDR template should be submitted via E-mail to ARIN at:

> *hostmaster@arin.net*

In order to ensure prompt and accurate processing of IN-ADDR requests, follow precisely the instructions below. Please do not modify the template nor remove the version number. IN-ADDR templates are automatically parsed. Errors in a template result in the template being returned for correction.

Please send only one template per message. In the Subject of the message, use the words: NEW IN-ADDR, MODIFY IN-ADDR, or REMOVE IN-ADDR, as appropriate.

Please do not send hardcopy registrations to ARIN. If you do not have an E-mail connection, you should arrange for your Internet Service Provider (ISP) to send E-mail applications to ARIN on your behalf.

When you submit a template, you will receive an auto-reply from ARIN with a ticket number. The ticket number format is:

> *NIC-<year><month><day>.<queue position>.*

Use the ticket number in the Subject of any message you send regarding a registration action. When the registration has been completed, you will be notified via E-mail.

All ISPs receiving from ARIN /16 CIDR blocks (Class B) which are greater than or equal to (>=)256 Class C's) will be responsible for maintaining all IN-ADDR.ARPA domain records for their respective customers. The ISP is responsible for the maintenance of IN-ADDR.ARPA domain records of all longer prefixes that have been delegated out of that block.

DETAILED INSTRUCTIONS FOR COMPLETING EACH IN-ADDR TEMPLATE FIELD

Section 0. Registration Action Type

N) New (M) Modify (D) Delete:

(N) New:

> *For new IN-ADDR registration, place an N after the colon.*

(M) Modify:

> *To modify/change an EXISTING record IN-ADDR registration, place an M after the colon. When "M" is selected, the current records will be replaced with the information listed in the template. Please provide a complete list of name servers in the order in which they should appear on the record.*

If the modification involves first registering a person or name server(s) not entered in the database, the instructions for completing Sections 2, 3, 4 and 5 apply. Search the WHOIS database for more information if you are unsure of the current information for the technical POC or name server(s).

The requested changes will be made if ARIN registry personnel determine that the modification request was issued by an authorized source. The issuing source may be a listed contact for the domain, others in the same organization, the current provider, or a new provider initiating network support.

(D) Delete.

To delete an existing IN-ADDR from your network record, place a D after the colon. List the IN-ADDR server and IP number and it will be deleted. The host entry will still exist in the global host tables.

Section 1. Network Record Information.

1a. Network Name.

Please supply the network name.

NOTE: The network name is not the domain name.

To verify an existing Network Name, use the searchable WHOIS database.

The Network Name is used as an identifier in Internet name and address tables. To create a network name, supply a short name consisting of a combination of up to 12 numbers and letters for the network. You may use a dash (-) as part of the Network Name, but no other special characters. Please do not use periods or underscores.

1b./1c. Start/End of Network Block.

1b. Start of Network Block.

If the network record is for a single network, enter the IP address of the single network here. Item 1c is then left blank. If the record is a block of IP addresses, enter the IP address of the start of the network block.

1c. End of Network Block.

If the network record is a block of IP addresses, Item 1c will be the last IP address of the network block.

If you received a block of IP addresses from your ISP, there may already be IN-ADDR servers on the parent block held by that provider. Please query your ISP before submitting an IN-ADDR request.

Section 2. Name and Postal Address of Organization.

2a. Name of Organization.

The network is considered to be registered to an organization, even if the "organization" is an individual. If you are an ISP submitting this request on behalf of your customer, please provide here the name and postal address of the organization that uses the IP address(es).

2b. Postal Address of Organization.

This is the physical address of the organization. Place the city, state, and zip code together on the same line below the Street Address or Post Office Box. Use a comma to separate the city and state. Do not insert a period following the state abbreviation. To change an address, please provide the new address information in this item, and flag the change in Section 6: Comments.

EXAMPLE:

111 Town Center Drive

Herndon, VA 22070

If the organization is located in a country other than the United States, please include the two-letter country code on the last line by itself.

EXAMPLE:

161 James Street

Montreal, QC H2S 2C8

CA

For the country entry, please use the two-letter country code found at: URL: [ftp://rs.arin.net/netinfo/iso3166-countrycodes]

NOTE: If you wish to make a change to an existing registered physical address of an organization, please note the change you want in Section 6: Comments.

Section 3. Technical Contact

The technical point of contact (POC) is the person responsible for the technical aspects of maintaining the network's name servers. The POC should be able to answer any utilization questions ARIN may have.

3a. User Handle (if known)

Each person in the ARIN database is assigned a user handle, which is a unique tag consisting of the user's initials and a serial number. This tag is used in database records to indicate a POC for a domain name, network, name server or other entity. Each user should have only one handle.

If the user handle is known, insert the handle in Item 3a and leave the rest of Section 3 blank. If the user's handle is unknown or the user has never been registered, leave Item 3a blank. The user's database record will be updated with any new information on the template.

3b. *Name (Last, First)*

　Enter the name of the Technical Contact in the format:

　　Last Name, First Name.

　Separate first and last names by a comma.

3c. *Organization.*

　Provide the name of the organization with which the Technical Contact is affiliated. Refer to the instructions for Item 2a.

3d. *Postal Address.*

　Refer to the instructions for Item 2b.

Section 4. Primary Name Server.

Networks are required to provide at least two independent servers for translating address to name mapping for hosts in the domain. The servers should be in physically separate locations and on different networks, if possible. The servers should be active and responsive to domain name server (DNS) queries prior to submission of this application.

ARIN requires that you provide complete information on your primary and secondary servers in order to process your registration request. Incomplete information in sections 4 and 5, or inactive servers will result in the return of the registration request.

NOTE: To change the name or the number of a registered name server, submit a separate IN-ADDR template requesting a modification of your IN-ADDR registration. Do this by placing an M after the Modify command in Section 0: Registration Action Type. New IN-ADDR registrations cannot be used to change the name or the number of a registered name server.

4a. *Primary Name Server Hostname.*

　Please provide the fully qualified name of the machine that is to be the name server.

　EXAMPLE:

　Use "machine.domainname.com" not just "machine" or just "domainname.com." Many reverse-authentication programs will not search for the nameserver if only the domain name is listed.

4b. *Primary Name Server Netaddress.*

It is suggested that the fourth octet of an IP address of a server should be neither 0 nor 255. The remaining 254 numbers in the fourth octet of the IP address are valid.

Section 5. Secondary Name Server(s)

5a./5b. Secondary Name Server Hostname/Secondary Name Server Netaddress.

Please refer to the instructions and examples in Items 4a./4b. above.

Copy Section 5 as needed to include all Secondary Name Servers. Do not renumber or change the copied section. A maximum of six domain name servers may be added to a network record.

Section 6. Comments.

Please use Section 6 to provide ARIN with all comments and any additional detailed updates relevant to your IN-ADDR registration not provided in Sections 0 through 5.

Sample Network Traces for DNS Resolutions

THIS APPENDIX DISPLAYS SOME VERY BASIC CAPTURES from the Microsoft Net Monitor utility. A fully capable version is included with the Systems Management Server as a part of BackOffice, allowing you to capture the traffic going to and from any machine on the network. A less-capable version comes with Windows NT Server that is able to trace traffic to and from the machine it's running on.

Network Monitor provides basic packet capture and decode capability. The figures presented in this Appendix have the header sections of the packets that were captured by the name server for several DNS queries submitted through nslookup.

DNS Query Trace: The Question

Figure E.1 shows the DNS question being sent for www.cnri.reston.va.us. Working down the header information, the listing starts off with Frame properties, Ethernet, IP, and UDP packet headers, and finally the DNS information. The highlighted line is the question in the DNS packet.

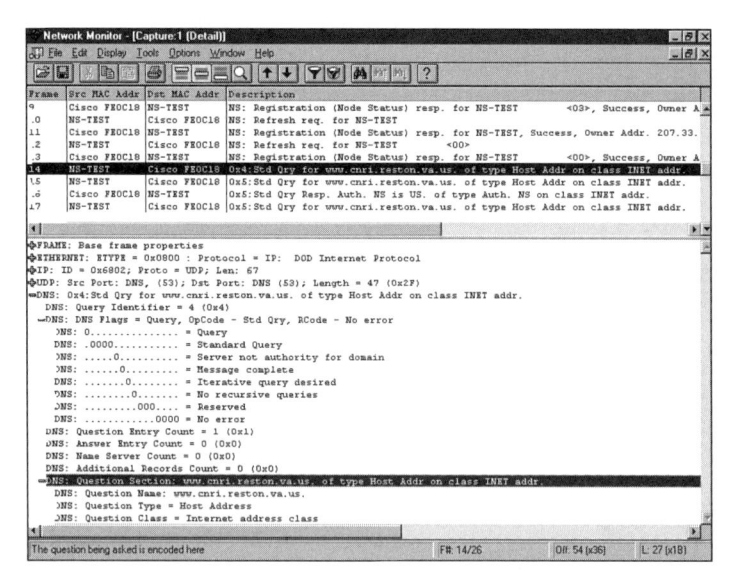

Figure E.1 Network Monitor trace of a DNS query for ww.cnri.reston.va.us.

From the information displayed, the packet can be identified as a DNS query for the Internet class host address of www.cnri.reston.va.us.

DNS Query Trace: The Answer

Figure E.2 displays the returned packet with the answer section of the query. Examining the lines for the DNS answer, the first thing that should be noticed is the fact that www.cnri.reston.va.us is actually a CNAME for www1.cnri.reston.va.us. The line following the declaration of the CNAME record provides the actual result of the query, that being the IP address of www1, aliased to www.

With the WINS lookup enabled, the DNS server can query for WINS registered hosts, and if they exist, report them as members of the Internet domain served by the name server.

DNS Query Trace: DNS Questions WINS

Figure E.3 shows the query for a host address being passed from the DNS server to the WINS server.

There are a couple of points of interest in this query. The first is the UDP header line where the source port is 53 (standard DNS). However, the destination port is 137 for the NetBIOS name service.

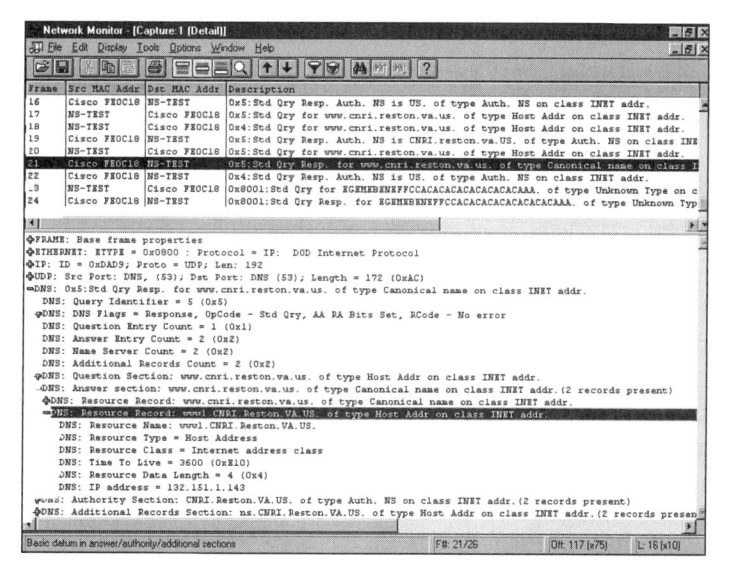

Figure E.2 Network Monitor trace showing an answer to the DNS query.

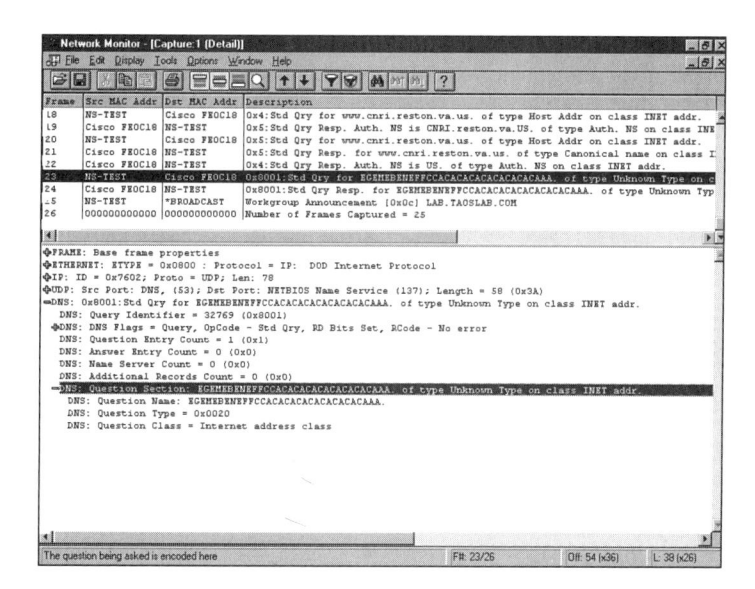

Figure E.3 Network Monitor trace showing how DNS queries WINS.

The second point of interest is that the name being used in the query is some encoded alpha-numeric string, and the type is "Unknown." Obviously, this is a problem. Microsoft has acknowledged it in KB article Q160828, "Network Monitor Parses DNS WINS Lookup Queries as DNS Packets." The article says that "…the Protocol column will say DNS even when the packet being sent to the WINS server is a NetBT packet destined for port 137." The article goes on to say, "Microsoft…[is]… researching this problem and will post new information here in the Microsoft Knowledge Base as it becomes available."

DNS Query Trace: WINS Answers DNS

In Figure E.4, the answer for the query, resolved through WINS, is displayed. Here again, some nonstandard information is being passed in the DNS packet. The same name is returned with a resource type equal to 20 (hex), which is an unknown resource type code in standard DNS, and the RDATA field that would normally contain an IP address isn't present. Instead, there's a series of numbers that look somewhat like a MAC address under the "Additional Resource Data" heading.

This answer is not very useful, and it's clear that there's hidden, undocumented information of some kind passing between the DNS and WINS server. The problem with this trace is that there really aren't any references to tell what is happening. The request goes to the WINS server and comes back with an answer, but how can anyone really be sure that the information is correct? And incidentally, the numeric string that came back from the WINS server is not a MAC address, as is evidenced by requesting the MAC address from a workstation:

```
> arp -d flamer.lab.taoslab.com

Net to Media Table
Device    IP Address                        Mask
Flags     Phys Addr
------    ------------------                ---------------
-----     ---------------
le0       flamer.lab.taoslab.com            255.255.255.255
00:20:af:f0:77:0e
```

Despite its shortcomings, Network Monitor is an excellent tool for administrators because it decodes and parses SMB (Server Message Block) and NetBT messages.

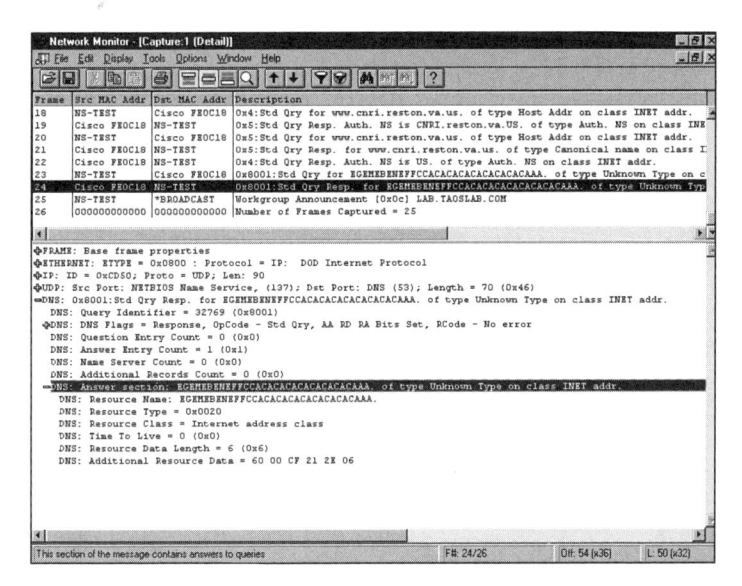

Figure E.4 Network Monitor trace showing how WINS answers DNS.

F

Resource Records and the InterNIC Cache File

THIS APPENDIX FURNISHES TWO KINDS OF INFORMATION, a list of Resource Records not found elsewhere in the book, and a sample of the InterNIC's root server cache file for your reference.

Resource Records

The Resource Record types documented immediately below are used infrequently compared with those in Chapter 7, "What DNS Knows." Refer to Chapter 7 for the more commonly used Resource Record types. In addition to an explanation of each RR type is its syntax for the boot file and an example showing how it's used. Note that the `<class>` and `<ttl>` fields for the Resource Records are reversible.

AAAA Records

AAAA (Address Records for a host using IPv6) or quad "A" Resource Records are the address record type for IPv6 Internet addresses. The syntax is basically the same as the standard A record:

```
<owner>      <ttl>     <class>     AAAA      <IPv6 address>
```

An example AAAA would look something like:
```
v6gtwy.taos.com.          IN     AAAA     1234:5678:abc:0:0:0:356:70
```

AFSDB Records

AFSDB (Andrew File System Database) Resource Records (experimental at this stage) are pointers for either AFS cell database servers or DCE authenticated name servers. AFS is a distributed network file system, for which the locations of all the filesets are stored in the cell database. Information about the location of DCE (Open Software Foundation distributed computing environment) services is obtained from the authenticated name server in a DCE cell. A cell is a group of hosts that share services. The syntax for the AFSDB record looks like:

    <owner>   <ttl>   <class>   AFSDB   <subtype>   <host>

where the `<subtype>` is a 1 for an AFS cell database, and 2 for a DCE authenticated name server. An example AFSDB record might look like:

    taos.com.   IN   AFSDB   1   afssrv.taos.com.

HINFO Records

The HINFO (Host Information) Resource Record was designed to provide some basic information about a host architecture or hardware type and operating system. Originally designed to aid clients when connecting to hosts with services like FTP, the HINFO record is now primarily used by local administrators to help keep track of machines on the network. The syntax is as follows:

    <owner>   <ttl>   <class>   HINFO   <cpu>   <os>

An example HINFO record might look like:

    flamer.taoslab.com.   IN   HINFO   PC   Win95

Note that the `<cpu>` and `<os>` types need to be enclosed in quotes if whitespace is going to be used.

ISDN Records

The ISDN (Integrated Services Digital Network) Addressing Resource Record (experimental at this stage) is designed to provide addresses for ISDN resources. The unique thing with ISDN, is the fact that the ISDN address is really a phone number. The Resource Record contains the telephone number with country and area code, and can also include a `<subaddr>` field, after the primary address (telephone number), to contain the telephone extension, if there is one. The syntax for the ISDN record is as follows:

    <owner>   <ttl>   <class>   ISDN   <ISDN-address>   <subaddr>

An example ISDN Resource Record could be represented as:

    pbx.taos.com.   IN   ISDN   14083302562   100

MB Records

The MB (Mailbox) domain record (experimental at this stage) was initially designed as a pointer to mail accounts in a DNS domain. The record never caught on for implementation, although the `<mailbox>` field in the SOA record uses the MB format specification. The syntax for the MB record looks like:

```
<owner>     <ttl>     <class>     MB     <mailbox domain name>
```

An example of the MB record might look like:
```
hknief.taos.com.     IN     MB     mailhost.taos.com.
```

MG Records

The MG (Mail Group) Resource Record (experimental in DNS at this stage, per the RFC) is another mail handling record that is very similar to the MB Resource Record. The purpose of the MG record is to provide a record for mail groups (also known as mail-lists). The syntax is essentially the same as the MB record, with multiple mailboxes listed under the mail group owner:

```
<owner>     <ttl>     <class>     MG     <mail group domain name>
```

A mail group (list) would look like:
```
sysadmin.taos.com.     IN     MG     hknief.taos.com.
                       IN     MG     gtal.taos.com.
                       IN     MG     mmasterson.taos.com.
```

MINFO Records

The MINFO (Mailbox Information) Resource Record (experimental at this stage) is very similar in function to the `Owner-<maillist>` and `<maillist>-response` aliases for many list manager software packages. The `<resp-mbox>` is the person responsible for list maintenance, and the `<error-mbox>` is the mail address where messages concerning errors should be routed. The formal syntax looks like:

```
<owner>     <ttl>     <class>     MINFO     <resp-mbox>     <error-mbox>
```

In an actual zone file, the record format could be represented as:
```
sysadmin.taos.com.     IN     MINFO     hknief.taos.com.     hknief.taos.com.
```

MR Records

The MR (Mailbox Rename) Resource Record (experimental at this stage) has the functionality that would be the equivalent of the redirected mail capability of the mail alias. It basically represents an alternate mail address for mail to be forwarded to, or for the mailer, which mail address to rewrite in the "To:" field. The basic syntax is represented by:

```
<owner>     <ttl>     <class>     MR     <new mbox>
```

In practical application, the entry in the zone file might look like:
```
hknief.isi.edu.     IN     MR     hknief.taos.com.
```

RP Records

The RP (Responsible Person) Resource Record (experimental at this stage) enables the administrator to designate, through the DNS, who is responsible for individual machines on a network. This can be a good or a bad thing depending on your job title and how the machine in question is performing. The syntax for the RP record looks like:

```
<owner>     <ttl>     <class>     RP     <mbox name>     <txt RR domain>
```

If this was implemented on an actual server, it could look like:
```
www.taos.com.    IN    RP    hknief.taos.com.    txt.taos.com.
txt.taos.com.    IN    TXT   "Help Desk - (408) 588-1296"
```

This record basically says that `hknief` is the responsible person, and further digging by querying the TXT record reports the phone number of the help desk.

RT Records

The RT (Route Through) Resource Record (experimental at this stage) looks like an MX record type, with the purpose of providing multiple addresses that packets may be routed through. If a host was not directly connected to the internet, but needed to have Telnet access, the idea that intermediate hosts could act as gateways for the session could be established with these RT records. Priorities can be specified to provide alternate routes, should one host fail. The syntax looks like:

```
<owner>     <ttl>     <class>     RT     <preference>     <intermediate-host>
```

In application, the record might look like:
```
internal.taos.com.    IN    RT    5     gateway.taos.com.
                      IN    RT    10    bkupgtwy.taos.com.
```

TXT Records

The TXT (Text) Resource Record (as with the RP Resource Record) enables the administrator to associate some text string with a particular record. The basic syntax for this Resource Record is:

```
<owner>     <ttl>     <class>     TXT     <text string>
```

Another example of the TXT record could give information about the location of a particular host:
```
www.taos.com.    IN    TXT    "Santa Clara Office"
```

WKS Records

The WKS (Well Known Services) Resource Record was designed to let outside agents know that certain hosts were providing specific services. The services are associated with the protocol (TCP or UDP) and the service type. The protocols may be any listed in the PROTOCOLS file (`\%systemroot%\system32\drivers\etc\protocol`). The

services can be any services below port 256 from the SERVICES file (\%system-root%\system32\drivers\etc\services). The syntax for the WKS record looks like:
```
<owner>      <ttl>      <class>     WKS       <address>  <protocol>  <service>
```

An example of WKS records might look like:
```
taos.com.            IN     WKS    207.33.46.130    tcp    telnet
                     IN     WKS    207.33.46.135    upd    domain
                     IN     WKS    207.33.46.140    tcp    smtp
```

X25 Records

The X.25 (X.25 Addressing) Resource Record (experimental at this stage), like the ISDN record, is designed to provide addressing for X.25 circuits. The address itself is actually an X.121 address for use in X.25 networks. The syntax is:
```
<owner>      <ttl>      <class>     X.25      <psdn address>
```

An example of an X.25 record could look like:
```
remote.taos.com.         IN     X.25    31547622562
```

The InterNIC Cache File

InterNIC's root cache file is automatically loaded into the DNS server during installation using the latest copy Microsoft received before distributing the server. The file's name is `cache.dns`.

Changes to the root cache records rarely occur, and changes that do occur usually have little or no effect on the functioning of other DNS servers. You can download the root cache file directly from the InterNIC at http://www.internic.net, and via FTP at ftp://rs.internic.net/domain/named.root.

The cache file contains the names and IP addresses of the root level servers. There's an NS record for each root name server and an A record as well, because the DNS architecture requires it. When the domain name system was first implemented, several name servers around the network were made root name servers. To simplify things and make it easier to recognize these important name servers, they were moved to the `root-servers.net` domain. For informational purposes you'll see, in each server's record, its old name—the one used before it was moved to the `root-servers.net` domain. The old name provides a clue to each server's actual location.

The `cache.dns` file contains entries like these:
```
; formerly NS.INTERNIC.NET
.                         3600000   IN   NS    A.ROOT-SERVERS.NET.
A.ROOT-SERVERS.NET.       3600000        A     198.41.0.4
;
; formerly NS1.ISI.EDU
.                         3600000        NS    B.ROOT-SERVERS.NET.
B.ROOT-SERVERS.NET.       3600000        A     128.9.0.107
;
```

```
; formerly C.PSI.NET
.                       3600000   NS   C.ROOT-SERVERS.NET.
C.ROOT-SERVERS.NET.     3600000   A    192.33.4.12
;
; formerly TERP.UMD.EDU
.                       3600000   NS   D.ROOT-SERVERS.NET.
D.ROOT-SERVERS.NET.     3600000   A    128.8.10.90
;
; formerly NS.NASA.GOV
.                       3600000   NS   E.ROOT-SERVERS.NET.
E.ROOT-SERVERS.NET.     3600000   A    192.203.230.10
;
; formerly NS.ISC.ORG
.                       3600000   NS   F.ROOT-SERVERS.NET.
F.ROOT-SERVERS.NET.     3600000   A    192.5.5.241
;
; formerly NS.NIC.DDN.MIL
.                       3600000   NS   G.ROOT-SERVERS.NET.
G.ROOT-SERVERS.NET.     3600000   A    192.112.36.4
;
; formerly AOS.ARL.ARMY.MIL
.                       3600000   NS   H.ROOT-SERVERS.NET.
H.ROOT-SERVERS.NET.     3600000   A    128.63.2.53
;
; formerly NIC.NORDU.NET
.                       3600000   NS   I.ROOT-SERVERS.NET.
I.ROOT-SERVERS.NET.     3600000   A    192.36.148.17
;
.                       3600000   NS   J.ROOT-SERVERS.NET.
J.ROOT-SERVERS.NET.     3600000   A    198.41.0.10
;
; housed in LINX, operated by RIPE NCC
;
.                       3600000   NS   K.ROOT-SERVERS.NET.
K.ROOT-SERVERS.NET.     3600000   A    193.0.14.129
;
; temporarily housed at ISI (IANA)
;
.                       3600000   NS   L.ROOT-SERVERS.NET.
L.ROOT-SERVERS.NET.     3600000   A    198.32.64.12
;
; housed in Japan, operated by WIDE
;
.                       3600000   NS   M.ROOT-SERVERS.NET.
M.ROOT-SERVERS.NET.     3600000   A    202.12.27.33
; End of File
```

Index

A

AAAA (Address Records for a host using IPv6), 307
accessing servers, 130-131
   DNS Spoofing, 224-225
   email security, 229
   firewalls, 225-227
   FTP, 228
   security, 133-134
   World Wide Web, 227-228
Active Directory, LDAP (Lightweight Directory Access Protocol), 29, 55
Address (A) records, 94, 102-103
addresses (IP), 4-5
   configuring clients for DNS, 190-191
   DNS name servers
      changing, 219
      editing configuration, 220-222
   mapping host names, 102-103
   multihomed servers
      connecting by preference, 168-169
      connecting with disabled NICs, 169
      mapping, 165-167
      queries, 167-168
   registration, 5
   remote systems, 71-79
   resolution, reverse lookups, 39, 100-102
   resource records, 5, 7
   WINS (Windows Internet Name Service) configuration, 180
AFSDB (Andrew File System Database) Resource Records, 308
American Registry for Internet Numbers, see **ARIN (American Registry for Internet Numbers)**
anonymous FTP, security, 228
answers, DNS queries, Net Monitor, 302-304

ARIN (American Registry for Internet Numbers), 294
   inverse mapping, registering, 295-300
   network numbers
      assignments, 294-295
      registering, 294-295

B

B-nodes (broadcast), NetBIOS computers, 42-43
BDCs (Backup Domain Controllers), 4
BIND (Berkeley Internet Daemon), 267
BIND configuration files, DNS servers, 139-140
Bind for NT, 267-268
BIND XFRNETS directive, 123-124
BIND-based name servers, 121-123
BindSecondaries Registry key, 122
boot files
   MS DNS, 123-124
   startup, DNS servers, zone transfers, 208
   storing WINDOWS NT configuration data, 82-83
   synchronizing DNS with Registry files, 83
BOOTP (BOOTSTRAP PROTOCOL), compared to DHCP (Dynamic Host Configuration Protocol), 252-253
broadcast method nodes, NetBIOS computers, 42
broadcast queries, NetBIOS name resolution, 25-26
BroadcastAddress parameter, NetBT, WINS (Windows Internet Name Service) configuration, 183

browsers
   Computer Browser service, 58
   LMB (local master browsers), 59
   browsing Windows NT networks, 177-180

C

caches, 111
   accessing root-level servers, 108-110
   DNS database, 202
   hits, 118-119
   InterNIC, 311
   misses, 119-120
   name servers, 86-87, 90-92
   names, NetBIOS, 24-26, 42
   queries, 134-135
canonical name (CNAME) records, 104-105
capacity, DNS servers, 128-129
characteristics, host names, 13-15
   RFC 1035, 14-15
   Windows (NetBIOS), 15-16
Cisco DNS/DHCP Manager, 265
clients
   configuring for DNS, 8, 185-187
      criteria for capacity, 128-129
      domain names, 188-190
      Domain Suffix Search Order, 191-193
      enabling DNS, 187-189
      host names, 188
      IP address order, 190-191
   configuring for WINS (Windows Internet Name Service), 171-174
      browsing on Windows NT networks, 177-180
      DHCP (Dynamic Host Configuration Protocol) servers, 175
      IP addresses, 180
      name registration, 175-176
      name-to-IP address mapping resolution, 177
      NetBIOS computer names, 180-181
      NetBIOS scope, 174-175
      NetBT parameters, 182-185
   DHCP (Dynamic Host Configuration Protocol)
      configuring, 253-254, 261
      integrating with WINS (Windows Internet Name Service) and DNS, 261-262
      options in server configuration, 259-261

   name servers
      cache hits, 118-119
      cache misses, 119-120
   reservations, 259-260
   resolving requests, 71-79
com, generic top-level domain name, 65, 196
commands
   DNS Manager
      New Host, 145
      New Record, 145-146
   NET SEND, 24
   NET VIEW, 24
   nslookup
      exit, 232
      finger, 232-233
      help or ?, 232
      ls, 233
      lserver, 233
      root, 233
      server, 233
      set, 234-239
Computer Browser service, 58
computer hosts, 4, 64-66, 141-144
configuring
   DHCP (Dynamic Host Configuration Protocol)
      clients, 253-254, 261
      servers, 257-260
   WINDOWS NT DNS servers, 139-150
Control Panel, installing DHCP (Dynamic Host Configuration Protocol) servers, 255-256
conventions, naming host names, 14-16
   Windows (NetBIOS), 15-16

D

databases, *see DNS Database tables*
datagram services, NetBIOS, 21
DCs (domain controllers), 58
DDNS (Dynamic DNS), 250
delegation, name servers, 110
   domains, 67-68
   (NS) records, 99-100

DHCP (Dynamic Host Configuration Protocol), 5, 251
  clients
    configuring, 253-254, 261
    configuring for WINS (Windows Internet Name Service), 175
    integrating with WINS (Windows Internet Name Service) and DNS, 261-262
  compared to BOOTTP, 252-253
  integrating with DNS, 251
  servers
    configuring, 257-260
    DHCP Relay Agent, 257
    installing, 254-256
DHCP Manager, server configuration, 257-258
  client options, 259-260
  scopes, 258-260
DHCP Relay Agent, 257
DhcpNameServer parameter, NetBT, WINS (Windows Internet Name Service) configuration, 185
Dig utility, 240-242, 266
directives, BIND XFRNETS, 123-124
distribution, host names, 11-12
DMB (domain master browsers), 59
DNS (Domain Name System), 3-4, 275-280
  combining with WINS (Windows Internet Name Service), 56-57
  configuring clients, 8, 185-187
    domain names, 188-190
    Domain Suffix Search Order, 191-193
    enabling DNS, 187-189
    host names, 188
    IP address order, 190-191
  domains
    hierarchy of hosts/domains, 4, 64-66
    top-level, 275-280
  host names, 4-5
    characteristics, 13
    distribution, 11-12
    Fully Qualified Domain Names, 16-17
    naming conventions, 14-16
    registration, 5
    resolution, 6-11
    resource records, 5, 7
    RFC 1035, 14-15
  integrating with DHCP (Dynamic Host Configuration Protocol), 251, 262
  integrating with WINS (Windows Internet Name Service)
    lookups, 158-160
    multihomed servers, 165-169
    name resolution, 154-155
    reverse WINS lookups, 162-165
    settings, 160-161
    testing WINS lookups, 161-162
    troubleshooting, 156-158
  Microsoft DNS
    communicating with other name servers, 121-122
    configuring boot files, 123-124
    integrating WINS (Windows Internet Name Service), 123
    migrating from BIND-based servers, 122-123
  monitoring in System event log, 200-202
  namespaces, 30
  name resolution methods, 40
    NetBIOS, 26
    query for NetBIOS names, 42-46
    query for non-NetBIOS names, 41-42
    query HOSTS and LMHOSTS files, 46-51
  non–Microsoft versions, 267
  process, 64
  provided by ISPs (Internet service providers)
    primary, 132-133
    secondary, 133
  purposes/limitations, 55-56
  WINS (Windows Internet Name Service) comparison, 154
  see also DNS name servers; DNS services
DNS database tables, 202
  RRs (Resource Records), 94
    address (A) records, 102-103
    Canonical name (CNAME) records, 104-105
    Mail Exchange (MX) records, 103-104
    name server (NA) records, 99-100
    pointer (PTR) records, 100-102
    Start-of-Authority (SOA) records, 96-99
    syntax format, 94-96

DNS database tables

WINS (Windows Internet Name Server)
   records, 105-107
WINS-Reverse records, 108
DNS Manager, 5, 123-124
  DNS menu, 140
  DNS server configuration, 139-140
    adding resource records, 145
    changing resource records, 146
    load balancing with round robin,
      147-148
    multihomed server support, 149-150
    notifying changes, 148-149
    zones, 141-144
  navigating, 140-141
  properties
    address (A) records, 102-103
    Canonical name (CNAME) records,
      104-105
    Mail Exchange (MX) records, 103-104
    name server (NS) records, 99-100
    pointer (PTR) records, 100-102
    Start-of-Authority (SOA) records, 96-98
    WINS (Windows Internet Name
      Service) records, 105-107
    WINS (Windows Internet Name
      Service)-Reverse records, 108
DNS name servers, 4, 266
  adding, 214-216
    primary zones, 216-217
    secondary zones, 217
  caching, 86-87, 134-135
  capacity, 128-129
  clients, resolving requests, 71-79
  configuring, 139-140
  domains
    number, 129-130
    subdomains, 131
  forwarders and slaves, 87-90
  host names
    characteristics, 13
    conventions, 14-16
    distribution, 11-12
    resolution, 6-11
    resource records, 5-7
  IP addresses
    changing, 219
    editing configuration, 220-222

ISPs (Internet service providers)
  providing DNS service
    primary, 132-133
    secondary, 133
load balancing with round robin,
  147-148
messages, sending, 114, 117-118
multihomed server support, 149-150
multiple zones, 212-213
number required, 130-131
notifying changes, 148-149
primary, 69, 82
  security, 133-134
  synchronizing DNS Registry and boot
    files, 83
  transferring data to secondary servers,
    70-71
  UNIX-style BIND configurations,
    83-85
  WINDOWS NT boot configuration
    data, 82-83
queries, Net Monitor, 301-302
  answers to queries, 302-304
  iterative, 38
  recursive, 36-38
  reverse, 39
  WINS (Windows Internet Name
    Service) server, 302-304
registering changes, 219-220
resource records
  adding, 145
  changing, 146
secondary, 69, 85-86
security for primary, 133-134
split-brain DNS, 135-136
types, 90-92
Windows resolvers, 35-36
  iterative queries, 38
  recursive queries, 36-38
  reverse queries, 39
zone transfers, 210-212
  Windows NT servers, 207-209
  WINS (Windows Internet Name
    Service) servers, 206-207
zones, 141-144, 217, 219
See also name servers
DNS Pro 5.6, 267-268
DNS Resolver, 266

DNS Spoofing, 224-225
DNS tab, TCP/IP Properties dialog box (Windows NT), 114-115
DNS Workshop, 266
DNS/BIND, RFCs (Request for Comment), 271-273
dnscmd, 266
DNSIND, 267
documentation, InterNIC domain registration, 282-293
Domain Name Registration Agreement, 219-220
domain name space, 185
Domain Name System, *see* DNS (Domain Name System)
domain Suffix Search Order
   qualifying names, 191-192
   setting with Registry, 192-193
   setting with text files, 192
domains, 64-66
   ADDR.ARPA, 295-300
   DNS (Domain Name System) servers, 4
      criteria for capacity, 128-129
      number, 129-130
      primary, 7, 69
      secondary, 7, 69
      subdomains, 131
      transferring data from primary to secondary, 70-71
   first-level, 275-280
   hierarchy, 66
   hosts, zones, 141-144
   name servers
      caching, 86-87
      determining types, 90, 92
      forwarders and slaves, 87-90
      primary, 82, 85
      secondary, 85-86
   names, 24, 281
      generic top-level domains, 196
      InterNIC (Internet Network Information Center), 186
      registering, 197-198, 281-293
      registering changes, 219-220
   resource records
      adding, 145
      changing, 146
   subdomains, 67-68

zones, 68-69
see also addresses
Dynamic DNS (DDNS), 250
Dynamic Host Configuration Protocol, *see* DHCP (Dynamic Host Configuration Protocol)

E

edu, generic top-level domains, 65, 196
email security, 229
EnableDNS parameter, NetBT, WINS configuration, 183
EnableLmhosts parameter, NetBT, WINS configuration, 184
error messages
   nslookup tool, 239-240
   see also troubleshooting
event logs, monitoring DNS service, 200-202
Event Viewer, monitoring DNS service, 200-202
exit (nslookup) command, 232

F

fields, DNS messages, 115, 118
files
   boot, MS DNS, 123-124
   HOSTS
      name resolution, 46-47, 50-51
      NetBIOS name resolution, 26
   LMHOSTS
      name resolution, 46-50
      NetBIOS name resolution, 25-26
finger (nslookup) command, 232-233
firewalls, 225-227
first-level domains, 65-66, 275-280
flat namespaces, NetBIOS, 29-30
forward lookup zones, 102-103, 142-144
forward queries
   iterative, 38
   recursive, 36-38
forwarders, 87-92, 114
FQDNs (fully qualified domain names), 16-17, 26
FTP (File Transfer Protocol) servers, security, 228

G-H

generic top-level domains, 196
gov, generic top-level domain name, 65, 196
H-nodes (hybrid), NetBIOS computers, 43-46
Help menu, DNS Manager, 141
help or ? (nslookup) command, 232
hierarchy, DNS hosts/domains, 64-66
HINFO (Host Information) Resource Record, 308
hint files, 108
host names, 4-5
   characteristics, 13
   distribution, 11-12
   Fully Qualified Domain Names, 16-17
   naming conventions, 14-16
   registration, 5
   resolution, 6-8
      resolvers, 7, 9
      reverse lookups, 9-10
      search order, 10-11
   resource records, 5-7
   RFC 1035, 14-15
host-to-address queries, 75-79
hosts, 4, 64-66, 141-144
HOSTS file
   name resolution, 46-47, 50-51
   NetBIOS name resolution, 26

I-J

IAB (Internet Architecture Board), 9
IANA (Internet Assigned Numbers Authority), 9
ICMP (Internet Control Management Protocol), 35
IESG (Internet Engineering Steering Group), 9
IETF (Internet Engineering Task Force), 9, 158
IMAP (Internet Message Access Protocol), email security, 229
In-addr (inverse address) zones, 142-143

In-ADDR.ARPA (domain), 295-300
info, generic top-level domain name, 196
Information Sciences Institute (ISI), 271
installing
   servers, DHCP (Dynamic Host Configuration Protocol), 254-256
   WINDOWS NT DNS service
      pre-installation checklist, 138
      steps, 138-139
      verifying TCP/IP stack configuration, 138
Internet
   domains
      ADDR.ARPA, 295-300
      first-level, 275-280
      names, 281
      registering, 281-293
   IP addresses, 4-5
      registration, 5
      resource records, 5-7
Internet Architecture Board (IAB), 9
Internet Assigned Numbers Authority (IANA), 9
Internet Control Management Protocol, *see* ICMP (Internet Control Management Protocol)
Internet Engineering Steering Group (IESG), 9
Internet Engineering Task Force (IETF), 9
Internet Message Access Protocol, *see* IMAP (Internet Message Access Protocol)
Internet Network Information Center, *see* InterNIC (Internet Network Information Center)
Internet Society (ISOC), 9
InterNIC (Internet Network Information Center)), 186
   cache files, 311
   domain names, 186,197-198, 281-293
inverse address (in-addr) zones, 142-143
inverse queries (reverse lookups), 39, 100-102

host name resolution, 9-10
WINS, 162-165
WINS (Windows Internet Name Service)-Reverse, 108
zones, 142-144
IP addresses, 4-5
configuring clients for DNS, 190-191
DNS name servers
changing, 219
editing configuration, 220-222
mapping host names, 102-103
multihomed servers
connecting by preference, 168-169
connecting with disabled NICs, 169
mapping, 165-167
queries, 167-168
registration, 5
remote systems, 71-79
resolution, reverse lookups, 39, 100-102
resource records, 5, 7
WINS (Windows Internet Name Service) configuration, 180
IP lease phases, DHCP (Dynamic Host Configuration Protocol) ? configuration, 253
IPC (interprocess communication) services of NetBIOS, 20-21
ipconfig utility, 244-245, 262
IPv6 (Internet Protocol version 6), 269
IPX/SPX, NetBIOS, 23
ISDN (Integrated Services Digital Network) Addressing Resource Record, 308
ISI (Information Sciences Institute), 271
ISOC (Internet Society), 9
ISPs (Internet service providers), DNS service, 199-200
primary, 132-133
secondary, 133
iterative queries, 38, 73-75, 113-114

K-L

keys (Registry), BindSecondaries, 122

lame delegation errors, 110
LAN Manager, 21
LAN Server, 21
LANs, NetBEUI (NetBIOS Extended User Interface), 21
LDAP (Lightweight Directory Access Protocol), 29, 54
LMHOSTS file
name resolution, 46-50
NetBIOS name resolution, 25-26
load balancing with DNS round robin, 147-148
localhost address, 84
lookups, WINS (Windows Internet Name Service), 158-160
reverse, 162-165
testing, 161-162
ls (nslookup) command, 233
lserver (nslookup) command, 233

M

m-nodes (mixed broadcast and point to point), NetBIOS computers, 43-44
Mail Exchange (MX) records, 103-104
mail security, 229
menus, DNS Manager, 140-141
messages, DNS
sending, 114, 117-118
TTL (time-to-live), 120
Meta IP DNS 3.1, 267
MetaIP, 268
MG (Mail Group) Resource Record, 309
Microsoft DNS
Active Directory services, 29
communicating with other name servers, 121-122
configuring boot files, 123-124
integrating WINS (Windows Internet Name Service), 123
migrating from BIND-based servers, 122-123
Microsoft Network Client for MS-DOS, configuring for WINS (Windows Internet Name Service), 172
Mil domain, 65
MINFO (Mailbox Information) Resource Record, 309

moving zone files, 110-111
MR (Mailbox Rename) Resource
  Record, 309
multihomed NetBIOS, 23
multihomed servers, 57-58, 165
  IP addresses
    connecting by preference, 168-169
    connecting with disabled NICs, 169
    mapping, 165, 167
    queries, 167-168
  supporting, 149-150
multiple zones, 212-213
  primary zone, 216-217
  secondary zone, 217

N

name caches, NetBIOS, 24-26, 42
name registration
  name refresh/release requests/responses, 176
  requests, 175
  responses, 176
  WINS (Windows Internet Name Service), 156
name resolution, 34-35, 71-72, 75
  broadcast, NetBIOS, 21, 24-26
  clients, 72-79
  DNS, 35-36
    iterative queries, 38
    recursive queries, 36-38
    reverse queries, 39
  DNS/WINS (Windows Internet Name Service) integration, 154-155
  methods, 40
    query for NetBIOS names, 42-46
    query for non-NetBIOS names, 41-42
    query HOSTS and LMHOSTS files, 46-51
  name-to-IP address mapping resolution, 177
  provided by ISPs (Internet service providers), 199-200
  WINS (Windows Internet Name Service), 35
name servers, 186
  BIND-based, 121-122
  caches
    hits, 118-119
    misses, 119-120

caching, 86-87, 111
delegation, 110
determining types, 90-92
DHCP (Dynamic Host Configuration Protocol)
  configuring, 257-260
  installing, 254-256
DHCP Relay Agent DHCP (Dynamic Host Configuration Protocol), configuring, 257
DNS database, 202
forwarders and slaves, 87-90
messages, TTL (time-to-live), 120
Microsoft DNS
  communication with other servers, 121-122
  configuring boot files, 123-124
  integrating WINS (Windows Internet Name Service), 123
  migrating from BIND-based, 122-123
multihomed, 165
  connecting by preference to IP addresses, 168-169
  connecting with disabled NICs, 169
  DNS support, 149-150
  mapping IP addresses, 165-167
  queries to IP addresses, 167-168
multiple zones, 212-213
  adding DNS servers, 214-216
  primary, 216-217
  secondary, 217
NS records, 99-100
number required, 198-199
primary, 82
  synchronizing DNS Registry and boot files, 83
  UNIX-style BIND configurations, 83-85
  WINDOWS NT boot configuration data, 82-83
queries, iterative and recursive, 113-114
root, cache files, 108-110
secondary, 85-86
security
  DNS Spoofing, 224-225
  email, 229
  firewalls, 225-227
  FTP servers, 228
  World Wide Web, 227-228

virtual, 150
WINS (Windows Internet Name
  Service), Windows resolvers, 35
zone transfers, 110-111, 205-206
  *DNS and WINS (Windows Internet
    Name Service) servers, 206-207*
  primary and secondary, 200, 210-212
  Windows NT DNS servers, 207-209
zones, properties, 217-219
see also DNS name servers, primary
  name servers; secondary name servers
name services, NetBIOS, 20-21, 24
names
  domains, 281
  hosts, 4-5
    characteristics, 13
    conventions for naming, 14-15
    distribution, 11-12
    Fully Qualified Domain Names, 16-17
    registration, 5
    resolution, 6-11
    resource records, 5-7
    RFC 1035, 14-15
    Windows (NetBIOS), 15-16
  NetBIOS
    characteristics, 30-31
    resource codes, 31-32
NameServer parameter, NetBT, WINS configuration, 184
NameServerBackup parameter, NetBT, WINS configuration, 184
NameServerPort parameter, NetBT. WINS configuration, 182
namespaces
  DNS, 30
  NetBIOS, 29-30, 174-175
navigating DNS Manager, 140-141
NBT (NetBIOS over TCP/IP), 22
nbtstat utility, 247
net domain, 65
Net Monitor, DNS queries, 301-302
  answers, 302
    WINS server, 302-304
    WINS server answers, 304
NET SEND command, 24
NET VIEW command, 24
net, generic top-level domain name, 196

NetApp filers, 22
NetBEUI (NetBIOS Extended User Interface), 21-23
NetBIOS (Network Basic Input/Output System), 20
  computer names, WINS (Windows Internet Name Service) configuration, 180-181
  future plans, 54-55
  history, 21
  host names, 15-16
  IPC (interprocess communication) services, 20-21
  multihomed servers
    connecting by preference, 168-169
    queries, 167-168
  name resolution, 24-26
    DNS, 41-46
    DNS/WINS (Windows Internet Name Service) integration, 154-155
  name services, 24
  names
    caches, 42
    characteristics, 30-31
    node types, 42-43, 46
    resource codes, 31-32
  namespaces, flat, 29-30
  RFCs (Request for Comment), 271-273
  scope, configuring clients for WINS (Windows Internet Name Service), 174-175
  SMBs (Server Message Blocks), 21-22
  TCP/IP, 22-23
  WINS (Windows Internet Name Service), 26
NetBT (NetBIOS over TCP/IP) parameters, WINS (Windows Internet Name Service) configuration, 182
  BroadcastAddress, 183
  DhcpNameServer, 185
  EnableDNS, 183
  EnableLmhosts, 184
  NameServer, 184
  NameServerBackup, 184
  NameServerPort, 182
  NameSrvQueryCount, 182
  NameSrvQueryTimeout, 183
  ScopeId, 185

NETINFO, 266
netlab utility, 243-244
netstat utility, 246-247
Network Appliance, CIFS (Common Internet File System) standard, 22
Network Basic Input/Output System, *see* NetBIOS (Network Basic Input/Output System)
Network Monitor, 265
networks
    adapters, IP addresses, adding/deleting second, 221-222
    numbers
        assignments, 294-295
        registering, 294-295
New Host command (DNS Manager), 145
nibble, 269
NIC Handles, 219
NICs (network interface cards), disabled, connecting to multihomed servers, 169
    see also multihomed servers
node types, NetBIOS, 42-43
    b (broadcast), 43-44
    h (hybrid), 43
    m (mixed broadcast and point-to-point), 44
    p (point-to-point), 44
nom, generic top-level domain name, 196
non-Microsoft DNS versions, 267
    normalized tables, WINS (Windows Internet Name Service), 28
notify directives, 111
notify option, 148-149
nslookup utility, 232, 262, 265
    commands
        exit, 232
        finger, 232-233
        ls, 233
        lserver, 233
        root, 233
        server, 233
        set, 234-239
    DNS Spoofing, 224
    error messages, 239-240
Nslookup4WWW, 266

O-P

Options menu, DNS Manager, 141
org generic top-level domain name, 65, 196
p-nodes (point-to-point), NetBIOS computers, 42-44
PDCs (Primary Domain Controllers), 4
Ping utility, 224, 242-243
pointer (PTR) records, 94, 100-102
POP (Post Office Protocol), email security, 229
ports, NetBIOS, 23
primary DNS name servers, 7, 69
    ISPs (Internet service providers), 132-133
    security, 133-134
    transferring data to secondary servers, 70-71
primary domain controllers, *see* PDCs (primary domain controllers)
primary domains, creating new, 142
primary name servers, 82, 90-92
    delegation, 110
    DNS database, 202
    multiple zones, 212-213
    number required, 198-199
    synchronizing DNS Registry and boot files, 83
    transferring files, 110-111
    UNIX-style BIND configurations, 83-85
    WINDOWS NT boot configuration data, 82-83
    zone transfers, 200, 205-206, 210-212
primary zones, 143-144, 216-217
print servers, multihomed, 58
private DNS servers, 12-13
problems
    DNS/WINS integration, 156-158
    utilities for troubleshooting
        dig, 240-242
        ipconfig, 244-245
        nbtstat, 247
        Netlab, 243-244
        netstat, 246-247

nslookup, 232-240
ping, 242-243
traceroute, 243
winipcfg, 245-246
see also error messages
protocols
  BOOTP (BOOTSTRAP PROTOCOL), compared to DHCP (Dynamic Host Configuration Protocol), 252-253
  DDNS (Dynamic DNS), 250
  DHCP (Dynamic Host Configuration Protocol), 5, 250-251
    clients, 175, 253-254, 261-262
    compared to BOOTP, 252-253
    integrating with DNS, 251
    servers, 254-260
  FTP (File Transfer Protocol) servers, security, 228
  ICMP (Internet Control Management Protocol), 35
  IMAP (Internet Message Access Protocol), email security, 229
  IPv6 (Internet Protocol version 6), 269
  IPX/SPX, NetBIOS, 23
  LDAP (Lightweight Directory Access Protocol), 29
    Active Directory, 55
  POP (Post Office Protocol), email security, 229
  SMTP (Simple Mail Transfer Protocol), email security, 229
  TCP/IP (Transmission Control Protocol/Internet Protocol), 3
    NetBIOS, 22-23

Q

QIP Enterprise 5.0, 268-269
queries
  caches, 134-135
  directing on multihomed servers, 167-168
  DNS, 114, 117-118, 301, 304
  inverse, 39
  iterative, 38, 113-114
  recursive, 36-38, 113-114
  reverse, 39

R

rec, generic top-level domain name, 196
recursive queries, 36-38, 72-79, 113-114
redundancy, DNS servers, 130-131
referrals, 114
registering
  domain names, 197-198, 219-220, 281-293
  host names, 5
  IP addresses, 5
  network numbers, 294-295
Registry
  configuring MS DNS, 123-124
  DNS servers
    startup, zone transfers, 208-209
    synchronizing with boot files, 83
    viewing entries, 222
  IP addresses, multihomed servers, 166-167
  keys, BindSecondaries, 122
  storing WINDOWS NT configuration data, 82-83
relay agents, DHCP Relay Agent, 257
reliability, DNS servers, 130-131
remote systems, clients, resolving requests, 71-79
Requests For Comments, *see* **RFCs (Requests For Comments)**
reservations, client, 259-260
reserved words, LMHOSTS.sam file, 50
resolution, host names, 6-8, 118
  resolvers, 7, 9
  reverse lookups, 9-10, 39
  search order, 10-11
resolvers, 73, 186-187
  host name resolution, 7, 9
  libraries, 114
  see also Windows resolvers
resource codes, NetBIOS names, 31-32
Resource Records (RRs), 5-7, 70, 94, 307
  AAAA, 307
  adding, 145
  address (A) records, 102-103
  AFSDB, 308

Canonical name (CNAME) records, 104-105
changing, 146
HINFO, 308
ISDN, 308
Mail Exchange (MX) records, 103-104
MG, 309
MINFO, 309
MR, 309
name server (NS) records, 99-100
pointer (PTR) records, 100-102
RP, 310
RT, 310
Start-of-Authority (SOA) records, 96-99
syntax format, 94-96
TXT, 310
WINS (Windows Internet Name Service) records, 105-107, 206-207
WINS (Windows Internet Name Service)-Reverse records, 108, 206-207
WKS, 310
X25, 311
reverse lookups, 39, 100-102
host name resolution, 9-10
WINS, 162-165
WINS (Windows Internet Name Service)-Reverse, 108
zones, 142-144
RFCs (Requests For Comments), 8, 14-15, 271-273
root (nslookup) command, 233
root name servers, cache files, 108-110
root-level domains, 65-66
Round robin, 147-148
RP (Responsible Person) Resource Record, 310
RRs, see Resource Records (RRs)
RT (Route Through) Resource Record, 310

S

scopeId parameter, NetBT, WINS configuration, 185
scopes, DHCP server configuration, 258-260

search order, host name resolution, 10-11
second-level domains, 65-67
secondary master servers, 110
secondary name servers, 85-86, 90-92
delegation, 110
DNS database, 202
DNS servers, 7, 69
ISPs (Internet service providers), 133
transferring data from primary servers, 70-71
multiple zones, 212-213
Notify option, 148-149
number required, 199
transferring files, 110-111
zone transfers, 200, 205-206, 210-212
secondary zones, 143-144, 217
security
DNS servers
access, 133-134
split-brain DNS, 135-136
DNS Spoofing, 224-225
email, 229
firewalls, 225-227
FTP servers, 228
World Wide Web, 227-228
server (nslookup) command, 233
Server List, multihomed servers, directing queries, 167-168
Server Message Blocks (SMBs), 21-22
servers
DNS name servers, 4, 266
adding, 214-217
caching, 86-87, 134-135
capacity, 128-129
clients, resolving requests, 71-79
configuring, 139-140
domains, 129-131
forwarders and slaves, 87-90
host names, 5-16
IP addresses, 219-222
ISPs (Internet service providers) providing DNS service, 132-133
load balancing with round robin, 147-148
messages, sending, 114, 117-118
multihomed server support, 149-150

multiple zones, 212-213
number required, 130-131
notifying changes, 148-149
primary, 69-71, 82-85, 133-134
queries, Net Monitor, 36-39, 301-304
registering changes, 219-220
resource records, 145-146
secondary, 69, 85-86
security for primary, 133-134
split-brain DNS, 135-136
types, 90-92
Windows resolvers, 35-39
zone transfers, 206-212
zones, 141-144, 217-219
name servers, 186
   BIND-based, 121-122
   caches, 118-120
   caching, 86-87, 111
   delegation, 110
   determining types, 90-92
   DHCP (Dynamic Host Configuration Protocol), 254-260
   DHCP Relay Agent DHCP (Dynamic Host Configuration Protocol), configuring, 257
   DNS database, 202
   forwarders and slaves, 87-90
   messages, TTL (time-to-live), 120
   Microsoft DNS, 121-124
   multihomed, 149-150, 165-169
   multiple zones, 212-217
   NS records, 99-100
   number required, 198-199
   primary, 82-85
   queries, iterative and recursive, 113-114
   root, cache files, 108-110
   secondary, 85-86
   security, 224-229
   virtual, 150
   WINS (Windows Internet Name Service), Windows resolvers, 35
   zone transfers, 110-111, 205-212
   zones, properties, 217-219
primary name servers, 82, 90-92
   delegation, 110
   DNS database, 202
   multiple zones, 212-213
   number required, 198-199
   synchronizing DNS Registry and boot files, 83
   transferring files, 110-111
   UNIX-style BIND configurations, 83-85
   WINDOWS NT boot configuration data, 82-83
   zone transfers, 200, 205-206, 210-212
secondary name servers, 85-86, 90-92
   delegation, 110
   DNS database, 202
   DNS servers, 7, 69-71, 133
   multiple zones, 212-213
   Notify option, 148-149
   number required, 199
   transferring files, 110-111
   zone transfers, 200, 205-206, 210-212
service packs
   Service Pack 2, multihomed servers
      connecting by preference, 168-169
      connecting with disabled NICs, 169
   WINDOWS NT, reapplying after DNS installation, 139
service resource codes, NetBIOS, 31-32
session services, NetBIOS, 20-21
set (nslookup) command, 234-239
set class option (nslookup set command), 235
set port option (nslookup set command), 236
set querytype option (nslookup set command), 237
set retry option (nslookup set command), 238
set root option (nslookup set command), 238
set srchlist option (nslookup set command), 238
set [no]d2 option (nslookup set command), 236
set [no]debug option (nslookup set command), 235
set [no]defname option (nslookup set command), 236
set [no]domain option (nslookup set command), 236

set [no]ignore option (nslookup set command), 236
set [no]port option (nslookup set command), 236
set [no]recurse option (nslookup set command), 237
set [no]search option (nslookup set command), 238
set [no]vc option (nslookup set command), 239
shop, generic top-level domain name, 196
slaves, 87-92, 114
SMBs (Server Message Blocks), 21-22
SMTP (Simple Mail Transfer Protocol), email security, 229
split-brain DNS, 135-136
Start-of-Authority (SOA) records, 94-99
stateful inspection, 225
subdomains, 66-67
   delegation, 67-68
   DNS servers, 131
subnets, DNS servers, criteria for capacity, 128-129
SYSTEM event log, monitoring DNS service, 200-202

T

TCP/IP (Transmission Control Protocol/Internet Protocol), 3, 22-23
TCP/IP Properties dialog box (Windows NT)
   DNS tab, 114-115
   virtual servers, 150
time-to-live, *see* TTL (time-to-live)
top-level domains, 65-66, 275-280
traceroute utility, 224, 243
transferring zone files, 110-111
Transmission Control Protocol/Internet Protocol, *see* TCP/IP (Transmission Control Protocol/Internet Protocol)
troubleshooting
   DNS/WINS integration, 156-158
   utilities

dig, 240-242
ipconfig, 244-245
nbtstat, 247
Netlab, 243-244
netstat, 246-247
nslookup, 232-240
ping, 242-243
traceroute, 243
winipcfg, 245-246
see also error messages
TTL (time-to-live), DNS messages, 120, 160-161
TXT (Text) Resource Record, 310

U

unique NetBIOS names, 24
UNIX
   BIND configurations for DNS primary name servers, 83-85
   Windows NT, compared, 266
untrusted hosts, 111
utilities, 265
   BIND, 267
   Cisco DNS/DHCP Manager, 265
   dig, 240-242, 266
   DNS Server, 266
   dnscmd, 266
   DNSResolver, 266
   DNSWorkshop, 266
   ipconfig, 244-245, 262
   MetaIP DNS 3.1, 268
   nbtstat, 247
   NETINFO, 266
   Netlab, 243-244
   netstat, 246-247
   Network Monitor, 265
   nslookup, 232, 262, 265
      DNS Spoofing, 224
      error messages, 239-240
      exit command, 232
      finger command, 232-233
      help or ? command, 232
      ls command, 233
      lserver command, 233
      root command, 233
      server command, 233
      set command, 234-239

nslookup4WWW, 266
ping, 224, 242-243
QIPEnterprise 5.0, 269
traceroute, 224, 243
winipcfg, 245-246, 262

V-W

View menu, DNS Manager, 141
viewing RFCs (Requests For Comments), 8
virtual servers, 150

Web sites
   domain names
      querying, 196, 198
      registering, 219
   RFC (Request for Comment), 271
   utilities, DNS, 243
web, generic top-level domain name, 196
Windows for Workgroups
   clients, configuring for WINS, 172
   names, 24
Windows Internet Name Service, *see* WINS (Windows Internet Name Service)
Windows NT
   TCP/IP Properties dialog box, DNS tab, 114-115
   UNIX, compared, 266
   networks, browsing, 177-180
Windows NT DNS servers
   boot configuration data, 82-83
   configuring, 139-140
   configuring with DNS Manager, 140
      adding resource records, 145
      changing resource records, 146
      load balancing with round robin, 147-148
      multihomed server support, 149-150
      notifying changes, 148-149
      zones, 141-144
   service, installing
      pre-installation checklist, 138
      steps, 138-139
      verifying TCP/IP stack configuration, 138

Windows NT Server clients, configuring for WINS, 172
Windows NT Workstation clients, configuring for WINS, 172
Windows resolution methods, 40
   query for NetBIOS names, 42-46
   query for non-NetBIOS names, 41-42
   query HOSTS and LMHOSTS
      interprocess communication services, 20
Windows resolvers, 34-35
   DNS servers, 35-36
      iterative queries, 38
      recursive queries, 36-38
      reverse queries, 39
   WINS servers, 35
winipcfg utility, 245-246, 262
WINS (Windows Internet Name Service), 20
   configuring clients, 171-174
      browsing on Windows NT networks, 177-180
      DHCP servers, 175
      IP addresses, 180
      name registration, 175-176
      name-to-IP address mapping resolution, 177
      NetBIOS computer names, 180-181
      NetBIOS scope, 174-175
      NetBT parameters, 182-185
   DNS servers, 206-207
   integrating with DHCP (Dynamic Host Configuration Protocol), 261-262
   integrating with DNS
      comparison, 154
      DHCP problems, 251
      multihomed servers, 165-169
      name resolution, 154-155
      reverse WINS lookups, 162-165
      testing WINS lookups, 161-162
      troubleshooting, 156-158
      WINS lookups, 158-160
      WINS TTL settings, 160-161
   integrating with MS DNS, 123
   name registration, 156
   NetBIOS, 25-26
   purposes/limitations, 55-57

records, 105-108
servers
   browsers, 59
   DNS queries
   multihomed, 58
   Net Monitor, 302-304
   Windows resolvers, 35
   zone transfers
WINS Manager, DHCP clients, 262
WINS Resource Records, 206-207
WINS_R Resource Records, 206-207
WKS (Well Known Services) Resource Record, 310
World Wide Web, security, 227-228

X-Z

X.25 (X.25 Addressing) Resource Record, 311
zone files, 94
   primary servers, transferring to secondary servers, 70-71
   secondary servers, 85-86
zone transfers, 110-111, 205-206
   caching, 111
   DNS servers
      primary and secondary, 210-212
      Windows NT servers, 207-209
      WINS servers, 206-207
zones, 141-144, 186
   domains, 68-69
   multiple, 212-213
   Notify option, 148-149
   primary, 216-217
   properties, 217-219
   secondary, 217

New Riders Professional Library

Windows NT TCP/IP
By Karanjit Siyan
1st Edition Summer 1998
500 pages, $29.99
ISBN 1-56205-887-8

If you're still looking for good documentation on Microsoft TCP/IP, then look no further — this is your book. *Windows NT TCP/IP* cuts through the complexities and provides the most informative and complete reference book on Windows-based TCP/IP. Concepts essential to TCP/IP administration are explained thoroughly, then related to the practical use of Microsoft TCP/IP in a real-world networking environment. The book begins by covering TCP/IP architecture, advanced installation and configuration issues, then moves on to routing with TCP/IP, DHCP Management, and WINS/DNS Name Resolution.

Windows NT Registry
By Sandra Osborne
1st Edition Summer 1998
500 pages, $29.99
ISBN 1-56205-941-6

The NT Registry can be a very powerful tool for those capable of using it wisely. Unfortunately, there is very little information regarding the NT Registry, due to Microsoft's insistence that their source code be kept secret. If you're looking to optimize your use of the registry, you're usually forced to search the web for bits of information. This book is your resource. It covers critical issues and settings used for configuring network protocols, including NWLink, PTP, TCP/IP and DHCP. This book approaches the material from a unique point of view, discussing the problems related to a particular component, and then discussing settings, which are the actual changes necessary for implementing robust solutions. There is also a comprehensive reference of registry settings and commands making this the perfect addition to your technical bookshelf.

Exchange Server Implementation and Administration
By Excell Data Corporation
1st Edition Fall 1998
450 pages, $29.99
ISBN 1-56205-931-9

If you're interested in connectivity and maintenance issues for Exchange Server, then this book is for you. Exchange's power lies in its ability to be connected to multiple email subsystems to create a "universal email backbone." It's not unusual to have several different and complex systems all connected via email gateways, including Lotus Notes or cc:Mail, Microsoft Mail, legacy mainframe systems, and Internet mail. This book covers all of the problems and issues associated with getting an integrated system running smoothly, and addresses troubleshooting and diagnosis of email problems, with an eye toward prevention and best practices.

Windows NT Performance Monitoring

By Mark Edmead
1st Edition Fall 1998
400 pages, $29.99
ISBN 1-56205-942-4

Performance monitoring is a little like preventative medicine for the administrator: no one enjoys a checkup, but it's a good thing to do on a regular basis. This book helps you focus on the critical aspects of improving the performance of your NT system, showing you how to monitor the system, implement benchmarking, and tune your network. The book is organized by resource components, which makes it easy to use as a reference tool.

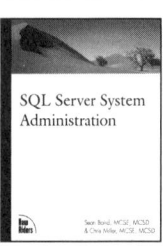

SQL Server System Administration

By Sean Baird, Chris Miller, et al.
1st Edition Fall 1998
400 pages, $29.99
1-56205-955-6

How often does your SQL Server go down during the day when everyone wants to access the data? Do you spend most of your time being a "report monkey" for your co-workers and bosses? *SQL Server System Administration* helps you keep data consistently available to your users. This book omits the introductory information. The authors don't spend time explaining queries and how they work. Instead they focus on the information that you can't get anywhere else, like how to choose the correct replication topology and achieve high availability of information.

Windows NT Thin Clients
Building Enterprise Solutions with Microsoft Terminal Server & Citrix Picasso

By Ted Harwood
1st Edition Winter 1998
500 pages, $29.99
ISBN 1-56205-944-0

It's no surprise that most administration headaches revolve around integration with other networks and clients. This book addresses these types of real-world issues on a case-by-case basis, giving tools and advice on solving each problem. If you use Citrix Picasso in your heterogeneous networking environment, this book is for you. The author also offers the real nuts and bolts of thin client administration on multiple systems, covering such relevant issues as installation, configuration, network connection, management, and application distribution.

Windows NT Technical Support

By Brendan McTague & George Neal
1st Edition Winter 1998
300 pages, $29.99
ISBN 1-56205-927-0

Well, you did it. You finally migrated your Enterprise network to Windows NT. Now what you need is a methodology, a logical way you can rigorously approach any problem, whether it's server or workstation related, and quickly get to it's root. That's what we asked Brendan and George, part of the group responsible for supporting Swiss Bank's worldwide NT enterprise, to put together for you. These guys have to support thousands of users on three continents —so they understand what technical support is. So why don't you read through their methodology, practice it on several of the sample work tickets included in the book, then go out and try it yourself?

Windows NT Security
By Richard Puckett
1st Edition Winter 1998
600 pages, $29.99
ISBN 1-56205-945-9

Swiss cheese. That's what some people say Windows NT security is like. And they may be right, because they only know what the NT documentation says about implementing security. Who has the time to research alternatives, play around with the features, service packs, hot fixes and add-on tools, and figure out what makes NT rock solid? Well, Richard Puckett does. He's been researching Windows NT Security for the University of Virginia for a while now, and he's got pretty good news. He's going to show you how to make NT secure in your environment, and we mean really secure.

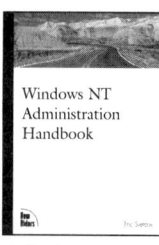

Windows NT Administration Handbook
By Eric Svetcov
1st Edition Winter 1998
400 pages, $29.99
ISBN 1-56205-946-7

Administering a Windows NT network is kind of like trying to herd cats—an impossible task characterized by constant motion, exhausting labor and lots of hairballs. Author Eric Svetcov knows all about it—he's administered NT networks for some of the fastest growing companies around Silicon Valley. So we asked Eric to put together a concise manual of best practices, a book of tools and ideas that other administrators can turn to again and again in administering their own NT networks. Eric's experience shines through as he shares his secrets for administering users, for getting domain and groups set up quickly and for troubleshooting the thorniest NT problems. Daily, weekly and monthly task lists help organize routine tasks and preventative maintenance.

MCSE Core Essential Reference
By Matthew Shepker
1st Edition Fall 1998
500 pages, $19.99
ISBN 0-7357-0006-0

You're sitting in the first session of your Networking Essentials class and the instructor starts talking about "*RAS*" and you have no idea what that means. You think about raising your hand to ask about *RAS*, but you reconsider—you'd feel pretty foolish asking a question in front of all these people. You turn to your handy *MCSE Core Essential Reference* and find a quick summary on *Remote Access Services*. Question answered. It's a couple months later and you're taking your Networking Essentials exam the next day. You're reviewing practice tests and you keep forgetting the maximum lengths for the various commonly used cable types. Once again, you turn to the *MCSE Core Essential Reference* and find a table on cables including all of the characteristics you need to memorize in order to pass the test.

Lotus Notes & Domino Essential Reference

By Dave Hatter & Tim Bankes
1st Edition Winter 1998
500 pages, $19.99
ISBN 0-7357-0007-9

You're in a bind because you've been asked to design and program a new database in Notes for an important client that will keep track of and itemize a myriad of inventory and shipping data. The client wants a user-friendly interface, without sacrificing speed or functionality. You are experienced (and could develop this app in your sleep), but feel that you need to take your talents to the next level. You need something to facilitate your creative and technical abilities, something to perfect your programming skills. Your answer is waiting for you: *Lotus Notes and Domino Essential Reference*. It's compact and simply designed. It's loaded with information. All of the objects, classes, functions and methods are listed. It shows you the object hierarchy and the overlaying relationship between each one. It's perfect for you. Problem solved.

Linux System Administration

By James T. Dennis
1st Edition Winter 1998
450 pages, $29.99
ISBN 1-56205-934-3

As an administrator, you probably feel that most of your time and energy is spent in endless firefighting. If your network has become a fragile quilt of temporary patches and workarounds, then this book is for you. For example, have you had trouble sending or receiving your email lately? Are you looking for a way to keep your network running smoothly with enhanced performance? Are your users always hankering for more storage, more services, and more speed? *Linux System Administration* advises you on the many intricacies of maintaining a secure, stable system. In this definitive work, the author addresses all the issues related to system administration from adding users and managing files permission to internet services and Web hosting to recovery planning and security. This book fulfills the need for expert advice that will ensure a trouble-free Linux environment.

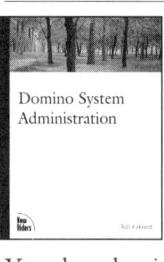

Domino System Administration

By Rob Kirkland
1st Edition Winter 1998
500 pages, $29.99
ISBN 1-56205-948-3

Your boss has just announced that you will be upgrading to the newest version of Notes and Domino when it ships. As a Premium Lotus Business Partner, Lotus has offered a substantial price break to keep your company away from Microsoft's Exchange Server. How are you supposed to get this new system installed, configured, and rolled out to all of your end users? You understand how Lotus Notes works — you've been administering it for years. What you need is a concise, practical explanation about the new features, and how to make some of the advanced stuff really work. You need answers and solutions from someone who's been in the trenches; someone like you, who has worked with the product for years, and understands what it is you need to know. *Domino System Administration* is the answer — the first book on Domino that attacks the technology at the professional level, with practical, hands-on assistance to get Domino running in your organization.

New Riders — We want to know what you think

To better serve you, we would like your opinion on the content and quality of this book. Please complete this card and mail it to us or fax it to 317-581-4663.

Name _____
Address _____
City _____ State _____ Zip _____
Phone _____
Email Address _____
Occupation _____
Operating System(s) that you use _____

What influenced your purchase of this book?
- ❑ Recommendation
- ❑ Cover Design
- ❑ Table of Contents
- ❑ Index
- ❑ Magazine Review
- ❑ Advertisement
- ❑ Reputation of New Riders
- ❑ Author Name

How would you rate the contents of this book?
- ❑ Excellent
- ❑ Very Good
- ❑ Good
- ❑ Fair
- ❑ Below Average
- ❑ Poor

How do you plan to use this book?
- ❑ Quick reference
- ❑ Self-training
- ❑ Classroom
- ❑ Other

What do you like most about this book?
Check all that apply.
- ❑ Content
- ❑ Writing Style
- ❑ Accuracy
- ❑ Examples
- ❑ Listings
- ❑ Design
- ❑ Index
- ❑ Page Count
- ❑ Price
- ❑ Illustrations

What do you like least about this book?
Check all that apply.
- ❑ Content
- ❑ Writing Style
- ❑ Accuracy
- ❑ Examples
- ❑ Listings
- ❑ Design
- ❑ Index
- ❑ Page Count
- ❑ Price
- ❑ Illustrations

What would be a useful follow-up book to this one for you? _____
Where did you purchase this book? _____
Can you name a similar book that you like better than this one, or one that is as good? Why? _____
_____

How many New Riders books do you own? _____
What are your favorite computer books? _____
_____

What other titles would you like to see us develop? _____
_____

Any comments for us? _____
_____
_____
_____

Windows NT DNS 1-56205-943-2

Fold here and scotch tape to mail

Place
Stamp
Here

New Riders
201 W. 103rd St.
Indianapolis IN 46290

How to Contact Us

Visit our Web site

www.newriders.com

On our Web site you'll find information about our other books, authors, tables of content, indexes, and book errata. You can also place orders for books through our Web site.

Email us

newriders@mcp.com

Contact us at this address:

- if you have comments or questions about this book
- to report errors that you have found in this book
- if you have a book proposal to submit or are interested in writing for New Riders
- if you would like to have an author kit sent to you
- if you are an expert in a computer topic or technology and are interested in being a technical editor who reviews manuscripts for technical accuracy

international@mcp.com

To find a distributor in your area, please contact our international department at the address above.

pr@mcp.com

For instructors from educational institutions who wish to preview Macmillan Computer Publishing books for classroom use. Email should include your name, title, school, department, address, phone number, office days/hours, text in use, and enrollment in the body of your text along with your request for desk/examination copies and/or additional information.

Write to us

New Riders
201 W. 103rd St.
Indianapolis, IN 46290-1097

Call us

Toll-free (800) 571-5840 + 9 + 4557
If outside U.S. (317) 581-3500 ask for New Riders

Fax us

(317) 581-4663